Islamic Gardens and Landscapes

PENN STUDIES IN LANDSCAPE ARCHITECTURE

John Dixon Hunt, Series Editor

This series is dedicated to the study and promotion of a wide
variety of approaches to landscape architecture, with special
emphasis on connections between theory and practice.
It includes monographs on key topics in history and theory,
descriptions of projects by both established and rising designers,
translations of major foreign-language texts, anthologies
of theoretical and historical writings on classic issues, and critical
writing by members of the profession of landscape architecture.
The series is the recipient of the Award of Honor in Communications
from the American Society of Landscape Architects, 2006.

Islamic Gardens and Landscapes

D. Fairchild Ruggles

UNIVERSITY OF PENNSYLVANIA PRESS | PHILADELPHIA

Publication of this volume was assisted by a generous grant from The Getty Foundation.

10 9 8 7 6 5 4 3 2 1

Published by
University of Pennsylvania Press
Philadelphia, Pennsylvania 19104-4112

LIBRARY OF CONGRESS CATALOGING-IN-PUBLICATION DATA

Ruggles, D. Fairchild.
Islamic gardens and landscapes / D. Fairchild Ruggles.
p. cm. — (Penn studies in landscape architecture)
Includes bibliographical references and index.
ISBN-13: 978-0-8122-4025-2 (hardcover : alk. paper)
ISBN-10: 0-8122-4025-1 (hardcover : alk. paper)
1. Gardens, Islamic. I. Title.
SB457.8.R85 2007
712.0917'67—dc22

2007023294

To my parents

Jeanne Françoise Peter Ruggles and Thomas Morrill Ruggles

Contents

Color plates follow page 28

Preface

ARDENS ARE AT ONCE highly meaningful, expressing the position of humankind with respect to the earth and cosmos, and utterly ordinary, reflecting the need to produce a food crop in order to survive the fallow season and plant anew another year. Moreover, the urge to garden, to domesticate the wild landscape by clearing it of all but selected plants, watering them, and tending them until they flower and bear fruit, is a basic human endeavor that requires few resources and no grand conceptual scheme. Although gardens and landscape works requiring complex irrigation or drainage systems may occur on a large scale and reflect either the ambition of kings or the ability of a community to organize itself, others are quite humble and occur spontaneously.

This book looks thematically at Islamic gardens and cultivated landscapes, placing them on a continuous spectrum with the city and architecture at one end and nature and wilderness at the other. The Islamic garden is a popular theme among architects and enthusiasts, and every year a new volume is produced with handsome illustrations of stunning gardens. However, a great many of these focus entirely on elite formal gardens, defining them as enclosed spaces that are geometrically laid out and interpreting their symbolic meaning narrowly as "paradise on earth." The removal of the garden from the broader context of landscape, agriculture, and water supply results in a limited and superficial view, giving extraordinary emphasis to religion and dynastic politics while ignoring other factors that contributed equally to garden form and meaning.

This is not a book about the origins of the Islamic garden or its formal properties. Unlike Islamic architecture—where we can observe highly recognizable forms in mosque, palace, and tomb design—in Islamic history there is really only one formal garden plan, with a few variations on it. This is the so-called *chahar bagh*, or the four-part garden laid out with axial walkways that intersect in the garden center, discussed in Chapter 4, and the various stepped terrace variations of it that proliferated in the Safavid and Mughal realms, discussed in Chapter 10 and throughout.

Gardens begin as secular endeavors, stemming from the practical need to organize the surrounding space, tame nature, enhance the earth's yield, and create a legible map on which to distribute natural resources. Three early chapters address these practical issues. Symbolic interpretations of the meaning of such domestication and fertility came later in the history of garden making, so that the good garden became a sign of human success, and a productive landscape a sign of divine favor. There have been several inspiring theological interpretations of gardens as signs of paradise for Muslims, but the evidence suggests that the actual early gardens were not regarded thus. In this respect, it is important to remember that while theology and history both seek the truth, they ask and answer different questions. With respect to the built environment and the interpretation of it, the questions that I attempt to answer here are purely historical.

One of the traps that writers about Islamic gardens often fall into is the emphasis on extant gardens, interpreting the historic past by means of easily visible and attractive gardens that have not been explored archaeologically and whose plantings are historically inaccurate. For instance, the Generalife Palace's Patio de la Acequía in Granada has been celebrated as a living and authentic Islamic garden, when in fact its soil levels and plantings are entirely modern. Among architects, historians, and site conservators there is a regrettable tolerance for botanical inaccuracy at historic sites, despite the fact that we now have an array of archaeological techniques to identify many of the plants and trees that were once grown there. Examples of successful garden archaeology help explain what we can and cannot learn about gardens from such approaches in combination with written texts and painted representations of gardens.

Equally problematic are the attempts to interpret the real gardens of this earth through the shimmering veil of Arabic and especially Persian verse; lacking historical reference and archaeological data, these are more successful as studies of poetry than as descriptions of actual gardens. The Taj Mahal has been studied thus: the references to judgment and the Throne of God in its program of inscriptions have prompted scholars to interpret the monument in compelling theological and political terms. But these Qur'anic inscriptions explain neither the unusual position of the tomb in the garden nor the relationship of the Taj complex to the pleasure garden on the river's opposite bank.

Finally, the garden form was such a powerful artistic form in many areas of the Islamic world that it was adopted by non-Muslims—such as the Rajputs of Mughal India—as a way of expressing alliance with Muslim rulers and thereby indicating a shared cultural identity that transcended their more obvious religious differences. The garden was not an exclusively Muslim production; it arose from a specific climate and set of techniques for controlling the landscape and thus reflected regional concerns that were common to all the peoples sharing that landscape. The point here is not that the garden was produced outside of religious and cultural contexts—indeed, the transformation of landscape is one of the most powerful expressions of the human experience, the awe at regarding the cosmos, and the fear and hope at contemplating death. But it is a fundamental argument of this book that neither religion nor culture alone can explain the meaning, mechanics, and productivity of that set of gardens that historians, in retrospect, label "Islamic."

Perhaps because the history of Islamic gardens was written, until quite recently, by persons who were outsiders to Islamic religion and culture, the range of scholarship on gardens varies from a kind of ahistoricity to insulting stereotypes.[1] While the worst of such endeavors can be dismissed as outrageous orientalist fantasy, one must wonder whether, in trying to re-create the experience of landscapes and inhabitants that vanished long ago, any historian is liable to project his or her own desires and expectations. For myself, I am aware of the attraction of representing Islamic Spain and Mughal India as successful melting pots of ethnicity and religion, as if the mingling of Islam, Christianity, Hinduism, Buddhism, and Judaism in those cultures could instruct the modern world. Cultural diversity and difference was a signal characteristic of the early Islamic world; yet while gardens reveal the diversity of plant material, their more powerful dimension is continuity. The evidence clearly shows that, while agriculture is deeply affected by political strife, the actual practice more often than not transcends political, religious, and ethnic boundaries. For this reason, it is almost impossible to distinguish between gardens made for Muslim and for Christian patrons in southern Spain in the thirteenth and fourteenth centuries. In general, agricultural innovations are quickly adopted when the benefits are recognized, provided the political and cultural climate allows it.

THE BOOK EXTENDS from the seventh through the twentieth centuries. Although the earliest chapters begin with the advent of Islam, they do not follow a strictly historical progression through the various successive dynasties. Instead, thematic grouping of issues in which subjects such as mythic gardens (Chapter 7) and manuscript representations (Chapter 6) are explored without trying to arrange all the sites in question into a neat chronological framework. The book focuses somewhat more on the landscapes of South Asia and Islamic Spain than elsewhere, partly because these areas have outstanding examples of extant gardens that have been well studied by historians and archaeologists, and partly because I am most familiar with these areas of the world. It does not extend into Southeast Asia or beyond Africa's northern coast simply because there is so little information on landscape design in those areas and because what material does exist belongs largely to the recent centuries, an era for which there is a surfeit of sites and gardens. The book ends with a list of Islamic Garden and Sites by geographical region, selected because they are historically important, well preserved, or representative in some way (especially in the case of nineteenth- and twentieth-century residential gardens, which are too numerous to list). Each garden and site in this section is illustrated by a plan or photograph and is followed by a brief bibliography.

For this volume I have supplied more than eighty plans, many corrected or redrawn for the first time. The ground plan is a useful tool for spatial analysis, but it reduces landscape to a world of architecture, plotted on flat paper, often with no indication of the topographic contours or ground water systems that may have been the principal determining factors in the garden's layout. Typically the garden is represented as distinct from the rest of the landscape, with only a minimal indication of whether it stands amidst a desert or a forest, on a mountaintop or a plain. Other shortcomings are that ground plans tend to show the garden in its original conceptual state, perhaps the only moment when a plan has any real meaning. Conversely, sections or views may envision the garden in an imaginary future moment when trees have matured and seasonal plants are in bloom. Nevertheless, given the lack of alternatives, I have reluctantly reproduced many such plans in the present volume. Most of the gardens discussed in the book appear in the later Gardens and Sites section, and readers should consult the plans that accompany these descriptions as they read the chapters.

The terms "Islamic" and "Muslim" appear throughout but are not interchangeable. The term "Muslim" refers to the believers of Islam, the religion conveyed by God through the Prophet Muhammad. It can also serve as a descriptor for mosques, practices, and concepts that directly reflect the religion. In contradistinction, the term "Islamic" is used broadly to refer to a community of Muslims as well as the set of social practices and material forms—their culture—that characterized not only these religious adherents but also the non-Muslims living in their midst. Hence, cities such as seventh-century Jerusalem, eighth-century Cordoba, late fifteenth-century Istanbul, and sixteenth-century Agra can be called Islamic, because they were ruled by Muslim governments that ensured the hegemony of Islamic cultural values. However, in each case, there were large numbers of non-Muslims—Byzantines and Jews in Jerusalem, and the adherents to the various sects that together are called Hinduism in Agra, for example. These lived in a predominantly Islamic culture and in some cases adopted many of the external signs of that culture, without departing from the beliefs of their own faith or renouncing their identity as Christian, Jew, or Hindu. Thus the religious term "Muslim" is a subset of the larger cultural rubric "Islamic."

Common era dates are used throughout, except where cited as hijra dates (H, the Islamic era) in primary sources. For the sake of clarity, especially for Western readers, Arabic, Persian, and Turkish words are pluralized with an "s."

Islamic Gardens and Landscapes

1   The Islamic Landscape

Place and Memory

ARDENS AND LANDSCAPE are elusive subjects, positioned in both space and time, yet belonging to neither one exclusively. The Islamic landscape is particularly problematic because there is the additional question of what defines it. The Islamic world is broad and diverse with different ways of cultivating the earth and organizing human society and such different histories that it can seem absurd to compare the Balkans with the Sahara, or riparian flood-based irrigation along the Nile with underground conduits supplying irrigation systems in Iran and Iraq or water storage systems in India (Fig. 1). Babur, the sixteenth-century founder of the Mughal empire, noted this when contrasting Hindustan (roughly equivalent to the modern nations of India and Pakistan) to his home territories around Kabul: "It is a strange country. Compared to ours, it is another world. Its mountains, rivers, forests, and wildernesses, its villages and provinces, animals and plants, peoples and languages, even its rain and winds are altogether different."[1]

Climate varies considerably in the many areas of the Islamic world. The Mediterranean is characterized by hot, dry summers and more moderate, moister winters. From Egypt to Tunisia the topography is mostly flat, but the snow-capped Atlas ranges with intervening broad plateaus extend from the western side of Tunisia through Algeria to Morocco. South of this is the Sahara desert, where temperatures can reach into the 130s F.

In comparison, northern India, western Pakistan, and Afghanistan are dominated by the Himalayas, a formidable barrier that rises to more than 7,500 meters (25,000 feet). These mountains drain into rivers that provide water for the vast Indo-Gangetic plain of northern India. The monsoon winds provide the other source of water. Syria and Iraq consist largely of low desert landscape, partially irrigated by the Tigris and Euphrates rivers. Over the course of millennia a river-based irrigation system was developed in this area in which water was drawn from a source upstream and carried by canal to a point at a lower elevation.

Just as the Islamic landscape is varied, the social traditions and historical identities of the peoples inhabiting these regions are also diverse, including Arabs, Berbers from northern Africa, Byzantine

FIGURE 1.
The Ardalaj stepwell (ca. 1498) near Ahmedabad has flights of steps leading to two deep wells. A pulley at ground level was used to lift the water to the surface.

3

Christians from the eastern Mediterranean, Persians from Iran, and Turkic peoples from the steppes of Central Asia, to name a few of the major groups. With the expansion of Islam from the eighth century onward into northern Africa and Iran, there were more and more Muslim communities in which Arabic was learned as a second language, not the language of the hearth but of the mosque and the government. In light of such diversity, one can certainly question the validity of "Islamic" as a coherent cultural label. Yet Muslims in both fourteenth-century Granada and fourteenth-century Cairo looked back to what they regarded as common roots in the holy places of the Arabian peninsula, and even Christians, Jews, and Hindus living in Islamic kingdoms often absorbed the culture to the extent that they adopted Islamic cuisine, music, dress, architecture, and literature without actually professing the Muslim faith. Trade and pilgrimage routes brought societies together, enabling people to travel and to exchange objects and ideas. Arabic literature is rich with travel accounts written by men who went by ship and caravan to the far ends of the Islamic world and beyond. For example, Ibn Battuta was one of the most determined travelers, his journeys taking him through Beijing, Calcutta, Bukhara, Constantinople, Granada, and Timbuktu between 1325 and 1354 (Fig. 2).[2] He recorded the new tastes, sights, and strange ways of the lands and peoples he encountered, remarking with equal interest on manners and monuments. In addition to describing society, these itinerant geographers observed the landscape in detail, often comparing one part of the Islamic world with another, the river landscape of Seville with the Tigris and Nile, or Baghdad with Cairo, in one sentence praising both. Even societies that had neither common borders nor the same spoken language perceived a mutual legacy and religious foundation in Islam, sharing the Qur'an as their holy book and the foundation for law and community organization.

Gardens are experienced by human beings who view them as spatial constructions and also apprehend them through the auditory and olfactory senses. As represented on paper

FIGURE 2.
Map of Ibn Battuta's travels. Ibn Battuta (1304-1368 or 1377) was one of the great itinerant geographers of the premodern Islamic world. He recorded his observations in his great work, *Tuhfat al-nuzzar* (The Treasury of Curiosities), usually known more simply as the *Rihlat* (Letters). (Ruggles and Variava after Robert Irwin)

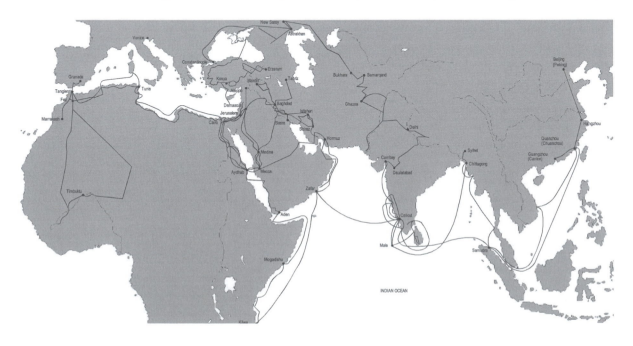

CHAPTER I

(the only record we have of many Islamic sites), a garden lacks the music of trickling water and bird song, yet Islamic gardens were often stocked with nightingales and doves that delighted listeners with their singing and cooing, and countless poems mention them. In describing a garden along the Caspian Sea, the great Persian poet Firdawsi wrote, "The nightingale sits on every spray/ and pours his soft melodious lay."[3] Another poet, Manuchihri, de-

FIGURE 3. Generalife Palace, Granada. At the fourteenth-century Acequía Court, pavilions looked down into the courtyard garden below as well as beyond to the dramatic landscape of city, cultivated countryside, and distant mountains.

scribed spring in a garden: "The dove is the muezzin and his voice is the call to prayer."[4] Gardens were also filled with the scent of flowers; a grove of orange trees in bloom is an intense sensory experience that envelops the person to the extent that one momentarily forgets sight and sound, closes one's eyes, and inhales. A great many trees and plants were cultivated in gardens, not only for their appearance but also for their pleasing perfume and the taste of their succulent fruit.

Furthermore, gardens can appeal to the senses through views and vistas, as well as hidden refuges. A view that looks straight along a level axis is entirely different from a panoramic view afforded by an elevated stance. In the Andalusian palace-city Madinat al-Zahra', the main reception hall was positioned in order to look outward in one direction to the garden, and from the gardens themselves one looked downward onto the grounds of the royal palace as well as the more distant farmed estates that stretched along the fertile river valley.[5] At the Alhambra, there were windows—miradors—whose sole purpose was to allow the palace residents to gaze out and down upon the surrounding city and distant mountain landscape (Fig. 3).[6] Yet in the plans of the Alhambra, where its various halls and pavilions are flattened onto one plane, the logic of the visual relationship among the halls and between the palace and the landscape cannot be discerned.

The emphasis on the architectural plan also implies a state of permanence. However, landscape is not a static work of stone, brick, and mortar: it is a living entity that provides a habitat for plants, animals, and people, no matter how artificially built and maintained that habitat may be. For this reason, it is helpful to adopt the approach of environmental scientists, who treat landscapes as interactive systems. Instead of the small enclosed object of garden history, the environmental scientist observes large swathes of landscape, for example, viewing the river as a system in which the activities upstream profoundly affect the quality of life downstream, the deforestation of one upland area leads to erosion of the topsoil and deleterious levels of silt in the streams and rivers below, and the pumping of large quantities of groundwater for agricultural irrigation ultimately depletes deep aquifers that cannot be recharged within a human lifetime.[7] Taking into account environmental factors, such as the variation in climate in the Islamic world (Fig. 4), all but requires such a perspective. This approach may seem entirely utilitarian and blindly ahistorical, but many

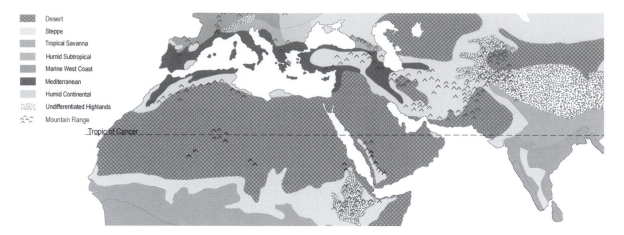

FIGURE 4.
Climate map of
Islamic world.
(Ruggles and
Variava)

environmental scientists are in fact deeply concerned about the preservation of historic landscape systems that were ecologically balanced and aesthetically pleasing.

The architectural model is more concerned with the landscape or garden as a work of art, and the environmental model is more concerned with the landscape as a functional system. The architectural historian inquires about form, typology, symbolism, patronage, and meaning within a linear historical context, while the environmental scientist inquires about cause and effect, and the balance between natural forces and cultural values in a cyclical temporal context. Both approaches have merit, and for this reason the book merges these perspectives to treat the landscape as both an object having material spatial presence and a performance unfolding in time.

The dimension of time appears most clearly in the growth cycle of plants within the garden. But time is also an important aspect of our visual experience of large and small landscape spaces. Landscape is generally too large to be apprehended in a single glance. It is rarely seen in its entirety but is revealed slowly as the individual moves through a site, down paths, under tree canopies, and around buildings. As the body moves through space, the head turns to look in one direction and then another, focusing on the distant and the close-at-hand, and finally scanning the full scene. In the Islamic context, the tension between the promise of a visual experience and its actual fulfillment is orchestrated by devices such as windows, doorways, and ornamental screens that temporarily curtail vision (see Figs. 28 and 53). To apprehend the view, the person is urged to step forward and train the eyes along a straight line, and then to make the visual sweep from side to side.[8]

While our experience of space is dynamic, the landscape itself also changes diurnally, seasonally, and over longer stretches of time. From one moment to the next, the view, sound, and scent change so that the same garden may appear quite different. The Mughal Emperor Jahangir experienced this when he visited Kashmir. He was accustomed to the summer vegetation enjoyed on previous visits, but in 1620 he saw the gardens for the first time in spring when they had a dazzling profusion of colorful spring tulips, narcissi, violets, and roses, as well as fruit trees in blossom.[9] The flowers themselves were not new, but erupted together in such quantities that they dramatically changed the appearance of the landscape.

Over years and sometime centuries, a garden designed for an anticipated appearance will grow and mature, its volumes expanding and its sightlines changing, sometimes fulfilling the original patron's intention, but at other times growing well beyond and even obscuring those intentions. Hence, one of the most powerful, romantic metaphors for the passage of time is the ruined garden whose neglect becomes a sign for loss, absence, a bygone era. Landscape is always both a living presence and a memory, a palimpsest of the real place and the collected, remembered images of it, and thus a merger of past and present. A remembrance is ultimately an experience of the present in which a memory or image substitutes for the actual past event to which we cannot return. The closest we can come to revisiting the past is to revisit the place where a past experience occurred.[10] Thus place plays an important role in memory.

One of the central tropes of early Arabic poetry was the place left behind, often associated with a lost love. For example, the most famous of the seven odes of Imru al-Qays begins: "Stop, friends, and weep for a love and a campsite at the edge of the sands of al-Dakhul and Haumal." The poet added detail to the memory: powerful winds, dry hollows, acacias, and the droppings of antelopes scattered "like peppercorns." The place was exquisitely drawn, yet it was recalled entirely from memory; when the poet recited his verse, he was no longer there. As he recounted his grief at parting, he lamented, "What is there left to lean on where the trace is obliterated?"[11] The campsite was real; yet it existed thereafter only in the mind of the poet (and now ours), the traces of sand and habitation erased by the wind.

Because of its ephemerality, the garden too was a favorite setting for nostalgic recollection. When the Andalusian poet Ibn Zaydun returned to Cordoba after a bitter civil war and an absence of many years, he camped in the halls of the abandoned caliphal city, Madinat al-Zahra', and recalled an old love affair. He compared the flourishing landscape of earlier days when "the flower gardens smiled with their silvery waters, like collars loosened from the necks of fair maidens" with the devastation and sadness of the present: "Now I enjoy the view of flowers to which my eyes are attracted, and dew weighs heavily on them—their stems are drooping."[12] The garden represented the trace of something gone and irretrievable, a love and an era that had slipped away, but that was recalled in the poet's return to the place. The theme of a lost golden age in al-Andalus was eventually transformed into a longing for al-Andalus itself (which succumbed to Christian rule in 1492) so that al-Andalus became the quintessential lost place.[13]

Even when building anew, the site selected for built architecture and gardens may be already redolent with meanings that the new construction embraces, redefines, or attempts to obliterate. In sites such as the Haram al-Sharif (Jerusalem) with its seventh-century Aqsa Mosque and Dome of the Rock, or the Fatih Cami built in Istanbul just after the Ottoman conquest, we can identify such an "iconography of the site." The Dome of the Rock (Qubbat al-Sakhra, finished 691) was built by the Umayyad caliph 'Abd al-Malik to cap a large rock on an elevated platform in Jerusalem (Fig. 5; and see Fig. 66); the platform was Mount Moriah, a place with deep meaning for Jews as the location of Solomon's Temple, Abraham's sacrifice of Isaac, and the birth and death of Adam. To Christians, it was significant as the site of the Temple's destruction. In time, the Haram al-Sharif platform gained ad-

ditional meaning for Muslims as the place from where the Prophet Muhammad was believed to have made his miraculous Night Journey and ascent into heaven, but its first significance in the eighth century appears to have been as a monument of conquest and symbolic appropriation.[14] The symbolic strategy of choosing that particular site for the first monumental work of Islamic architecture relied on the meanings attached, by means of memory, to that unique place.

The Fatih Cami was built between 1463 and 1470 in Istanbul by Sultan Mehmet II, called Fatih ("Conqueror"), following the taking of Constantinople in 1453 (Fig. 6). A few minor mosques existed in the city prior to conquest, but this was the first great imperial mosque complex after the fall of Byzantium, and its hilltop location and majestic size clearly announced the presence of Islam and Ottoman identity through publicly visible built form.[15] One of Mehmet's primary motivations in choosing that site was surely the opportunity to claim Constantinople's skyline, but it must have been considerably enhanced by the knowledge that the mosque would be superimposed on the derelict site of the Holy Apostles and would use material quarried from that venerable Byzantine monument, where the Byzantine emperors from the ninth century onward had been buried. For both the Dome of the Rock and the Fatih Cami, considerations of a site's natural elevation went hand in hand with the recognition of already inscribed meanings that contributed to the meaning of the new monument.

The naming of places can enhance the association between present and past or, more specifically, between a place here and now and another more historically or geographically distant. The Romans used the technique to evoke the memory of successful military campaigns in their villas of leisure and retirement. At his villa in Tibur (Tivoli, 118–138 C.E.), Hadrian sought to represent the monuments of the world that he had seen in his career as emperor, and so the estate had an Athens, Nile, Thessaly, and even Hades guarded by a statue of Cerberus. Similarly, Muslim rulers gave names to locations that were intended to evoke historic and mythic places. Some repeated names referred not to specific sites as much as general architectural forms: the *hesht behesht* type used by the Timurids and Safavids was an octagon containing eight bays (the name means "eight paradises") encircling a central space, and the *chihil situn* type was a hall or porch lined with columns (literally, "forty columns").[16] The cities of Isfahan and Kashan had Chahar Bagh avenues lined with gardens: *chahar bagh* is a term that originally described a specific four-part garden layout with axial walkways meeting in the center but later acquired a more general meaning of "garden."[17]

But the Safavids of seventeenth-century Iran were also quite conscious of earlier Timurid antecedents, and so when Shah Suleyman I (r. 1666–1694) chose the name Hesht Behesht for one of his pavilions in Isfahan, he was identifying not only a typology but also making reference to Tabriz, where there was an earlier Hesht Behesht (1466–1478) laid out by a

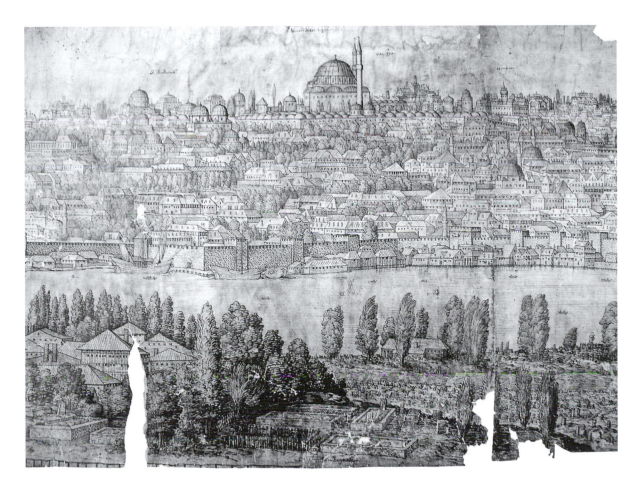

Timurid patron. Similarly, the multicolumned Chihil Situn was both a common Safavid architectural type as well as a reference to the Chihil Situn of Samarkand in Timur's day.[18]

The Timurids, too, liked to name gardens after older places with historic prestige. Indeed, in the late fourteenth century Timur surrounded Samarkand with estates bearing the names of great Muslim cities: Shiraz, Baghdad, Damascus, and Cairo (Misr).[19] The connection to the other great cities was further enhanced by bringing artisans from them to work at Timur's court in Samarkand, and the traveler Clavijo wrote that "trade has always been fostered by Timur with the view of making his capital the noblest of cities: and during all his conquests wheresoever he came he carried off the best men of the population to people Samarkand, bringing thither together the master-craftsmen of all nations." He further remarked that Samarkand became overpopulated to the extent that there was not enough housing for all the Turks, Arabs, Moors, Greeks, Armenians, and Indians.[20]

Mughal palaces had halls called the Shish Mahal (chamber with mirror mosaic) and Shah Burj ("royal tower"), and these too were generic types rather than references to known monuments. But in the sixteenth century, toponymy specifically evoked a distant place for the people of Agra when the Mughal emperor Babur built gardens irrigated by running water and supplied by waterwheels along one bank of Agra's river: the locals nicknamed the area Kabul. In this case, since the native population had never seen Kabul, the name

FIGURE 6. Melchior Lorichs made a panoramic drawing of Istanbul in 1559 when he visited the city. The great Ottoman imperial mosque, the Fatih Cami, stands out on the urban skyline, its dome and minarets visible from the Bosphorus's opposite shore (which was covered with gardens) both because of its tremendous size and its prominent site on one of Istanbul's seven hills. (Leiden University Library, BPL 1758)

was probably not intended to imply similarity to the other place but rather to identify the newly developed area with the invaders who had come from Afghanistan.[21] It is significant that first the invaders and then the place were identified according to geographic origins. Hence, although distant and distinct, Kabul and Agra were joined in the persons of Babur's followers.

When the Mughal emperor Shah Jahan built the Shalamar Bagh of Lahore in 1641, he was reproducing a well-known type of stepped garden as well as making a specific reference to an earlier Shalamar Bagh in Kashmir to which he had made significant additions in 1630. The connection between the two was thus both generic and particular. Through naming, references were made not only to the historic past but also to mythic places such as Iram, a beautiful city intended to rival paradise. Hence one poet, praising a garden made for the Qajar ruler Fat'h 'Ali Shah (1797–1834) at Tehran, wrote: "This garden Iram is comparable to the old garden Iram."[22]

Just as naming can create associations with other places, material objects transferred from one site to another can endow a new site with some of the symbolic or even physical attributes of the first. The Ottomans created a chamber of relics in the Topkapı Palace (Istanbul) in which they collected various keys, locks, and rainspouts from the Kaaba in Mecca, an imprint of the Prophet's footprint, and earth from his tomb in Medina. These forged a material connection between the ruling dynasty and the Prophet, a link that was especially meaningful since, unlike many other Muslim rulers, the Ottomans could not claim to be *sharifs* (descendants of the Prophet). The objects created an association not only with Muhammad, but also to the Kaaba, a uniquely central place in Islamic faith and history. In particular, the handful of sacred earth in the Topkapı unites Istanbul physically with the Prophet's Mosque.

Finally, the act of visiting a historic site can forge a link between present and past. Al-Mu'tamid, king of the province of Seville (1169–91), made a trip to the abandoned palace of Madinat al-Zahra' in nearby Cordoba soon after he became ruler. In so doing, he temporarily placed himself in what had been the seat of power of the much larger, more prosperous Umayyad kingdom of al-Andalus (756–1031) and made a claim to its legacy and authority, for despite the palace's evident ruin, it had historical and contemporary significance as a place that evoked the memory of deceased kings and a lost golden age.[23] The Fatimid caliphs of Cairo in the eleventh century also understood the power of claiming a place. They began the practice of weekly parades through the city, visiting in turn each of the great congregational mosques—'Amr, Ibn Tulun, al-Azhar, and al-Hakim—so as to attach their physical presence to the buildings and thus to the quarter of the city and the historical period to which each belonged.[24] Although in theory these monuments and indeed the entire city belonged to the Fatimids, that fact could be maintained only by showing the caliph's movement toward the actual place and his praying within it. The concept of ownership and authority was grounded at the site.

While performance, ritual, and human memory attach meaning to a place, at the same time interpretation and meaning can be guided by a site's preexisting physical character. Rivers flow naturally in one direction; the Himalayas receive copious precipitation while the Sahara receives none. Human society can certainly alter these characteristics, leveling mountains, changing the course of rivers, and managing water through irrigation and drainage, and there are few (if any) landscapes that have not been imprinted by human society in some way. Indeed, we can know a landscape only by entering into it, whether bodily or by the act of adopting an aerial or earthbound perspective onto it, and thereby reproducing it in terms of a human perceptual experience. But this does not change the fact that when a society seeks access to a heavenly place perceived to be "on high," the natural phenomenon of a mountain (or perhaps a meteorite that has fallen from the sky) provides that axis between the earthly and spiritual worlds. We give these places meaning, but to some extent they also shape *us*, imposing limits to the possibilities of human existence on the land, which we then seek to challenge. Unlike architecture and painting, then, the work of designing and building landscape and gardens begins on terrain that already has contour, temperature, moisture, and sunlight, and our attribution of meaning to these characteristics is socially produced by event and memory. Islamic gardens and landscapes through time have expressed this intersection of nature, design, and history.

2   Making the Desert Bloom

Transforming an Inhospitable Earth

ISLAMIC CIVILIZATION BROUGHT dramatic changes to the landscape it inhabited. With the skillful acquisition and transportation of water, the parched lands of the Middle East and northern Africa flourished with human-made verdant oases that not only transformed the economy with their agricultural products but also became a powerful form of cultural expression. The techniques employed to effect this transformation originated among the ancient Persians and Romans. But Muslim communities implemented them more broadly for a complex web of motivations having to do with the system of land ownership and labor, inheritance laws, taxation, urban growth, and an idealized vision of country life.

The first Muslims came from the inland desert of the Arabian Peninsula. They were the followers of the charismatic leader from Mecca, Muhammad (570 or 571–632), who in about the year 610 experienced a revelation in which God conveyed to him a new vision of the world. This and subsequent revelations, communicated orally to him over the course of the next twenty years, comprise the Qur'an. The messages that Muhammad, as God's prophet, preached to the people of Mecca angered those entrenched members of Meccan society who did not want to submit to the changes demanded by the new religion, causing Muhammad to flee for his life to Medina. There the faithful gathered to pray in his house, a rectangular enclosed compound with a thatched roof on palm trunks along the southern wall, that was the prototype for the first congregational mosque (Fig. 7). For centuries thereafter, congregational mosques followed this model of a hypostyle, roofed prayer hall oriented to Mecca, preceded by a walled open-air courtyard.

The Muslims of Muhammad's generation were a small cluster of Arab traders and urban merchants in Mecca and Medina with little or no farming experience. But in the mid-seventh century the Muslim armies led by the Umayyads (661–750), the first hereditary dynasty in Islam, conquered the lands that are today known as Syria, Jordan, Israel, Palestine, Lebanon, Iraq, and most of Iran, and the burgeoning population of Muslim converts began to include city dwellers, nomadic tribespeople, and settled farmers. By the early eighth century, this territory extended from Syria westward across northern Africa to Morocco and the Iberian Peninsula, and eastward through Iran to central Asia.

The Muslims inherited practical and intellectual knowledge from the Roman past, the built landscape of which they now inhabited; they learned also from their diverse brethren,

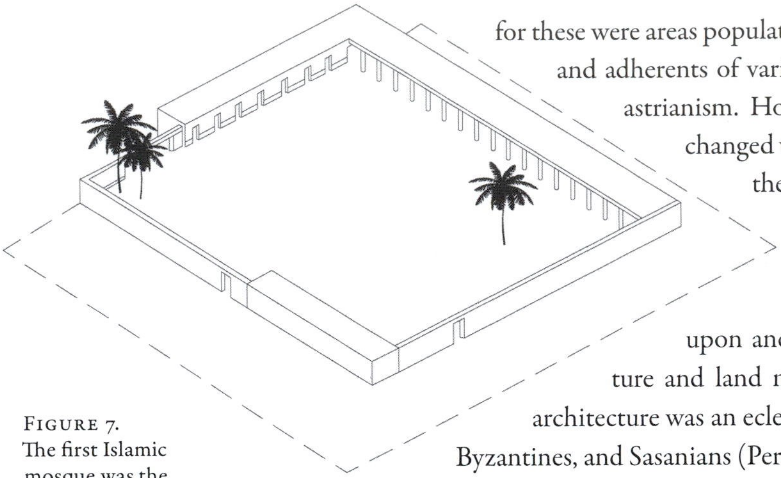

FIGURE 7.
The first Islamic
mosque was the
Prophet's own
house, a large open
enclosure with a
roofed area along
one or more sides,
built about 622 C.E.
in Medina. These
characteristics
of a vernacular
Arabian dwelling
became the model
for subsequent
congregational
mosques. (Ruggles
and Variava after
Sauvaget)

for these were areas populated by Byzantine Christians, Jews, Copts, and adherents of various polytheistic religions such as Zoroastrianism. However, while human cultural practices changed with the advent of Islam, many aspects of the land itself did not, for the climate of the Mediterranean rim has not changed significantly in the past two thousand years. Thus, early Muslims could build upon ancient and existing knowledge of agriculture and land management techniques. Much as their architecture was an eclectic mixture of motifs from the Romans, Byzantines, and Sasanians (Persian dynasty, 226–640 C.E.), so too their agriculture drew from many traditions.

The newly conquered Islamic world was a predominantly arid landscape (the Arabian peninsula, Syria, Jordan, the Anatolian Plateau, much of Iran, and all but the coast of North Africa) where small amounts of rain fell seasonally but not regularly even during the supposed wet season. Drought-tolerant crops like dates and olives flourished.[1] But crops requiring water, such as fruit, many grains, and especially vegetables, could be grown only seasonally, as rainfall or irrigation permitted. In the desert, rainfall—on which irrigation was also dependent—often does not occur for several years, and the occasional rain that does fall fails to soak the desert hardpan. Desert soil has a high rate of evaporation and runoff so that only 10 percent of the water that falls actually penetrates into it.[2] Hence, for rainfall to have an effect, it must be collected, stored, and distributed in a managed network.

The economic benefits of irrigation technology were quickly learned in Islam, whose rulers, landowners, and farmers could observe and improve upon Roman and Persian precedents. In many cases, Muslim communities did not build new hydraulic systems as much as they resuscitated and extended existing irrigation works. Ironically, however, although Arabic intellectual history was legitimated by its claim to ancient foundations, the historians of the first centuries of Islam seldom acknowledged the material and architectural debt to the Roman empire. It is only through close archaeological study that we can ascertain, for example, that the stretches of aqueduct built outside Cordoba (Spain) in the tenth century predated the patron who took credit for building it.[3] The engineers of Islamic Cordoba simply rebuilt a much older system that had previously served the multitude of Roman villas stretching between the mountains and the fertile banks of the Guadalquivir River.

Irrigation by means of a predictable, dependable supply of water could transform the desert from wasteland—or at least ground with extremely limited productive value—to a prosperous landscape of small agricultural estates that gave forth enough food to sustain permanent residential communities as well as to exchange in trade (Fig. 8). The skill in obtaining and using water allowed the Islamic domestic agricultural economy to flourish, and it stimulated surpluses that could be traded with other lands, forging a strong link between the countryside and market centers. Thus an intimate relationship of mutual dependency developed between the rural and city dwellers.

As a result of irrigation, Syria and Jordan bloomed with agricultural estates that appeared like islands of greenery amid the arid, ocher-colored landscape. Some of these, like Jabal Says, built between 707–15 about 105 kilometers southeast of Damascus (Syria), had very limited water supplies (Fig. 9). The water for Jabal Says came from a nearby volcanic mountain. In the extinct volcano's 2.5-kilometer-long crater, a seasonal spring and shallow lake collected water that was then stored in three cisterns. Replenished by winter rains, these supplies were enough to allow a single short growing season and to nourish drought-tolerant trees like the olive. The resulting agricultural production sustained a community with a residential *qasr* (fortified residence) or caravanserai, mosque, bath, farmhouses, and large granary.[4]

Qasr al-Hayr West (al-Gharbi) was built for the prince Hisham of the Umayyad family in 724–27 in arid landscape about 60 kilometers west of Palmyra. It was known in his day as al-Zaytuna, meaning "olive." Its palace, bathhouse, and caravanserai stood within a walled rectangular enclosure (1,050 by 442 m) devoted to irrigated agriculture and olive trees. Water was obtained from an underground canal, called a *qanat*, that carried water from a third-century Roman dam, 16 kilometers to the south. There was also a seasonal stream and a semicircular stone barrage (2.75 m thick) with sluices.[5]

Qasr al-Hayr East (al-Sharqi) was an oasis settlement built by Umayyad patrons in the years 700–730 northeast of Palmyra (Fig. 10).[6] It consisted of an extensive walled enclosure (about 7 square km) with buildings for the permanent residents as well as a caravanserai for transient merchants. In the former, the archaeologists excavated a room with heaps of olive pits—clear evidence that the economy of the estate was based on olive production and processing, perhaps augmented by some fruit and other seasonal crops. It is also possible that arboriculture coexisted with hunting, the enclosure serving as a small animal preserve with grassy feed. Irrigation was achieved by trapping the rain-fed seasonal stream, called a *wadi*, within the low enclosure walls. At the north and south ends of the enclosure, enormous sluices controlled the water's ingress and egress. The north sluices, which had thick walls and narrow openings, could be blocked up with

FIGURE 8.
Most of Syria is steppe. It appears to be desolate and barren for most of the year, but when the rains come — sometimes not for several years in a row — the desert erupts with vegetation. The baths of Qusayr ʿAmra (711-15), seen here, were fed by a seasonal stream that was exploited so that, in the eighth century, the landscape was greener than it appears today. (Ruggles)

rocks and earth to form a dam to contain the water, thus creating an artificial reservoir. The site had only one canal which ran from the northeast portion of the enclosure to the southwestern portion, and no other signs of irrigation canalization, which has led some historians to suggest that the site could not have served an agricultural purpose.[7] But the water collected from rains and the wadi extended the cultivator's ability to irrigate an orchard of relatively drought-tolerant trees. The south sluice gate, which was originally five meters high and had larger openings, allowed the water to escape quickly when the floods were too violent. Qasr al-Hayr East's simple but effective system of walls and sluices ensured the maximum use of rainfall which, when it fell, came in torrents and quickly washed over the hard-packed earth. By trapping the water and using it slowly over the course of many weeks, allowing it to percolate deep into the soil, inhabitants made longer periods of irrigation possible, altering the natural "all or nothing" water supply so as to improve growing conditions.

Khirbat al-Mafjar was a far more luxurious site. Built around 739–43 near Jericho by the Umayyad al-Walid II before he became caliph, it was a well-appointed but unfinished palatine complex consisting of a large, walled courtyard through which one passed to reach the palace proper, mosque, handsome bathhouse, and large roofed fountain. Water flowed from nearby springs via a Roman aqueduct and was stored in a tank that stood on ground 24.5 meters higher than the palace and 700 meters distant. As it coursed toward the palace's cisterns and baths, it turned the wheels of various mills. Below the palace on its east side, a buttressed wall formed an irregular enclosure of approximately 150 acres. The grain grown in this area was probably ground by the mills above.[8]

These sites, whether aristocratic palaces like Khirbat al-Mafjar and Qasr al-Hayr West or more functional working estates like Jabal Says and Qasr al-Hayr East, relied on the acquisi-

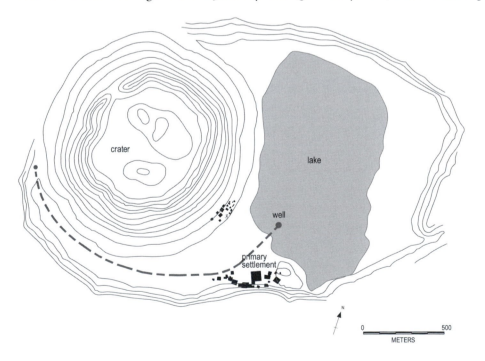

FIGURE 9.
Jabal Says, built between 707 and 715 in the Syrian desert, was a settlement of farmhouses, a bath, mosque, and a caravanserai or formal residence that was entirely dependent on the waters collected in its artificial lake. (Ruggles and Variava after Sauvaget)

FIGURE 10.
Qasr al-Hayr East
(700–730) was an
agricultural settle-
ment in Syria that
produced olives
from its orchards
and sustained a
permanent resi-
dential community
that lived in the
large structure
seen here.

tion and manipulation of water for their survival. By augmenting seasonal or groundwater supplies, water systems created flourishing oases that were both profitable and handsome. The primary function of the water was to irrigate crops that were sent to the cities for trade; the secondary purpose was to provide pleasure in the form of the fountains and basins that adorned the courtyards and the immersion pools in the bathhouses. Most of these estates fell to ruin centuries ago, and now only the footings of walls and chunks of broken stucco and stone remind us of what once stood there. It is no wonder that earlier architectural historians mistakenly called them "desert estates" and typically presented them as architectural ground plans with no reference to the hydraulic infrastructure and vegetation that was their raison d'être. When arranged in chronological sequence, their plans do show the typological development of an Umayyad formal design of large palace or residential building, but they fail to disclose the much larger landscape context to which the architecture responded. Together, these estates created a complex web of water and land management that changed the landscape of the eastern Mediterranean and that was one of the keys to the political and economic success of Islam in its first century and a half.

Water is extremely difficult to transport because it is heavy, hard to contain, and evaporates quickly in a hot, dry climate. But there are various ways to supply water to an irrigation system. The most efficient is to use canals and natural gravity to carry the water from a high point of collection, such as a cistern or lake, to a lower point of delivery into the irrigation network. Such a system relies on exact measurement of the canal's slope, the techniques for which have been known and in use since the beginning of large-scale agricultural settlement. The ancient Romans were masters of hydraulic engineering and built impressive aqueducts that carried water long distances across topographically irregular terrain through the landscape and into major cities, such as the Aqueduct of Valens built in fourth-century Con-

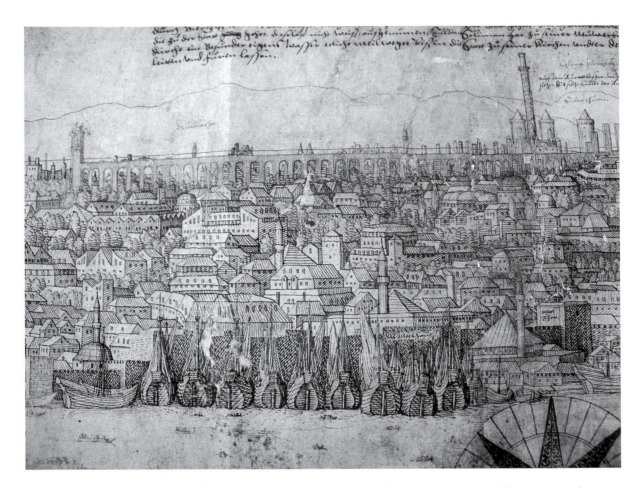

FIGURE 11.
In Melchior Lorichs'
panorama of
Istanbul, the Roman
Aqueduct of Valens
(325 C.E.) is clearly
visible. It still stands
today, a testament
to the endurance of
Roman engineering.
(Leiden University
Library, BPL 1758)

stantinople (Fig. 11).[9] Precise geometrical calculations were required for aqueducts because water carried at too steep an incline quickly becomes a torrent that overflows the walls of the canal bed, while water refuses to move along too level an incline, collecting in pools and stagnating. Roman aqueducts littered the Mediterranean landscape, and early Islamic civilization, which embraced the sciences of mathematics, geometry, astronomy, and surveying, proved highly efficient at building and repairing such waterworks.

Some of the most ingenious manipulations of water, both in terms of collection and display, occurred in al-Andalus, the Islamic kingdom in the southern half of what is today Spain and Portugal. An offshoot of the Syrian Umayyad dynasty ruled al-Andalus, from the capital city Cordoba, between 756 and 1031. Cordoba was surrounded by a belt of farm estates, many owned by Umayyad princes and high-ranking court officials, which embellished the landscape and enriched the coffers of the state, transforming al-Andalus from a backwater province into a bustling commercial and cultural center. The first such estate was built north of the city and called al-Rusafa, after the Syrian palace estate of the same name where the Hispano-Umayyad ruler 'Abd al-Rahman I had spent his youth before emigrating to al-Andalus. But the grandest of the estates was Madinat al-Zahra', built beginning in 936 and continually augmented and renovated until its destruction by fire and human violence in 1010.

Madinat al-Zahra' received water from a branch of the Valdepuentes Aqueduct that appears to have been partly new construction and partly a reuse of an aqueduct built in the Roman period.[10] The 18.6-kilometer-long aqueduct, which ran down from the mountains northwest of the palace, was graded to flow at a steady rate, and where the land was irregular, the water was carried on bridges to maintain a constant slope. Indeed, Cordoba was amply supplied by aqueducts that had been built in the Roman period and continued to flow in the eighth century and later; the remains of these can still be seen in the outlying countryside as well as in the now urbanized area that formerly lay just west of the city walls (Fig. 12). Elsewhere in the Mediterranean, a slightly different technique likewise transported water across long distances but, instead of traversing ravines with horizontal bridges, it employed vertical shafts that together behaved as a siphon (Fig. 13, bottom). The siphon's advantage over the aqueduct was that it used considerably less brick and stone.

A less costly but more labor-intensive technique lifts the water from its source in buckets or large scoops. For example, the Castillejo of Monteagudo, near Murcia in twelfth-century al-Andalus, stood on an isolated hilltop which could not possibly have trapped enough rainwater to sustain the irrigated courtyard garden in its center. Instead, the water for drinking and irrigating was lifted upward to a considerable height by means of a variant of a waterwheel called a *saqiya*.[11] In the case of a saqiya, numerous containers hang along the length of a chain or rope loop which is attached to a horizontal bar (like an ordinary yard well) (Fig. 13, top, and Fig. 14). The horizontal bar has a cogwheel at one end that is rotated by a larger horizontal cogwheel which is turned steadily by a draft animal, such as a mule or

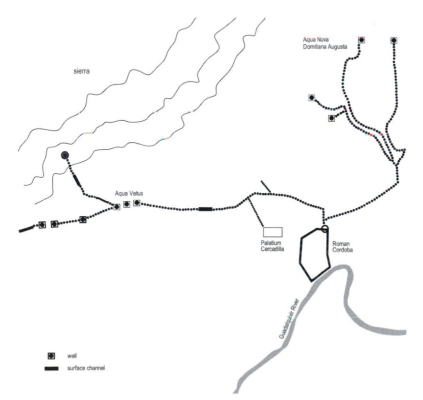

FIGURE 12. The Roman hydraulic system of aqueducts and wells was extended in the Islamic period to serve the city and agricultural estates of Cordoba. Its primary arteries are shown here. (Ruggles and Variava, after Ventura Villanueva)

FIGURE 13.
Top: waterwheel
with chain of
buckets; middle:
a series of two
shadufs; bottom:
siphon (Ruggles
and Variava, after
Thorkild Schioler)

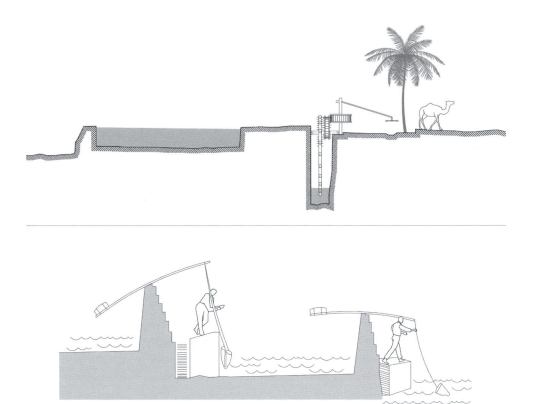

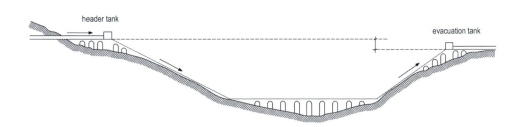

ox, which walks around it in continual circles. As the buckets tilt at the highest point, the water splashes into a raised canal and from there flows to the agricultural field, garden bed, or basin where it is to be used. This system is ideal for lifting water from a deep but confined source, like a well or cistern; although water is transported in relatively small quantities, it can be lifted from a very low point of storage to a very high point of delivery.

Another water-lifting device was the *shaduf*, consisting of a long lever with a bucket at one end and a counterweight or handle at the other (Fig. 13, middle). This was used extensively in ancient Egypt to raise water from the river to the fields along its banks. The lever system is less efficient than the wheel because it moves very little water at a time and requires a human being to dip, raise, and guide the bucket from the river to the trench from where the water will flow into the field. Sometimes shadufs are used in stacked sequences, lifting water from one level to the next, as shown in the diagram. This system is best suited for low-lying areas such as the Nile River valley where the source of water is not far below or far away from the fields where it will be used in cultivation. When the waterwheel was introduced from the Near East in the eighth century, it gradually replaced the shaduf,[12] but shadufs are still used by small farmers today on a limited scale because they are inexpensive and easy to build.

A third lifting device is the noria (*na'ura*), a water-wheel with attached buckets (typically eight) that circulate, dipping into the source below, which may be a river or reservoir, and then, as the wheel rotates, rising to dump their contents into a canal that carries the water to the field or garden. The noria wheel operates much like the saqiya but it is less costly since locomotion is provided either by a yoked draft animal (in which case it may be called a *dulab*) or, in rivers, by the natural water current. Waterwheels that take advantage of river propulsion are the most economical and rapid means of lifting water into an irrigation system, although their effectiveness is limited because they can lift water no higher than the diameter of the wheel itself.[13] They lift more water in the winter, when streams are swollen and their currents run fast; in the summer, when irrigation water is badly needed, their output is greatly diminished. In areas of low technology, such wheels are still used today.

FIGURE 14.
This Egyptian waterwheel has ceramic pots tied to its rim. As the wheel turns, the pots scoop water from the irrigation canal and then dump it into a small channel leading into an agricultural plot.

In each of these cases, machinery must be built and either animal or human labor used to raise relatively small amounts of water from the source to the point of delivery into the irrigation system. Hence, the benefit of cultivating crops using irrigation must be offset against the cost of labor and the capital investment of construction. Furthermore, the supply of water cannot be very far from the field that it irrigates.

An altogether different means of transporting water to an irrigation system, which was able to deliver large amounts of water over long distances, was the *qanat*. A qanat is a subterranean tunnel that carries water from an elevated source where the water supply is constant, such as a mountain with melting winter snows, to a lower point that may be more than 30 kilometers away. At Qasr al-Hayr West, a Roman dam provided the source of water, and a qanat brought the water to the residential and agricultural complex 16 kilometers distant. Qanats were used in Iran during the Achaemenid Empire (sixth to fourth centuries B.C.E.), and probably earlier, although it is uncertain whether earlier qanats were drainage channels for mining runoff or true irrigation conduits. These qanats were clearly still in use during the Islamic period, for in the ninth century a congress of Muslim jurists was convened in Khurasan to compile a book on water law and qanat regulations.[14] Qanat technology spread to Syria, the Arabian Peninsula, and India; the Romans carried it across northern Africa, and Muslims brought the technique to the Iberian Peninsula and Sicily.

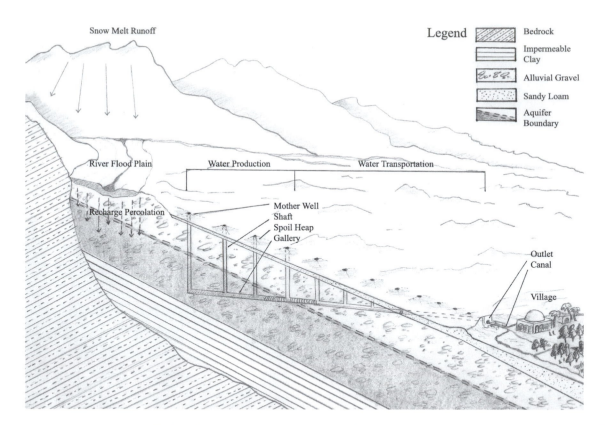

Snow Melt Runoff

Legend

Bedrock

Impermeable Clay

Alluvial Gravel

Sandy Loam

Aquifer Boundary

River Flood Plain

Water Production

Water Transportation

Recharge Percolation

Mother Well
Shaft
Spoil Heap
Gallery

Outlet
Canal

Village

FIGURE 15.
Qanats allowed water to be transported great distances. A mother well is sunk at the foot of a mountain where the water table is naturally high, and from there, a large horizontal water tunnel is dug in the direction of a village. The tunnel declines steadily in order to encourage flow, but at a lesser decline than the water table itself. At the qanat's destination many kilometers distant, where the water table is much lower, water flows copiously. (Schleicher for Ruggles)

To build a qanat, a vertical mother well is dug down into the high water table at the foot of a mountain (Fig. 15). A horizontal tunnel is extended from this, running at a very slight slope that declines less than the water table itself and less than the surface of the land above ground. Eventually the tunnel meets the land surface where it spews forth its water many feet above the natural water table. A series of vertical shafts allow aeration of the tunnel as well as access for the regular maintenance that must be performed to keep the tunnel from collapsing. The initial investment in construction is extraordinarily high, but the wonder of the system is that, once constructed, no human or animal labor is required to move the water because it flows like a natural stream. The qanat transports large quantities of water, twenty-four hours a day, often providing irrigation to an entire settlement, and in arid areas, the qanat has the advantage over above-ground aqueducts or seasonal wadis because the water does not evaporate.[15] Thus, in the dry landscape of Syria and Iran, as well as across northern Africa, qanats were used through history to transform the desert by providing farms and orchards with abundant quantities of necessary water (Fig. 16).

However, qanat systems require large teams of skilled laborers and are expensive to build, even when the costs are spread incrementally across generations of workers. Furthermore, they encompass large areas and require enormous planning for the initial construction phase, followed by a consistent collaboration among community members to maintain the tunnels and allocate the water thus obtained. Planning and regulation on such a large scale had to be supervised by either a central director or communal committee with the authority and power to draft labor and to levy taxes in order to pay for it. It also required a viable system of apportionment so that the benefits of the hydraulic system could be fairly distributed. In some areas of the Islamic world, water allocation was measured in units of time proportional to the amount of land owned so that each parcel of land might receive water for one half day a week. In other areas, such as Damascus (Syria) and Valencia (Spain), the farmers took turns, so that each farmer was entitled to open the sluice gate to his field for as long as necessary to flood the land, whereupon the next farmer would take a turn, and so on until the rotation was complete. A third system prevailed in lands with constant water scarcity due to the lack of rivers: for example, in the Yemen and oasis communities, water rights were a utility measured in units of time that could be sold or traded as commodities, regardless of land ownership.[16]

Hydraulic systems in the Islamic world varied in size from the farmer's individual well to a community-served *qanat*. But with any form of irrigation in which multiple users partook of the same resource, whether a river-based canal network or a qanat, social mechanisms were necessary to oversee the acquisition and allocation of the resource. When the inevitable disputes arose, institutions such as specialized administrators and courts with informed judges had to resolve the conflicts. Some historians and anthropologists have proposed that the installation and regulation of such a water distribution system provoked one of the earliest forms of large-scale political organization, in which a central despot garnered forced labor to build the irrigation system which then was a valuable resource that he controlled.[17] Others have countered that water, as a resource held in common, led to community organization around mutual interests at local level.[18] There is no doubt that in arid climates water resources were political and economic issues of the highest importance, although it is by no means clear that the only response was political repression. Indeed, an alternative result was cooperation and consensus (and a tightly woven social fabric of interdependency), with the farmers and land owners paying the costs and in return reaping the immediate benefits of hydraulic installations that were linked to form large-scale systems.

Since most of the histories in the pre-modern period were written for caliphs and sultans and contain little information on ordinary people, it is hard to assess how much

FIGURE 16.
A qanat can transform an arid landscape, producing an artificial oasis of cultivated fields and orchards in the midst of harsh desert. But as it passes under the desert's surface, only the openings of its vertical holes are visible. (Dale Lightfoot, Oklahoma State University)

of the potential benefit of capital-intensive investments in irrigation accrued to the agriculturalists themselves. Certainly the surpluses produced by a bumper crop allowed individuals as well as the government to store grain against times of famine, thus ensuring stability, and they probably also sparked a demand for luxury goods in the market, which in turn increased the importance of such a market center in the regional trade network. According to court chroniclers across the lands of the early Islamic world, a clearly broadcasted sign of beneficent sovereignty was the construction of a hydraulic system that would serve, first, the gardens of the palace and then the surrounding farms and the city's public drinking fountains. The importance of the act is demonstrated by the historians and geographers of the early centuries of Islam who, in their descriptions of major historic events and landscape features, repeatedly praised such irrigation canals and fountains as signs of a civilized community.

In Abbasid Iraq, the vizier Mu'awiya ibn 'Abdullah maintained that the costs of building and maintaining waterworks should be the responsibility of the government.[19] But in actual practice, this varied according to whether the property thus improved was state land, known as *kharaj*, or belonged to the cultivators themselves, known as *sulh*. When the caliph al-Mahdi (r. 775–785) built a canal in Wasit, the farmers who received the new water supply paid for it through their taxes, which were doubled. The Abbasids (749–1258) conquered huge territories in the late eighth through tenth centuries and were confronted with the problem of supervising diverse and sometimes distant lands. They required expert knowledge in engineering and in land management, such as that provided by Abu Bakr Ahmad ibn Wahshiyya (d. 870), Abu'l-wafa al-Buzjani (d. 997), and Ya'qub b. Ibrahim Abu Yusuf (d. 798).[20] The government not only installed hydraulic infrastructure but sometimes even dictated which crops should be grown in order to maintain economic stability and avoid wasting land.[21] Their investments to improve farmland yielded profits that allowed them to construct at an unprecedented scale and luxury.

The Abbasid city of Samarra in the mid-ninth century is an example of the vast expenditures given over to construction for supporting a water supply in new capital cities. The funds and manpower came from the immense booty and thousands of slaves captured in the wars waged by the Abbasid dynasty in the expansion of the Islamic empire. With deep financial pockets, the Abbasid caliphs undertook one of the greatest architectural follies in world history: a palace complex larger and more sumptuous than anything built before. Searching for a place to realize grandiose ambitions, the Abbasid Caliph al-Mu'tasim moved his court out of the capital city of Baghdad in 836 to Shammasiyya first and then Qatul, eventually locating in Samarra along the Tigris River. Baghdad had been well suited to settlement because of its canals bringing water from both the Tigris and the Euphrates rivers, and so its inhabitants had water in abundance and were able to plant not only many date palms but also fruit trees and gardens.[22] But none of the new sites was selected with water supply in mind—indeed, the engineers were called in only after each site was chosen—and the delivery of water quickly became a troubling concern.[23]

In their settlement along the Tigris and Euphrates rivers, the Abbasids generally availed themselves of existing canals dating from the Sasanian period. But among the necessary elements of the infrastructure for the palatine complex at Samarra was a new canal to bring water from the Tigris. For this canal, entire villages were bought up and removed, a colossal undertaking that was estimated by the chronicler Ya'qubi to cost an extraordinary one and a half million dinars.[24] However, this canal did not supply enough water for the sprawl of residences, bathhouses, and palaces with gardens, fountains, and pools since the same chronicler relates that in most houses, human carriers delivered water from the river.[25] Similarly in the eighth-century Egyptian city of Fustat, where the annual flooding of the Nile made canals seasonally undependable, water was transported by pack animal to man-made reservoirs from where carriers would deliver the water to small tanks in individual households.[26] But Fustat did not pretend to match the scale of Samarra. After fifty years, the system of getting water by canals and drawing it from the Tigris in buckets proved insufficient, and for this and other political reasons the Abbasids quit Samarra and returned to Baghdad.

The harnessing of water resources—when it was done wisely and with foresight—enabled agriculturalists to farm areas on the Islamic map previously suitable only for transient animal herding. Landscapes that today appear barren and desolate supported pockets of irrigated agriculture at one time, and indeed, the desert of Syria and Jordan is littered with the remains of architectural sites from the Umayyad era, such as Qasr al-Hayr East, built of stone, mud brick, and wood (in areas where no trees are present today). Such places are proof that the arid terrain, which in any case was more steppe (arid with limited seasonal rainfall) than true desert, was once fertile and capable of supporting permanent settlements of considerable sophistication. Olives were the primary crop, but grapes were also significant, with Christians consuming most (but not all) of the wine produced.[27] The "greening" of Syria and Jordan began during the Hellenistic age, accelerated under the Romans, and declined in the seventh century due to social turbulence associated with the Arab conquests. However, under the Umayyads, these lands were redistributed and the hydraulic infrastructure repaired so that agriculture could thrive again. In northern Iraq, the Muslims initiated new agricultural development on the Syrian model of manorial estates serving both Muslim and Christian markets.[28]

The Islamic success in irrigation and farming in the steppe permitted more and more permanent settlements that served as artificial oases mediating between the desert and the domesticated agricultural lands outside cities such as the Umayyad capital, Damascus. The desert was populated by nomadic tribes who lived by herding goats, camels, and sheep and plundering small towns and merchant caravans; the urban centers had the densest population of consumers and great markets where agricultural produce was sold. Intermediary settlements such as Qasr al-Hayr East and Jabal Says, as well as princely palaces such as Khirbat al-Mafjar, Mshatta (Jordan, a temporary residence), and the bathhouse Qusayr 'Amra (Jordan), provided meeting places where Umayyad rulers could entertain the autonomous tribal chiefs whose support was necessary in the first two centuries of the Islamic state. Until 750, the settlements also served as visual markers of the political territory of the Umayyad caliphs, after which they were absorbed in the new and much more extensive empire of the Abbasid caliphs, centered around their new capital city of Baghdad.

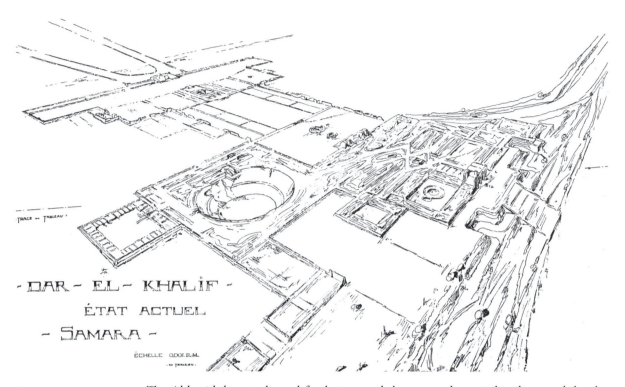

- DAR - EL - KHALIF -
ÉTAT ACTUEL
- SAMARA -

TRACE au TABLEAU

ÉCHELLE 0.001. P.M.
au TABLEAU

FIGURE 17.
In this view of the Dar al-Khilafa, Samarra, drawn in 1913, a tripled arched portal stood on a broad terrace at the head of the enormous flight of steps at the Samarran palace. From here, there was a sweeping view of gardens and pools at the foot of the stairs, a channel that led to small pavilion on the banks of the river, the river itself, and the less densely settled landscape on the opposite bank. (Henri Viollet)

The Abbasid dynasty leaned further toward the east and was imbued as much by the cultures of Iraq and Iran as by the echoes of the Mediterranean-focused Roman Empire. Both because of their more eastern character and because they succeeded an already established Islamic dynasty, the Abbasids held an attitude toward the land that was markedly different from that of the Umayyads. Whereas the Umayyads faced the problem of how to define Islam with visible symbols that would represent the religion and the dynasty, the Abbasids inherited an already recognizable stock of symbols and mechanisms for the display of Muslim identity. For example, one established architectural type was the hypostyle mosque plan—a rectangular enclosure with a roofed prayer hall of columnar supports derived from the Prophet's House in Medina—while another type was the royal reception hall with a domed throne chamber signifying sovereignty. Under the Umayyads, garden design had also begun to develop into a fixed set of forms, and one of the principal signifiers in garden symbolism was water. The Umayyads conspicuously displayed water in large fountains, handsome bathhouses, and of course the gardens themselves, where flowers and foliage were a visible sign of the nurturing capacity of water. Their Abbasid successors used both land and water even more recklessly in their huge palaces at Samarra. Both the Balkuwara Palace (see Sites), built 849–59, and the Dar al-Khilafa (Fig. 17), built around 836, stood on the bank of the Tigris, so that while the palaces could be approached by land at one end, they were also reached by water at the other.[29] The river façades of these palaces consisted of elevated halls or pavilionlike portals with the space between the architecture and the riverbank filled with cultivated gardens traversed by water channels and punctuated by pools so that the river was integrated into the aesthetic experience of the landscape. In the palaces' great interior courtyards, water also played a prominent role in centrally placed fountains, the spray of which must have been a welcome refreshment in Iraq's blistering heat. Because no vegetation remains from these palaces, which today are dusty archaeological relics, the presence of water canals and fountains is a clue to a verdant splendor that we can only imagine. But it is not purely imaginary, for we know that water, both artificially supplied and in its natural riverine form, gave life and as such was an object of spectacle and delight. Indeed, poetry describing the Abbasid palaces mentions water-wheels propelled by ostriches in gardens planted with narcissus, myrtle, and saffron.[30]

In later periods, architects continued to attend to the natural conditions of landscape. A palace or palatine city such as Samarra, or the Mughal palatine city Fatehpur-Sikri in sixteenth-century India, required careful planning and a cautious use of water. Fatehpur-Sikri has no flowing water today and its gardens have disappeared because the hydraulic systems—inadequate to begin with—were allowed to deteriorate when the palace was abandoned not long after it was built. Those water supplies that still exist are needed by the local community for basic functions such as drinking and bathing. Samarra and Fatehpur-Sikri are examples where the engineers appear to have miscalculated, for the water resources were barely enough to sustain cities in those arid areas. But at the edge of the Iranian desert, near Kashan, the sixteenth-century Bagh-i Fin palace still has running water that courses through its water channels and nourishes its plants (Plate 1). The water is brought to the palace and surrounding agricultural fields via the original qanat, so that both architecture and landscape continue to be dependent upon the same precious resource.

PLATE 1.
Bagh-i Fin, Kashan.
In this earliest
surviving Safavid
garden, the water
channels are lined
with blue tile which
contrasts with the
cream-colored
stone and the dark
green of the tree fo-
liage. Water seems
abundant, but it
is in fact carried
to the site across
a long distance by
an underground
conduit called a
qanat. (Yasamin
Bhadorzadeh)

PLATE 2.
Acequía Court,
Generalife Palace.
A long channel
forms the central
axis of this court-
yard, punctuated
at each end by a
low marble basin
with a jet. Although
a narrow band of
pavement bisects
the channel midway
and divides the
garden into four
discrete parts, this
may not be original.
Today the planting
bears little relation
to that of the
Islamic period in
Granada and the
surfaces of beds
are 70 centimeters
higher than
formerly.

PLATE 3.
Tomb of Humayun,
Delhi. Although
built of local In-
dian red sandstone
incised with white
marble, this mauso-
leum's domed form
and classic Persian
hesht behsht plan,
was a clear refer-
ence to the Mughal
dynasty's Timurid
roots.

PLATE 4.
Casa de Contratación, Alcazar, Seville. The walls that line the deeply sunken quadrants of this garden are lined with overlapping blind arches of brick. The water channels are carried at a much higher level, set within the walkways, meeting at the garden center in a pool with a jet (that has been considerably restored). The elevated paths and channels facilitated irrigation, while the plants were set at a lower level so that their blooms would barely reach the surface of the pavement.

PLATE 5.
This Mughal manuscript illustration from 1595 depicts a garden divided into grassy quadrants by water channels bordered by spring flowers. On one side, a raised platform projects out into the river, offering views to the opposite bank, while a cutaway section of the wall shows a waterwheel propelled by oxen. (British Library, Or. 12208, f. 65a)

PLATE 6.
In this page from *Bayad wa Riyad,* the only Andalusian manuscript with narrative illustrations, waterfowl swim in a pool with bronze horsehead spouts while a hare is poised to leap up the steps. Above, a vine twists and climbs along a trellis. The story is a romance: the other illustrations depict a lutist serenading ladies, a despondent lover, and courtly scenes, most of them in garden settings. (Biblioteca Apostolica Vaticana (Vatican) VAT. AR.368)

PLATE 7.
The *Khamsa* of Nizami is a collection of five long poems by Iran's greatest poet of the twelfth century. In this illustrated copy from 1595, a group of men sit outside city gates. In the foreground, a leafy vine grows over a cage trellis, carefully placed alongside a small brook in order to water the roots of the plants. (British Library, Or. 12208 [40b])

PLATE 8.
A basin is set on the backs of twelve lions in the center of the cross-axially divided courtyard of the Court of the Lions, Alhambra. The garden's original planting is not known, and it has been variously replanted in the past hundred years —sometimes quadrants of flowers, other times a few shrubs interspersed on bare earth—but it is believed that the fourteenth-century soil level was considerably lower than at present.

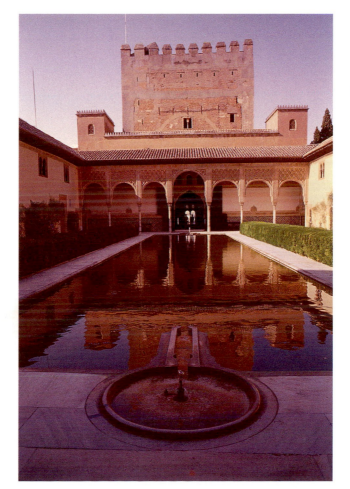

PLATE 9.
At the Alhambra, a smooth sheet of water occupies the center of the Court of the Myrtles, mirroring a reflection of the imposing Comares Tower (housing the Hall of the Ambassadors). At either end, small jets spout water into round basins, the emanating circles of which make a pleasing and dynamic contrast to the placid rectangle of the pool.

PLATE 10.
Centrally planned
with a fountain
in the shape of an
eight-pointed star,
the garden of the
Palace of Pasha
'Abd al-Kari in Fez
(1860), celebrates
geometry yet avoids
the cross-axial
planning of a
chahar bagh.
(Mercedes Maier)

PLATE 11.
Mughal garden
estates were built
all around Lake
Dal in Kashmir and
were reached by
either a lakefront
road or boat. The
climate was utterly
different from that
of the Indian plains.
Bulbs flowered in
the spring and sum-
mer, and hundreds
of fountain jets
sprayed water into
rushing channels.
The magnificent
topography of lake
surrounded by
steep snow-capped
mountains provided
spectacular land-
scape vistas.

PLATE 12.
While most paintings of gardens depict ideal settings that are useful only as genre scenes, this manuscript illustration (1663) shows the Mughal emperor Shah Jahan in a place that can be easily identified as Nishat Bagh, Srinagar (Kashmir). Water is central in the image, passing between rectangular borders divided into discrete square beds. (RAS Persian MS 310, 21b in Titley and Wood).

PLATE 13.
The *Maqamat* by al-Hariri show lively scenes of ordinary life such as a preacher in a mosque and the return of pilgrims from the hajj. In this manuscript of 1237, a cemetery is depicted with mourners amidst domed tombs. (Bibliothèque Nationale de France, Arabe 5847, folio 29v)

خوب می نماید خیلی باغ خوبی طرح شده و در ظرف خوب

کوه سفید نکهار واقع شده در میان نکهار و سنکش وسطه

PLATE 14.
In this ca. 1590
manuscript of
the *Baburnama*,
Babur supervises
the planting of the
Bagh-i Wafa, which
teems with colorful
plants, birds, and
human beings. It is
especially remark-
able for the gridded
architectural plan
held by the supervi-
sor, the first known
example of such
planning in Islamic
landscape history.
(Victoria and
Albert Museum)

PLATE 15.
This illustrated
Safavid copy of the
Haft awrang, a set
of poems by the late
Timurid acclaimed
poet, Jami, was
made for Ibrahim-
Mirza in 1556-67.
In this scene of a
garden plundered
by an insensitive
city-dweller, the
plants are rendered
in exquisite detail.
(Freer Gallery of
Art, Smithson-
ian Institution,
Washington D.C.:
Purchase, F1946.12,
fol. 179b)

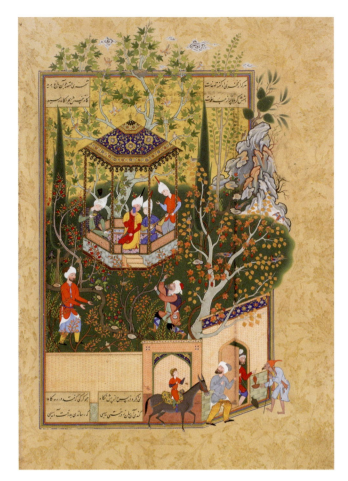

PLATE 16.
Dig Palace's huge
central garden is
laid out as a simple
chahar bagh with
raised channels
and walkways and
recessed beds that
are today filled
with grass. The Ke-
sav-Bhawan, in the
background here,
frames the view be-
yond the garden to
the artificial lake.

PLATE 17.
On the uppermost terrace of the Udaipur City Palace, the Amar Vilas courtyard is planted with lush vegetation and leafy trees that surround a central square tank. It appears today as it did in eighteenth-century paintings of court life. (Jennifer Joffee)

PLATE 18.
The plantings in the Bagh-i Bulbul have not received serious historical study, but the late-seventeenth-century Hesht Behesht pavilion still stands with some of its original wall tiles intact. Like other Safavid pavilions, nature is invited inside through large arched openings that align with the axes of the garden. (Yasamin Bahadorzadeh)

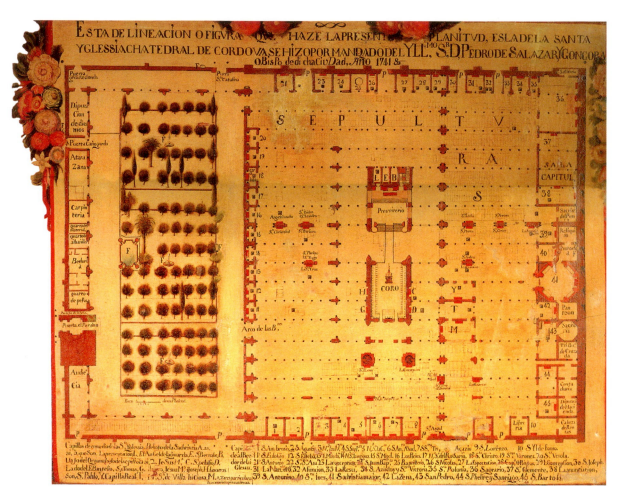

PLATE 19.
This 1741 painted
representation of
the Great Mosque
of Cordoba shows
orange and palm
trees planted at
regular intervals
in the courtyard.
While these are not
the same trees that
grew in the eighth
century, they are
evidence of
continued cultiva-
tion and renewal.
(Cathedral of
Cordoba Archives)

PLATE 20.
In the Chella
Necropolis, Rabat,
the *zawiya* is
organized around
an open courtyard
with a deep rect-
angular pool in its
center, colorful
zellij tile on the
floors and walls,
and scalloped
marble basins at
either end. The se-
ries of small cham-
bers that surround-
ed this space served
as dormitories for
the residents. A tall
minaret dominates;
to one side there
is a mosque and a
cemetery.

PLATE 21.
The white marble
Tomb of I'timad al-
Daula stands in the
center of a classic
chahar bagh, one
of many such hand-
some garden estates
on the banks of the
Yamuna River in
Agra. Mausolea and
residential pavilions
were typologically
similar, as were the
gardens in which
they stood, perhaps
because mausolea
were conceived
as eternal dwell-
ings and gardens
celebrated life on
earth even as they
were reminders
of the rewards of
paradise.

PLATE 22.
Seen in the monsoon fog, the Aiwan Pavilion at Shalamar Bagh, Lahore, stands on the central terrace. Water flows along the garden's long central channel, running beneath the pavilion's floor and pouring over a wide chadar flanked by large-scale chini khana panels. In front, a raised dais placed on the central axis provides a refreshing place from which to enjoy the spectacle of splashing water. (James L. Wescoat, Jr.)

PLATE 23.
The handsome Khass Mahal stands on an elevated terrace above the Anguri Bagh in Agra Fort. Water fills the scalloped basin in the center of the terrace, flows through a broad channel lined with gray and red marble in a zigzag pattern, and falls over a chini khana. Seventeenth-century accounts mention that niches such as these might be filled with brightly colored marigolds and roses during the day and flickering oil lamps at night. (Photo by the author)

PLATE 24.
Jahangir's Quadrangle, a courtyard of concentric rectangles, was the largest in the Lahore Fort's private quarters. Like the other Mughal forts, the imperial quarters were aligned along one wall of the fort and enjoyed exterior vistas. (James L. Wescoat, Jr.)

PLATE 25.
Built by a wealthy American in the late 1930s in Honolulu, Shangri La is neither pastiche nor homage. Rather, it interprets Mughal and Persian (seen here) garden and architectural concepts through the filter of modernism. The result balances smooth and textured surfaces, ornament and pure geometry.

PLATE 26.
Although built by
a Rajput (Hindu)
patron, the style
of this interior
courtyard garden at
the Amber Fort is
thoroughly Mughal.
It is divided into
an ornate chahar
bagh with flying
walkways and water
channels that flow
over a chadar and
chini khana.

PLATE 27.
Cairo's Azhar Park,
completed in 2005,
combines both
modern purity of
form with historic
references. Water
runs beneath or
along the central
walkway in jets,
channels, and oc-
casionally a flowing
chadar, reminiscent
of Andalusian and
Persian palace gar-
dens. In side areas,
sunken beds with
central fountains
are quotations of
classical Ottoman
gardens. Through-
out, the views along
the powerful axis
and beyond the
site to the sur-
rounding city are
breathtaking.

3   The Science of Gardening

Agricultural and Botanical Manuals

S THE ISLAMIC LANDSCAPE changed considerably during the eighth and ninth centuries, government administrators, landowners, and farmers took notice. The Islamic political map expanded to include new areas of the world with different climatic conditions and agricultural practices. This, in combination with the expansion of trade networks, first in the Mediterranean basin and subsequently along the land routes to central Asia and the east, stimulated the exchange of botanical specimens and farming lore. In the eighth, ninth and tenth centuries, while northern and western Europe slumbered in an age only partially enlightened by the Carolingian renaissance, the Islamic world, which in the ninth century stretched from the Iberian peninsula across North Africa to the eastern shores of the Mediterranean and beyond the Tigris and Euphrates river valleys to Afghanistan in central Asia, enjoyed a brisk economy. The need to manage and exploit newly conquered domains spurred an interest in land management and agronomic literature among the military aristocracy. This culture likewise produced a large wealthy class whose greatest worldly ambition, it would seem, was to own a fine house in the country and pen verses in praise of flowers and songbirds.[1]

In addition to an appreciation for the beauty of nature, these landowners, who might own property that they worked themselves or rented out for others to farm, paid serious attention to the practical aspects of maintaining their land. Not only did the property owner and the cultivators of the land have an interest in increasing the yield of crops, but the state did too, for rents and taxes were often paid in the form of a percentage of the harvest. In Egypt, records beginning in the ninth century indicate that centralized state controls, although imposed to ensure the accurate assessment of taxes, resulted in improvements in agricultural practice and long-term planning for the population's needs for food.

As a result of the interest of the ruler, elite property owners, and tax officials, a written literature on the science of agriculture soon developed in those countries with flourishing agricultural economies, especially al-Andalus under the Umayyad and taifa (small splinter kingdoms) dynasties, Coptic and Muslim-ruled Egypt, and the Yemen under the Rasulid dynasty. The first texts were calendars or almanacs instructing how and when to plant and botanical dictionaries describing plants (usually wild) and their curative properties.[2] These important compendia contained a wide range of information, including how to

FIGURE 18.
In addition to
identifying and
cultivating herbs,
a physician had to
serve as pharmacol-
ogist. In this scene
from a manuscript
illustration of the
De materia medica
of Dioscorides, a
physician, seated
below the jars
stored in his attic,
boils a concoction
while his client
waits patiently.
(The Metropoli-
tan Museum of
Art, Cora Timken
Burnett Collection
of Persian Minia-
tures and Other
Persian Art Objects,
Bequest of Cora
Timken Burnett,
1956 [57.51.21])

preserve foods and recipes for herbal medicines
(Fig. 18). The earliest extant Islamic calendar is
a ninth-century text by Ibn Masawayh, a physician from Iraq.[3] Better known, because it was
translated into Latin at an early date, is the Andalusian *Calendar of Cordoba* (*Kitab al-anwa'*),
composed sometime between 967 and 976.[4]
Although written in Arabic for Muslim patrons,
the *Calendar of Cordoba* and subsequent calendars employed the Christian calendar and Latin
names for the months because the solar reckoning system of the Christians was more suitable
for agriculture than the shorter lunar calendar
of Islam in which the months occurred in different seasons each year. Indeed the first chapter of
the late thirteenth-century Yemeni treatise *Milh
al-malaha* begins, "The first thing here is the
knowledge of the solar year."[5] The eclecticism of
the almanacs reveals the adjustments that were
made between the pan-Islamic culture (its calendar and feast days) and the actual regional prac-
tices of communities that were by no means exclusively Muslim. Studies of the Egyptian
almanacs indicate that they drew from diverse sources: astronomical information from
Arabic sources, material on food and healing from Hellenistic sources, and material on administration and religious festivals from local Islamic and pharaonic sources.[6] Numerous
calendars dating from (or attributed to) the tenth through the fourteenth centuries have
been discovered in Morocco, al-Andalus, Tunisia, Libya, Egypt, and the Yemen.[7] From the
Yemen alone, eight almanacs have been identified, dating from 1271 through the fifteenth
century (and probably more await discovery).[8]

A second group of texts were botanical treatises, which identified plants with useful
pharmacological properties and described the healing concoctions that could be made
from them. These texts were at first based on Hellenistic and Roman precedents, such
as the *De materia medica*, a treatise on plants with medicinal value and medical practice written about 78 C.E. by Dioscorides, a physician in the Greek army. The utility and
popularity of this treatise is demonstrated by the fact that during the medieval era Greek
copies—some of them handsomely illustrated—were found in the Byzantine court, as in
the mid-tenth-century illustrated manuscript that belonged to the Emperor Constantine
Porphyrogenitus (Fig. 19),[9] as well as translations and glosses into Arabic that were made
subsequently for Muslim rulers. Galen's *De simplicium medicamentorum temperamentis et
facultatibus*, written between 129 and 200 C.E., was equally well known in the Arab world.

The botanical manuscripts were quite specific with respect to their written descriptions
and divided plants according to taxonomic classifications: *jins* for genus, *naw'* for species,

and *sinf* for variety.[10] They were sometimes, but not always, illustrated. While theoretically these pictures offer some of our first glimpses of nature and its representation in the early centuries of Islam, unfortunately the illustrations rarely have enough detail to allow us to identify them with known botanical specimens. Some of the inexactitude can be blamed on the process of manuscript production. A text was produced for oral delivery at first and then, if important and valuable enough, it would be copied down. As demand for its contents increased, more copies would be made and circulated to new patrons and libraries and sometimes, as in the case of the Dioscorides, even sent to new countries where the plants it described did not necessarily grow, or if they did, had a different form and appearance. Although the copyist system was well regulated to preserve the integrity of texts, with licenses and certificates of correct transmission, the illustrations were not as carefully controlled.[11] Details were sometimes lost, either because the artist did not understand the botanical specifics of the plant being rendered or because he drew from a picture rather from a specimen of a real plant.

Some of the pictorial unreliability can be attributed to the way that images were produced to begin with. They were intended to supplement the text in a secondary capacity and were not intended to substitute for the written description. In a world where geographers sometimes wrote lengthy descriptions of lands they had never visited, trusting in the descriptions written by earlier geographers, it is not hard to imagine that a botanical illustrator might find it perfectly reasonable to use a stylized and schematic rendering of a plant to accompany a far more detailed written description. And can we assume that early illustrators even looked at the plant while painting it? This changed by the time of the great Mughal, Safavid, and Ottoman painting ateliers from about the sixteenth century onward, when landscape scenes and plant "portraits" reveal the artist's meticulous observation (see Chapter 10), but in the earlier era, the plants were rendered more schematically.

Baghdad and Isfahan were centers for the botanical sciences in the ninth through eleventh centuries, with major treatises also produced in Cairo, Tunis, and the provincial capitals of al-Andalus. Although the treatises began as translations and glosses of classical texts, they were soon surpassed by editions based on the actual study of native plants. Long before Linnaeus, botanists in the Islamic world were organizing plants into morphological groups and studying the wonders of nature, both at home and abroad, on the basis of direct personal observation. These studies sometimes combined empirical and comparative methods, as in al-Andalus where one botanist acknowledged the importance of the supple-

FIGURE 19. A flower, bud, stem, and roots of a rose are illustrated on this page of the Dioscorides manuscript made for the Byzantine emperor Constantine Porphyrogenitus. (The Pierpont Morgan Library, New York. MS M.652, f.142 verso)

mentary information given to him by travelers reporting on specimens seen firsthand in India, Constantinople, the Yemen, Khurasan, and China.

Occasionally travelers carried actual specimens with them, which led botanists to try their hand at domesticating exotic plants such as new varieties of figs and pomegranates near Malaga (Spain) in the eighth century and in eleventh-century Toledo and Seville.[12] The singer Ziryab, who went from the Abbasid court at Samarra and Baghdad to the court of the Hispano-Umayyads in 821, introduced many novel fashions in dress, music, etiquette, and cuisine: he was the first to gather and eat asparagus in al-Andalus, perhaps because he had already learned to do so in Iraq.[13] However, the asparagus that was grown for the Abbasid table was itself a domesticated exotic: the original plants came from the Jordan valley.[14] Similarly, the sultans of the Yemen obtained fruit trees from Saladin in Syria in the twelfth century, as well as coconut trees, mango trees, grape varietals, rice, and rare plants from other foreign sources.[15]

The botanical treatises and calendars were followed by a third form of agricultural literature: the *Kitab al-filaha*, or book of agriculture, which was not so much a new genre as a shift in focus, from calendrical reckoning based on observation of the stars and planets in order to determine the correct time for seasonal activities, to more practical instructions regarding not only when but also how to plant, irrigate, fertilize, and reap.[16] Such manuals had numerous classical precedents. Pliny the Elder (23/24–79 C.E.) wrote *Naturalis historia*, an encyclopedia treating, among other things, kitchen gardens, irrigation, the preparation of the soil, and plants for cultivation as well as description of the appearance and use of wild plants. Running to thirty-seven volumes, this immense work was based more on earlier literary works than on farming experience. But Columella's *De re rustica*, written around 60–65 C.E., was informed by existing writings as well as actual work on his father's estate.

The earliest known Arabic agronomic text is Ibn Wahshiyya's *al-Filahat al-nabatiyya*, written in 904 C.E. in Iraq, although it was based on late antique and Arabic sources and claimed to be a translation of a Syriac text.[17] It was more concerned with social philosophy than practical method, and thus does not compare with the more scientific manuals produced later. At its loftiest, it provides a blueprint for the agricultural society: "Preserving people in a laudable condition depends on farmers and fieldworkers who are at the root of all this and its support and matter. Because of this they are the most excellent of all people. . . . Next we will speak about the king, kingship and its means of subsistence. The owners of estates and farmers are also the support of the king and of his subsistence, and they elevate his kingship and keep intact its means of subsistence."[18] But in general it is anecdotal and superstitious. At its earthiest, it suggests that human copulation will aid the grafting of a branch from one tree onto the trunk of another.[19] A copy of the *Nabatiyya* reached al-Andalus in the tenth century and was probably the catalyst for new agricultural manuals there. References in later Andalusian agricultural manuals indicate that one was written in the third quarter of the tenth century by one of the authors of the *Calendar of Cordoba*, although not even its title survives.[20] The next earliest text was the *Abridged Book of Agriculture* (*Mukhtasar kitab al-filaha*) written by Abulcasis (al-Zaharawi) in Cordoba sometime between 975 and 1013–14.[21] Many of these included plants lists that provide a sense of the basic repertoire of plants in cultivation in a given area and historic period. Ibn Bassal's eleventh-century agricultural treatise, for example, names 177 species that included basic foods such as lentils and onions, spices such as basil and cumin, cereals such as millet and sorghum (the list appears incomplete in this area), and ornamentals such as the viola and oleander (see table).[22] In the Yemen, four agricultural

acacia
almond
amaranth (2 varieties)
apple mint
apricot tree
artichoke
ash (3 varieties)
asparagus (3 varieties)
asparagus bean
balsam tree
barley
basil
beet
bindweed (3 varieties)
bitter apple (*citrullus vulgaris*)
black cumin
black mustard
black pepper
bottle gourd
box thorn
bramble
broccoli (*brassica oleracea*)
broom
broom (*retama sphaerocarpa*)
broomcorn
bugloss
cabbage
caper bush (2 varieties)
caraway
cardoon
carob tree
carrot
celandine
chamomile (*anthemis* and 2 varieties of chamaemelum)
chestnut
chick pea
chicory
citron
coco grass
common anise
common apple
common balm
coriander
cotton (2 varieties)
cowpea
crocus (saffron)
cucumber
cumin
cypress
cyprus-turpentine (*pistacia terebinthus*)
date palm

dock
dyer's broom
eggplant
elm (2 varieties)
esparto grass
fig tree
flax
foxtail millet
frankincense tree
garden pea
garlic
gingerbread palm (*hyphaene thebiacca*)
golden-shower (*cassia fistula*)
grape (wine)
hackberry
hazelnut
henna
hollyhock
hyacinth bean
jasmine
jujube
kale
laurel
leek
lemon
lentil
lettuce
madder
madonna lily
mahaleb
maiden hair fern
mallow (*althaea*, 2 varieties)
matricary
melon
millet
morning glory
mulberry (2 varieties)
mullein
myrobalan
myrrh
myrtle
narcissus (4 varieties)
nut sedge
oak tree
oil grass (*cymbopogon schoenanthus*)
oleander
oleaster
olive tree
onion
orach
orange (*citrus aurantium*)

panic grass
paradise tree
parsnip
peach
pear
pepper grass
pine tree
pistachio tree
plum tree
pomegranate
poplar (2 varieties)
poppy (2 varieties)
privet
purslane
quince
radish
rape
reed
rice
rose
rue
rush (*lygeum spartum* and *juncus*)
safflower (2 varieties)
sea onion
sesame
snake melon
snowbell (2 varieties)
soft rush
sorghum
spinach
stock
strawberry tree (*arbutus unedo*)
sweet cherry tree
sweet marjoram
sycamore
thistle
thyme
vetch (3 varieties)
viola
wallflower
walnut
watercress
watermelon
wheat
white lupine
white mustard
wild peas
wild teasel
willow (4 varieties)
wormwood
yellow sweet clover

manuals were written during the rule of the Rasulid dynasty (1229–1454). These also listed plants cultivated specifically in the lands of Yemen, with a great emphasis on the major crop of dates, but at least one also included information on the olive and betel, neither of which were widely planted.[23]

Whereas almanacs are often rather dull schedules of seasonal activities, the manuals are surprisingly interesting, even today, for readers with a practical interest in gardening. For example Abu'l-Khayr, writing in eleventh-century al-Andalus, explains the best way to propagate olives, which was one of Spain's staple crops (Fig. 20). The farmer cuts a shoot ten to twelve palms long and plants it where the olive tree is to grow permanently, sticking the shoot in a hole with pebbles spread around the base, filling the hole with earth, and leaving a surface depression to catch water. But, not content with just one method, the author also explains how to make a small branch sprout roots by sticking it in the earth without detaching it from the mother tree, as well as how to sprout an olive tree from a seed so that its stem will be thick as a finger in four years. While he cites the work of others, he also advises the reader: "We have had the experience of doing this ourselves."[24] It was necessary to discuss multiple ways of plant reproduction because one method might yield very different results than another. In the date palm (*phoenix dactylifera*), propagation by seed and cross-pollination does not yield predictably satisfactory results because, of the young trees thus produced, less than 5 percent bear good fruit. Hence, date palm trees, which like the olive could be grown under arid conditions, are likewise most commonly cultivated by cutting suckers (which sprout near the base of the trunk).[25]

Abu'l-Khayr also explained the principle of crop rotation, stating that one parcel of land can produce a crop of flax followed by either wheat or barley, and he discussed the interplanting of complementary crops, specifically grapes with olive trees.[26] But Ibn Wafid, who lived in eleventh-century Toledo, specifically warned against the interplanting of beans with fruit trees because it harmed the flavor of the fruit.[27]

Some of the manuals explain the strategic positioning of houses and gardens. Abu'l-Khayr recommended planting on terrain that slopes to the south because it has the most hours of sunlight. Ibn Wafid advised: "The best place in the farm for building houses is the highest place because of the fact that they will neither be flooded nor totally dry and the run-off will help provide water to the rest of the farm and its gardens and fields. And it is preferable that the houses be built on a riverbank and that their doors and windows open eastward. This is because the east winds are more salubrious than the winds from the west, and also because the heat of the sun removes the ill effects of bad air. The houses

FIGURE 20. Mechanization has changed the practice of olive culture, but Andalusia continues to be a major producer of olives, grown on stock that has not changed significantly since the Roman era.

should be tall and broad with wide doorways so that they are well-ventilated. In this way their inhabitants will be most healthy."[28]

One curious feature of the manuals is that some were written in verse, probably so that they could be more easily remembered. The Islamic world in the tenth through twelfth centuries was shifting from oral to written culture, in part because of the availability of a cheap new medium: paper. Although a treatise on agriculture was written down and probably copied several times, it is also likely to have been read aloud in scholarly groups and may have circulated in the form of a memorized text. Such was the twelfth-century manual of Ibn Luyun, written in a simple rhymed meter that, while it never impressed the great poets of the day, would have caught the ear of a moderately well-educated landowner interested in agronomy. Similarly, an anonymous calendar from Granada in the fifteenth century was written in lines of staccato brevity, surely to avoid taxing the memory of the audience for which it was composed. In the Yemen, related works on health and the months of the year, such as the seventeenth-century work by Ahmad b. Abi Bakr al-Zumayli, were written in verse for analogous reasons.[29]

The crop plants mentioned in these manuals are also named in crop registers, which have been studied for Rasulid Yemen (1229–1454),[30] and in notarial documents, such as those from fourteenth- and fifteenth-century Sicily.[31] (Although Islamic rule had ended with the Norman invasions in the third quarter of the eleventh century, agricultural practice and indeed much of Sicilo-Norman culture continued to reflect Islamic habits.) The contracts between landowner and farmer usually stipulated not only the rental fee but also the provision of water and even techniques of cultivation. Since rents were often paid in the form of a percentage of crop yield, the landlord had as much of an investment in realizing a good harvest as did the farmer himself.

In Iran, the science of agronomy was likewise recorded in treatises such as the anonymous *Yavaqit al-'ulum* (1117), Fakr al-Din al-Razi's *Jami al-'ulum* (1179–80), and Shams al-Din Amuli's *Nafayis al-funun* (1340). Like their Mediterranean equivalents, these were based on much older sources, such as Galen, Plato, Pliny the Elder's *Natural History*, and the sixth-century *Geoponica* of Byzantine Cassianus Bassus (translated into Persian by the tenth century).[32] They offered information on bee-keeping, horticulture, arboriculture, the storage of crops, and other things useful to farmers. Some, such as the sixteenth-century *Irshad al-zira'a*, were written in verse not only to facilitate memorization but also to enhance the scientific merit of the work through the display of literary prowess. The fact that such treatises could travel as broadly as they did in the Islamic world suggests that the specific application of a treatise's contents to a particular regional landscape mattered less than the authority of the ancient authors.

Collectively, this body of literature demonstrates the importance of agriculture, both as a set of traditional procedures practiced by humble laborers and as a science studied by scholars with various levels of ability in languages, astronomical calculation, and botany. However, it is difficult to imagine precisely for whom the manuals and treatises were written: certainly not the sweat-stained farmers who dug the earth. But it is equally hard to imagine that a fairly expensive manuscript copy of a how-to manual on the diverse ways of propagating, pollinating, and grafting would have been of immediate use to a member of the intellectual class who alone was wealthy enough to afford it. A botanical manuscript that was hand-copied on parchment would have been a luxury item that no farmer could have owned. Possibly the Arabic and Persian literature on gardening and farming that arose in the tenth through twelfth centuries was written to document an already flourishing agricultural landscape by recording fairly new changes in farming techniques such as irrigation, and by preserving knowledge about the planting of seeds and cuttings, preparation of the soil, and application of new types of fertilizer. In other words, the almanacs and manuals may have registered changes in practice that had been recently adopted by ordinary farmers and which benefited both them and the elite class of literate land owners. But at least in al-Andalus, there is also evidence to the contrary—that this literature was one of the catalysts for change, originating from the Islamic culture of comparative science and learning, and resulting in the pursuit of new plant specimens and actual botanical experimentation that transformed daily agricultural practice.[33]

By the tenth century (earlier in al-Andalus) the Islamic Mediterranean began to experience a dramatic economic, scientific, and social transformation. Improvements in agricultural techniques—of which the most profound was the acquisition, storage, and distribution of water for irrigating the land—led to a boom economy. New plants and new techniques were quickly adopted by entrepreneurial farmers eager to make profits. Often they were led by the caliph or ruling prince himself, who through the collection of taxes was able to perceive the benefits of investments and innovation. For example, in his palatine city of Samarra, near Baghdad, the Abbasid Caliph al-Muʿtasim (r. 833–842) established gardens which he stocked with palm trees from elsewhere in Iraq. A chronicler of the time reported, "They sowed all sorts of plants, scented or edible, as well as greenery: the earth had lain fallow for thousands of years so everything they planted there grew well."[34] To this he added that the gardens, orchards, and fields were then taxed so that they contributed to the caliph's coffers.

The ruler sponsored botanical research and subsidized the writing of treatises in order to study and stimulate the improvements and to urge the economy toward even greater prosperity. Some rulers took a direct, personal interest in new plant varieties. For example, during the reign of the ʿAbbadids in Seville in the eleventh century, an observer reported that a peasant from a nearby village presented the ruler with four enormous melons that "weighed so much that the man could hardly carry them in a basket on his head." He continued: "The Sultan was very much surprised to see such fine fruit, and began to question the peasant, who answered that those melons did not always grow to so great a size, but that they could easily be obtained of those dimensions by cutting off all the branches of the plants but ten, and then supporting the stem by means of props of wood."[35] This technique of selective pinching or disbudding, familiar to any medieval or modern kitchen gardener, caught the attention of the ruler because it was an opportunity to improve agriculture and thus both the regional cuisine and economy.

Economic considerations were clearly important and could outweigh cultural and religious values. Less than a hundred years earlier, the Caliph al-Hakam II (r. 961–976) had wished to ban viniculture in al-Andalus in order to discourage its principal product, wine, but as the grape was one of the peninsula's major crops, his advisors hastened to dissuade him.[36] In Samarkand, the Emperor Timur (r. 1370–1405) ordered flax and hemp to be grown for the first time because he foresaw a need for rope fiber for building and tents.[37] His descendant the Mughal Emperor Akbar (1556–1605) enjoyed touring the fields of Kashmir to observe the autumn saffron harvest, not only because the crocuses were lovely but also, presumably, because of the satisfaction derived from witnessing a crop ready to be reaped.[38]

Although most rulers could appreciate economic profit, not all understood the agricultural cycle and its specific processes. When the Abbasid Caliph al-Muqtadir (r. 908–932) wanted to stage a party in a palace courtyard filled with narcissus, one of the gardeners wished to lay dung on the beds to prepare the soil where the bulbs were to be planted, according to standard practice. But the caliph was outraged that a place where he would sit should be fertilized with animal excrement. When the gardener explained the purpose of the manure, the caliph commanded that it be mixed with musk to ameliorate the smell.[39] In contrast, the Mughal Emperor Jahangir was a keen observer of landscape and its ecological processes, and understood basic issues such as the grafting of trees to produce tasty fruit on sturdy root stock, the role of mulberry trees in silk production, and the difference between species (wild) and domestic lilies.[40]

Innovation and change apparently drove authors, botanists, and patrons to record everything known about the science of agriculture in the late ninth and tenth centuries, but the opposite seems to have occurred in Herat (Afghanistan) during the last years of the Timurid dynasty (1370–1506 and dwindling thereafter) where the political and social conditions were quite different. There, an agricultural manual written in Persian in 1515 documented an active agrarian system that was threatened by destructive changes. The *Irshad al-zira'a* (*Guide to Agriculture*) seems to have been occasioned by an agrarian crisis following Uzbek invasions of Khurasan and internal shifts in leadership. Its author was Qasim b. Yusuf Abu Nasri, the accountant in charge of lands from which the rents and crops supported the shrine of 'Abdullah Ansari in Herat. The guide sought to explain the management of farmland, which required knowledge of mathematics, geometry, financial accounting, agricultural practice, and hydraulic engineering, the latter a necessity in the Khurasan area where Herat is located. Qasim b. Yusuf apparently had no personal expertise in agriculture, and so he consulted "experienced people" among the peasants.[41]

Early medieval scientific literature tends to emphasize received knowledge rather than experimentation and discovery, although in later periods we have seen some instances of authors claiming personal knowledge through observation. While the literature describes agricultural practices, it rarely describes the layout and appearance of actual gardens. One aspect of gardening preserved in the treatises that is entirely absent from the gardens themselves is the actual gardener. In Spain we know that Abu Ya'qub Yusuf, the Almohad ruler of Seville, hired three men to design and supervise his magnificent Buhayra gardens that were arrayed east of the city in the late twelfth century. The first of these was Ibn Basu, who had also served the ruler as the architect of the Great Mosque's minaret. The second was a judge, Abu'l-Qasim Ahmad ibn Muhammad, and the third was the imam of the mosque, Abu Bakr Muhammad ibn Yahya.[42] They were entrusted with surveying, preparation of the soil, and plans for cultivation—in essence all the practical applications that the treatise writers described. One can imagine that it is these kinds of individuals—highly educated, yet involved in directing actual practice—who may have made the most use of texts such as the agricultural manuals.

Much more is known about the Iranian horticulturalist Mirak-i Sayyid Ghiyas, who served the Timurid ruler Sultan Husain-i Bayqara Mirza (r. 1469–1506). He belonged to a family of important landscape designers who flourished in Iran from the mid-fifteenth century and much of the sixteenth. He was born and lived in Herat and learned from his father, in the traditional manner, the science of agronomy, irrigation, and architectural construction. As landscape architect to the sultan, he supervised the construction of gardens and garden architecture where all three areas of expertise were necessary and where aesthetic considerations and actual productivity were equally valued. The Uzbek invasion of 1507 led to upheavals that culminated in Safavid rule and a more hostile political climate. On more than one occasion Mirak-i Sayyid Ghiyas's lands were seized, and at one point he was imprisoned, although he was soon back to work and offering advice to the author of the *Irshad al-zira'a*. He eventually left for India, where between 1526 and 1530 the conqueror Babur (r. 1526–1530) was in need of a professional landscape architect for his works in Dholpur and Agra. By 1540, Mirak-i Sayyid Ghiyas had moved to Bukhara, where he served as landscape architect to the Uzbek khan there until his death sometime after 1550.[43]

Treatises were clearly one means by which scientific information traveled from one Islamic society to another, a role that was greatly increased when paper was developed and adopted as the cheapest medium for writing, replacing parchment for the copying of all works but the Qur'an. But the biographies of the Andalusian aesthete Ziryab, Mirak-i Sayyid Ghiyas, and others demonstrate that the individuals themselves were equally important as agents of transmission. The landscape architects and gardeners who moved with the vicissitudes of conquest and new opportunities brought theoretical information with them, which was the material for much of Qasim b. Yusuf Abu Nasri's *Irshad al-zira'a*, as well as conveying their practical knowledge of how to get the work done.

The fact that there were so many written works on medieval Islamic botany, agriculture, and land management reveals the acute interest of farmers, scholars, and princes in the cultivated landscape. A few of the manuals describe the ideal organization of a garden, but for more specific information on layout, actual plantings, and meaning we must look at the gardens themselves as recorded through descriptions, surviving remains, and archaeological excavation.

4   Organizing the Earth

Cross-axial Gardens and the Chahar Bagh

SLAMIC GARDENS WERE not created *ex nihilo*. Like the religion of Islam and the culture that was born out of it, there were prior layers that help explain how Islam developed as it did. The earlier and contemporary societies of Byzantium, the Sasanians, and the city-dwelling Arabs and Jews expressed the relationship between humankind and the earth through the making of gardens, and thus to understand the form and meaning of early Islamic gardens, it is instructive to examine the ancient gardens of southwestern Asia and the Mediterranean. Of course these precedents do not wholly explain the gardens of Islam, because historical practices do not unilaterally explain later disruptions and innovations such as those that occurred when Arab farmers adopted better irrigation and agricultural techniques. But the techniques for producing a bountiful crop transcend religious boundaries, and adherents to the new religion did not generally invent but rather adapted existing customary agricultural practice as well as the formal organization of gardens, imbuing the latter with a new political and spiritual meaning. Neither history nor geography alone can explain landscape formation: they were equal forces and must be considered together.

One of the hallmarks of Islamic gardens is the four-part garden laid out with axial walkways that intersect in the garden center. This highly structured geometrical scheme, called the *chahar bagh*, became a powerful metaphor for the organization and domestication of the landscape, itself a symbol of political territory. However, the cross-axial plan was not the only means of organizing the garden. In imperial, subimperial, and ordinary house gardens, the space might be as simple as a paved courtyard with a fountain or sunken basin surrounded by potted plants. It might take the form of a single long rectangular bed with a central watercourse, as at the Generalife's principal garden (Plate 2), or multiple beds aligned end to end in terraces on a sloping hillside as occurred in the Mughal Nishat Bagh in Kashmir (see Sites). And just as one architectural plan may yield buildings with strikingly distinct appearances due to the use of different materials and manipulation of structural elements, as in the case of the Tomb of Humayun (Plate 3) and the Taj Mahal (see Fig. 76), so may a four-part garden plan. It may have deeply sunken quadrants planted with shrubs whose leaves just barely reach the surfaces of the elevated paths (Plate 4), or shallow expanses of sturdy turf suitable for sitting (Plate 5). At the beginning of the seventeenth century in Mughal South Asia, the simple rectilinear geometry of the chahar bagh and its water basins was embellished and transformed by elaborate curvilinear and stellar patterns.

Until recently, historians believed that when used in historical texts, the term *chahar bagh* referred literally to a garden divided into four parts, or a multiple of four. Thus, when the term appeared in a historical account of gardens, one assumed that it described a garden with quadripartite form. However, a study of sixteenth-century Bukhara showed that the term was used more loosely in that context than historians had imagined, so that the term *chahar bagh*, as well as other Persian labels such as *baghcha*, *bustan*, and *rabaz*, could refer to gardens of various sizes, shapes, functions, and importance.[1] In earlier periods, it is more likely that the term *chahar bagh* referred specifically to a four-part garden, but we should nonetheless be wary of equating the words with the form. At the same time, we should be cautious in assigning an Islamic identity to this garden type because the concept of quadripartite planning preceded Islam; versions of it appeared in both Mediterranean and Persian history.

The ancient precedents for formal garden planning can be seen at sites such as Pasargadae, the Achaemenid capital of Cyrus the Great (559–530 B.C.E.) in Iran, where the royal garden contained a rectangular garden bed opposite the throne hall (Fig. 21). Stone water channels with regularly spaced rectangular basins on three sides of the garden bed, as well as the axis of sight extending from the throne room through the center of the garden, suggest that the space may have been divided cross-axially by intersecting watercourses.[2] The practical purpose of such divisions was to distribute irrigation water to the four quadrants of the garden. However, the evidence for a cross-axial plan is not conclusive, and with so few standing remains for the excavators to study, the argument depends partially on reading backward from the quadripartite layout of Islamic sites more than a thousand years later. But whether or not incised channels apportioned the space into equal quadrants, it is quite clear that sightlines could establish visual axes that implied a four-part geometry.

For the Roman period the archaeology is more complete and examples more numerous, owing to the preservation effect of the layers of pumice stones and volcanic ash spewed by Vesuvius in 79 C.E. onto the sites of Pompeii and Herculaneum and the surrounding area. Those gardens had large pools, water channels (sometimes spanned by slender marble bridges), arbors, fountains, statues and handsome murals depicting vegetation, birds, and ephemeral structures such as wooden trellises, fences, and pavilions. In addition to flowers, there were climbing vines and topiary trees and shrubs such as myrtle, cypress, and plane trees. A wide

FIGURE 21.
In Pasargadae, the palace of Cyrus the Great (559–530 B.C.E.) had a royal garden that may have been divided cross-axially by intersecting watercourses. The throne pavilion was positioned in the center of the northwest wall, giving the royal occupant an extensive view. (Ruggles after D. Stronach)

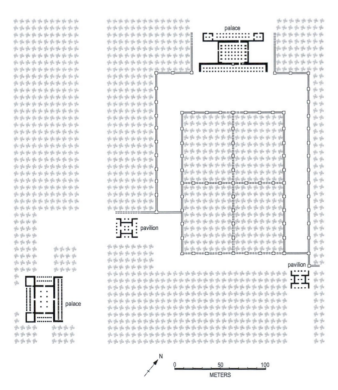

variety of fixed types of formal gardens responded to their specific rural, urban, or maritime context; some were enclosed by colonnades while others extended generously between architecture and the landscape.

Often Roman gardens were organized around a single linear axis, such as the house of Marcus Loreius Tiburtinus (Fig. 22) in Pompeii. From a terrace at the north end, water cascaded through a long channel down the length of the garden, flanked by an arbor on either side. The midpoint of this axis was marked by a pergola and fountain, and the interruption of the axis midway by a pool in this manner hints at the possibility of an intersecting axis. However, in Roman gardens the lateral axis was not developed with walkways or channels. The Foro Boario ("Cattle Market"), which was divided into four unequal quadrants by intersecting paths (Fig. 23), is a rare exception, but it was a large working vineyard, probably with vegetables planted in the four feet of space between the vine stems. It was not a formal garden.[3]

By the imperial Roman period (after 31 B.C.E.) the peristyle garden consisting of an enclosed courtyard surrounded by a portico, sometimes with fountains, became an expected feature of grand houses.[4] Often one wall of enclosed gardens was embellished with murals of plants and birds that visually extended the space and indulged the Roman taste for illusionistic imagery and scenes from myth, while at the same time giving the impression of a large house with many adjoining courtyards. Scenes of wild animals suggested the presence of a hunting park or *paradeisos*, a concept introduced to the Greco-Roman world as a result of Alexander the Great's conquest of Persia (334 B.C.E.).[5] These wall paintings were lifelike, but it is debatable whether they constituted true trompe-l'oeil since the paint, subjected to the sun, rain, and flying dust, would have borne the visible scars of its outdoor location. On the other hand, the plaster usually had an extraordinary finish intended to counteract such deterioration. Part of the pleasure was surely the willingness to acquiesce momentarily to the suggestion of a verdant yet unattainable space beyond the garden at hand, in which the leaves of real trees were juxtaposed with painted foliage.

Islamic garden designers followed the Roman model of geometrically laid out gardens with central axes in the form of walkways and watercourses, but they did not embrace the colorful garden murals and the embellishment of green spaces with copious figural statuary. This was not due to strictures against the representational arts, as is commonly supposed. Although imagery of human and animal beings in mosques and tombs was forbidden so as to prevent the temptation of idolatry, in nonreligious contexts figural imagery was allowed; indeed, Islamic palace halls and bathhouses such as Khirbat al-Mafjar were often adorned with images of flowers, prancing animals, musicians, and even nude women, and garden settings did have fountains with animal shapes.

FIGURE 22. In this house of Marcus Loreius Tiburtinus in Pompeii, a cross-axial plan was implied by the position of a fountain and arbor halfway down the central channel. However, the four-part layout was not formally inscribed as intersecting axial walkways. (Ruggles after Jashemski)

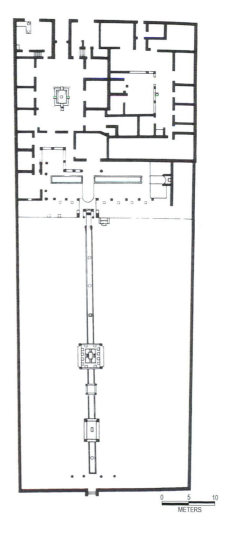

0   5   10
METERS

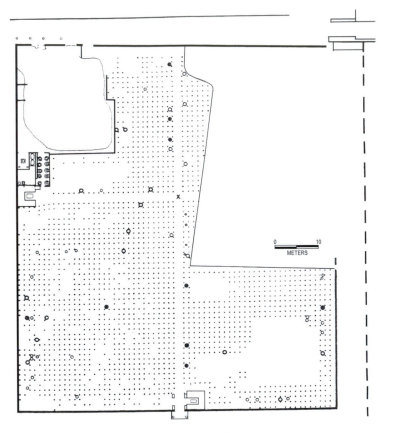

However, because there was no religious context for figural imagery and no drive to manufacture images of saints, the art of portraiture and three-dimensional sculpture did not develop with the same enthusiasm as it did in Christian Europe. Instead, Islamic gardens were more often adorned with fountains, trellises, lavish displays of water, and—in rarefied palatine environments—stunningly theatrical transformations of natural vegetation by the application of gilding, rich textiles, and gems.

The earliest surviving Islamic gardens, built in the Umayyad period and the first two centuries of Abbasid rule (from the seventh to the mid-tenth century), were enclosed by walls and most of them were structured with axial walkways. Most of the early Islamic formal gardens belonged to palace environments where their sensuous perfumes, colors, and cooling breezes contributed to the beauty and comforts of the material world. Some of the most famous Islamic gardens today are associated with tombs, but these are relatively late gardens, dating from the sixteenth century. And although in the first centuries of Islam, some mosque courtyards were planted, this was only in the simple sense of rows of trees, introduced for shade and to provide fruit to pay the building's custodian.

At the gleaming, gypsum-walled city of Rusafa, archaeologists discovered a garden which they assigned to the reign of the Umayyad caliph Hisham (724–43). If their dating is correct, this is the earliest Islamic garden exemplar. Outside the walls and to the south of the walled city was a stone palace with a large garden enclosed by mudbrick walls. In the center, at the intersection of two beaten plaster walkways, stood a square pavilion of stone. The pavilion was raised above the surrounding garden on an elevated plinth and access was possible by three steps on each of the four sides (see Sites).[6] The axial walkways and the apertures in the pavilion's walls and surrounding arcade indicate that the pavilion was designed for an elevated view of the garden with distinct vistas in the four cardinal directions.

The placing of pavilions at a garden's nucleus in order to position the viewer centrally eventually became a trope in Islamic palaces where they became an expression of sovereign power. In eleventh-century Lashkari Bazar in Afghanistan (see Sites), where the palace complex consisted of a series of large walled courtyards, at least one such court had a centrally placed, raised pavilion that probably provided pleasing views from its second-story terrace.

FIGURE 23. While the Foro Boario (Pompeii, 79 C.E.) was divided by walkways into quadrants, it was not a pleasure garden but a working vineyard with fifty-eight trees and vines that were staked and regularly spaced 1.2 meters apart. (Ruggles after Jashemski)

In seventeenth-century Isfahan, the Chihil Situn and Hesht Behesht pavilions stood at the heart of walled gardens of the palace precinct (see Sites).

Not all these gardens had a true quadripartite layout consisting of four beds divided by axial pavements. In some of them the cross-axial layout was merely suggested by the central position of the pavilion and the centrally placed openings of doorways in the enclosure walls. For example, at Lashkari Bazar, the enclosure adjoining the central palace was organized by axes that extended from the ramped entrances on each of the central cruciform pavilion's four sides. These led to corresponding ramps or stairs piercing the enclosure walls. Whether visually implied or inscribed with stone pavement, the cross-axial plan appears almost entirely in palatine settings and appears to have been a prerogative of royal patrons.

FIGURE 24. The irrigation canals in the Agdal, a richly cultivated area outside of Marrakesh, are modern, but the method of diverting water from one channel to another by means of simple blockages is timeless.

On a practical level, the four-part cross-axial plan was adopted for palatine gardens because, just as in the agricultural landscape, it provided a sensible means of irrigation. Water was typically introduced from a single source such as the endpoint of an aqueduct, a reservoir or water-lifting apparatus, and distributed into a network of canals that reached the four quadrants, flooding each for a few hours or at least long enough to penetrate into the soil at the roots of the plants. It was directed through small earthen or tile-lined canals by opening some entrance points and blocking others with mud and stones, a practice which can still be seen today, as in the agricultural fields in the outskirts of Marrakesh (Fig. 24).

This irrigation network and the subsequent dividing of the landscape into slightly sunken beds became the organizing principle for the palatine garden. However, in the palace, the scale was reduced so that the four-part garden was a concise representation of the system

FIGURE 25. A qanat brings water to the Bagh-i Fin, Kashan, a Safavid estate in Iran. The axial water channels that flow throughout the gardens provide both practical irrigation and sensory pleasure. (Yasamin Bahadorzadeh)

of irrigated plots of the larger agricultural landscape. The quotidian irrigation canals and wells that provided the water for the agricultural landscape were elaborated as decorative water channels and fountains in palace gardens, as in the Safavid Bagh-i Fin, built about 1587 near Kashan (Fig. 25 and Plate 1) and the Nasrid Generalife Palace in Granada. Similarly, the palace garden's exotic plant varieties, imported at great cost from foreign lands, were a reflection of the rich diversity of crops for cultivation—sorghum, hard wheat, rice, banana, sugar cane, eggplant, cotton, artichokes, and varieties of citrus—that people

enjoyed as a result of agricultural innovations and exchanges in the early Islamic world and continuing into so-called Age of Empires (the Ottomans, Safavids, and Mughals).[7]

Even devices such as trellising, in which vines and long-branched fruit trees are trained to grow on a structure that raises the fruit from the ground and reduces the potential for rot, also served as display in pleasure gardens where they created living walls alive with flowers, sweet fruit, and singing birds. An illustration from one of the few Andalusian manuscripts with representations of gardens, the *Bayad wa Riyad*, shows a garden with a pool and a domed kiosk to one side, while to the left a figure leans forward while grasping one of the structural supports of a trellis (Plate 6). A sinuous vine climbs up to enmesh its foliage in the cagelike roof of the latticework structure; perhaps there was a wall trellis as well, but because the illustrations lack background detail, no such element is depicted. Similar cage trellises are used in vineyards today in Spain (Fig. 26). A crude trellis on forked upright supports can also be seen in an illustration in a late sixteenth-century copy of the *Khamsa* of Nizami (Plate 7). Trellising, irrigation, fertilization, pruning, pinching, and grafting were necessary procedures for both agriculture and pleasure gardens, and it is in the translation from the purely utilitarian farm to the perfumed, colorful, and exotic garden that the expressive function of gardens lies. Gardens distilled the elements of the greater landscape, with all of the attached political, economic, social, and religious meanings, into a form that was intended for the pleasure as well as comprehension of an elite group of court patrons.

Although historians often treat the four-part garden as a quintessential and ubiquitous Islamic plan, this is a misleading representation made on the basis of incomplete evidence. Almost all the gardens that have been archaeologically recovered from the first several centuries of Islam belonged to royal palaces, and while it is true that most of those gardens were quadripartite, this is by no means a complete representation of the full spectrum of gardens in the Islamic world.[8] Very few early Islamic dwellings of more ordinary character have been excavated and studied, but in those cases, there is no evidence of four-part plans.

For example, the excavations of the ruined city of Fustat (Egypt) which flourished in the Tulunid (868–905) and Fatimid (909–1171) periods, yielded no dwellings having courtyards with quadripartite divisions. Thirty-nine small urban residences were excavated at Fustat where space was at a premium in the dense urban fabric. The houses were organized around central open-air courtyards; nineteen of them had either one or two water basins and eight had garden beds. One of the grander houses (number VI) in the Fatimid period had a courtyard that measured approximately nine by fourteen meters, with a rectangular tank that abutted a garden bed five meters in length (Fig. 27). In a chamber off the *iwan* (a hall with three sides, open on the fourth) on the north side of the courtyard, water was piped by underground pipes into an ornamental basin, from which it flowed down a textured chute, along an open-air channel that dropped in level at

FIGURE 26.
In medieval paintings and in agricultural practice today, as seen here in Galicia (Spain), vines are trained on wall trellises or cages in order to keep the fruit off the ground and to prevent rot.

the point where the iwan opened toward the courtyard, finally reaching the courtyard pool. The waters of this large pool cooled the enclosed microenvironment during the long hot season, while the bed of flowers and shrubs delighted the eye and filled the air with pleasant scents. Alongside the pool a larger shrub—possibly a tree—provided shade from the sun overhead.[9]

The non-aristocratic dwellings at Fustat are a welcome exception to the general bias in archaeology toward monumental architecture, which is invariably better preserved than humbler dwellings of ephemeral materials such as mudbrick and wood, and which, because of its elite patrons, tends to yield objects prized by collectors and museum curators. Furthermore, the powerful patrons who commissioned works of history and literature in which gardens were described were the wealthy rulers dwelling in enormous palace complexes with reception halls and pavilions set amidst large gardens. Naturally, literary attention was more often paid to their elite gardens than to the residences of mere merchants and court officials of middle rank. Because of these archaeological and historical preferences for "high" palatine architecture, we know considerably more about the form and meaning of royal gardens than their humbler contemporaries.

The first such palatine garden was the already-discussed Umayyad garden at Rusafa in Syria in the second quarter of the eighth century. The second example of a cross-axial garden plan for which

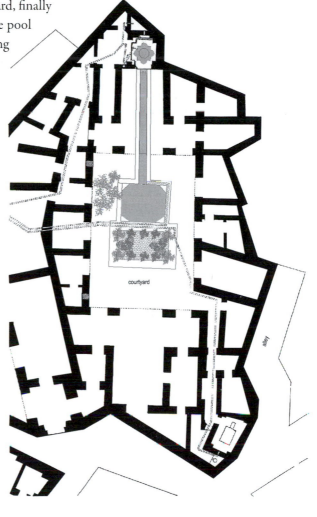

FIGURE 27.
In Fustat (Egypt), several of the houses (House VI is shown here) had central courtyards with water basins surrounded by planting that included shrubs or even small trees. (Ruggles and Variava, after Baghat and Gabriel)

there is archaeological evidence occurred at the great Abbasid city of Samarra in Iraq in the mid-ninth century. Balkuwara, one of the palaces at Samarra built by the Abbasid caliph in 849–59, had three large courtyards that appeared to have been divided into equal quadrants by paved walkways on the plan drawn by the archaeological excavator, Ernst Herzfeld, in the twentieth century. While the interest of the Abbasid patron in the cross-axial arrangement of garden is clear from the axial location of the side entrances in the two adjoining gardens, it is cannot be ascertained that this layout was expressed in the form of four distinct garden beds.[10] In other words, the cross-axial plan which Herzfeld drew appears to have been partly conjectural.[11]

The next instance of an archaeologically verifiable quadripartite garden occurred at the Andalusian palace city, Madinat al-Zahra' (see Sites). The Hispano-Umayyad caliph built Madinat al-Zahra' approximately five kilometers from the walled capital city of Cordoba

FIGURE 28.
The Salon Rico in
Madinat al-Zahra'
was closed on its
side and rear walls,
where it abutted the
retaining wall of
the esplanade just
behind and above
it. But its southern
face opened toward
the ornamental
pavilion opposite,
set within the Up-
per Garden. The
Salon Rico was
reconstructed in
the mid-twentieth
century but only
a few pillars have
been resurrected
from the pavilion.

beginning in 936. It was an enormous double-walled complex that was draped in three terraces down the lower slope of a mountain. The upper terrace consisted of residences for the caliph and his family as well as high-ranking court officials honored to be permitted to live in close proximity to the caliph. Among these was the rich-ly ornamented reception hall recon-structed in the late 1950s and dubbed the Salon Rico (Fig. 28).[12] This hall consisted of three naves on columns bearing horseshoe arches and opened via a transverse hall and a similar screen of columns and arches to a large cross-axial garden (Fig. 29). The garden was divided into unequal quadrants by walkways. Facing the Salon Rico along the central axis was a smaller pavilion that probably mirrored it on a reduced scale. Intervening between the two was a large pool, deep enough to have held fish—according to the chroniclers, large numbers of fish (pre-sumably for human consumption) were stocked in at least one of the palace's huge pools. From either pavilion, a viewer saw the reflection of the other in the shimmering surface of the pool, so that the architectural effect was both illusionistic and utterly real.[13] A second cross-axial garden on a lower level almost duplicates the upper one, but the lower one has not been thoroughly explored by archaeologists (Fig. 30).[14]

At least five quadripartite gardens were built in the twelfth century in Islamic Spain and Morocco. Four gardens have been excavated, and three of them are either still visible or restored in the Seville Alcazar. One, in the present-day Casa de Contratación which is attached to the west side of the former Islamic palace, consists of twelfth-century fabric that is still in excellent condition although over-restored by conservators a few decades ago: the four quadrants are sunken to a depth of two meters and irrigated by water distributed in canals running along the walkways (which, on the basis of stylistic similarity with the Alcazar's Patio de las Don-cellas, appear to be fourteenth century in date) (Plate 4).[15] An archaeological survey found that jasmine and orange trees had been planted in the beds. At one end of the garden there are vestiges of an even older eleventh-century garden with sunken pools. Elsewhere in the same palace complex another twelfth-century garden, known as El Crucero, had four quadrants sunken to an extraordinary depth of five meters, also planted with orange trees, the topmost branches of which were level with the

FIGURE 29.
In the Upper
Garden, Madinat
al-Zahra', the axial
layout was articu-
lated by walkways
that surrounded
and traversed the
four-part garden;
these in turn were
lined by channels
that carried water
to each quadrant.
(Ruggles and
H. Wilke)

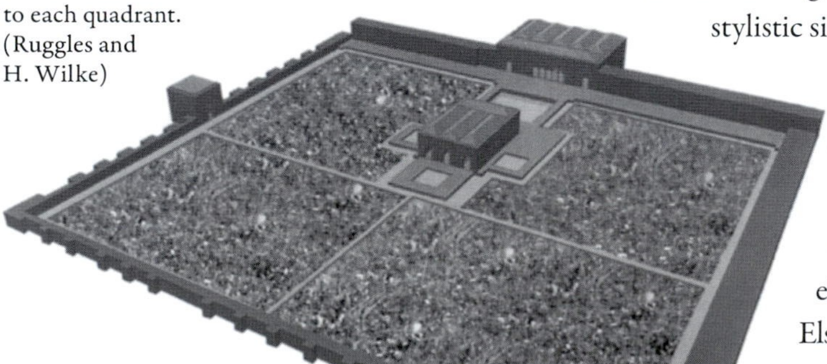

surrounding walkway.[16] The Patio del Yeso, which consisted of a square courtyard with a large rectangular pool in its center lined by low shrubs and ornamented with an arcade on columns along the south wall, also belongs to this period (see Sites). Finally, the Patio de las Doncellas (Court of the Maidens), a courtyard belonging to the period of Pedro the Cruel (r. 1350–69), has recently been excavated to reveal a fourteenth-century sunken courtyard bisected by a raised central channel (see Sites).[17] The courtyard belongs to multiple periods and it is unclear whether the central channel was flanked by garden beds, but the presence of interlacing arches along the walls of the sunken areas closely resembles those in the garden of the Casa de Contratación.

The earliest dated cross-axial garden in Morocco was discovered when the remains of an Almoravid palace were unearthed beneath the second Kutubiya Mosque in Marrakesh.[18] The former palace was revealed to have contained a courtyard with a small quadripartite garden, ten and half meters long, with sunken beds divided by beaten plaster walkways and surrounded by an elevated walkway (see Sites). The palace was built in the years 1106–42 and destroyed when a mosque was erected in its place between 1147 and 1162.

The Castillejo of Monteagudo, built in eastern Spain between 1147 and 1172, likewise had a central courtyard divided cross-axially (see Sites).[19] Although the walls have long since collapsed, the surviving foundations reveal that the fortified palace was built around an open courtyard divided into equal quadrants by walkways and water channels. The hilltop site lacked sufficient natural water to nourish the garden, and so water was raised by noria from cisterns below.

FIGURE 30. Although the Lower Garden of Madinat al-Zahra' occupied a level fourteen meters below that of the Upper Garden, it mirrored the latter's cross-axial layout.

The quadripartite plan became a powerful symbol of sovereignty in the Maghreb (the Arabic name for western North Africa) as well as elsewhere in the Islamic world. It seems to have developed in the Islamic West as a legacy of the Umayyad dynasty that first ruled Syria and then, when its leading family members were assassinated by a competing clan in 749, moved to the Iberian Peninsula where they ruled until approximately 1031. The legacy was so enduring and influential that it was embraced by subsequent Muslim dynasties in Morocco and Spain.

The Alhambra Palace, a huge hilltop complex poised above the Nasrid capital of Granada, was built during the thirteenth and fourteenth centuries by members of the Nasrid dynasty (1230–1492) at a time when the Muslim grasp of the Iberian Peninsula had been seriously weakened by foes from the Christian north. The Alhambra had a cross-axial garden in the Court of the Lions (and possibly others that simply do not survive), consisting of four sunken garden beds surrounded and crisscrossed by paved paths (Plate 8). Where the paths intersect at the garden center, an elegant basin is held aloft on the backs of twelve stone lions (Fig. 31). Water runs toward the Lions Fountain from inlaid basins in the kiosks that project from the east and west ends of the courtyard, and it flows as well from larger basins in the chambers off to the north and south sides. These axial currents meet in the

FIGURE 31.
The Lions Fountain
at the Alhambra
stands at the inter-
section of the two
axes that define the
courtyard's chahar
bagh. The lions are
age-old symbols of
might and sover-
eignty and here may
refer to the Nasrid
patron's steward-
ship of the land as
he controls precious
water resources.

garden center, where water (driven by gravitational force from natural sources in the mountains above the city) pours from the mouths of the lions.

The nearby Generalife Palace had a garden that predated the Court of the Lions. The Generalife's Acequía Court, so named for the water channel (*acequía,* from the Arabic *saqiya*) that runs down its center axis, was built during the first decade of the fourteenth century. Here the plan was elongated so that it is almost four times as long as it is wide. Although the presence of a narrow walkway across the center creates a chahar bagh, like the Court of the Lions, spatially it more closely resembles the Court of the Myrtles (Plate 9) with arcaded pavilions at each end that mark the ends of the long central volume of water. Moreover, it is not certain that the narrow walkway is original to the fourteenth century. Excavations revealed that the quadrants were sunken seventy centimeters below the level of the pavements and were probably planted with a low carpet of vegetation with some larger shrubs.

In the period when the Umayyads ruled Syria and later when the Hispano-Umayyads ruled the Iberian peninsula, the cross-axial garden was a powerful symbol of territory, possession, and sovereign rule. The palatine garden served as a metaphor, not only for the organization of the landscape, but also the political economy. The sovereign sat in a central location, either in the middle of the garden or overlooking its primary axis, and looked across the meticulously gardened space, much as a landowner supervised the cultivated fields. The productive fields yielded crops that enriched the farmers and landowners, while at the same time providing tax revenues that allowed the ruler to construct extravagant palace complexes adorned with multiple gardens. The inscription of human activity on the landscape as a whole was a sign of civilization, and within that the palatine pleasure garden was a sign of sovereign territory.

Four hundred years later in Granada, the political and economic conditions that had led to the transformation of the landscape and by extension the aestheticization of that process in the design of formal gardens was a thing of a past. But although the Nasrid sovereign's ability to maintain rule and secure his kingdom's borders was constantly tested by enemies, the initial meaning of the garden metaphor continued to resonate. To some extent garden-making had become an automatic gesture, like the celebration of a religious holiday by agnostics who do not believe the theology that prompts its observance. But in another sense, the generous proportions of the Generalife's Acequía Court, and the four-part layout of the Alhambra's garden in which growling lions guard the fountain, the symbolic source of water, continued to have a powerful meaning as a metaphor for the organization and possession of the land. The potency of the four-part plan no longer stemmed from an ability to express change and new conditions of authority, power, and ever-expanding territorial presence; instead, at this date in history, it had become an established and familiar type that referred to a distinguished precedent—Cordoba.

The four-part plan was certainly not the only formal garden type, for in South Asia, the gardens of Kashmir had terraces stepped along a linear axis. Nor was it universally adopted by royalty to express power, for in Morocco, the vast area of twelfth- and thirteenth-century gardens at Agdal on the south side of Marrakesh was a royal development configured as a series of enclosed orchards organized in an approximate grid (see Sites). One of the most vehement expressions of this underlying geometrical order can be seen in the nineteenth-century palace of Pasha 'Abd al-Kari in Fez. The climbing vines and flower beds in its main courtyard are kept within an interlocking stellar design that delights in brilliantly colored *zellij* tile (Plate 10). The gardens of the Ottoman Empire were more sensitive to the natural topographical variation of their sites and thus did not impose an artificial grid. But whether adhering to the quadripartite model or not, gardens in all other areas of the Islamic world have a strong sense of geometrical order.

5 Trees and Plants

Botanical Evidence from Texts and Archaeology

ARDENS ARE EPHEMERAL. While the pavement slabs and stone or brick walls of a garden may survive through centuries of neglect, its trees, shrubs, and flowers will wither and reseed haphazardly, interspersed with weeds and volunteer species that were not original to the site. Given that living matter cannot be recuperated as easily as the more enduring forms of architecture, how then can we re-create the botanical contents of historic gardens? We have seen that treatises from as early as the tenth century list the plant varieties cultivated in a given period and region, but these rarely provide information about the arrangement and density of the plants within the garden. The descriptions of geographers, court historians, and travelers who saw a garden site or the vegetation of a region in its prime are useful, but these can be flawed by the writer's ignorance of unfamiliar species. In any case, written descriptions are seldom sufficiently detailed to allow a modern historian to identify planting arrangements. Similarly, manuscript paintings show lively compositions of plants in gardens, but the scale is not accurate and the observation of the individual species ranges from the botanically accurate to the abstract and schematic. Nonetheless, plant lists, descriptions, and manuscript illustrations are often the best evidence that we have for reconstructing the botanical contents of a historic site. In a very few cases, actual archaeological excavation and analysis has been carried out. Together, texts, pictures, and archaeological excavation can give a sense of the character and planting of historic gardens.

Islamic gardens are seldom excavated for botanical remains and soil composition because the means to do so have only recently become available, such investigations require a sophisticated level of expertise, and they are extraordinarily expensive for the amount of information that they yield. Instead, archaeologists typically investigate a garden's buildings, identifying the structure and date of paved walkways and stone or mud brick walls. Rarely is any attempt made to examine the soil itself to distinguish between rocky subsoil and the richer earth of the garden bed, hidden under layers of debris from later periods. Ironically, when archaeologists do excavate such soil levels, they destroy the integrity of the very subject they wish to investigate. Fortunately, within the past decade or two archaeologists have begun to employ noninvasive techniques with which they can explore soil without digging it up and destroying its structure. These include visual analyses such as ground-penetrating radar, remote sensing with proton magnometer, and aerial photography, as well as chemical analyses such as soil phosphate surveys, and magnetic enhancement to determine changes in soil composition.[1]

Archaeologists of the Roman period have been the most successful in identifying garden plans, plant species, and plant organization in gardens. At Almedinilla, a prosperous community in the Iberian peninsula devoted to olive growing in the Roman period as well as today, excavations at the large estate of El Ruedo revealed a simple nymphaeum and broad channel that flowed into and through the dining hall and from there into a large storage tank outside the walls of the house proper. On the other side of the house, excavated pits indicate the former presence of trees, perhaps to give shade. Even more information is known about the Roman gardens of Pompeii, Herculaneum, and Stabiae, due to the unusual circumstance of the eruption of Mt. Vesuvius in 79 C.E. that buried those cities under a sheet of ash. The volcanic event fossilized people in the midst of daily life, preserving urban architectural fabric as well as city gardens and the orchards and estates of the surrounding countryside. Beginning in the late 1960s, Wilhemina Jashemski began to work with botanists and other experts to examine the pollen and the fossilized plant matter and ash deposits in root cavities to identify the cultivated plants of late Republican Rome.[2] Archaeologists were thus able to detect not only the permanent stone pavements, wells, and walls of a garden enclosure, but also the spacing of plants, the presence of wooden stakes, and the variety of plants grown in a given plot. It was a remarkable feat that stimulated a new branch of archaeology.

However, the techniques developed by the archaeologists working in Pompeii and Herculaneum were of limited application since they had an unusual subject in the form of plants "preserved" by burning and ash deposits. While they promised the hope that a similar archaeological method could be applied to sites such as Madinat al-Zahra', which was burned during a bitter political conflict in 1010, the preliminary investigations attempted there have yielded information about soil levels but relatively little specific identification of the plants grown in the tenth century. There are few garden sites that make good candidates for archaeological investigation because the soil is rarely left undisturbed by subsequent generations of gardeners and farmers. Once the earth has been plowed anew, the structure disappears and the botanical matter rapidly decomposes.

Madinat al-Zahra' is unusual in this respect, for after the palace estate was sacked and burned, the city of Cordoba collapsed inward and its outlying villas were abandoned. Not only did the buildings of Madinat al-Zahra' fall as a result of the fire, but its gardens also failed to regenerate with the collapse of the irrigation system. Within a period of a few years, the palace became the haunt of solitary shepherds; their flocks grazed on the weedy vegetation without disturbing the soil beneath. The palace was frozen in time ironically, preserved by the very conflagration that had destroyed it. Although the stone pavements, ashlar blocks, and marble ornament were stolen from the site in the early fifteenth century for reuse in the building of the monastery of San Jerónimo,[3] as well as other sites, the extensive grounds of Madinat al-Zahra' lay virtually untouched for most of their subsequent history because farmers had little interest in the sloping terrain, preferring the flatter lands along the river below. It was not until the mid-twentieth century that the soil was again overturned when modern gardens were planted with no pretense to historical veracity.

Somewhere below the present blanket of earth and debris, the tenth-century garden of Madinat al-Zahra' awaits investigation. Archaeologists might be able to find the original soil level with deep pockets indicating the presence of shrubs and trees, and they might also discover broken ceramic pots that were used in transplanting, as mentioned in Arabic texts of the period.[4] They might find vessels for transporting water, coins (useful for dating), and gardening tools such as trowels, pruning knives, leveling devices (*murjiqal* in Arabic), and claws for lightly scratching the soil (*shanjul*).[5] It might even be possible to discover the identity of the actual plants cultivated there, and indeed, attempts at archaeobotany have been attempted in recent years with both illuminating and disappointing results.[6] On the one hand, by examining the pollen contents of core samples the botanists were able to determine that the original level of the Upper Garden of Madinat al-Zahra' lay at a depth of 90 centimeters below the present ground level (although due to the ground slope, gardening activities, and previous archaeological excavation, in some areas of the garden the present soil level appears to be the original surface).[7] However, their pollen samples found only varieties that were native to the region and could have blown in over the garden wall.[8] It is important to continue trying to identify the plant species themselves, but the information gained through this kind of selective core sampling will not explain the organization of plants within gardens.

The Generalife (1302–1308) and the Court of the Lions (1370–90) at the Alhambra are sites where the gardens were excavated as a consequence of modern catastrophe. When a fire in the Generalife in December 1958 compelled the site director to rebuild one end of the Acequía Court, the architectural fabric of the north pavilion was stripped of its modern accretions, revealing Islamic material. More important, the garden at that end of the courtyard was also explored. The garden is an elongated chahar bagh formed by a central water channel crossed midway by a narrow band of pavement. Vigorous jets—added by the architect Prieto Moreno at mid-century—line this channel, and there are water basins at the ends of the channel as well as marking the central intersection. The garden is enclosed by arcaded pavilions at either end, and along its western wall seventeen arches originally opened onto the landscape that fell away in stepped terraces below. A salient mirador with nine apertures (a miniature version of the Hall of the Ambassadors) projected from the center of this wall (see Sites).

The excavations revealed the original pavements of the Islamic-era walkways as well as the water conduits that linked the water channel's central fountain to the mirador along the west wall.[9] The former soil surface of the quadrants was discovered at 70 centimeters below these pavements (which were already lower than the present pavement level). This soil layer was buried so deeply that when the Alhambra and Generalife were claimed by the government in the twentieth century and cleaned up for a modern generation of tourists, the gardeners had not needed to dig into the fourteenth-century layer, innocently leaving its structure intact for archaeologists to examine at a later date. The fourteenth-century soil layer was thin—about 45 centimeters—indicating that only plants with shallow root systems were cultivated there. However, there were excavations in the soil made for the root balls of significantly larger plants—and indeed in the sixteenth century an observer saw orange trees and myrtles growing there.[10] The jets crisscrossing the central channel today were added in the modern era, but it is possible that the garden originally had at least a few jets with high arcs, for the water pressure from the mountains above the Generalife was more than adequate for such propulsion. According to one sixteenth-century witness, the pressure in one of the courtyards caused a jet to spout "diez brazas" (ten yards) in the air.[11]

Garden archaeology has often occurred as an unanticipated byproduct of other excavations. This was the case in the Alhambra's Court of the Lions, built in 1370–90. The courtyard (28.5 by 15.7 m) consists of a chahar bagh formed by the intersection of marble walkways that carry water channels to a central fountain of twelve lions bearing an inscribed basin on their shoulders. The courtyard is surrounded by an arcade of slender columns that project in kiosks at the east and west ends. When work was carried out here in the mid-twentieth century, one of the archaeologists noted that there was an observable difference in the soil character at a depth of approximately 80 centimeters.[12] To this information regarding the depth of the formerly sunken quadrants, we can add a sixteenth-century traveler's description of six orange trees that grew high enough to stand beneath.[13] The sunken beds and plantings in the Court of the Lions roughly match the discoveries at the Generalife: but because the archaeologist's report was recorded casually as an oral history, the precise chronology of the discoveries cannot be assessed.

In the eastern part of the Islamic world, the Bagh-i Babur in Kabul has tremendous importance as one of the few extant gardens designed by Babur, founder of the Mughal dynasty, and also as his burial place (see Sites). It was surveyed just before 1972 with the idea of restoring it but actual work was not undertaken until 2002–5.[14] Its fifteen terraces, hydraulic structures, and buildings—which date to various periods between the sixteenth and twentieth centuries—were examined and selectively restored. However, the site is huge and specific botanical excavation was not undertaken.

FIGURE 32. Excavations carried out in the Mahtab Bagh, built between 1632 and 1643 on the riverbank opposite the Taj Mahal in Agra, revealed a sandstone pool in a lotus shape on a raised terrace along the river, whose edge was marked by a wall capped with domed chhatris at either end. (James L. Wescoat, Jr.)

Another of Babur's gardens, the Bagh-i Nilufar, an early garden complex in Dholpur made in 1527–30 (see Sites), was excavated to reveal a complex partially carved from a natural plateau of red sandstone, its channels incised in the bedrock. The site was large and included many courtyards and esplanades with pools in the shapes of lotuses as well as a stepwell to collect water, an aqueduct, a bathhouse, and a pavilion.[15] Although the water system and architectural structure of the garden were identified, there were no botanical remains to investigate.

It can be difficult, time-consuming, and thus very costly to ascertain historical plantings, and archaeologists often do not even try. At Humayun's Tomb, a Mughal commemorative garden in Delhi built in 1565 or 1569, excavations completed in 2003 found that the large quadrants that are currently planted with turf were originally planted with clover. However, because the site today is enjoyed as a public park, the restorers decided to retain the more resilient grass, to which they added historically correct trees and vines such as mango, lemon, orange, neem, pomegranate, hibiscus, and jasmine.[16]

In Agra, excavations were recently carried out at an enigmatic garden on the opposite bank of the Yamuna River from the Taj Mahal. The Mahtab Bagh (Moonlight Garden) was built between 1632 and 1643 by Shah Jahan in conjunction with the construction of the Taj (see Sites). Led by Elizabeth Moynihan, a team of archaeologists and botanists studied the history of the site, which was all but washed away by the flooding of the river, and excavated its remains. They found the stone rims of pools, pavements of terraces, the remains of a riverfront retaining wall whose *chhatri*-capped end pavilions still stand, and a network of irrigation channels and storage reservoirs (Fig. 32). The form of the garden was reconstructed and some of the woody species grown in the area were identified. Pollen sampling yielded no results, but there were burned wood remains of trees such as cypress, red cedar, chirunji (cashew), jujube, and the night-blooming champa. With the exception of celosia (cockscomb), the archaeology yielded no information about more ephemeral botanical materials.[17] It was an exciting attempt to unearth a lost garden of great architectural importance, yet the successive floods had washed away the level of the soil where the key botanical remains might have been preserved.

Botanical matter rarely endures and soil structures seldom remain undisturbed. But water systems are more likely to survive, both because they are made of permanent materials like brick and stone and because an irrigation system that produces water continues to be used and maintained. For example, the Agdal Basins that collected and stored water on the outskirts of Marrakesh still fill with water, although in addition to historic gardens they now also serve agricultural fields (see Sites). The larger irrigation network to which the basins belong now have concrete conduits, but the traditional system of blocking off the arms of a split channel in order to divert water into first one and then another plot of land can still be witnessed. This technique for irrigating agricultural fields and garden beds is seen throughout the Islamic world today and historically, and it is the reason why the plots are typically sunken as opposed to raised (in the European manner) (Fig. 33). Water is allowed to flow into a bed, flooding it for several hours until the water penetrates the soil and

waters the roots of the plants. The water is then redirected to the next bed and so on until the cycle begins again at the first bed.

Because the plants in gardens are dependent on a water source that may be distant, archaeological analysis of hydraulics can take the form of a broad geographic survey. For instance, to understand the agricultural productivity of Tunisia in the Islamic period, one must look at the continued use of Roman systems such as the aqueduct that

FIGURE 33. In some areas of the world, farmers still use the methods of cultivation of their ancestors, in part because they lack the capital to industrialize production. The field shown here (in Champaner, India) has been divided into geometrical plots by means of raised earthen ridges that contain the water while it floods each square.

FIGURE 34.
The second-century
C.E. nymphaeum
of Zaghouan's
"Temple des Eaux"
poured water into
a conduit com-
prised of surface
channels and raised
aqueducts until it
reached Carthage
(Tunis). Its water
continued to flow
well into the Islamic
period.

emerged from a spring-fed nymphaeum in Zaghouan and flowed 90 kilometers to supply the cisterns of Carthage in the second century C.E. (Fig. 34). It was cut several times but was rebuilt and put back into service in 698 and again in 1267.[18] Southward in Kairouan, the medieval historian al-Bakri wrote that there were fifteen reservoirs built in 724–43 on the outskirts of the city by order of the Umayyad caliph Hisham.[19] In the ninth century, the Aghlabid governors expanded the system, which served the city as well as its surrounding gardens. The presence of these basins and others has been confirmed by modern archaeologists. They were circular or polygonal in shape, often preceded by a smaller basin that served to trap waterborne sediment (a filtration technique employed by the Roman engineers for the Zaghouan aqueduct as well). The largest of these surviving artificial reservoirs is a huge forty-eight-sided polygon (128 m diameter), with a central platform that once provided an island for a pavilion. This main basin decanted into a seventeen-sided basin (37.40 m across). It was supplied both by seasonal rainwater (scarce in Tunisia's arid climate) and an aqueduct that brought water from a range 39 kilometers to the west. The aqueduct no longer flowed to the basins in the 1950s, but a seasonal stream still supplied the main one.[20] The fact that water continued to fill some of Kairouan's basins may be due to the continued importance of the town as a tourist destination and a shrine center; nearby, the tenth-century basins of the abandoned Raqqada are dry.

Archaeology as it has been practiced to date has yielded useful information regarding the form and hydraulics of historic gardens, but it has been less successful in identifying flowers and shrubs and their arrangement within the garden. Fortunately, this data appears in scientific and descriptive texts, although these must be used with caution since such texts were rarely written as guides and descriptions of actual gardens. The botanical treatises and agricultural manuals discussed in Chapter 3 not only named the plants grown by farmers, they sometimes provided illustrations to aid in identification and instructions for cultivation as well. These were generally plants with utilitarian value. Even flowers which today are loved for their appearance were cultivated in the medieval period both as an aesthetic choice and for culinary and pharmacological uses. Perfumes were produced not only for the pleasure of their heady fragrances but also as part of a general regimen of health (akin to the popularity of aromatherapy today). Thus, a shrub such as the rose might be cultivated in gardens for its beauty and fragrance while at the same time grown as a farm crop for use in the perfume industry. Cordoba was renowned for the roses that grew on the hillsides outside of town. One observer wrote, "Indeed their numbers are so surprising, that although a *roba* [*ruba'*] (five-and-twenty pounds weight) of rose leaves will at times fetch at Cordoba four dirhems, or perhaps more, which makes it a great source of revenue to proprietors, yet no one prevents the people from plucking them on his grounds."²¹ Saffron is another marketable commodity that was mentioned by both Andalusian and Mughal historians (and remains a significant crop in Kashmir today); it was harvested from crocuses that might also be appreciated for their colorful appearance in autumnal gardens.²²

There is one flower in particular, admired for aesthetic beauty and regarded as the prize of any garden, for which there is considerable written documentation. This is the tulip, which became a symbol of the Ottoman dynasty in the imperial period. The name derives from *tulbend*, or turban, which the closed petals seemed to resemble. The tulip had humble origins as a meadow flower in Turkey, Iran, and Central Asia.²³ Exported to northern Europe in the mid-sixteenth century, the trade in tulips (both from Turkey and back again from the Low Countries) stimulated the economy, causing the rise and fall of individuals as they gambled fortunes on obtaining rare specimens. Taxes were imposed, and, to curb market speculation, prices of some tulips were fixed by the government. Sultan Selim II loved the flower and in 1574 he ordered 50,000 from Aziz (now part of Syria) for his gardens in Istanbul; in such quantities, these must have been species tulips obtained from the natural landscape.²⁴ By the reign of Ahmed III (1703–1730), tulips with unusual colors and patterns were so passionately sought after that the first half of the eighteenth century in Ottoman Turkey is known as the Lale Devri, or "Tulip Period." The flower is not only mentioned in descriptions of Ottoman palaces and country estates, it also appears in the textiles, manuscripts, and ceramic ornament of the time (Fig. 35).

A great many flowers are named in poetry, often in metaphors where the myrtle stands for hair, fruit for full breasts, the almond for the beloved's eye, and so on.²⁵ In the great Persian epic the *Shahnama*, the poet Firdawsi offered such a description of a woman: "Her cheeks were as red as pomegranate blossoms and her lips like its seeds, while two pomegranates grew from her silver breast. Her eyes were like the narcissus in the garden, and her eyebrows stole the blackness from the crow's feathers. She is a Paradise to look upon."²⁶ Such overblown descriptions are not useful in re-creating the appearance of gardens, but other poems

FIGURE 35. Stylized swaying tulips, like the lithe form of youthful bodies, adorned Ottoman textiles and ceramics such as this tall cup. (anonymous collection)

specifically described the garden flowers and the experience of being in such spaces, albeit from an idealized perspective. For example, when the Andalusian king al-Mu'tamid (1095) was exiled from his capital, Seville, to a town near Marrakesh, he recalled with sad longing his former palace's Zahir and Turayya halls, named for constellations and planets, and its gardens:

> I wonder whether I shall ever spend a night,
> With flower gardens and water pools around me,
> Where green olive groves, far-famed are planted,
> Where the doves sing, the warbling of birds resounds,
> In the Zahir on the heights, refreshed by soft rain,
> The Turayya pointing at us, we pointing at it,
> The Zahi looking at us with its round Sa'd as-su'ud,
> Jealous of each other, like a beloved and a lover!
> All this is now hard, not easy to attain:
> Yet, whatever God wishes to pass, is easy to bear![27]

These literary references to gardens were never intended to serve as maps indicating what was planted where, but they give a sense of the general characteristics of a garden—olive groves, doves, flowers, and pools—and do provide an important insight into audience reception and the prominent place of nature imagery in Islamic discussions of beauty.

Many of the descriptions of gardens found in heroic epics and courtly poetry have evocative descriptions of gardens, the plants grown within them, and cultivation techniques. For example, the Umayyad regent al-Mansur's al-'Amiriyya palace outside of Cordoba was praised in detail by a poet who saw roses, chamomile, narcissus, anemone, and basil there.[28] When the ninth-century historian al-Ya'qubi described Samarra, he praised at length the magnificent palm trees that "reached to the sun."[29] Mehmet II the Conqueror's Greek biographer described the sultan's gardens at his palace in Edirne as well as the gardens of the Topkapı Palace in the second half of the fifteenth century, extolling the variety of flowers and fruit trees, abundantly irrigated and stocked with singing birds.[30] In 1620 the Mughal emperor Jahangir observed the Kashmiri custom of covering roofs with soil in order to plant tulips, commenting, "It looks really beautiful. . . . This year the tulips bloomed exceptionally well in the palace garden and on the roof of the congregational mosque."[31] Shah Jahan's court biographer repeatedly commented on the thick stands of evergreens and plane trees in Kashmir, as well as the scarlet lotus which bloomed in the waters of Lake Dal and the willows which grew along its shores.[32] The poet Ibn Zaydun in eleventh-century al-Andalus gave a description of artificial pollination. In the voice of a palm tree he wrote, "You have nourished my spirit; gather, then, the first fruits. The fruit of the palm tree belongs to he who pollinates it."[33] The concept of sexual fertilization of plants was known to both poets and agronomists, for one agricultural manual author wrote about two date palms in Cairo that, when separated by a wall, ceased to bear fruit for two years. He explained that the trees were enamored of each other and could not bear to be apart, and that when the wall was dismantled, the love-sick trees recovered.[34]

Similarly, European travelers, intent on recording geography, social customs, architecture, and botany, described the flowers they saw in Turkey, Iran, Central Asia, and India. For example, in the seventeenth-century John Chardin mentioned seeing tulips, anemones, red ranunculus, jonquils, daffodils, lilies, violets, jasmine, and fritillaria (crown imperial), as well as many varieties of rose in his travels through Central Asia. His contemporary, François Bernier, commented sourly on the landscape of India in general, but when he accompanied the entourage of the Mughal emperor Aurangzeb during a three-month visit to Kashmir in northern India, he greatly admired the landscape (Plate 11). He saw varied and lush vegetation that included apple, pear, plum, apricot, and walnut trees, as well as tall aspens and poplars, and noted "fields of rice, wheat, hemp, saffron, and many sorts of vegetables, among which are intermingled trenches filled with water, rivulets, canals, and several small lakes."[35]

Travelers' accounts tend to discuss plants and the impression of landscape, and botanical and agricultural texts list plants and explain cultivation, but seldom do these describe planting arrangements with any degree of detail. Fortunately, there are some exceptions. In twelfth-century al-Andalus, Ibn Luyun wrote a treatise in verse in which he recommended making sunken beds for gardens where water was scarce, which was the prevailing practice in al-Andalus and the Maghreb for flood irrigation. He cited the standard size as 12 by 4 cubits, although he recommended smaller dimensions for gardens requiring more irrigation.[36] He also gave instructions on the placement and design of the estate garden:

> With regard to houses set amidst gardens an elevated site is to be
>   recommended, both for reasons of vigilance and of layout;
> And let them have a southern aspect, with the entrance at one side,
>   and on an upper level the cistern and well,
> Or instead of a well have a watercourse where the water runs underneath
>   the shade.
> And if the house have two doors, greater will be the security it enjoys
>   and easier the repose of its occupant.
> Then next to the reservoir plant shrubs whose leaves do not fall
>   and which [therefore] rejoice the sight;
> And, somewhat further off, arrange flowers of different kinds,
>   and further off still, evergreen trees,
> And around the perimeter climbing vines, and in the center of the whole
>   enclosure a sufficiency of vines;
> And under climbing vines let there be paths which surround the garden
>   to serve as margin.
> And amongst the fruit trees include the [common] grapevine similar
>   to a slim woman, or wood-producing trees;
> Afterward arrange the virgin soil for planting whatever you wish to prosper.
> In the background let there be trees like the fig or any other
>   which does no harm;

And plant any fruit tree which grows big in a confining basin so that its mature growth

May serve as a protection against the north wind without preventing the sun from reaching [the plants].

In the center of the garden let there be a pavilion in which to sit, and with vistas on all sides,

But of such a form that no one approaching could overhear the conversation within and whereunto none could approach undetected.

Clinging to it let there be [rambler] roses and myrtle, likewise all manner of plants with which a garden is adorned.

And this last should be longer than it is wide in order that the beholder's gaze may expand in its contemplation.[37]

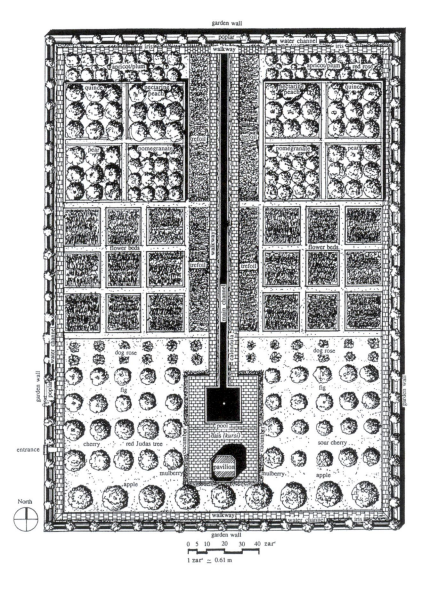

FIGURE 36.
Irshad al-zira'a
(Maria Subtelny)

The sixteenth-century *Irshad al-zira'a* by Qasim b. Yusuf Abu Nasiri was more specific. This Persian treatise was based on earlier agronomic sources and interviews with actual farmers in Herat, as well as some firsthand experience.[38] Herat was an ideal landscape for agriculture and was densely planted with farms and gardens even within its immediate suburbs, where both utilitarian agriculture and pleasure gardening relied on irrigated cultivation within small enclosed spaces.[39] The *Irshad al-zira'a* contained the typical chapters for agricultural treatises: types of soils, optimal times for planting, the cultivation of cereals, legumes, and vegetables, and planting method, propagation, and grafting. But, perhaps because of the close relationship between farm and garden techniques, it also includes a chapter on the plan of an estate garden that gives precise measurements for the dimensions of pavilions, platforms, and pools as well as their respective relationships on a plan.

The *Irshad al-zira'a* recommends that the garden wall should enclose an inner perimeter three zar' wide (a variable unit, between 60 and 73 cm) with an encircling row of Samarkand poplars, followed by a water channel one zar' wide, the inner edge of which should be planted with irises (Figs. 36 and 37). Next there should be an underground water channel (also three zar' wide) capped by a walkway, followed by a border of one zar' filled with irises along the edge of the walkway.[40] Next come apricot trees spaced eight zar' apart on mounds, interplanted with red roses and peach trees, followed by plum trees grafted onto apricot stock. A water channel flanked by walkways that cap subterranean channels should flow down the center of the garden into a pool placed twenty zar' in front of a raised pavilion at the garden's south end. This channel should be lined with calendula, iris, and other flowers. The garden should descend from this pool in four terraces planted with fruit trees, and below this there should be garden beds planted with varieties of crocus, violet, iris, narcissus, rose, tulip, anemone, jasmine, Judas tree, red poppy, waterlily, althaea, pink, and amaranthus, as well as others.

The Mughal *Bayaz-i khwushbu'i* (Sweet-smelling Notebook) of 1628–38 is similarly detailed, although here the emphasis is not on technique but on land management. It says that a regular rectangular bed (*kiyari*) for a formal garden (*baghcha*) should have a proportion of 3:2. It states the number of ordinary and specialized gardeners (perhaps designating the distinction between labor and horticultural expertise), wells, and oxen (draft animals) necessary to tend a garden of a certain size, giving multiple examples. In one case, it says that a garden of the princess Jahanara had an area of 56 *bigah* (a bigah equals three-fifths of an acre), sixty regular gardeners and fifty-six royal (specialized) gardeners, sixty cattle, and three wells and twelve buckets (perhaps indicating a saqiya wheel that drew water via buckets attached to a chain on an axle).[41]

FIGURE 37. The *Irshad al-zira'a* was a sixteenth-century late Timurid agricultural treatise. Subtelny's plan of the garden described in *Irshad* (opposite) is different from Alemi's plan (below), yet the drawings were made from the same detailed text. (Mahvesh Alemi)

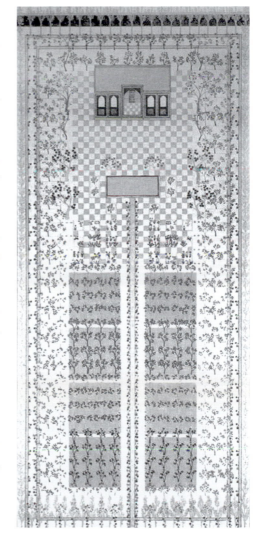

Although earlier manuals such as Ibn Luyun's in Spain had prescribed the layout of an ideal garden, the late Timurid *Irshad al-zira'a* differs from these in that it gives actual dimensions, rather than variable proportions. The specificity of measurements may indicate that it was based on an actual garden, or it may be explained by the roughly four-hundred-year gap between them and the increasing shift from proportions to numerical measurements in the later era. The *Bayaz-i khwushbu'i* is similarly precise with respect to the labor and necessary equipment, and indeed the Mughal text refers to actual gardens with the names Maula Mahal, garden of Jahanara, Dahrah-i Kalani, and garden of the Nur Saray. Yet, despite the enumeration of gardeners, wells, and numerical or proportional garden measurement, these descriptions ultimately rely on words to represent a three-dimensional, material body. There is a translation from a spatial to a grammatical syntax that assumes that the reader already knows the sort of garden under review and can read the missing information between the lines of text. Four hundred or a thousand years later, the sense of familiarity with the original form is lost, and with it has vanished essential information about gardens. Indicative of the inadequacy of these written works in representing the gardens they describe are the images made by two twentieth-century scholars of the garden described in the aforementioned *Irshad al-zira'a*. These use the same textual description of the garden to produce different representations so that, although the facts supporting each artist's rendering are the same, the interpretations made by them vary significantly. They are immensely useful—and quite lovely—as visualizations, yet they are not windows onto an actual garden. This is the predicament of every modern reader: how to read written texts for information on material and visual form.

6 Representations of Gardens and Landscape

Imagery in Manuscript Paintings, Textiles, and Other Media

ANUSCRIPTS FROM THE thirteenth century onward depict landscapes and gardens in styles that range from schematic scenes lacking spatial depth to meticulously rendered landscapes, rich with detail and convincing observation. Because manuscript painting is a visual medium, it would seem to have an advantage over written descriptions of gardens. But are the images in manuscripts any more accurate or complete than those of texts? To what extent can paintings be used as transparent windows onto lost places? It is not always clear from a manuscript or album painting whether an artist was representing an actual garden with observable and recognizable features (which he may or may not have seen), as in the case of the Mughal painting where the seated man is clearly Shah Jahan and the garden with a channel flowing over a panel of *chini khana* niches is identifiable as the Nishat Bagh in Kashmir (Plate 12); or, whether he was rendering an ideal or imagined garden or genre type. The use of paintings as evidence to reconstruct actual garden form can be problematic, because they are subjective representations filtered through an artist's eyes and imagination and rendered according to visual codes that reflect cultural norms. And yet, for an art form as ephemeral as the garden, painted scenes can capture transitory conditions and, more important, reflect the response of those who experienced them.

The earliest representations of plants are found in scientific treatises where schematized renderings are preferred over accurate depictions of natural features such as asymmetry and life-cycle phases such as the bud stage. The *De materia medica* of Dioscorides (see Fig. 19), for example, was richly illustrated with painted representations of lettuce, gentian, calamint, viola, and cumin, among others. However, because the images were typically copied over and over from other pictorial sources rather than observed from life, a modern botanist might find it difficult to identify plants on the basis of the illustrations alone in some manuscripts. Textiles and vessels of ivory, silver, and glazed ceramic likewise depicted plants, stock image types, and ornamental motifs in an era before narrative painting. Some of these media, such as the *mina'i* ware (ceramic with stain and overglaze painting) produced in eastern realms of Islam, had a close relationship to manuscript illustration and had sequential scenes that suggest an emerging interest in storylines. The figures typically dominate the scene in these early illustrations, so that there is little space given over to details of setting; where vegetation is included at all, it is typically decorative rather than informative in a scientific sense. Artists representing gardens and landscape in scenes with narrative content took liberties with scale and detail because they were more concerned with the story itself than the accuracy of botanical detail or garden design, and yet much can still be learned from manuscript illustrations, especially the richly detailed and elegantly rendered book and album paintings from the sixteenth century onward.

The *Kalila wa Dimna* and the *Maqamat* are two early texts with thirteenth-century illustrated copies in which vegetation begins to play a pronounced role. The *Kalila wa Dimna* was a set of moralizing fables composed around the year 300 in India, introduced to Iran in the mid-sixth century and translated into Arabic two centuries later.[1] The tales take place outdoors with animal and human protagonists and landscape settings that often seem to take precedence over narrative action and human figures. In the early and mid-fourteenth-century manuscript illustrations, the trees are rendered schematically, and yet there is some attempt at differentiation to show variety: some have palmate leaves while others have branches painted with horizontal black lines to create partitions; the fruit and blossoms are blue and red, in bud stage and in full bloom. The ground is represented in green stripes that occasionally burst with bladed leaves and flowers. In one image, a hare and a lion look into a pool of water, the lion mistaking his own reflection for a rival (Fig. 38). In this scene from a fourteenth-century *Kalila wa Dimna*, the landscape shows two trees, a body of water, variegated land forms, and the ground line of grass. As is common in Islamic painting, the scene pushes beyond the red line that defines the right-hand margin of the field of text, while on the left, the tip of the hare's tail and plump red fruit also break the border. It is as though the energy of the scene could not be contained by its rectangular frame. A manuscript copy made less than forty years later shows a more delicately articulated landscape with diminutive figures of which one scholar has observed, "the artist's use of landscape could almost be criticized for being . . . at the expense of the figures in the drama."[2]

The *Maqamat*, or "Assemblies," of al-Hariri (1054–1122) consisted of fifty stories told about a cunning yet foolish character, Abu Zayd, and the tricks he played on people with his eloquence. Not only their humor and narrative excitement appeal to modern audiences, but also the representations of quotidian life in a library, mosque, pharmacy, caravanserai, and cemetery, among other settings, in the various illustrated manuscripts (Plate 13). The landscape is similarly varied and interesting. In one, a fruit-laden palm tree leans provocatively in front of a minaret

FIGURE 38. The early illustrations of the *Kalila wa Dimna*, of which there are many manuscript copies, reveal an interest in landscape, although the details are minimal and the settings simple. (Oxford, Bodleian Library, MS Pococke 400 folio 51 verso)

while villagers go about their daily work and animals drink from a stream bordered by vegetation (Fig. 39).³ Below, two camels, one with mouth open to reveal teeth, tread on a field of flowers. Indeed, in this image, the architecture and landscape provide the only frame of the pictorial field. These images do not purport to represent real villages, and yet they are so rich in detail that they do seem like windows to the past: the world that they reveal is delightfully ordinary.

The *Kitab al-diryaq* (Book of Antidotes) of Pseudo-Galen, written and illustrated in 1199, likewise shows an interest in the realism of outdoor settings. One scene shows the main character, a physician, seated in the upper left observing agricultural activities while his servant bears a tray of food (Fig. 40). The rest of the image is taken up by laborers working with a spade, sickle, thresher, winnowing tray, a six-tined hay fork, and draft animals. Reading from left to right and top to bottom, according to the natural sequence of work, the field is represented first as an orange mass with wavy lines to show that the earth has

FIGURE 39.
This scene from the *Maqamat* of al-Hariri, a manuscript copied in 1237 in Baghdad, is an energetic and evocative depiction of village life. (Paris, Bibliothèque Nationale de France)

been dug, and subsequently as a golden mass of grain. From both the tilled earth and the crop of grain, a few tall plants emerge with either tight yellow or feathery orange "flowers." The juxtaposition of the mature plants with the rest of the landscape is illogical, suggesting that the artist copied the scenes of labor from another source, perhaps ceramics or metalwork, either without fully understanding the agricultural cycle or simply unconcerned with correct temporal sequence.⁴

While these manuscripts indicate that the natural landscape was already a subject of interest for early manuscript painters, later illustrations begin to depict more complex courtly scenes where landscape and garden settings are important to set the tone of the narrative and are integral to the plot itself. For instance, the *Bayad wa Riyad* offers a glimpse into palatine gardens where in some scenes an audience listens to music and in another a lover throws himself despondently alongside the banks of a running river. Although the love story is set in Iraq, the only existing copy was written in Maghrebi script and has been dated to thirteenth- or fourteenth-century Spain on the basis of paleography and the architecture depicted in the illustrations.⁵ In one scene, the protagonist Bayad plays a stringed instrument called the 'ud, while court ladies listen with drinking cups and a flask, seated in a garden overlooked by towers with miradors.⁶ The vegetation is schematic with brown or green branches that yield individually articulated, identical green leaves and terminate in round red fruits. As in some of the representations in the *Kalila wa Dimna*,

FIGURE 40.
This scene from the
*Book of Antidotes
(Kitab al-diryaq)*
of Pseudo-Galen,
painted in 1199,
shows cyclical ag-
ricultural activities,
much like a
European "labors
of the month."
(Paris, Bibliothèque
Nationale de
France)

the grassy ground is painted as a dense blanket of wavy green lines. We can identify these repeated techniques for representing landscape as visual codes that were distinct from attempts at verisimilitude. However, despite the schematization, there was a clear desire to convey specific information about the plants in this and other illustrations in the manuscript, for the green striped ground surface terminates with red dots, indicating a grassy turf intermingled with wild flowers. Illustrations in the *Maqamat* manuscripts also show conventional red dots to indicate blooms, but because the grassy stems are more individuated and the red blooms are not symmetrically aligned, the *Maqamat* illustration appears more naturalistic.

Another scene from the *Bayad wa Riyad* manuscript shows a garden with a central pool with paddling waterfowl, fish, and the outlines of what might be swimming turtles (Plate 6). To the left, a trellised vine climbs sinuously upward while to the right, ladies converse in a pavilion indicated by a single arch on red marble columns. The scale of the human figures is exaggerated so that their heads almost reach the peak of the arch and one of them stand above the trellis, a hand resting lightly on its upper surface. Water streams into the pool from fountains in the shape of horse or deer heads. In the background, a compact tree grows from grassy ground once again indicated with wavy green lines topped by tiny red blooms. The architecture is depicted with rich detail, so that the viewer sees that the pool is surrounded by a flying walkway that projects over the surface of the water, and that the trellis rises to a finial in the form of a metal ball.[7] Spatial recession is suggested through overlapping surfaces; but at the same time, the plane of the pool's surface tilts upward so that it is seen from above instead of in profile. The treatment of spatial volume and the relative scale of architecture, people, and flora make no pretense to naturalism; yet the complex scene is represented with sufficient clarity that it can be read and understood.

The Mongol invasions of the mid-thirteenth century caused great destruction and the dispersal of established centers of painting in central Islamic lands, but also renewal and an infusion of artistic ideas from eastern Asia that spread beyond the borders of Mongol rule into Mamluk Syria and Egypt. Under Ghengiz Khan (ca. 1162–1227), the Mongols united a vast empire that extended from eastern China to Iran and the Caucasus Mountains. On the death of the emperor and the fragmentation of his empire into four smaller but still huge territories, the Mongol Il-khanids (1256–1353) ruled Iran, profiting from their close familial ties to the other three dynasties. They established a stable administration that encouraged economic prosperity and a renaissance of the arts. In particular, they were keen patrons of the book arts and manuscript painting flourished, especially copies of the *Shahnama*, the great Persian heroic epic with lively stories of open-air battle, intrigues, and love that lent themselves easily to illustrations. Of these, at least ten fourteenth-century copies exist.[8] Under the Il-khanid rulers, a new style of painting developed in which Chinese influences were particularly evident in the rendering of landscape.[9] Space began to be depicted with receding planes to suggest depth of field; ground lines were uneven; and the landscape gained a new emotional tone so that craggy rocks, gnarled trees, and scrolling clouds enhanced the drama of the text. (A much later example of Chinese-style clouds can be seen in the illustrated *Haft awrang*, Plate 15.) Moreover, because the books were produced on a larger scale than previous illustrated manuscripts, the paintings were larger and included more descriptive detail. Sometimes human figures and their steeds filled the page to the degree that there was little room left over for extraneous details of the natural setting or sky (rendered in gold, brilliant red, and deep blue).

In late fourteenth-century Iran, the pictorial arts were refined with lighter colors and figures represented in smaller scale so that the landscape's spatial volume seemed more convincing. Timur, the founder of the fifteenth-century Timurid dynasty (1370–1506) in Iran and Central Asia who was himself descended from Ghengiz Khan, passed on to his successors a taste for beautifully illustrated books. By this time, luxury books were objects of avid inter-

est and were often given as political gifts or traded. The book arts rose to a high level and with them the status of the artist and the emotional depth of the imagery. In a manuscript painting by the great Bihzad, who served the Timurid ruler Sultan Husayn Mirza (r. 1470–1506), a dragon clings to a bare tree and a stream (once bright silver but now tarnished to gray) wanders; landscape spills out of the left-hand margin of the page, and a tree trunk, rather than an abstract edge, provides the composition's frame (Fig. 41). This breaking of the frame suggests an uncontained energy and in this case may have served as a coded sign for naturalism, much as the vanishing point and a raking light in an otherwise dim chamber were signs for naturalism in European painting of the Renaissance and baroque periods, respectively. In both cases, these were conventional signs that were understood and shared by artists and viewers of the period. By the end of the Timurid period, the space within the frame was increasingly layered with a distinct foreground, middle ground, and background of overlapping trees, topographic elements such as rocks and hills, and human and other animal figures, enhancing the scene's appearance of three-dimensionality and thus verisimilitude.

FIGURE 41. "Bahram Gur Slays a Dragon," *Khamsa* of Nizami (copy dated 1442), was painted by Bihzad, 1493, Herat. In this Timurid manuscript illustration, a dragon emerges from a dark cave and clings to a dead tree—a harbinger of his fate at the hands of the hunter Bahram Gur. A silver stream wanders through the rocky desert in the right foreground. (British Library, Add. 25900, fol. 161r)

Not only were the pages filled with handsome polychromatic painting, but the broad margins of the paintings or text block pages might also be filled with exquisitely drawn scenes with a more subdued or monochrome palette. A black ink drawing from the 1403 *Diwan* of Sultan Ahmad Jalayir shows a continuous landscape with a figure driving a pair of oxen in a marshy field bordered by cattails in the lower right corner, while waterfowl paddle in the pools of water (Fig. 42). On the left margin, an elderly man with a staff walks next to a woman bearing an infant, while overhead geese fly with wings outstretched. There is dynamic movement in the figures and an intense sense of atmosphere in the wind-driven clouds and leafy stalks of the landscape below. The landscape's animation owes nothing to colorful paints or gleaming gold: it is the close attention to detail that brings it to life. In other manuscript paintings, those components could include everyday scenes of bathing and barbering, artisan activities, manual labor, architectural construction, and love and leisure enjoyed in a garden setting. The lifelike qualities of such scenes was evidently much appreciated by viewers: when a master asked his two companions to describe what they saw in a certain landscape painting, the first replied, "Master, when I saw those blossoming flowers, I wanted to stretch out my hand, pick one and stick it in my turban." The other said, "I too had the same desire, but (then) it occurred to me that if I stretched out my hand, all the birds would fly off the trees."[10]

Similar monochrome ink paintings are seen in the margins of the 1595 Mughal copy of the *Khamsa* of Nizami (Plate 7). Lions, gazelles, hares, and birds are pictured in a landscape of varied flowers and plants, trees, and an almost surreal mountain crag. Although well observed and enlivened by realistic references, these scenes from the *Diwan* and the *Khamsa* nonetheless often belonged to genres, within which the audience was already primed to recognize such stock human types as the hero, lover, and fool and such stock themes as predator attacking prey. The purpose of naturalistic detail was to attract the eye and delight the senses; it did not necessarily mean a realistic depiction of a historic or unique event.

In addition to illustrated manuscripts with narrative cycles, individual works on paper were produced and subsequently compiled in albums by collectors. From the mid-sixteenth century onward, artists increasingly made paintings for sale on the open market and attached prominent signatures that enunciated their individual identities as artists.[11] Many of these were genre scenes such as images of painters' workshops; others were portraits of plants and individuals; and still others were pages of fine calligraphy. The art of painting for albums and narrative texts that flourished in Iran and Central Asia was eagerly adopted by patrons of the Ottoman dynasty, especially after the conquest of Constantinople (1453), and by the Mughals of South Asia (1526–1858). These new patrons supported large schools of painting and calligraphy, attracting or sometimes forcibly relocating artists to work for them at their palace courts. As artistic style and the patron's connoisseurship became a hallmark of individuality, they also collected the work of older artists, pasting those paintings into existing books and albums.[12]

From the sixteenth century onward, painters in Iran, Turkey, and South Asia frequently rendered flowers with such detail that the varieties can be identified today: in Mughal miniatures alone we see carnation, cockscomb, crocus, delphinium, heliotrope, hollyhock, hyacinth, jasmine, larkspur, lotus, marigold, narcissus, oleander, stock, tuberose, violet, and wallflower as well as a wide variety of flowering shrubs and trees.[13] These meticulously observed depictions in manuscript and album paintings provide clues to the interrelationship of specific plants and architecture in the garden, and yet the coded nature of representation—entangled in style, influence, technique, symbolic reference, and audience re-

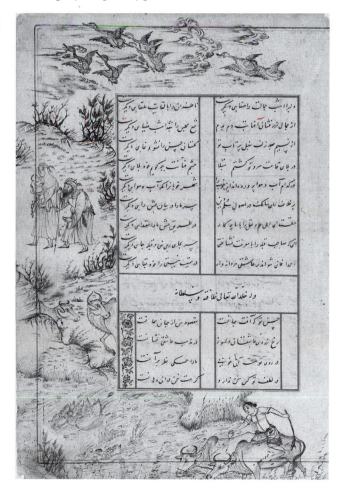

FIGURE 42. This finely drawn pastoral scene from the *Diwan* of Sultan Ahmad Jalayir, 1403, is similar to the scenes in the margins of Plate 7. The artist, who may have been 'Abd al-Hayy, worked for one of the Il-khanids' successor dynasties that ruled Iraq and Azerbaijan. (Freer Gallery of Art, Smithsonian Institution, Washington D.C.: Purchase, F1932.30)

ception—means that paintings did not give unmediated access to the gardens of the past. How high did the plants grow? Were flowers planted in thick clusters to create masses of color or were they scattered evenly across a grassy bed? Questions of size and distribution are difficult to answer on the basis of painted imagery because, as we have seen, the scale of illustrations was often distorted to give heightened emphasis to human activity or to compress larger structures to fit the limited confines of the manuscript page.

For example, the often reproduced image from a copy of the *Baburnama* from about 1595 that shows the Mughal emperor Babur supervising the laying out of the Bagh-i Wafa depicts the four garden beds of a chahar bagh, but they are miniaturized to an impossibly small scale (Plate 14). The quadripartite structure of the garden plan was clearly of greater importance than the correct proportions of the plots, the depth of the water channels, and the size of the garden enclosure. And yet, despite its manipulation of scale, the image does show that a variety of fruit trees were grown along the inner face of the enclosure walls while smaller plants were cultivated within raised plots, and it contrasts this organized treatment of nature with the wilder landscape beyond the garden walls where plants and animals emerge from rocky crevices. Moreover, the panel held in the hands of the architect whose back is turned to allow the viewer to peer over his shoulder reveals that the garden was planned using a regular grid, as is modern architectural practice today.[14] This and other illustrated copies of the *Baburnama* manuscript provide welcome insight into Mughal garden planning and patronage, but they must be used with considerable caution because the intended political purpose of the pictures—to glorify and authenticate the beginnings of Mughal rule in South Asia—differs from the role that modern historians assign to them. Although the original text of this manuscript was composed by Babur in the form of a memoir written in his own hand, its handsome illustrations were added only to the new manuscript copies that circulated seventy-five years after his death. Thus, as James Wescoat pointed out, although they purport to represent a garden from Babur's era (and have been used to illustrate the form and appearance of that garden by many modern historians), in actuality they reflect garden design in the later age of Akbar, who commissioned illustrated copies of the *Baburnama* to legitimate the foundation of the empire.[15]

Some manuscripts correctly show the techniques by which plants were cultivated. We have already seen that the *Bayad wa Riyad* shows a garden with a multi-branched vine climbing a pergola (Plate 6). The fact that this was a ubiquitous technique for viniculture is attested to by the appearance of trellises in manuscript illustrations from other areas of the Islamic world as, for example, the illustrated scene from the late sixteenth-century Mughal copy of the *Khamsa* of Nizami, which shows a city with pavilions that open to a landscape of dense trees, slender cypresses, a rocky stream with ducks, and grapevines trained within a cage of interlacing horizontal supports (Plate 7).[16] In this scene of courtly entertainment with musicians, a man in the foreground is adjusting the slats of the trellis. Ottoman manuscripts also show domed pergolas that provide the frame for climbing vines.[17] Ibn Battuta in the fourteenth century saw betel trees grown on cane trellises in the Yemen, and the French traveler François Bernier mentioned seeing trellised walks in the gardens of Kashmir in 1665.[18] In addition to architectural structures bearing vines, trees could provide natural support. A Safavid copy of the *Haft awrang* (Plate 15) made in the mid-sixteenth century shows a vine climbing through the strong branches of a tulip tree or sycamore, a technique that appears often in manuscripts with garden scenes and that is still practiced today throughout the world.

In addition to well-tended gardens, manuscripts also contain scenes with undomesticated landscapes, such as sixteenth-century illustrations in the *Shahnama* where a hero encounters his enemy or a demon or hunts in a wilderness depicted with brilliant colors. The landscapes are rendered in much larger scale relative to the persons positioned within them; people and animals hide in the craggy mountains amidst rocks to which gnarled trees cling. Skies are rendered in blue, often with clouds and even a sun or moon. The landscape bursts out from the margin as if its seething energy cannot be subdued by the frame's rigid geometry. In a different sense, the *Khamsa* of Nizami also depicts an undesigned landscape, distinguishing between the orderly garden within the walls and the more turbulent landscape without. These are wonderfully illustrated scenes of nature, but while they reflect an interest in plants and trees and landscape as a whole—especially its potential for emotional expression—they do not provide evidence for planning and design.

With respect to planted and tended landscapes, Islamic manuscripts show two kinds of arrangements, the meadow garden and the more deliberate formal garden. Although praised for their sensory appeal as places for the enjoyment of color, fragrance, and sound, neither the meadow nor the formal garden depicted in manuscripts was made purely for pleasure. The trees that bloomed in bright colors and yielded heady scents also produced edible fruit that was harvested and either bestowed as a salary to the garden staff, or given as a gift to the lord's many retainers and dependents. In the 1556–65 copy of the *Haft awrang*, the garden is fecund: teeming with nesting birds and tree boughs heavy with fruit. In the lower right corner of the painting, a gardener gives a cluster of grapes to a passing beggar. Indeed, the abundant harvest yielded by such gardens was surely one aspect of the pleasure and satisfaction enjoyed therein.

The first of the two garden types is a naturalistic country landscape with wildflowers scattered across a grassy meadow. Although seemingly artless, the landscape is by no means uncultivated. The *Haft awrang*'s scene shows a city dweller who, wandering uninvited into such a garden while spending a day in the country, trampled the ground in his haste to pick the apples, pomegranates, and grapes that are brightly depicted on gracefully swaying trees. The space is enclosed and gated and has a beautiful canopied tent erected on a raised hexagonal platform where four figures sit at leisure with drinking cups and a stringed instrument. The trees are large and vigorous, weaving behind and in front of the painting's rectangular frame and blocks of text. Along the upper right-hand margin, a stream emerges from a rocky outcropping and then meanders behind the tent-pavilion, through the garden, and around the fruit and cypress trees, its border occasionally marked by a small boulder. Although there are no permanent buildings, formal rows of flowers, or ornamental fountains, and although the stream does not provide an organizing axis for the garden composition, the landscape is nonetheless the creation of a gardener, as evidenced by his presence, holding a spade, at the gate in the lower right. This is confirmed by the text that accompanies the image: when the intruder, approached by the owner, asked if he had erred, the owner replied: "You have destroyed in a moment what took years to create!"[19] Thus, while the garden has an informal appearance, imitating a meadow with scattered flowers and trees growing randomly, and perhaps reflecting a rural context, the narrative reveals that it was in fact planned and managed.

The other type of garden displayed in paintings was the enclosed courtyard, bounded by high walls and containing built structures, permanent water features such as canals and fountains, and a garden space subdivided geometrically into smaller plots. These sites, regardless of whether they were located in the remote countryside or a city, had a distinctly architectural character to which the garden responded with what landscape architects today call hardscape—tile and stone pavements—and structural elevation. In manuscript representations, the architecture and garden are mutually permeable, so that trees are glimpsed through windows and iwans (arched niches), and gardens are overlooked by upper-story balconies and permanent pavilions. In such spaces, planting occurs in rows, water enters through stone-lined channels, and plots are organized symmetrically. This was precisely the kind of planting scheme advocated in the *Irshad al-zira'a*. Although that text reflected an Iranian context, Mughal manuscript illustrations contain the best instances of garden formalism.

An imperial Mughal manuscript dated to 1595 shows the planting layout of a palace garden enclosed by red sandstone walls (Plate 5). The garden stands on a riverbank and in the distant background, there are clusters of reddish-hued buildings within strong gated enclosures—possibly a view of Agra in the sixteenth century before Jahangir, Nur Jahan, and Shah Jahan had made their additions and renovations. From the garden's enclosure wall a raised circular platform of white marble projects on sturdy supports above the river's coursing waters (pavilions at gardens along Agra's Yamuna River had similar platforms and terraces for enjoying the views of the river and the opposite bank). The plantings are represented in refreshing and colorful detail. The garden quadrants are filled with green turf except along the edges where neat rows of crocuses and tulips are aligned on stepped borders. Some of the borders are slightly raised by red sandstone walls, as at the base of the circular terrace; elsewhere the demarcation and changes in level are less clear. In addition to flowering bulbs, four cypresses grow in circular containers at the corners of the basin with the fountain jet. These are companion-planted with spring-blooming trees such as plum and cherry, with white and red blooms. The circular containers may have been meant to create raised ground for seating, or more probably they held water around the roots of the plants to facilitate irrigation.[20]

The garden's working system is also depicted, for in the background, water is lifted up to the garden from the river via a waterwheel connected by an axle and cogs to a vertical shaft that is rotated by two water buffalo. Here a portion of the garden wall appears to have been removed by the artist to reveal the hydraulic mechanism of the noria, and the ground plane has been tipped upward to show the circular path of the animals. The water from the noria pours into a circular tank and flows from there through raised channels that crisscross the garden. These channels form an asymmetrical chahar bagh that appears to continue beyond the right-hand margins of the painting (although as it is a right-hand page, there is no such extension). The channels are interrupted by square basins at the termini of the axes, as well as one round basin with a multipronged jet positioned just in front of the circular riverfront terrace. As in the illustration of Babur supervising garden construction in the *Baburnama*, the scale here is condensed to show as much of the garden and as many figures as possible.

While the chahar bagh layout could be staged at a grand scale in large gardens, the underlying concept of the grid was often realized on a smaller scale in small courtyards or where the separation of plants in discrete beds was desired. The 1663 Mughal manuscript illustration of Shah Jahan in the Nishat Bagh shows the garden behind him as a simple grid with no discernible cross-axis (Plate 12). A broad water channel courses from a pavilion in the background, through three raised stepping stones that allowed a person to pick his or her way carefully across the water, and over a ledge adorned with tiered rows of chini khana niches, splashing into a pool with playing jets. The emperor sits in the foreground on cushions and carpets adorned with floral motifs. The watercourse divides the flower beds into two groups of twelve units each. It is unclear whether the beds were created by partitions of cut sandstone that were on level with the beds or raised them above the surrounding garden. The use of stone framing in this garden, built in 1625 by the empress Nur Jahan, predates by about ten years the prevailing taste for ornate tracery during the reign of Shah Jahan, as seen in the Anguri Bagh (1628–37) of the Agra Fort (see Fig. 86) or the Taj Mahal (1632–43) (see Fig. 85).

The Mughals ruled over a population of Muslims but also various sects of Hinduism (and to a lesser extent, Buddhists and Jains), and among these Hindu contemporaries, the Rajput princes of Rajasthan were patrons whose taste influenced and also reflected that of the Mughals. Especially in the realm of secular palatine architecture and gardens, it can be difficult to identify a specifically Muslim or Hindu identity in the shared vocabulary of water channels, fountains, and pavilions. In a large chahar bagh, broad swathes of turf (possibly consisting of mixed vegetation) might be used, as at the eighteenth-century Dig Palace near Bharatpur (Plate 16), but just as often, the garden took the form of a partially paved floor covered with a grid of deep recesses. This was the case at the Amar Vilas garden of the City Palace of Udaipur (Plate 17), and it is also a technique represented in paintings. It is possible that these basin-like recesses, which are most in evidence in Rajput contexts, contributed to the Mughal taste for beds divided into dense grids since, like the latter, they imposed a powerful geometry to which the individual plants were subordinate. However, artistic production in Mughal South Asia can rarely be traced to a single cultural point of origin. Manuscripts show sunken beds with rectangular and scalloped profiles in depictions of both the Rajput and the Mughal gardens. Clearly the grid was an organizing principle in both, although it is unclear whether the Rajput sunken basins derived from the Mughal chahar bagh, or whether the Mughals intensified the geometry of the chahar bagh as a result of seeing the Rajput manipulation of surface pavement. The manuscripts are a problematic form of evidence, because they were made to delight the patron, not to satisfy the historian.

Therefore, when using manuscript paintings to recuperate lost garden forms, we must exercise caution and recognize that actual gardens and representations of gardens follow distinct systems of signage and representation. Yet in some respects, the two visual forms seem to share a geometrical aesthetic that asks viewers to read visual forms as a series of interconnected flat surfaces, rather than the volumetric spaces. Although this emphasis on flatness is an aspect of Islamic visual culture that has been analyzed in the scholarly literature on painting, it is rarely mentioned with respect to garden-making. Yet, throughout the Islamic world, landscape architects often planted shrubs and plants at such a depth below the pavement level that their blooms and foliage could be seen from above only as horizontal surfaces. In a quadripartite garden with sunken beds of a half meter or more, one can imagine the plants extending upward toward the sun, their colorful flowers just reaching the level of the floor pavements. To a viewer seated on cushions on the ground, looking at a low angle toward the garden, each bed might appear as a horizontal surface of evenly interspersed flowers, not unlike a carpet laid on the floor or the surface of still water in a large basin, as in the Alhambra's Court of the Myrtles. Nonetheless, the superior perspective did not completely prevent the perception of other volumes and planes. Indeed, ornament such as blind arcades, painted stucco, carved sandstone, and inlaid marble applied to the interior walls of the garden beds, as for example in the Casa de Contratación garden in Seville, indicates that the viewer was expected to see these surfaces too, enjoying the play between horizontal and vertical.

This garden aesthetic parallels that of early Islamic architecture. Architecture in the first centuries of Islam was structurally simple with thick walls that stood by virtue of sheer mass and heavy buttressing, but the walls were covered with richly colored tile, marble panels, gleaming mosaic, and textured stucco so that the perceptual complexity outshone the relatively straightforward structure (as in the Dome of the Rock; see Fig. 5). Similarly, gardens were perceived not as volumetric structures but as surfaces that one looked across and beyond to more distant views. The vegetation certainly had volume, especially in the case of trees like cypresses, palms, and flowering oranges that draw the eye upward to gaze upon bladelike leaves, a canopy of fronds, or a burst of richly perfumed, brilliant white blossoms. But the flowering plants themselves—the margaritas, narcissus, roses, and violets—were usually confined to rectangular beds that were sunken sufficiently below ground surface that the flower heads were best seen from above, not as individual or massed shapes, but as dashes of color in a green carpet. This way of planting a garden is seen in actual sites as well as in manuscripts.

Although the formal "carpet" approach appears to have been used extensively, it was not universal, for there were many other ways of planting and organizing gardens in the diverse areas of the Islamic world through history. Paintings also show the formal planting of bulbs in rows and the scattering of flowers across an open field where the viewer sits not above but on the ground level itself. Nonetheless, the taste for horizontal surfaces was a prevalent mode of garden design and perception that had its complement in other arts such as painting and textiles. The shared aesthetic is not merely the product of one two-dimensional medium (painting) representing another (landscape), for the archaeology of surviving sites confirms the spatial arrangement of sunken beds that would have been perceived from above by viewers positioned on elevated walkways and terraces. The experience of being in the garden, whether an actual site or a representation in art, seems always to inform the selection and arrangement of its components.

7 Imaginary Gardens

Gardens in Fantasy and Literature

RABIC POEMS AND narratives, and even Islamic religious texts, often describe gardens in fantastic terms. Although gardens with golden palm trees that bore emeralds for fruit existed only in the imagination, others in which tree trunks were wrapped with golden textiles were quite real. The latter did not attempt a convincingly natural style; to the contrary, the whole point of the theatricality was to evoke the imaginary and mythic, and to test the limits of credulity. But the imaginary and the real cannot be easily separated, for each contributed to the realm of the other. Ironically, while literary descriptions exaggerated the elements of the gardens that they described to the point of impossibility, real gardens were enhanced with strange devices so as to measure up to the opulent hyperbole of mythic gardens. Thus, the fantastic gardens of the mind are important not only as ideals, but also because they inspired the design of actual gardens and the recording of those gardens in literary description.

The idea of a wondrous garden of gold and precious jewels had two meanings in the Islamic world. On the one hand, paradise was envisioned as such a place, and since paradise was the reward promised in the Qur'an to faithful Muslims for having lived a pious life on earth, that garden was fundamentally good. To desire to attain such an eternal place was a worthy ambition that encouraged adherence to the laws of God. However, there were other gardens and courtyards that teased the imagination in the elaborate and opulent artifice of the flora and fauna and that led only to perdition. Such gardens were signs of folly, impiety, and in the most extreme cases, the arrogant desire to compete with original creation. To some extent, this ambivalent response to landscape extravagance is a symptom of the human condition: one wishes to control the excesses of nature and to make the world better and safer, and yet doing so threatens the relationship between God and humankind. There is a delicate balance between, on the one hand, defying God by tampering with creation, and, on the other, fulfilling the divine mandate to serve as the stewards of the earth (Qur'an 2:30). Humans naturally seek to improve their lot and to survive natural disasters, but at what point does improvement transgress the bounds set by God? The double meaning of fantastic gardens, paradisiac or satanic, reveals this inherent tension.

Iram is an example of fantastic architecture and gardens that led its owner to perdition. Mentioned briefly in the Qur'an (89:7) and a fuller narrative given in the *Thousand and*

One Nights (nights 276–279), Iram was a legendary city in which the patron overstepped the limits of pride and ambition and suffered for it.[1] It was built by Shaddad, who had read a description of the pavilions and gardens of paradise in ancient books and vowed to build such a place, commanding his men: "Go ye forth therefore to the goodliest tract on earth and the most spacious and build me there a city of gold and silver, whose gravel shall be chrysolite and rubies and pearls; and for support of its vaults make pillars of jasper. Fill it with palaces, whereon ye shall set galleries and balconies and plant its lanes and thoroughfares with all manner [of] trees bearing yellow-ripe fruits and make rivers to run through it in channels of gold and silver."[2] He assembled the greatest architects, engineers, and craftsmen and, exploring the entire world, they finally "came to an uninhabited spot, a vast and fair open plain clear of sand-hills and mountains, with founts flushing and rivers rushing, and they said, 'This is the manner of place the King commanded us to seek.'"[3] For three hundred years they toiled to build for him the foundations, pavilions, and fountains with water channels, all adorned with jewels, pearls, silver, and gold and contained within high, massive walls. But Shaddad, who had dared to try to rival paradise with his city, was struck down by God before he could enter the gates. Thereupon all roads to the city were hidden, so that, although the city of dreams continued to exist in mineralized perfection, it was not seen by human eyes.

The story of the Copper (or Brass) City in the *Thousand and One Nights* is a similar tale of profligacy and pride. Sheherazade, the narrator, related that Musa ibn Nusayr (governor of the Maghreb) and a guide went looking for magical brass bottles from the time of Solomon and were directed to the Copper City.[4] The walled city had twenty-five gates, none of which could be opened by Musa or his men. Eventually Musa looked over the walls from a nearby hilltop and saw a great, handsome city "with dwelling places and mansions of towering height, and palaces and pavilions and domes gleaming gloriously bright and sconces and bulwarks of strength infinite; and its streams were a-flowing and flowers a-blowing and fruits a-glowing."[5] Marveling and weeping at the fate of the beautiful city, Musa sent some of his men to scale the walls, but each one perished in the attempt.

Finally a guide, Shaykh 'Abd al-Samad, succeeded in gaining access by uttering an invocation to God that protected him from the city's curse. When Musa and his men entered the city, they saw unimaginable wealth—it was heaped with jewels, precious metals, rich silken textiles and brocades, and rare spices. Passing into one palace, Musa found a great hall with four gold, silver, and colored pavilions in its corners. "In the heart of the hall was a great jetting-fountain of alabaster, surmounted by a canopy of brocade, and in each pavilion was a sitting-place and each place had its richly-wrought fountain and tank paved with marble and streams flowing in channels along the floor and meeting in a great and grand cistern of many-coloured marbles."[6] In subsequent pavilions the men found caskets of pearls, gems, richly colored brocades, damascened weapons, crystal platters, pearl-encrusted goblets, and a floor of shining marble inlaid with gems that looked like a shimmering surface of water. At last they came upon a couch on which lay a damsel, dead, although stunningly beautiful, her eyes seemingly glistening with life. The other inhabitants of the palace were likewise lifeless but perfectly preserved.

Various tablets found in the Copper City told its story and one admonished its reader in verse:

> Consider how this people their palaces adorned
> And in dust have been pledged for the seed of acts they sowed:
> They built but their building availed them not, and hoards
> Nor saved their lives nor day of Destiny forslowed.

It concluded:

> The tombs aloud reply to the questioners and cry
> "Death's canker and decay those rosy cheeks corrode!"
> Long time they ate and drank, but their joyaunce had a term
> And the eater eke was eaten, and was eaten by the worm.[7]

The story is a gruesome reminder of the ephemerality of life on earth. However, although the sight of death in every hall was disturbing and repugnant, the description of the treasure encountered there is tremendously appealing, and the fascination with a world of mineralized splendor lingers despite the message that such a place may be dangerous and the work of Satan. The role of luxury is ambiguous in these descriptions, and one sign of this is the shimmering floor. It recalls the famous meeting of King Suleyman (Solomon) and the Queen of Sheba in Suleyman's legendary palace of colored marble with columns of white and transparent crystal and floors paved with turquoise and glass tiles. According to the Qur'an (27: 44), when the Queen came to pay homage to him there, she thought the highly polished floor of the lofty structure was water and lifted her skirts, exposing her legs.

The illusion of a gleaming structure in which solid mass appears as water served as a literary model for real pavilions and palaces in the Islamic period.[8] Hence, when a domed pavilion was built for al-Ma'mun, the ruler of Toledo (1043–75), in which water poured over the sides of a crystal structure that stood amidst a lake, the trompe l'oeil of solid crystal turned to water echoed the illusionism of Suleyman's mythic palace.[9] Just as literature may quote earlier works, buildings also quote their architectural ancestors, and the educated and culturally sophisticated members of the court that marveled at the Toledo pavilion— transparent so that one could not distinguish between water and solid form—would have seen it as a reference to Suleyman, the archetypal wise king of antiquity, that was surely intended to underscore the sovereign identity of the present king, al-Ma'mun.

According to the Qur'an, the inhabitants of paradise will recline on couches studded with gold and gems, attended by big-eyed maidens:

> In gardens of tranquility;
> A number of the earlier peoples,
> And a few of later ages,
> On couches wrought with gold,

Reclining face to face.

Youths of never-ending bloom will pass round to them

Cups and decanters, beakers full of sparkling wine,

Unheady, uninebriating;

And such fruits as they fancy,

Bird meats that they relish,

And companions with big beautiful eyes

Like pearls within their shells . . .

Gushing water,

And fruits numberless,

Unending and unforbidden . . . (56: 12–33)[10]

The *hadith* (sayings of Muhammad) elaborate upon the architecture of paradise in more detail, describing pavilions made of one enormous pearl and gem-studded palaces with glowing floors of mother-of-pearl, sometimes laid with rugs woven from pearls, rubies, and lapis lazuli with stripes of silver and gold.[11] Dazzling environments such as Iram and the Copper City could represent greed and the insane desire to outdo God, but because some of the same imagery was applied to paradise in the Qur'an and the hadith, the splendor was not *inherently* evil. Therefore, although the patrons of the gardens and palaces with bejeweled and illusionistic architecture that were built in Egypt, Iraq, the Maghreb, al-Andalus, and South Asia were occasionally criticized for their profligacy, those same palaces may also have been understood as tacit references to the unseen worlds of paradise or Iram. Indeed, the references were sometimes explicit. For example, in the early eleventh century, Persian poets likened the Ghaznavid palaces (of which only Lashkari Bazar, near Bust, still exists) to other mythic and sacred sites, including Iram;[12] and in the eleventh-century Saljuq court, a poet could describe a palace with hyperbole: "Iram its highest degree, Shaddad's seven [palaces'] worth."[13] The preceding chapters have argued that the prevailing concerns of garden patrons in the first centuries of Islam were worldly—more political and economic than spiritual. But at the most elite level of society, where wealth was virtually limitless and patrons could exercise their imaginations, they could repudiate the reality of the agricultural landscape—especially its harsh realities of drought, plague, and failure—by creating an ideal world that far surpassed ordinary conditions.

The gardens of Iram and paradise rely on the human imagination to envision what the eye cannot see. As myths or divinely conceived places, they existed in a state of perfection untested by human experience. But there were actual gardens that achieved similar effects in which natural vegetation was painted or draped to create the illusion of a special world where pearls grew on trees. The palace of the caliph al-Muqtadir in early tenth-century Samarra was an example of such theater in the garden on the occasion of the arrival of the Byzantine ambassador in 917. Upon entering, the ambassador was led ceremonially through a succession of great halls, corridors, and courtyards where he saw richly apparisoned horses and a hunting park of wild animals. He was brought to the New Palace where there were gardens with a metal-rimmed pool surrounded by four hundred tall palm trees dressed with painted textiles hanging from golden hoops and yielding magnificent dates. Orange trees ringed the garden. From there the visitors went to the Tree Court where, in the middle of a great pool, stood a tree with eighteen gold and silver branches with multicolored leaves that fluttered as if in the breeze. On the tree limbs, gold and silver birds twittered and sang. Finally they arrived in the hall where the caliph awaited them. When the caliph gave the order, a tree miraculously emerged from the ground, growing until it filled the dome overhead. Mechanical birds sang while at ground level fountains spouted rose water and musk perfume.[14]

Palaces such as these surely gave rise to the mythic palaces of the *Thousand and One Nights*, and it is no coincidence that the architecture and the narrative tale (or the sources from which later versions of the tales were extracted) belong to the same period. The Copper City tale evolved from an early ninth-century Andalusian text that captured the awe and puzzled reaction of the Muslim conquerors to the strange but marvelous Visigothic and Roman character of the Iberian peninsula.[15] It expressed a real response to the encounter between civilizations and the experience of the exotic, and it struck a familiar note not only in al-Andalus but further east as well. Showing nature as bizarre was a common strategy to emphasize the difference between familiar and foreign or ancient places. The Persian epic poem the *Shahnama*, composed by Abu al-Qasim Firdawsi around 1010 for the Ghaznavid ruler Mahmud in central Asia (and drawing from earlier oral sources), consisted of a series of heroic battles, wondrous adventures, and romances. In one scene the warrior Rustam was received at court by the ruler who sat in a garden beneath a fabulous tree with a silver trunk, golden leaves, and gems. It bore quince and orange fruit simultaneously, and contained musk and wine in its hollow trunk.[16] A significant difference between actual palace complexes and scenes such as this in the *Shahnama* or the *Thousand and One Nights* is that whereas Rustam and the Copper City were mythic stories from the realm of literature, the Samarra palaces were quite real. Although little remains of them except the medieval chroniclers' words, which were probably as exaggerated as any description of a valiant adventure into the unknown, the palaces were not a storyteller's invention. There are too many historical mentions of extraordinary halls and gardens in disparate areas of the early Islamic world to discount them as pure fable.

Although al-Muqtadir's Samarra garden quickly became the stuff of legend, it may have been inspired by historic antecedents. For example, the Byzantine emperor Theophilos in the first half of the ninth century had a golden tree with mechanical singing birds.[17] Near Fustat (in modern Cairo), Khumarawayh ibn Tulun (884–896), who ruled in the name of the Abbasid dynasty, built a country palace with gardened courtyards. Palms, fruit trees, waterlilies, manicured myrtle, roses, basil, saffron, and exotic plants were brought from as far away as Khurasan and thrived there, and peacocks and other beautiful birds roamed freely. But to control nature by cultivating a splendid garden was not enough: the patron had the palm trunks sheathed with copper that was gilded so that it would not tarnish, and his engineers hid lead tubing under the metal sheathing and piped water upward so that the palms sprouted not only fronds but a spray as well. The water fell into basins and from there flowed through the rest of the garden. Elsewhere in the palace there was a golden chamber

FIGURE 43.
Excavated at the
great Umayyad
palatine city,
Madinat al-Zahra',
near Cordoba, this
bronze stag was one
of many marble and
metal sculp-
tures that
adorned
the basins
in its court-
yards and
gardens.
Water was
piped upward
through the
animal's body
and poured
through
its open mouth.
(Museo Arque-
ológico y
Etnológico de
Córdoba)

with a large tank filled with mercury on which Ibn Tulun, an insomniac, slept on an inflated leather mattress.[18]

The scholar Von Grunebaum saw a parallel develop-ment in poetry. He identified a shift from the stock roman-ticization of nature in the Umayyad period, to a greater emphasis on individual gardens and the poet's individual perception in the Abbasid period. In the mid-eighth century, the taste for na-ture—romanticized but grounded in reality—shifted to a taste for the fantastic, where plants were likened to jewels and stars to pearls.[19] Perhaps this change in the attitude toward nature chal-lenged garden architects to re-create the effects in actual gardens; but it is also possible that the verse may have changed as the poets witnessed the architectural extravagances in which the Abbasids were known to have indulged.

In al-Andalus, there are historical descriptions of extant gardens in which the patron's whims were similarly gratified. At the late tenth-century Cordoban palace Madinat al-Zahira (not to be confused with another Cordoban palace, Madinat al-Zahra'), the ruler al-Mansur had a large pool in which grew a profusion of wa-terlilies. When al-Mansur was visited by the ambassadors of a potentially hostile neighbor who wished to assess the strength of his kingdom, he ordered that silver and gold chunks be inserted into the buds while they were still closed in the cool early morning. Later that day as the waterlilies opened to the sun, the blooms were gathered up and presented to the guests who could not have failed to comprehend the metaphor. Seeing that the flowers of al-Andalus miraculously yielded silver and gold, they realized the extent of al-Mansur's resources and were suitably impressed.[20]

The spectacle of gold-blooming flowers at Madinat al-Zahira, an effective device for rep-resenting economic power, was not hard to produce. But in other gardens, more sophisti-cated mechanical skill was required to make inanimate objects move and speak. In one of the fountains at Madinat al-Zahira, water poured through the mouth of a black amber lion wearing a necklace of white pearls, while another basin held croaking tortoises.[21] The tortoises may have been alive, but given the Andalusian predilection for zoomorphic fountains, it is quite possible that they were fabricated of bronze and made sounds as water was forced through their internal pipes. In the Mediterranean, such spouts and fountains shaped like animals abounded, from at least the Roman period, enjoyed presumably because of the pleasing illusion of life that the water introduced to the otherwise inanimate form.[22] In the twentieth century, the excavations of Madinat al-Zahra' led to the dis-covery of a small bronze stag that served as a fountain (Fig. 43). One can imagine the sculpture poised at the edge of a pool, spewing water from its mouth. Two bronze rabbits from eleventh- or twelfth-century Egypt likewise functioned as fountain spouts,

FIGURE 44.
A rabbit is
an appropri-
ate theme
for a garden
setting; this
bronze sculpture
(measuring 15 cm
high) functioned
as a fountain spout.
(Stuart Cary Welch)

water entering via a square hole in each animal's belly and pouring from its mouth (Fig. 44). Every gardener knows the rabbit's insatiable appetite for tasty vegetation; the lively body of the rabbit, poised as if ready to leap and run, is incised with swirling scrolls, suggesting the dense foliage or climbing vines of its natural context.[23]

The palatine city Qal'a Bani Hammad (founded 1007–8) in Algeria had terraced gardens and, in one of its palaces, an enormous rectangular pool where water spectacles were staged, the boats launched from a sloping ramp (see Sites). In the dry mountainous climate, the storage and distribution of water was necessary to support food production in the surrounding area. The harnessing of water to serve the court's needs was displayed in various ornamental fountains, translating an act of necessity into visual delight. Many of the fountains were zoomorphic, such as the bronze fragment of a quadruped's foot and a basin with a framed sculptural relief of a lion on each side in which the animal's mouth forms a water jet.[24]

At the Alhambra palace in Granada, twelve stone lions support a basin in the Court of the Lions (see Fig. 31). The date of the lion figures and their disposition with the present basin is much debated by historians, but there can be no doubt that animals, and especially lions, were a popular fountain motif in the Nasrid court of Granada in the thirteenth and fourteenth centuries, as well as in previous Andalusian and Maghrebi courts.[25] In addition to the aforementioned, zoomorphic spouts and fountain fragments have been excavated at eleventh-century Elvira (near Granada), tenth-century Beni-Khalled (the Maghreb), and tenth- or eleventh-century Cordoba. Elsewhere in Granada, a cousin of the Alhambra's lion figures stood in the courtyard of the Maristan (hospital); in the twentieth century it was given a more scenic placement alongside a pool in the Partal Palace at the Alhambra (Fig. 45). A fragmentary lion figure with its internal water pipe still visible is in the San

FIGURE 45.
The fountain statue in the Partal Palace is similar to the set of twelve in the Court of the Lions elsewhere in the Alhambra, although its placement here is not original. The water spewing from this beast's maw lent the figure a vitality that encouraged the viewer to imagine a real lion.

FIGURE 46.
One of the clocks
described and
illustrated in this
manuscript copy
of the *Treatise of
Pseudo-Archimedes*
manuscript was an
elaborate fantasy of
silver birds perched
on the branches of
a copper tree set be-
tween two mounds.
On the hour, forced
air would cause
serpents to emerge
from the mounds
and the birds to
twitter and screech.
(Redrawn by
Variava)

Francisco Convent at the Alhambra, and there are two stone lions, originally made for a palace in the Azares quarter of Granada, now in the Casa de Moneda.[26]

To pipe water through an inert stone sculpture requires hydraulic skill of a very basic kind, making the illusion of animation easy to achieve. But many fountains were engineered to do more than simply pour. Birds could be fashioned to sing and whistle, and they and other animals could be crafted with moving parts (Fig. 46). While few of these ingenious garden devices survive, we can find the plans for their design in a genre of treatises written about amusing contraptions called *automata*. These devices appeared to operate by perpetual motion, but they relied on the same engineering principles and the same power source as irrigation systems and waterwheels. Among the earliest automata manuscripts are a ninth-century Arabic manual on mechanical devices called the *Kitab al-hiyal* by three brothers called the Banu Musa bin Shakir,[27] the treatise of Pseudo-Archimedes (compiled between the tenth and twelfth centuries), and the treatise on clock-making by Ridwan al-Sa'ati writen in 1203.[28] In turn, these early Arabic texts owed a considerable debt to Hellenistic and Byzantine precursors.

The best known of the Arabic treatises is *The Book of Ingenious Mechanical Devices* by al-Jaziri, completed in either 1204 or 1206 in east central Turkey.[29] One sign of the immense popularity of al-Jaziri's treatise on automata is the existence today of at least eleven partial or wholly surviving copies, including one made for a Mughal dynast and one made as late as the eighteenth century. The treatise is divided into six categories on subjects such as clocks, drinking vessels, and pitchers and basins for phlebotomy and washing. Category IV is "On the construction in pools of fountains which change their shape, and of machines for the perpetual flute," and Category V is "On the construction of machines for raising water from standing water which is not deep, and from a running river."[30] The explanations, quite specific and clear in their own right, were greatly enhanced by the 173 accurately drawn illustrations that accompanied them (illustration 174 was a list of letters).

The description of a hand-washing machine instructs the reader to make a four-columned pavilion with a dome (a removable lid) topped by a bird finial; the pavilion is attached to a base on which kneels a slave holding a pitcher in the right hand and a towel and comb in the left. Soldered to one side of the platform is a basin with a duck. When the reservoir below the dome is filled with water, the water is conducted through a pipe hidden within the figurine's body toward its pitcher, displacing air which rushes up through a different pipe to make the bird whistle (like a tea kettle). The water in the pitcher causes it to tip, pouring its contents into the basin below. This water collects in the basin and the duck appears to drink it as it drops through another hidden pipe into a second reservoir hidden in the base. As water accumulates in the container, a bucket attached by a rope to the figurine's hand is filled, causing the hand to extend with the towel and comb.[31] Another illustration explains the mechanics for raising water with two waterwheels (Fig. 47). Although the instructions refer to a small toy with a wooden figure of a cow, the mechanics are the same as large waterwheels used to supply water to gardens and farms. While in all cases, the descriptions indicate that mechanical toys of tabletop size were intended, there is no reason why such engineering skill could not be realized on an expanded scale for garden settings. Thus the automata treatises allow us to imagine how the extraordinary gardens with gilded palms, bejeweled vegetation, mechanical birds, and exuberant waterworks may have been created and also how such amazing devices, which required expert skill in design and fabrication, could and did move through Islamic, Byzantine, and western European contexts. Indeed, there was a rich tradition of automata in Byzantine palatine gardens, but since the Byzantine palaces date to the same period as the Abbasid gardens, it cannot be ascertained which one begat the other.[32]

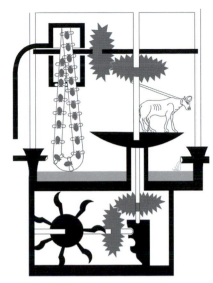

FIGURE 47.
In this diagram from al-Jaziri's *Treatise*, a cogged wheel attached to a vertical shaft rotates a horizontal axle to which a loop of buckets are attached. The diagram illustrates one of the automata that entertained educated audiences in the medieval period, but the engineering principle is that of a noria realized on a small scale. (Redrawn by Variava)

The illustrations made for the early copies of the *Kitab al-hiyal* are particularly interesting for a garden historian because they show hydraulic devices with sculptured figural spouts. One such picture shows a machine with spouts in the shape of two rams' heads and another shows a lion head spout (Fig. 48). This entertaining mixture of technology and figural animation that pleased courtly audiences on a small scale was also realized in architectural environments, as seen in a painting from the *Bayad wa Riyad* manuscript from thirteenth- or fourteenth-century Islamic Spain (Plate 6). Although the figures of the human beings, the swimming ducks, and the rabbit were meant to suggest living creatures, the horse heads spewing water into the pool were sculptures like those depicted in the diagrams of the *Kitab al-hiyal*. Historians of technology have redrawn many of the machines in order to explain how they worked, and in so doing, the mechanically extraneous depictions of animal figures and waterspouts are omitted. However, because these figures resemble those in manuscript images of gardens and as well as surviving fountains such as those from the Maghreb, they provide important evidence that the devices were used in actual garden settings.

Imaginary gardens and their real-life evocations can be found in all periods and places in Islamic history. For example, in the court of Timur in Samarkand (ca. 1405), the tent of his principal wife had a golden oak tree with golden birds pecking at gemstone fruit.[33] Babur, in his memoirs of the conquest of Hindustan (Pakistan and India) in the second quarter of the sixteenth century, described a party in Kabul at which he saw a willow tree with branches decorated by gilded leather strips. He confessed that he could not discern whether even the willows

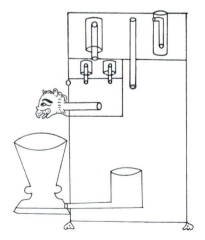

FIGURE 48.
The lion head spout in this automata diagram from the *Kitab al-hiyal* was of less interest to the engineer who consulted the manuscript than the instructions for constructing the pump. But similar spouts, animated by the water that poured through them, delighted the audiences of gardens in Spain and the Maghreb from the tenth through fourteenth centuries. (Redrawn by Variava)

FIGURE 49.
The finely carved
white basin in the
Rang Mahal was
filled with water
from the Nahr-i
Behesht (River of
Paradise), a channel
that flowed through
the royal pavilions
of the Delhi Fort.

themselves were real and said, "They looked fantastic."[34] The Ottomans also loved artifice
and theatrical displays. In 1582, a festival celebrating the circumcision of Sultan Murad III's
son included a parade with floats that included large trees and an enormous tulip made of
colored paper.[35] A similar festival held in 1720 included four large models of gardens made
of sugar: a manuscript image of this shows a variety of fruit-laden trees, tulips, cypresses,
pavilions, birds, and even fountains spouting water.[36] At the Delhi Fort, the royal pavilion,
the Rang Mahal (1639–48), had a shallow pool in the shape of a flower in bloom with blossoms and foliage in colored-stone inlay (Fig. 49). One observer wrote that when the pool
was filled with rippling water, "the foliage of the inlay work appears to wave to and fro."[37]
This pool was fed by a broad water channel called the Nahr-i Behesht ("river of paradise")
that flowed through the baths (*hammam*) and all of the pavilions aligned along the Fort's
river edge. The Italian visitor Manucci wrote that the Emperor Shah Jahan ordered the
channel to be stocked with fish wearing golden rings strung with rubies and pearls around
their heads.[38] These were theatrical ruses intended to amaze, delight, and persuade the
viewer, but artificial devices could serve another purpose: to bring the garden's ephemeral
effects into the surrounding buildings and make them permanent.

In gardens of pleasure and commemoration the concept of an artificially preserved
gardened universe was often made a reality. For example, the walls of the Salon Rico at
Madinat al-Zahra' were stuccoed with intertwining vines bearing stylized leaves and fruit.
In Agra with a technique called *pietra dura*, representations of plants in colorful stone
were inlaid on the white walls of the garden tomb of the Mughal empress's parents, the
tomb of I'timad al-Daula (finished 1628, Fig. 50), as well as the Taj Mahal (1632–43). The
imagery of vegetation was thus extended onto the very fabric of the building, prompting
the emperor's court poet to write: "They have inlaid stone flowers in marble, / Which sur-
pass reality in color if not in fragrance."[39] Such floral wall decoration hardly measures up
to the fabulous descriptions of gem-studded palaces at the beginning of this chapter; yet

it suggests that in palatine reception halls as well as funerary gardens, the desire to blur the distinction between the real and the artificial was present, and in the funerary context perhaps it was intended to convey the concept of eternal life.

Not only the walls, but also the carpets that typically covered the floors of garden pavilions and palace halls contained floral motifs. In Iran from the sixteenth century onward, carpets began to represent gardens divided into a chahar bagh arrangement with rivulets of zigzagging water and parterres with trees, flowers, and birds, the architectural elements presented in plan while the floral elements appear in profile. These textiles brought the illusion of nature into the architectural environment and thus extended the garden experience (Fig. 51).[40]

Architecture and garden had a fluid spatial relationship because of the floral imagery that decorated the floors and walls of building interiors but also because the spaces themselves were ambiguous: pavilions, especially under the Safavids (1501–1736) and Qajars (1779–1924), opened to their surroundings through large arches (called an *eyvan* in Persian, or *iwan* in Arabic) or multicolumned porches (called *talar*), such as in the Chihil Situn pavilion in the palatine quarters alongside Isfahan's Chahar Bagh Avenue and the Palace of Mirrors (now vanished) situated along Isfahan's riverbank (Fig. 52). Standing in a large garden (the original form of which has not been thoroughly studied), the Chihil Situn pavilion admitted its surroundings into the interior in several ways. A person seated on the carpeted and cushioned floor of this pavilion could gaze on the colorful images of vegeta-

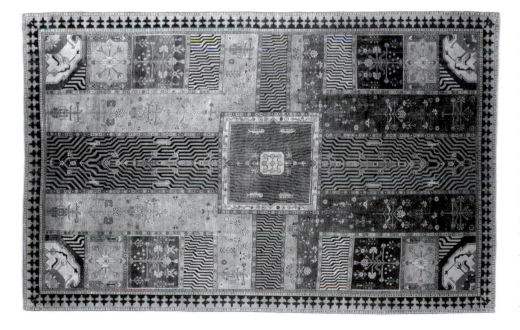

Figure 51.
Carpets such as this early eighteenth-century example from Iran brought the garden aesthetic indoors so that the company could sit amidst flowers, enjoying views of the cultivated surroundings, yet be protected from the sun. (Brooklyn Museum of Art. 84.140.16. Bequest of Mrs. Joseph V. McMullan, gift of the Beaupre Charitable Trust in memory of Joseph V. McMullan)

FIGURE 52.
An 1867 engraving of the Palace of Mirrors, Isfahan, shows a pavilion, similar to the Chihil Situn, with an open *talar* porch that gave views toward the riverbank. The pavilion no longer exists. (P. Coste)

FIGURE 53.
The Hesht Behesht pavilion in Isfahan (in an 1867 print) was like an enormous fountain from which water spouted in a central jet and then flowed beneath the floor, into basins, down ornamental cascades, and into the pools of the surrounding garden. (P. Coste)

tion on the tiles of the walls and floors, as well as the actual flowers and plants growing outside in the garden. The talar porch served as a canopy that defined the space of the viewer and shielded him or her from the hot sun; but because it had no walls, it invited a panoramic view of the broad water channels and vegetation outside. The fountains and basins that brought the waterworks of the garden under the roof of the pavilion further extended the experience of nature. Similarly, fountains played in the seventeenth-century Hesht Behesht pavilion in Isfahan, their overflow running to the edge of the structure's raised floor where the water cascaded down a chute into the garden's canals (Figs. 53 and 54). The arched shape of the eyvans framed the views of the surrounding garden so that interior and exterior were joined in one visual field (Plate 18). The intentional ambiguity of architecture and landscape, embellished and served by the same waters, was enhanced by wall stucco and tile representing lush vegetation and pretty birds, and by the floor's thick carpet that imitated the geometrically laid out beds, canals, and plants of the garden surrounding the pavilion.[41]

FIGURE 54.
The *eyvans* (large arched apertures) of the Hesht Behesht framed the view of the garden on all sides. In garden pavilions such as this, nature was represented in wall tiles and carpets on the floors, and the real flowers, trees, and birds were never far away. (Yasamin Bahadorzadeh)

In a similar vein, we can consider the fruits made of steel and decorated with gold damascene or etching that were popular in Iran from the seventeenth through nineteenth centuries. The decorative objects are only slightly larger than life size: the etched-steel apple pictured here (Fig. 55) had a diameter of almost eleven centimeters.[42] With leaves, stems, and in some cases hooks, the objects could easily have been suspended, and one can imagine such fruit, glinting in metallic perfection, innocent of the mold, bugs, and rot to which worldly fruits succumb, either gathered in a bowl or perhaps hanging from a tree bough—whether real or contrived—in a garden that rivaled those of Iram and Samarra.

To make an environment with a carpet of ever-blooming flowers, silver fruit, and birds that sang on command required tremendous wealth, and it is unlikely that any but the richest and most powerful patrons could call them into being. Such gardens were expressions of cultural and economic status and there cannot have been many of them. But fantastic gardens evoked another human desire as well. The creation of a permanent garden that did not fade seasonally and was unaffected by drought and frost embodied the concept of mastery, includ-

FIGURE 55.
Artificial apples and pears, popular in the eighteenth and nineteenth centuries, may have been displayed in bowls as ornament or suspended from trees to mimic hanging fruit. This nineteenth-century example of a etched-steel apple is from the Qajar period, Iran. (Walter Denny)

ing control over the most frightening experience, death. Just as the ruler or any landowner of means transformed the earth by installing irrigation systems and collecting plants from near and far with which to stock his garden, the defeat of the natural cycle of the changing seasons was yet another sign of his worldly control. God *created* nature, but the good steward was empowered by God to control nature. That mandate is summarized in the Qur'anic statement that God places humankind not just upon the earth, but *over* it as its manager: "He made for you all that lies within the earth" (2:29). In the next verse God says to the angels, "I have to place a trustee on the earth," and then gives Adam knowledge and the power to name all the things of the earth.[43] The fantastic gardens of the imagination and their real-life imitations seem deceptively frivolous, worldly, and exaggerated, but their very artificiality held a powerful symbolism because they evoked a world of excess and wonder where nature was transformed by human endeavor, subjected to human control, and made perfect and permanent. In this sense, like paradise, they may ultimately have promised the triumph over death of life eternal.

8   The Garden as Paradise

The Historical Beginnings of Paradisiac Iconography

THE THEME OF PARADISE in the previous two chapters arose with respect to fantastic and ideal gardens in the literary imagination, and the sumptuous gardens of the royal courts. In this chapter and the next, we will consider paradisiac symbolism in mosques and tomb gardens.

Paradise is envisioned as a garden in Muslim thought, and the Qur'an gives a fairly detailed description of it. According to one verse: "The semblance of Paradise [*janna*] promised the pious and devout (is that of a garden) with streams of water that will not go rank, and rivers of milk whose taste will not undergo a change, and rivers of wine delectable to drinkers, and streams of purified honey, and fruits of every kind in them, and forgiveness from their Lord" (47:15).[1] Other verses describe gardens and springs (44:52), an endless variety of fresh fruit suspended within easy reach (44:55 and 55:54), garments of brocade and silk (44:53), carpets (55:54), and companions with large dark eyes (44:54). One passage describes two gardens with shady boughs traversed by flowing springs, as well as two other gardens with dark green foliage, fruits such as dates and pomegranates, and two gushing fountains (55:46–68). The specificity of these descriptions helps us to imagine the visual appearance of paradise as well as the sensation of eternal life there. Because paradise is described as a shady garden with four gardens and four streams, it might seem logical to assume that this provided Muslim architects with the blueprint for the Islamic chahar bagh. But the four-part division and the metamorphosis of the simple irrigation canal into a defining element in garden organization predates Islam, as we saw in Chapter 4. Hence, it is not the form that reflects a specifically Muslim conception of paradise, but rather the description of paradise that reflects a preexisting vocabulary of garden forms.[2]

One of the unfortunate consequences of the disciplinary separation of Islamic studies from studies of Jewish and Christian culture (and the methodological division of geography and knowledge into the invented categories of East and West) is that when scholars ask why certain forms and concepts arose in a given cultural context, they tend to look for the answers internally. Thus, the issue of how and why the chahar bagh form originated has appeared to many historians to have a solid answer within Islam and specifically in the Qur'an. But Islam, born in the seventh century, flourished in the eastern Mediterranean where Roman and Byzantine Christianity as well as Judaism also flourished, and both the material culture and the religion of Islam owe much to these neighboring peoples (and indeed, many of the early Muslims were converts whose cultural formation had been as Jews, Christians, and polytheists). The Qur'an contains many of the same stories as the Bible, and its exegetes occasionally drew information from the Bible of the "People of the Book." For example, the Qur'an briefly mentions the garden of Eden: "And we said to Adam: 'Both you and your spouse live in the Garden, eat freely to your fill wherever you like, but approach not this tree or you will become transgressors.' But Satan tempted them and had them banished from the (happy) state they were in" (2: 35–36).[3] The repetitions and parallels are regarded by Muslims as indication of the Qur'an's corrective, rather than derivative, nature.

Muslims lived in close proximity with Jews and Christians; they fought over the same resources—land, cities, people, trade routes—and not only observed each other's cultural practices but also adopted many of them. They shared many religious practices, such as monotheism, oriented prayer, and iconoclasm. Additionally, the keen interest among early Muslim scholars in classical mathematics, astronomy, optics, pharmacology, and hydraulic engineering is proof that the sciences were studied regardless of the historical cultural source.[4] Of course, the early Muslim leaders defined themselves self-consciously in terms of their ideological difference from Christians and Jews; yet one of the great strengths of early Islam was that Muslims did not hesitate to appropriate useful ideas and techniques from diverse sources, particularly Byzantium.

There is no evidence in the first four centuries of Islam that gardens were consciously designed with four quadrants and four water channels in order to imitate paradise as the Qur'an described it. Indeed, in literary descriptions and in actual built sites, most gardens belonged to palaces where the environment was decidedly impious, characterized by political display, wine-drinking, intrigue, and sexual encounters. Even in those rare cases where gardens were attached to early mosques, where a note of paradisiac symbolism might be expected to resound, the historians of the period were silent with respect to religious meaning. This is not to say that references to paradise are absent in their descriptions of the world around them—they frequently praised handsome towns and fertile landscapes as paradisiac—but they did not ascribe such meaning to individual gardens.

FIGURE 56. Trees have been planted in the courtyard of the Great Mosque of Cordoba from the beginning of the ninth century continuously to the present day. The congregational mosques of Malaga and Seville were similarly planted.

The earliest mosque where planting is known to have occurred is the Great Mosque of Cordoba, where trees were planted in the courtyard at least as early as the first decade of the ninth century (Fig. 56).[5] This mosque was begun in 785–87 by 'Abd al-Rahman I, an Umayyad prince who had grown up in Syria and escaped the assassination of his family members there by fleeing to al-Andalus. In its first phase the mosque had eleven aisles, and in the next two hundred years the prayer hall was extended southward several times, a new *mihrab* (niche indicating the direction of prayer) was built, a bridge was built to link the prayer hall to the emir's palace (located west of the mosque), the courtyard was faced with arcades, and a new minaret was added to the courtyard wall opposite the entrance to the prayer hall. The last Islamic phase of the mosque was the expansion of both the prayer hall and courtyard in the eastern direction by eight aisles in 987–88, whereupon the courtyard measured 120 by 60 meters (see Sites). Significant changes also occurred to the building after 1236 when Cordoba was conquered by Christians and the building was converted to a church with tombs, chapels, and ultimately a great central altar.

Numerous eleventh- and twelfth-century authors described the changes made to the mosque's fabric by various patrons, but although the plan, structure, and decoration of the mosque and its furnishings were reported with evident admiration, regrettably the courtyard was mentioned only in regard to its dimensions and surrounding arcades.[6] A rare exception is a brief line in a twelfth-century description that says that a variety of trees were newly planted there, but for the most part, the built structure had perceived value whereas the vegetation growing in its courtyard was dismissed as unimportant.[7]

Although there are few textual sources describing the courtyard, the material fabric reveals the phases of its development. In the earliest phase, the courtyard had no arcades (*riwaqs*). The arcades that today encircle the interior were added sometime before 951-52, prior to the construction of the tall new minaret in that year, and the façade of piers alternating with two columns was added to "finish" the arcades, also prior to the minaret's construction.[8] The mosque had a fountain for ritual ablutions in its courtyard, the water for which came from the rainwater running off the prayer hall's roof (Fig. 57) that then drained from the courtyard into an underground tank.[9] The water was raised to ground level by an animal-powered wheel and distributed via shallow channels dug in the soil to irrigate the trees planted in the courtyard. In 967 the supply of water was augmented when a large stone canal with lead piping was constructed between the mosque and the mountains which lay northwest of Cordoba. An observer remarked that it "flowed into the mosque's irrigation canals and ablution basins on the east and west sides," an indication that by this time the courtyard required two fountains, perhaps due to the larger numbers of Muslims using the mosque.[10] In 991–92 larger, deeper cisterns were dug in the courtyard floor.[11] Excavations in the twentieth century have revealed the presence of one large underground cistern with an underground water channel entering the courtyard in the northeastern corner.[12]

The sources do not state whether the courtyard was originally planted with fragrant orange trees, as is currently the case, but we know that its trees were fruit-bearing and can surmise that the trunks were planted in straight rows aligned with the columns of the prayer hall, as is the case today. Although the courtyard is now paved, it was originally earthen, like the floor of the prayer hall itself. In 1557, by which point the mosque had been converted to a church, sweet and sour orange trees, lemons, and limes were planted there.[13] A 1741 plan in the Archive of the Cathedral of Cordoba shows the courtyard with three fountains and a tank, and planted with regularly spaced trees—perhaps oranges—with foliage forming a compact ball, with a few cypress and palms interspersed (Plate 19).

FIGURE 57.
Deep runnels
between the gables
of the Cordoba
Mosque's roof drain
rainwater into the
courtyard. Where
the runnels meet
the edge of the roof,
they project as great
spouts.

Why were trees cultivated in the mosque? Did they satisfy a worldly desire for shade and food, or were they were supposed to remind the Muslim worshippers of the paradise awaiting them? A legal opinion rendered in the eleventh century by one of Cordoba's leading Muslim jurists, Ibn Sahl, refutes the paradisiac explanation. Ibn Sahl (d. 1093), served as secretary to the *diwan* of the *qadis* (a panel of judges) in Cordoba beginning in about 1051, and in that capacity he had access to all the juridical and notarial records of the city.[14] These he consulted to answer questions posed to him by other judges as well as the administrators (*muhtasibs*) responsible for the day-to-day management of the city regarding cases under review. The decisions he rendered were constructed on the judgment of previous authorities, with the conflicts in their juridical positions exposed and assessed.[15] When asked for a legal opinion regarding the planting of trees in mosque courtyards, Ibn Sahl gave the following opinion:

> [Regarding] the planting of trees in the courtyard of mosques.
> Ibn 'Attab [d. 462/1069], may God have mercy upon him, did not approve of planting them or any vegetation at all in the courtyards of mosques. He criticized this and forbade the practice and uprooted [the trees] when he could do so. Ahmad b. Khalid mentioned that he himself asked Ibn Waddah [d. 287/900] about a tree that was in the courtyard of a mosque, and he replied: "My preference is that it be chopped down and not allowed to remain in it. I have not seen any tree in the mosques of the cities [*amsar*], either in Syria or any other place." Ahmad b. Khalid asked, "If the tree is there, in your opinion is it permissible to eat [the fruit] from it?" Ibn Waddah replied, "To the contrary, only the [muezzin?] can do so on account of the doubt [*shubha*] that is attached to this and I myself would not eat from

it." Ahmad Ibn 'Abd al-Barr [d. 338/959] mentioned in his *History* in the entry on Saʿasʿa b. Sallam that he, meaning Saʿasʿa, was the leader of prayer in Cordoba, and said, "During Saʿasʿa b. Sallam's lifetime, trees were planted in the congregational mosque, and this is the doctrine of Awzaʿi and the Syrians, but Malik and his followers say that it is reprehensible [*yakrahunuhu*]. Saʿasʿa died in the year 192 [807–8]."[16]

Of the five authorities from the ninth through eleventh centuries whom Ibn Sahl cited, all disapproved of the practice of planting mosque courtyards with vegetation. The earliest of his cited authorities affirmed that trees were indeed present in the courtyard in the early ninth century and that under Maliki law (which came to prevail in al-Andalus) such a thing was "reprehensible," a strongly censorious legal term.[17] Clearly, although trees were to be found at the Cordoba mosque in the ninth, tenth, and eleventh (and sixteenth and eighteenth) centuries, the Islamic legal authorities, who based their opinions on both the interpretation of theological precepts and prior case law, did not interpret the trees as paradisiac symbols or indications of piety.

Twentieth-century historians, however, have always tended to read Islamic gardens in a religious light, associating the cultivated garden with its water channels and fountains with the garden of paradise. Although, as we shall see in the next chapter, many later Islamic tomb gardens *were* deeply imbued with paradisiac symbolism, the interpreters of religious law in Cordoba did not interpret mosque "gardens" as such. It is far more likely that the trees in the courtyard were cultivated for the fruit that was given to the building's caretaker in recompense for tending the prayer hall and grounds. This custom was similar to the division of capital and yield in a perpetual endowment (called *waqf*), a legal structure which dated from the days of the Prophet Muhammad, who advised one of his followers that the administrator of such an endowment was entitled to its "fruits." (The modern English term is *usufruct,* from the Latin term meaning "use of the fruit.") Hence, in the legal case concerning the Cordoba mosque, one of the pressing questions put to the jurists was whether or not it was permissible to consume the fruits cultivated in that environment. There was no mention of the mosque or its trees as waqf—although both buildings and trees could be so entailed—and so it is unclear whether the legal question pivoted on the question of usufruct or the reprehensibility of the trees themselves. Nonetheless, there is a long tradition of patrons bestowing the fruit of their lands upon designated servants and followers as gifts and salary, and a document dated 1557 shows that, in the Christian period at least, the fruit from the Cordoba cathedral (formerly the mosque) was indeed given to the custodian.[18]

Cordoba was not the only Andalusian or Mediterranean mosque with a cultivated courtyard. At least one Cairo mosque in the eleventh century had palm trees in its courtyard. An inscription from one such building (which no longer exists) stated: "These palm trees that are within the mosque are all for the Muslims and they should neither be sold nor bought."[19] In his extensive travels in the mid-fourteenth century, Ibn Battuta reported seeing a mosque in Tabriz with a courtyard planted with trees and climbing jasmine.[20] When Ibn Battuta traveled to al-Andalus he reported that the congregational mosque of Malaga had an open courtyard planted with tall orange trees.[21] In 1586, a visitor to the Mosque of Seville (built 1172–82) noted that the courtyard had a large central fountain and was still planted with a thick grove of orange trees and fruit-bearing palm trees, planted in rows and irrigated.[22] Of course, by then Seville had been in Christian hands for more than three hundred years: the trees may have been a new addition to the old courtyard, which was kept even after the prayer hall was razed in order to build the present cathedral in the fifteenth century.[23]

The planting of trees in religious settings has a very long history in the eastern Mediterranean, for Psalm 92 of the Bible says that the "righteous shall flourish like a tree in a courtyard of the Temple." It is possible that some early Islamic mosques acquired this characteristic from extant churches, much as they took spolia, appropriated sites, and even adapted ritual practices. In the eastern Mediterranean, mosques of the Umayyad dynasty were sometimes built in close proximity to gardens, as for example, the Umayyad Mosque of Damascus (begun 705 or 706 and completed 715), which was built near an earlier Byzantine palace from which it was separated by a garden or open ground. The Umayyad Mosque of Aleppo (begun 715) was constructed in the gardens that formerly belonged to the Byzantine cathedral. In Fustat (Egypt), the Mosque of 'Amr (built 641–42) was supposedly surrounded by gardens and vineyards. The late twelfth-century traveler Ibn Jubayr saw palm trees in the Medina Mosque, and mosques in Cairo were frequently planted with trees acccording to the early fifteenth-century eyewitness al-Maqrizi.[24] Pages from a Qur'an manuscript from the Great Mosque of San'a' (the Yemen), dated to the late seventh century, show a mosque with trees flanking its mihrabs. It is unclear whether the image depicts live trees or representations of them in mosaic or painted stucco, but whether real or symbolic, this early mosque was clearly "planted."[25] Although Ibn Sahl's ninth-century jurist stated that he had never seen trees in Syrian or other mosques, one of the mid-eighth-century Syrian jurists had said that tree plantings in mosques were permissible, implying that he was familiar with such practices. The connection between the landscaped setting of early mosques and Byzantine churches deserves closer attention and is far from proven by these disparate mentions of trees in religious environments; at present it is sufficient to note that at least one ninth-century Byzantine church was surrounded by enclosed and irrigated gardens with fountains.[26]

The Cordoba mosque had live, fruit-bearing plants, but mosques might also be symbolically "planted" with mosaic and carved stucco representations of vegetation. Such plant representations occurred early in areas with a strong Byzantine presence, such as Jerusalem, Damascus, and Medina in the seventh and early eighth centuries. The expansions to the Cordoba mosque in the tenth century likewise had mosaics with inscriptions and plant motifs adorning the mihrab and the dazzling dome overhead (Fig. 58), prob-

FIGURE 58. The mosaics of the Cordoba Mosque were made in 965 by a Byzantine master invited to the court of the Andalusian caliph al-Hakam II. Mosaic floral ornament embellishes the voussoirs of the mihrab's horseshoe arch and more vegetal decoration fills the stucco spandrels.

CHAPTER 8

ably to create a visual association with Cordoba's supposed progenitor, the Umayyad Mosque of Damascus, which had an extensive mosaic program depicting trees and landscape covering the walls of its courtyard, its freestanding treasury chamber, and the façade of the transept leading to the qibla wall and mihrab (Fig. 59).[27] Unlike the problematic trees in Cordoba's courtyard, the architectural ornament of tall trees and endlessly scrolling vegetation, some of which framed the mihrab itself in Cordoba, was probably understood as a reference to paradise. Unfortunately, while works of art may survive the centuries, the response of the viewer rarely does and, with the exception of a few captious jurists, we seldom know how the viewers of art interpreted what they saw.

Fortunately, there is one instance where the paradisiac reading is secure, because history has preserved a rare interview with one of the artisans who worked on the mosaics (now lost) added at the time of the expansion of the Prophet's Mosque in Medina between 705 and 715. The man said of his handiwork, "We made it according to the picture of the Tree of Paradise and its Palaces."[28] If the plants in the Medina mosaics represented paradise (or an image of it), then it can be deduced that the mosaic scenes of gardened cities and leafy vegetation adorning the courtyard walls of the Umayyad Mosque of Damascus, built in the same period, and the interior walls of the Dome of the Rock in Jerusalem, built 690–92 (Fig. 60), were similarly intended.[29]

FIGURE 59. The courtyard façade of the Umayyad Mosque of Damascus (begun 705 or 706 and completed 715) was entirely covered with rich mosaics. Those at the entrance to the transept, or mihrab aisle, depict trees with thick foliage.

The question then becomes: what is the precise relationship between the real trees and the mosaic representations of them? We have seen that Islamic history and myth contain many examples of artificial gardens made of fabulous materials. Although real and artificial gardens are materially and symbolically distinct, historians too often regard real gardens and garden representations as if they were the same. To understand how they differ, it helps to shift our focus from the representation of nature, to the nature of representation. The Medina artisan's statement and the historian's recording of it confirm that the pictures of trees and vegetation at Medina, and probably Damascus and the Dome of the Rock, were signs intended to provoke an image of paradise in the viewer's mind. Eventually, this paradisiac signage was imported into the Great Mosque of Cordoba when, in the course of tenth-century expansions, the walls, vaults, and, above all, the mihrab were adorned with mosaics and carved wall panels depicting intertwining vines and leafy vegetation. But the living trees in the mosque courtyard of Cordoba were different because they did not represent paradise to the official interpreters of religion and law, and, despite their location in a highly meaningful place, they did not partake of that building's complex and meaningful signage system.

What is the shift in conditions that makes a mosaic rendering of a tree connote paradise and a live tree not? Apparently, a tree could refer to paradise only if it was already

FIGURE 60.
A mosaic of scrolling vines encircles the inner rim of the dome of the Dome of the Rock (690–92) in Jerusalem. Although the motif had Hellenistic precedents, in this context it has been interpreted as making reference to Paradise. (Robert Ousterhout)

converted into a pictorial representation. The tree image in the Damascus mosaic is a representation of a tree (a denotative function) as well as a representation of paradise (a connotative function). The living tree is the referent that underlies the signifier (Damascus mosaic) that produces the signified (paradise). The semiotic equation appears simple, but it is all too easy to confuse signifieds, referents, and signifiers, and indeed, the slippage from referent to signifer to signified is part of the power of the sign. The mosaic was not a real tree; it was a manipulated image created expressly to elicit the sign. In contrast, the real tree, which may have been planted by human hands in deliberate rows or may have seeded itself by chance and grown haphazardly, was not created expressly to serve as a sign. While it has retroactively become so in a later age, in the eighth through eleventh centuries it was not yet recognized as a symbol of anything.

If live gardens were not acknowledged as references to the religious concept of paradise through the eleventh century, then when did such gardens acquire this meaning? That question is explored more fully in the next chapter's discussion of tombs, but at least part of the answer can be found in the development of mosques in fourteenth-century al-Andalus and India. In Granada, capital of al-Andalus under the Nasrid dynasty (1230–1492), there are three known examples of small mid-fourteenth-century mosques for individual prayer in which the oratory is not fully enclosed but opens to its environment via windows. One belonged to the *madrasa* (theological college) in downtown Granada, today part of the university and facing the cathedral. Founded in 1349 by the Nasrid sultan Yusuf I (1333–54), the madrasa would have had a library, dormitories, and at least one lecture hall; all that remains is the diminutive and much restored prayer chamber. This elegant oratory had an ornamented mihrab flanked on either side by double arched windows (Fig. 61). Although the windows have been blocked up in the modern era, they formerly opened toward the exterior which may have been gardened because, in addition to Qur'an verses and a foundation inscription, there was a poem near the door to the stairway that began: "Behold this garden of fine appearance."[30]

In the Alhambra palace complex, atop a high hill overlooking Granada, there were two oratories used by the sultan and the elite members of his court. One, attached to a public audience hall called the Mexuar, projects at an odd angle from the palace's exterior wall. It was largely destroyed by an explosion in the sixteenth century, but its position indicates that on the northeast wall, perpendicular to the qibla wall, there was a large window with panoramic views of the landscape around and below the Alhambra. The other, called the Mihrab Tower (Torre del Mihrab), built in 1333–54, was located just south of the Torre de las Damas which is all that remains of the Partal Palace's residential fabric (Fig. 62).[31] A door on the northwest side leads into the prayer chamber with its qibla wall and mihrab opposite the entrance; the north and south walls are adorned with shallow niches framing double windows. The south window allowed the worshipper to admire the gardens of the Partal (now with modern plantings and lacking some of its original architecture) while the north window offered a magnificent vista of green valleys and hills.

A fourteenth-century historian wrote that Granada adorned itself with garden palaces like bracelets. In addition to their famous country villas, the Nasrid sultans were also known for their opulent lifestyle and religious laxity. While one might surmise from the inviting mosque windows that these rulers were more interested in the splendors of the world around them than the performance of prayer, a more indulgent interpretation might be that for them the splendors of this world were but a reflection of God's bounty. Indeed, the Qur'an instructs the faithful that the creator provides the rain that makes the grain, date palms, grapes, pomegranates, olives, and foliage grow and admonishes: "Look at the fruits, how they appear on the trees, and how they ripen. In all these are signs for those who believe" (6:99).[32]

Nasrid Granada was surrounded by snow-capped mountains on one side and a fertile agricultural plain on the other, and the city's immediate environs included the densely populated Albaicin and suburbs with orchards, vineyards, gardens, and handsome pavilions.[33] Its temperate climate was excellent for agriculture and animal husbandry, as many Muslim geographers noted. However, with a population in the fourteenth century estimated at between 50,000 and 100,000, it was one of the most populous cities in Europe, in large part due to the influx of Muslims escaping northern regions conquered by Christians. Despite its productive farms, the city could not sustain itself.[34] It imported large quantities of grain, which may have been balanced by the export of refined commodities

FIGURE 61.
A small prayer chamber is all that remains of Granada's madrasa founded by the Nasrid sultan Yusuf I in 1349. The twin windows formerly provided views to the exterior.

FIGURE 62.
This small oratory (1333–54) in the Torre del Mihrab, Partal Palace, Alhambra, has windows on both side walls that encourage a wayward gaze, distracting the faithful from prayer or perhaps encouraging the appreciative contemplation of God's creation.

such as silk and dried fruit as well as by Granada's role as a commercial entrepôt, mediating between Islamic North Africa and northern Spain.[35] Granada could not claim agricultural superiority after the twelfth century, but it still prided itself on cultural brilliance and a better natural climate than any of its European or North African competitors. Surely the sight of such a perfect environment could have been interpreted as a sign of God's generosity. Moreover, territory was not an abstract concept in the medieval world: to gaze upon one's kingdom and its distant horizons was an act that confirmed possession, stewardship, and ultimately sovereign identity. The juxtaposition of the act of prayer with the act of looking at landscape may have confirmed and combined the sultan's roles as both faithful subject and earthly representative of God.

Similarly in South Asia at approximately the same period, the sultans of the Tughluqs (1320–1414), Lodis (1451–ca. 1526), and other regional dynasties often constructed mosques with windows piercing the side wall or even the qibla wall itself. For example, in Delhi, the Hauz Khas educational complex was built in 1352 on elevated ground with a mosque that had openings on its qibla and side walls to permit the worshipper to enjoy views, albeit restricted, of the landscape below (see Sites). The landscape consisted of a large reservoir surrounded by trees and visited by animals and birds. Not only did the residents of this complex have visual access to nature, but they could also descend to the reservoir by a double stairway that led down from the mosque's principal mihrab, a distinctly unusual arrangement. Likewise at Champaner, the Gujarat city ruled by the Beghara dynasty in the fifteenth and early sixteenth century, the Jami Masjid and many of the other mosques had prayer halls with screened windows that looked onto the enclosure surrounding the hall and its courtyard. Moreover, most of them had roof terraces above the prayer hall with balustrades and benches. These furnishings were not intended for the muezzin, who in any case would have climbed the stairway not to the roof but to the top of the sanctuary's portal; instead they seem to have been intended for the use of individuals—perhaps the students studying at the mosque—who could thus climb to the rooftop to enjoy the refreshing breezes and to gaze upon the striking scenery of the encompassing forest and the great Pavagadh mountain that towered over the city (Fig. 63).

FIGURE 63. Like many of Champaner's mosques, the late fifteenth-century Nagina Masjid has a rooftop terrace with a walled surround and benches from where the surrounding palatine city and fertile agricultural landscape could be contemplated.

In more ordinary, undated mosques of India there are some with a single tree emerging from the center. The tree may have been read as a symbol of resurrection, but it may also have been co-opted from Buddhist and Hindu symbols of the cosmic tree, such as the Bodhi tree and the pipal, respectively, with roots in ancient animistic beliefs.[36] It would be unduly restrictive to assign only one meaning to trees, gardens, and landscape views, for among a population of diverse religions, ethnicities, and social status such as in South Asia from the thirteenth century onward, there would not have been one unilateral response to any cultural form. But we have already seen that one of the Islamic meanings associated with gardens was paradise, and this symbolism could have had some resonance in South Asia where Hindus regarded groves, rivers, mountains, springs, and tanks of water as sacred sites frequented by deities.[37] The Hindu concept of sacred vegetation and water, which was associated with rejuvenation and sacred crossings (*tirthas*) from one state of being to the next, including that of life to death and rebirth, complemented the Islamic idea of the paradisiac garden. Hence, the Muslim rulers of the sultanate period, who ruled over a majority Hindu population, may have adopted such symbols as a deliberate strategy to make themselves more universally comprehensible to the mixed population of their kingdoms.

The Lodi sultans built numerous domed tombs and at least one mosque in the Bagh-i Jud gardens of Delhi, which today comprise an extensive public park (called the Lodi Gardens) with paved paths connecting the architectural monuments. Although the density of settlement and built fabric in the Lodi period can only be guessed at, there is evidence that at least in some cases the architecture and the garden setting were conceived together. The Jami Masjid of Sikander Lodi (1494) was a single-nave mosque attached to a high-domed building called the Bara Gumbad (Fig. 64).[38] The original function of the Bara Gumbad is unclear—it may have been intended as a tomb—but it was subsequently used as a portal to the mosque. This portal, mosque, and the columnar hall opposite formed an open-ended ∪, the open space of which served as a courtyard that was raised above the rest of the landscape by several steps. Piercing the side walls of the prayer hall were projecting balconies with windows which, although open today, may once have been screened by ornamental *jali*

FIGURE 64. The Sikander Lodi Mosque (1494) stands today in the Bagh-i Jud (or Lodi Gardens), a public park in a picturesque style. But even in the fifteenth century, the large window at one end of the prayer hall allowed the worshipper to look up from prayer and see a semi-natural landscape.

tracery. These screens would have partially blocked the vision to the exterior, but if one stood close enough to look through them, they framed a view of the verdant environment outside the prayer hall.[39] The opening of the mosque through windows on the side or qibla walls was an anomaly in Islamic architecture generally, but it was a fairly common feature in sultanate architecture of South Asia.

Further south and a century later, 'Adil Shah Ibrahim II (1580–1627), who flourished in the Deccan at the time that the Mughals ruled northern India, built

FIGURE 65.
The Ibrahim
Rauza complex in
Bijapur consists of
a mosque facing
a tomb across an
ornamental ablu-
tion tank. From the
sides of the prayer
hall (built in 1620),
windows provide
views to the sur-
rounding enclosed
garden seen here.

the Ibrahim Rauza complex (finished 1626) west of the city walls of Bijapur. The ensem-
ble consists of a walled gardened enclosure with a raised rectangular plinth in the center
on which stand a mosque and mausoleum, facing each other across a tank of water with
a central fountain. Although the two principal buildings are of different sizes and functions, their matching façades enhance the harmony of the composition. As in the sultanate mosques further north, the side walls of the mosque have projecting windows so that
the worshipper is easily diverted from inward thoughts of submission to God and instead
gazes upon the pleasing scene of the garden to either side of the prayer hall (Fig. 65). Such
a juxtaposition of prayer and worldly views would have been permissible only if the view
enhanced the act of prayer. Although, as we have seen, the palatine gardens of earlier centuries were secular metaphors of princely stewardship and territorial control, and the earliest
examples of mosque plantings were frowned upon by Muslim jurists, clearly the juncture
of garden with mosque and tomb had a popular appeal in India in the sultanate period and
thereafter. In this context, the garden surrounding the place of prayer may have become a
reminder of the afterlife that awaits the faithful, in much the same way that a prayer rug
with motif of flowers suggests the gardens of paradise.

In Ottoman Istanbul it was common for mosques to have adjacent gardens that served
as cemeteries. Mehmet II's tomb in the Fatih Cami (1460–73) stood in a garden beyond
the qibla wall, while in the courtyard that preceded the prayer hall, four cypress trees encircled a fountain, an arrangement that Muslim observers read as a metaphor for the gardens of paradise.[40] Although the form of the arrangement derived from the Hagia Sophia's
atrium (now missing), which likewise had cypresses around a central fountain,[41] the plantings in the mosque were given a specifically Muslim theological interpretation. As imperial
Ottoman mosques began to expand to include an array of services that included hospitals,
soup kitchens, madrasas, and libraries, an outer enclosure court planted with trees and
grassy turf provided a common ground on which to organize the various buildings. A late
eighteenth-century drawing of the Suleymaniye complex (1550–57) shows trees planted
in both the outer enclosure and the mosque courtyard.[42] Here and in many other mosque
complexes, a funerary court with the tombs of the patron and family members stood on

the qibla side of the prayer hall (see Sites). Similarly, the Yeni Valide Mosque complex in Istanbul had cypresses, pines, and plane trees planted within its enclosure walls.[43]

Evidently in Islamic Spain, India, and Ottoman Turkey, where gardens were beloved by patrons whose palaces were famed for their formal and informal uses of landscape, nature was welcomed into the spaces reserved for religious worship. However, garden symbolism did not expand from a territorial metaphor to one of piety and salvation purely as a result of this integration—indeed, at Cordoba we saw that the inclusion of vegetation in a mosque setting met with official disapproval, although there were pragmatic reasons for continuing the practice. Rather, as the next chapter demonstrates, the shift in meaning occurred as a result of the placement of tombs and commemorative structures in garden settings that allowed the living faithful to glimpse a foretaste of the afterlife where the deceased enjoyed nature at its most perfect.

9 The Here and Hereafter

Mausolea and Tomb Gardens

Lthough the Qur'an and various hadith describe paradise as a garden, and although the mosaic and stucco representations of trees and nature in mosques were evidently intended to call to mind the garden of paradise, we have not yet seen evidence that actual gardens in the first four centuries of Islam were interpreted as representations of Paradise. This is because living gardens did not take on a specific paradisiac meaning until they were used as the settings for tombs, at which point, in addition to their role as visible signs of God's bounty to the living, they were metaphors for the perfect gardens of eternity where the faithful dwelled.

Like gardens, Muslim tombs have a problematic history. Although the hadith condemn the building of tombs, and Muhammad himself set the example of requesting burial in an unmarked grave in one of the chambers of his house, tombs eventually became one of the most ubiquitous of Islamic architectural forms. Yet neither the pre-Islamic Arabs nor the Sasanians of Iran and Mesopotamia were tomb builders. Given the theological aversion to tomb building in Islam, and the lack of immediate precedents, we can ask: from where did the concept and models come? The most likely model for Muslim tombs in Syria and the eastern Mediterranean were the centrally planned, square, round, and octagonal Roman mausolea and Byzantine tombs and martyria (monuments marking the site of martyrdom, grave, or relics of a Christian saint). Excavations at the Roman tombs at Scafati (Italy) showed that they were enclosed and gardened with pools,[1] but there is little evidence elsewhere in the Roman world for mausoleum gardens, possibly because historians of antiquity have been too distracted by the magnificent villa gardens to look for more modest plantings attached to tombs. Because of the influx of Turkic peoples coming into Iran and Iraq as mercenary soldiers, prisoners of war, and slaves beginning in the Abbasid period, Iran (and eventually Syria and Egypt) may have absorbed some of the Turkic practice of funeral ceremonies and covering tombs with tents, but theories as to garden settings for these tombs are speculative.

While the Umayyad burial practices are not well known, at least some of the Abbasids chose burial in garden settings with structures marking the burial sites. For example, in the second half of the eighth century, when Harun al-Rashid's wet nurse died, he bought "land for her in a garden next to the Wadi l-Qanatir on the banks of the Euphrates. She was buried there and a *qubba* built over her grave."[2] The oldest identifiable Muslim tomb, the Qubbat al-Sulaybiyya, also dates to the Abbasid period.[3] Built in Samarra in 862, it has excavated remains that reveal a centrally planned square structure with a dome and ambulatory. Although the grave is that of a Muslim caliph, the patron was his mother, a Byzantine princess, and hence this tomb may possibly reflect a Christian desire for grave marking and commemoration. However, by this date, the Byzantine emperors were no longer buried in individual mausolea; indeed, the idea of a free-standing mausoleum did not survive beyond late antiquity. In the ninth century, Byzantine emperors were interred at the Church of Holy Apostles in Constantinople, and persons of nonimperial but distinguished blood were similarly buried not in mausolea but in the narthex or private chapel of a church.[4] This preference for interment in church settings suggests that while Byzantium may have supplied the formal architectural models for Islamic mausolea, it did not provide the social practice of the individual imperial tomb.

The Dome of the Rock (begun 685–86 or 687–88) is the earliest Islamic model for centrally planned commemorative buildings (Fig. 66; also see Fig. 5). It takes the form of two concentric octagonal ambulatories that wrap around a domed central space. In the center is a great rock that Muslims in later centuries associated with the Prophet's mystical Night Journey from Mecca to "the farthest Mosque" (believed to be the Haram al-Sharif) (Qur'an 17:1) as well as his ascent to heaven.[5] Although it memorializes an event rather than a grave, the inscription of a circle on the ground nonetheless designates a place of singular and central historical importance; the conceptual axis that rises vertically from the circle's center through the apex of the dome forms an *axis mundi* that connects the earthbound place with heaven. However, while the architectural typology of such memorial structures in Islam may begin with the Dome of the Rock, the typology of tomb gardens does not, since the Haram al-Sharif in Jerusalem, where the Dome of the Rock is situated, is a paved platform with no gardens.

The personal motivation for funerary commemoration is due to the special ability of the dead to act as intercessors for the living. Saints in particular occupy an intermediate space between life and death in the theological imagination, enabling them to mediate between God and the faithful supplicant.[6] Although we can only speculate about the earliest models and sources for Muslim tomb construction, we do know that by the eleventh century, Iran and Egypt had large numbers of tombs dedicated to members of the ruling dynasty and, increasingly, to venerated individuals.[7] Egyptian tombs were often clustered together in large areas, as for example at Fustat and the Aswan necropolis, both dating to the Fatimid period (909–1171). The tomb was a sign of conspicuous consumption among individual patrons of moderate wealth and might be lavishly decorated. Some of the imagery consisted of cypresses (evergreen and thus a sign of eternal life), peacocks, and domes (symbol of heaven and paradise); and although there is hardly any evidence, it is possible that some of these

FIGURE 66.
The Dome of the Rock (finished between 690 and 692) adapts the Byzantine martyrium plan to mark one of the most important places in Islam's religious and political history. (After Creswell)

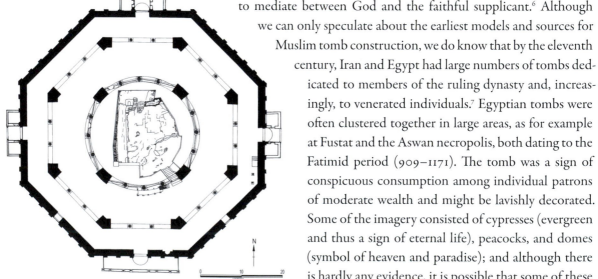

N

0   10   20
METERS

diminutive buildings were set amidst informal landscape environments, not gardened so much as graced by a few trees or flowering shrubs. Paradisiac imagery predominates in the ornament, but the Qur'anic inscriptions of these tombs tend to be about the imminence of death (Sura 21:35 and 3:185) and not the pleasures waiting in paradise.[8]

Archaeology and historical sources reveal little about the landscape context of early tombs and grave sites. It stands to reason that since they were freestanding structures, often in cemeteries with no other building types, the land around them was open and seasonally green. One of the words for a tomb in Arabic is *rawda*, a term which also means garden, although without giving any sense of formal planning. A *Maqamat* manuscript from Baghdad (1237) shows an interment in a cemetery with domed mausolea overhung with dense branches (Plate 13), pictorial evidence for the informality of funerary planting.

Probably the cemetery of the Umayyads in the Cordoba Alcazar looked something like this in the ninth and tenth centuries. It was called the Rawda by contemporary sources, indicating that it had some kind of planting or natural greenery. The Rawda was a simple open-air enclosure, but if there were large mausoleum structures or gardens, none of the historians made note of them.[9] Similarly, in fourteenth-century Granada, the Nasrid rulers were buried in a small enclosure adjoining the Court of the Lions in the Alhambra Palace. This cemetery consisted of graves in an open-air setting as well as a two-chambered tomb.[10] Despite the inferred or demonstrable presence of vegetation in these Muslim tomb gardens, we do not know if the gardens were cultivated to the extent of having caretakers who actively weeded and watered them. Although the cemetery area east of Fustat had a water system adequate to sustain baths and a pool in the early tenth century, the tomb enclosures do not seem to have been irrigated.[11] Without regular tending and irrigation, the great cemeteries of Cairo, Fustat, and Aswan in Egypt, which received virtually no rainfall, would have been dry and brown.

The necropolis of Chella was built between 1310 and 1334 on a hill just outside the walls of Rabat (Morocco) and was used for the interment of members of the ruling Merinid family (1196–1465). It consists of a crenellated pisé wall with an entrance gate flanked by towers. Partway down the sloping rambling landscape of Roman ruins and Merinid-era graves, there is a rectangular enclosure (44 by 29 m) containing tombs, two prayer halls, a minaret, and a *zawiya* (a residential retreat for prayer). In this walled area, the Mosque of Abu Yusuf was preceded by a courtyard that served as the entrance to the funerary complex. To the northeast, the zawiya had two stories of small residential rooms and, at its center, an open courtyard with a rectangular pool ornamented at either end by scalloped marble basins embedded in the tiled pavement (Plate 20). The southeast end of the courtyard led to a small prayer hall for the residents, and off to the southwest side of the zawiya was an open area with long rectangular tombstones marking the graves of the Merinid deceased.

Although the necropolis is a romantic relic today and infrequently visited, it still gives a sense of how landscape was incorporated informally in elite religious foundations. The tombstones were aligned with the body so that the deceased, when positioned on his or her side, faced Mecca (Fig. 67). In 1922, Basset and Lévi-Provençal noted the remnants of walkways in the area of these graves and the larger tomb of the patron, Abu'l Hassan, and sug-

FIGURE 67.
In the Chella
Necropolis, these
gravestones of
Merinid fam-
ily members were
once tended by
the inhabitants
of Chella's zawiya.
Although the mark-
ers themselves are
simple, the entire
setting served as
a funerary and
commemorative
complex.

gested that there were once gardened parterres.[12] The cemetery may possibly have been planted with flowers and shrubs selected for beauty or scent; water was very close by and vegetation could easily have been irrigated by surface channels or even handheld containers carried by the zawiya residents who tended the grounds.

The setting of a shrine or funerary cluster amidst gardens became commonplace in the Maghreb. The sixteenth-century royal Saʻadian graves in Marrakesh rest in pavilions in a garden setting (which today is no longer original). In the late seventeenth century, the shrine of Tangier's patron saint Sidi Muhammad al-Hajj al-Baqqal, located outside the medina (the old walled city), was supported by a waqf document dated 1714 that endowed not only the shrine buildings but also its extensive surrounding gardens. This became the preferred place of burial in that city because of the proximity to the saint and his spiritual blessing (*baraka*), and the stands of trees encircling the shrine and cemetery were regarded as sacred.[13]

The informal landscape setting for graves was not solely a Maghrebi phenomenon, however; it is seen also in manuscript illustrations representing Ottoman burials in funerary complexes. As multiple buildings with diverse purposes were juxtaposed in endowed complexes (*kulliyes*) from the thirteenth century onward, the landscape became an increasingly important neutral ground on which to position the mosque, *turbes* (tombs), hostels, and auxiliary structures. Particularly among the Ottomans, the great kulliye establishments such as the Suleymaniye, Selimiye, and Yeni Valide Cami had large yards separating the various functions. A manuscript illustration from the *Tarikh-i Sultan Suleyman* (1579) shows the burial of Sultan Suleyman in a walled courtyard next to the already completed tomb of the sultan's wife, Hurrem (d. 1558) (Fig. 68). The grave is dug directly in the earth under a temporary canopy, and the grounds of the enclosure are depicted simply as green turf with small clusters of red blooms, perhaps tulips.[14] Although the restrained kind of landscape depicted here may be due to the sixteenth-century style of pictorial representation, it is also quite likely that the context of the two tombs at the Suleymaniye made no grand aesthetic claims in the Ottoman era. Today, however, the tombs of the Suleymaniye and similar imperial foundations are densely surrounded by slab gravestones with vertical markers, interspersed with roses and flowers, some of which are planted directly in apertures in the gravestone itself (see Sites).

At what point did Muslim tombs shift from informal settings to formal gardens, and when did the meaning of paradise become intentional and explicit? Tombs, despite their obvious eschatalogical and paradisiac resonance, do not seem to have been endowed with formal gardens until considerably after the garden had been developed as an art for palaces and sites of pleasure. And in Ottoman Anatolia, order in the garden was never achieved through dominant axial water channels and geometrically arranged sunken parterres. Instead, Ottoman gardens adapted more flexibly to the natural topography. Elsewhere in the Islamic world, garden pavilions often took the form of square or centrally planned free-standing structures open on all sides, designed expressly to offer the pleasure of enjoying the sight, scent, and music of the surrounding environment. However, just as houses could become the final resting place of the deceased—the Prophet himself was buried thus at home—garden pavilions could be similarly transformed. Garden pavilions take many forms, as do tombs, but the Rusafa garden pavilion in Syria exemplifies a type that has a central plan, domed or pyramidal roof, and entrances or apertures on some or all sides. Similarly, the pavilion that stood in the center of the Upper Garden of Madinat al-Zahra' was a square that appears to have had openings on all four sides. Hence, although there was radical transformation in meaning, the functional shift from pleasure pavilion to commemorative mausoleum required nothing more than the addition of a cenotaph.

In the Islamic west, one such conversion is well documented. The Hayr al-Zajjali, which stood outside the walls of Cordoba, was a pleasure garden that belonged to a prosperous but nonroyal family at the end of the tenth or early eleventh century.[15] An observer wrote that in the first half of the eleventh century, the owner, the vizier Abu Marwan al-Zajjali and his companion used it for "the gratification of the senses" and "the pleasures of sobriety and inebriation."[16] Although the garden no longer exists, its multicolored pavilion, white marble courtyard, basin, water channels, and plantings were described as follows by this same writer in the second half of the eleventh century: "The garden [*rawda*] has files of trees symmetrically aligned and its flowers smile from open buds. The foliage of the garden prevents the sun seeing the ground; and the breeze, blowing day and night over the garden, is loaded with scents."[17]

The owner was eventually buried in the garden; and not long thereafter, in 1035, his friend was interred there as well. At that point, the Hayr al-Zajjali changed from being a pleasure garden to both a pleasure garden and a cemetery with two sepulchers; the same garden plan and architectural structures served equally for both purposes.[18] The functions of worldly pleasure and eternal commemoration are not so different as might appear: the inebriating food and drink enjoyed by the living revelers was like the fruit, fowl, and wine that the deceased would eat and drink in the company of dark-eyed companions called *houris* in paradise, and the Hayr's shade, fruit, and running water channels likewise mirrored those of paradise. Both the living garden and the garden of paradise are sites of pleasure. The difference is that one is ephemeral and created by human labor, while the other is eternal and bestowed by God to reward the faithful.

Tombs abounded in Central Asia and northwestern Iran from the tenth century onward, in part due to strong pre-Islamic Turkic traditions of commemorative architecture. These tombs are typically free-standing towers or domed squares, cylinders, and octagons surrounded by more modest graves and grave markers.[19] Although the structures have been studied by architectural historians and conservators, little attention has been paid to the surrounding space, so that we do not know whether or not the tomb enjoyed a green setting and whether that setting was informally landscaped or carefully organized into beds divided by pavements and water channels.

But in the case of the tomb of Sultan Sanjar, built around 1152 in Merv (Seljuq period), there is reason to believe that the tomb stood in a garden context (see Sites). Since the distinguished Russian archaeologist G. A. Pugachenkova studied it in mid-twentieth century, it has received attention as one of many key points in the typological development of tomb complexes, with little consideration of its spatial context. The tomb, which stands in semi-ruins, consists of a large square base from which rises a tall dome, fourteen meters high, in which the exterior transition from base to dome is mediated by an arched gallery. The tomb was attached to a mosque and is notable not only for its monumental size but also as the first securely dated example of such a mosque-tomb combination. However, it is also important as an early example of a formally landscaped tomb. A late nineteenth-century visitor, Edmond O'Donovan, sketched a plan of the tomb precinct that shows its quadripartite setting, and he described it as standing in the center of a large enclosure at the point where two axial pavements intersected.[20] Although O'Donovan's testimony does not serve to date the quadripartite setting to the twelfth century, the fact that the sultan's tomb belonged to a complex that included a palace supports the hypothesis that the original tomb stood in a chahar bagh because palaces were often adorned with formal gardens with fruit trees and flowers.

When the tomb stands in an enclosed garden, especially when the garden is cross-axial and quadripartite, the design of building and landscape respond to each other so that the axes of the garden meet at the position of the tomb, and the tomb's own internal axes extend into the surrounding landscape. This integrated conception of architecture and landscape is quite different from the casual siting of the mausoleum or pleasure pavilion in a verdant, flowered environment in which the relationship is one of random juxtaposition. In India during the sultanate period, the Khalji dynasty (1290–1320) sponsored a complex in Mandu (Madhya Pradesh province) that consisted of a congregational mosque, the tomb of Hushang Shah, and a domed madrasa with a garden stretching along its east side. Although the tomb did not sit amidst the garden, the group of structures was conceived as a single entity along a symmetrical axis in which the garden was a fully planned element. Today the garden is abandoned, but one can imagine that, like the grounds of Bijapur's Ibrahim Rauza complex, it was formerly a verdant and possibly flowered environment.

In contrast, the Hauz Khas madrasa-mausoleum complex in Delhi was developed over time (see Sites). Although it ultimately possessed a sophisticated and beautiful integration of built form and landscape, this was the result of successive building campaigns and not a single underlying initial plan. It began simply as a huge reservoir built by a ruler of the Khalji dynasty (r. 1296–1316). In 1352, a two-storied madrasa and mosque were built on a natural elevation in the reservoir's southeast corner by Firoz Shah (r. 1351–88), the most prolific builder of the Tughluq dynasty. The complex was intensely cultivated and had single-storied, airy pavilions. Water was the predominant feature of the site, and in Delhi's seasonally dry climate the sight of the lake below as well as the artificially sustained greenery above must have been an impressive and satisfying experience. To this environment of study, prayer, and pleasure, the tomb of Firoz Shah himself was added in 1388. Like the Hayr al-Zajjali, the gardens preceded the mausoleum, but unlike the Hayr, they were already imbued with a character beyond that of simple worldly delight.

Similarly, a Tughluq garden at Vasant Vihar (south Delhi), in the late fourteenth–early fifteenth century received its tomb at a later date.[21] The complex comprised a rectangular enclosure of twelve hectares, with an area of stepped terraces (Fig. 69). On a lower terrace, raised stone watercourses with wells and cisterns could have sustained garden planting; on the next terrace stood a mosque; and the highest level had a domed pavilion with an open platform on one side that allowed a view over the terraces below, which were probably gardened. About a hundred years later during the Lodi period, a tomb was attached to this pavilion's north side. Although there are no signs of formal four-part planning, the garden was more than simply a natural setting; it was an irrigated, stepped enclosure. Furthermore, the position of the tomb at the edge of the uppermost terrace, next to a viewing platform, suggests that the site was carefully considered in order to maximize the possibility of a view onto the lower gardens.

At the Timurid shrine complex at Gazur Gah (Afghanistan) the main shrine has an informal relationship with its gardens (see Sites). Built in 1425, with various other tombs added during subsequent decades, the shrine consists of a walled enclosure with four iwans facing inward toward the tomb of the Sufi Shaykh 'Abd Allah Ansari. A walled, semi-enclosed area of gardens extended west from the shrine and tombs and in it stood a kiosk (possibly two). Its purpose, based on comparisons with similar Timurid structures elsewhere, was probably that of a garden pavilion, serving as a place where visitors to the shrine could rest and enjoy the agreeable environment. The greenery would have been irrigated by canals that were built between 1451 and 1469 to nourish gardens near the shrine.[22] The precise chronology of the buildings relative to the landscape elements is uncertain, but two aspects of the site's gardens are noteworthy. First, the informal organization suggests that neither the garden nor its pavilion was essential to the shrine's functional purpose or architectural design. They were appendages, if not in the strictly chronological sense, then in the sense of the overall design. Second, visitors who came

FIGURE 69. Although today hardly anything can be seen at the late fourteenth- or early fifteenth-century site, Vasant Vihar (Delhi) was formerly terraced with a pavilion and tomb at its summit.

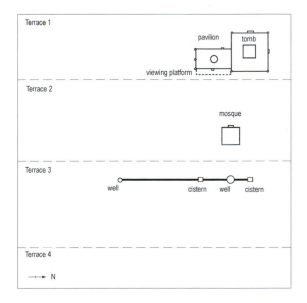

THE HERE AND HEREAFTER

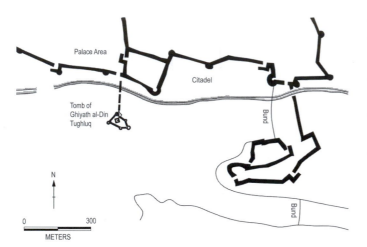

Palace Area

Citadel

Tomb of
Ghiyath al-Din
Tughluq

Bund

Bund

N

0   300
METERS

FIGURE 70.
The red sandstone
tomb of Ghiyath
al-Din (1320–1325)
in Tughluqabad
(Delhi) occupied a
fortified island in
an area that could
be flooded in times
of stress.

to pray at the shrine could relax afterward in the parklike setting, possibly enjoying a picnic much as families do today at the Mt. Auburn Cemetery (Cambridge, Massachusetts) and the Tomb of Humayun (Delhi). Interestingly, at Gazur Gah the gardens appear secondary to the main element, the shrine, whereas the reverse occurred in Cordoba's Hayr al-Zajjali where the gardens were the preexisting foundation to which the memorial component was added.

The practice of garden burials may have begun earlier, but the custom proliferated among the sultans of Delhi. As early as 1210, Qutb al-Din Aybak, the first of the Mu'izzi dynasty, was buried in a garden.[23] As we have already seen, the Tughluq ruler Firoz Shah was buried in the garden of a large complex in the mid-fourteenth century, and the rulers of the Lodi dynasty of Delhi built numerous domed tombs in the Bagh-i Jud gardens, many of which are still standing today (see Sites).

Some tombs were surrounded by water so that the relationship of the garden to its occasional tanks and basins was reversed: the water dominated the space and vegetation was limited to an island or pushed to the perimeter. The Tughluq ruler Ghiyath al-Din (r. 1320–25) built such a tomb near his fortress in Tughluqabad (now part of greater Delhi) (Fig. 70). Dams and sluices trapped the rains so that in the monsoon season the water formed a moat around the tomb, which was reached by a raised causeway. Similarly, the great tomb of Sher Shah Sur (d. 1545), the founder of the Afghan Suri dynasty, stands in the center of an artificial lake on a stepped square platform that is reached by a causeway on its north side (Fig. 71).[24] *Chhatris* (domes raised on pillars) in the corners and on projecting balconies provide views from the octagonal tomb toward the surrounding water and landscape. The equally monumental mausoleum of his son and successor, Sultan Islam Shah (d. 1554), was similarly situated. Whereas palaces and fortresses were located near water because the inhabitants needed a ready supply, in a tomb the water and the vegetation that it nourished may been intended to suggest the perennial abundance of paradise. At the same time, it is important to remember that just as tombs could serve multiple functions as places for both relaxation and commemoration, they also belonged to a larger landscape system in which utilitarian purposes coexisted with aesthetic and spiritual values.

The delight in allusion and illusion was a pronounced feature of Mughal architecture where there are many pavilions set amidst pools. Babur, who launched the Mughal dynasty when he led his army from Kabul (Afghanistan) across the Himalayas into the plains of northern India in 1525, always preferred the mountainous landscape of his native land to the flat and drier plains. When he died in 1530, he was temporarily buried in Agra in a garden on the banks of the Yamuna River but was later given a permanent resting place in a garden of twelve terraces in Kabul (see Sites). The first monumental imperial Mughal tomb was built not for Babur, therefore, but for his son, Humayun (r. 1530–40 and 1555–56). Furthermore, the tomb of Humayun was built after the Mughal dynasty was finally secure, and after the death of the Mughals' greatest rival for Delhi, the aforementioned Sher Shah Sur, whose successors were unable to retain control. The young Akbar (r. 1556–1605) built the tomb both as a memorial to his deceased father and as the first great statement of empire and dynasty.

FIGURE 71.
This monumental tomb of Sher Shah Sur, the archrival of the Mughal Emperor, Humayun, was built in Sasaram in 1545. Qur'anic verses on its exterior refer to the faithful quenching their thirst upon entering paradise, a selection chosen perhaps to refer to the tomb's lake setting. (Catherine Asher)

The Tomb of Humayun, built 1562–71, launched a new type of imperial Mughal tomb that would have numerous copies in subsequent generations. Its *hesht behesht* plan (eight bays encircling a central ninth bay) and imposing double-shell dome construction recall the huge magnificent domes of Timurid Iran and Central Asia, while the materials of construction and ornament—red sandstone crisply incised with white marble—were obtained from native South Asian quarries (Plate 3). The monument thus drew attention to its historic roots and source of political legitimacy, while at the same time it clothed itself in the colors of the local landscape.[25] The mausoleum's garden setting was a classic walled chahar bagh with a central garden pavilion—here a tomb—from which radiate the four axial walkways that define the plan (Fig. 72). The quadrants are subdivided into grids of eight squares, the ninth being occupied by the corners of the enormous tomb platform. Water channels run down the center of the pavements, swelling at each intersection to fill square basins. As the visitor approaches the tomb from the walkways leading from any of the four gated entrances, the tomb appears to expand in size and majesty, while at the same time it is reflected in these shimmering pools of water.

Like the architectural form, the garden setting likewise drew from two traditions. The chahar bagh plan was a Timurid organizational concept, introduced by Babur, who employed it for pleasure gardens.[26] But the plants that flowered there must have been local varieties: perhaps the red and white oleander, hibiscus, and semitropical fruit trees that struck Babur as rare and beautiful when he encountered them for the first time in South Asia. The building of the tomb was innovative in that the imported Timurid structural forms were expressed in regional materials; however, the concept of burial in a landscape setting, as we have seen, was neither a Mughal innovation nor a Timurid import, since the sultans of Delhi already had a long tradition of such funerary architecture.

Subsequent monumental Mughal tombs were set in chahar baghs: the tombs of Akbar (Sikandra), Jahangir (Lahore), Nur Jahan (Lahore), I'timad al-Daula (Agra), Shah Jahan and Mumtaz Mahal (Agra), and Aurangzeb's wife (Aurangabad). Despite the unchanging formula of a tomb set within a four-part garden, the form of the mausoleum itself could vary considerably. For example, the structure of Akbar's Tomb at Sikandra (finished c.

FIGURE 72.
The Tomb of
Humayun (Delhi)
stands at the center
of a vast chahar
bagh, subdivided
into smaller squares
by broad walkways
flanking narrow
water channels.
At their points of
intersection, the
channels meet at
rectangular pools.

1613) was an unusual hodgepodge in which the five stories seem not to correspond to one another; yet it stands within a classic cross-axially divided garden (Fig. 73). Even though only one monumental gate provided entrance to the enclosure, the power of the grid was such that false gates were built at the ends of the axial walkways to complete the expectation of symmetry provoked by the chahar bagh plan. In contrast, the tombs of Jahangir (d. 1627) and Nur Jahan (d. 1645) near Lahore and Maryam al-Zammani (d. 1623) in Sikandra were of the modest platform type, while the Tomb of Humayun and Shah Jahan's Taj Mahal had ostentatious double-shell domes. The Tomb of I'timad al-Daula and his wife (parents of the empress Nur Jahan) had a hesht behesht plan that was realized with an altogether different elevation: instead of a massive bulbous dome, the second story consists of a platform bearing a rather small, rectangular canopy dome and four short chhatri-topped minarets.[27] The layout of the chahar bagh was more consistent, but some variation within the four-part plan was possible. For example, the Tomb of I'timad al-Daula consisted of four simple quadrants, but quadrants of Humayun's Tomb and the Taj Mahal were subdivided into smaller units. Typically the tomb stood at the center of the chahar bagh, but the Taj Mahal's mausoleum was unusually placed at one end of the garden on an elevated platform.

By the sixteenth century, there was a sufficiently wide repertoire of architectural and garden forms that patrons could choose among several available types. There was some degree of chronological development in which innovations led to design changes or new preferences (as we shall see in the next chapter), but for the most part multiple typologies existed concurrently and were adopted according to each patron's taste.[28] As for significance, the garden by this point had gained a powerful and pervasive meaning as an earthly reflection of the paradise to come. Just as the deceased body rested on earth in a shady garden environment, so too the soul enjoyed an eternity of leisure, ever-verdant vegetation and fruit forever ripe. The tomb was a metonymic stand-in for the deceased, and the tomb garden represented paradise. Not only did Arabic and Persian poetry celebrate the garden in this sense, but even the selective use of Qur'anic passages in architectural inscriptions insisted on a paradisiac meaning. For example, on the great entry gate of the Tomb of Akbar, Persian inscriptions (by 'Abd al-Haq) equated the tomb garden that the reader was about to enter with the gardens of Eden and paradise:

Hail, blessed space happier than the garden of paradise!
Hail, lofty building higher than the divine throne!
A paradise, the garden of which has thousands of Rizwans as its servants,

The garden of which has thousands of paradises for its land.
The pen of the mason of the divine decree has written on its court:
These are the gardens of Eden, enter them to live forever.[29]

The Taj Mahal was covered with Qur'anic passages on its exterior, framing the iwans. These selections were eschatological in theme, proclaiming the power of God and warning of the arrival of the Day of Judgement.[30] The monumental entry gate at the south end of the Taj Mahal likewise bore inscriptions from the Qur'an, including the sura "The Dawn," which concludes:

O you tranquil soul,
Return to your Lord, well-pleased and well-pleasing Him.
"Enter then among My votaries,
Enter then My garden."[31]

Whether poetry or Qur'an verses, the presence of a text made explicit the symbolic role of garden form, especially the chahar bagh. Thereafter, the connection between garden and paradise became commonplace so that it entered the collective imagination and became part of garden discourse, whether or not there were inscriptions present to remind the viewer. Once the idea of the garden as paradise became a cliché, it became so ubiquitous that even the most secular gardens claimed to be paradises. Thus the Shalamar Bagh in the Mughal's favorite summer resort in Kashmir was inscribed with a Persian verse (by Jami): "If there be a Paradise on the face of the earth, it is here, it is here, it is here."[32] The reference to paradise was surely meant in a literary rather than theological sense, for the imperial garden had neither a prayer hall nor a tomb to justify the association with the afterlife. It was enjoyed as a place for entertainment, leisure, and sensory pleasure, and when used in such a setting, the paradise metaphor was intended as hyperbole, suggesting that the garden was immeasurably beautiful. Even today, people around the world will describe a place or an experience as "heavenly" without intending specifically religious meaning.

In addition to large tombs set within formally planned gardens, there is another kind of tomb that has no garden and yet embraces nature in an implicitly paradisiac sense. These are the simple graves, open to the sky, that were popular in seventeenth-century India as a revival of an earlier orthodox burial custom. Babur himself was initially buried quite simply in one of the gardens along the Yamuna River's banks. The word used in a contemporary source to describe this tomb is *mazar*, meaning a sanctuary or place that one visits, derived from the Arabic word for "visit."[33]

FIGURE 73. In the imperial Mughal tradition, the Tomb of Akbar (Sikandra) stands in an enormous chahar bagh, called the Behishtabad (Abode of Paradise) in the *Akbarnama*. But the mausoleum itself departs from the earlier model of Humayun. Rather than the classic Timurid dome, the stacked trabeated layers and massing of chhatris in Akbar's tomb recall residential architecture.

FIGURE 74.
A decade or more
after his death in
1530, Babur's body
was moved to this
site in Kabul. Over
a hundred years
later, Shah Jahan
enclosed the tomb
with a marble *jali*
(screen), a style
than was repeated
in Jahanara's tomb
in Delhi. (Charles
Masson, 1842)

It does not describe a building type, and this lack of evidence for a permanent structure marking the gravesite is the only information we have about Babur's first interment. In any case this was only a temporary burial, for ten to fourteen years later his body was removed to Kabul where it was buried in a large garden of fifteen sloping terraces with water channels flowing from one level to the next (see Sites). The tomb of Babur's granddaughter was added at a later date, and circa 1645, Shah Jahan rebuilt portions of this Bagh-i Babur in Kabul, enclosing both tombs with a marble screen.[34] A representation of the tomb made in the mid-nineteenth century shows a tomb of the *hazira* type: a simple grave on a slightly raised platform surrounded by a walled enclosure (Fig. 74).

The hazira became a popular type during the lengthy reign of Emperor Aurangzeb (r. 1658-1707). Aurangzeb was a pious, austere follower of Islam who had inherited an empire of diminished resources. His patronage was directed more toward religious structures than palaces as he turned away from the more ostentatious Mughal forms of display and luxury, especially those derived from Hindu sources such as the ceremonial daily appearance of the emperor in the palace *jharoka* (balconied window). He was a devoted student of theology and was known to have memorized the entire Qur'an. He was clearly ambivalent about the practice of erecting monumental tombs and stated that tomb visiting was contradictory to orthodox Islam, although he contributed to the maintenance of existing royal and saintly tombs, had a hand in the preservation of a thirteenth-century mausoleum in Delhi, and commanded his son to build a mausoleum for his mother, Aurangzeb's wife, in Aurangabad.[35] This tomb of Rabi'a Daurani (also known as the Bibi-ka Maqbara) was finished in 1660–61, four years after the empress's death in 1657, and was modeled on the

Taj Mahal (although using less costly materials, substituting plaster for marble).

But other burials built during this period were of the modest hazira type, placed in *dargah* (shrine) settings where the deceased could partake of the blessings of the saint around whose tomb such complexes arose. The tomb of Jahanara (d. 1681), built in the last years of her life, was located in the dargah of the saint Nizam al-Din in Delhi. It consisted of a white marble cenotaph surrounded by a handsomely carved marble screen (4.8 by 13.6 m) in the fashion of a hazira enclosure, so that one can look through the gate as well as the jali screen (Fig. 75). The enclosure is more than two and a half meters high and was originally surmounted by a slender minaret in each corner. Although the floor of the small enclosure is paved, the cenotaph has a deep depression on its horizontal face to allow planting. A marble slab inscribed with a pious verse rises vertically at the head of the cenotaph: "Let nothing but the green [grass] conceal my grave. The grass is the best covering for the tombs of the poor in spirit; the humble; the transitory Jahanara, the disciple of the holy men of Chist; the daughter

FIGURE 75. The Tomb of Jahanara (built just before 1681) stands in a densely built *dargah* (religious complex) in Delhi. Its white marble walls of pierced jali screens protect a simple slab tomb from the center of which a vine climbs, as if yearning for eternity.

of the Emperor Shah Jahan; May God illuminate his intentions. In the year 1093 [referring to the hijra date]."[36] Nearby are the similarly screened graves of the Mughal prince, Mirza Jahangir, and Emperor Muhammad Shah who ruled a vastly diminished Mughal kingdom between 1719 and 1748. The vines that grow from these three cenotaphs have woody stems that twist sinuously and cling to the upper edge of the screen so that from outside, the gravesite has the appearance of an enclosed garden.[37] Whether grass or vines were originally intended for the grave is less important here than the use of greenery to suggest the piety of orthodox burial and the heavenly destination of the deceased. Similarly, Aurangzeb commissioned his own tomb just before he died in 1707 at the dargah of Shaykh Burhan al-Din in Khulabad, near Aurangabad. His was a simple grave that, like Jahanara's, consisted of a horizontal stone cenotaph with a depression in its top that was "filled with earth, in which fragrant herbs have been planted."[38]

The conceptual union of the garden with the Qur'anic paradise was achieved as soon as tombs began to be placed within garden environments. It was the mausoleum—not piety or Qur'anic associations—that created the link with the afterlife, for we have seen that prior plantings of vegetation in mosques did not call to mind paradisiac meanings. However, once the connection was made between the deceased on earth and the soul in heaven, and between the earthly garden and the paradise described in the Qur'an, the two became virtually inseparable. The reference to paradise occurred most spectacularly in the great imperial tomb-in-chahar-bagh complexes of the Mughals, but it was also evident in simpler tombs where the concept of a soul's departure for heaven was expressed through the upward reach of a vine.

10 A Garden in Landscape

The Taj Mahal and Its Precursors

ISTORIES OF Islamic gardens have traditionally focused on the garden as an enclosed, bounded entity with a definition as precise as that of a building. While this is a successful strategy for considering some aspects of the garden such as patronage and typology, it excludes other aspects of garden-making such as views, the ecological issues of water management and botany, and the ways that an enclosed garden can respond spatially to the surrounding topography. Therefore, in this chapter, instead of comparing the various ways that botanical exchange, fantasy, memory, and design affected gardens and sites throughout the Islamic world, we will focus on a single site—the Taj Mahal—and examine its response to specific elements in its own landscape context and the way that it reflects previous experience of garden design in markedly different landscapes elsewhere in South Asia.

The Taj Mahal (Fig. 76) is a large funerary complex with a garden that is usually treated as a self-contained construction bounded by rectangular walls; yet its unusual position on the edge of a river raises broad-ranging questions of landscape, hydrology, topography, and view. Ironically, although no building has become more emblematic of the Mughal house than the Taj Mahal, it may not have been originally intended to serve as an imperial tomb. It was built between the years 1632 and 1643 for the Emperor Shah Jahan's favorite wife, Arjumand Banu Begam, known as Mumtaz Mahal (1590–1629), from whence comes the popular calque "Taj Mahal." The emperor himself was ultimately buried there, having built no other tomb for himself, and this fact, together with the stern content of the Qur'anic verses on its exterior and the enormous size and cost of construction, has led some prominent scholars to propose that it was intended to serve as his own mausoleum.[1] It is unlikely that such a prolific builder as Shah Jahan would have overlooked the necessity of a building himself an imperial tomb. However, the fact that the central placement of Mumtaz Mahal's cenotaph forced the subsequent placement of the emperor's off-center and west of hers suggests that, at least at the time of the queen's death, the emperor did not foresee that he would eventually be buried there as well and would be relegated to a spatially subordinate position. Whether or not the Taj was built to serve as Shah Jahan's own tomb, it became de facto an outstanding monument in the series of imperial Mughal mausolea.[2]

Obtained in fair exchange from the Rajput noble Raja Man Singh (of Amber), the land used for the tomb and garden was situated on the banks of Agra's Yamuna River, which was

already thoroughly inscribed with both pleasure and tomb gardens, such as the Bagh-i Nur Afshan (now known as Ram Bagh) and the Tomb of I'timad al-Daula. History records that he was genuinely devoted to Mumtaz Mahal, devastated by her death a mere three years after his accession to the throne, and commenced procuring the land and planning the great tomb in the period immediately following her death.[3] The funerary precinct forms a rectangular enclosure running 567 meters north-south and 305 meters east-west with the mausoleum occupying the central position on a terrace elevated at the northern end.[4] The monumental white marble tomb follows a nine-bay hesht behesht plan with a large open central chamber for the cenotaphs topped by a bulbous double-shell dome (the actual sarcophagi are buried below ground directly beneath). Each face of the tomb consists of a huge iwan flanked by two tiers of smaller iwans and enframed by Qur'anic inscriptions. The minarets of the mausoleum are separate from the tomb itself and placed at the four corners of the mausoleum's plinth, enhancing the building's tranquil majesty and visual clarity. The plinth on which the tomb and minarets stand rises from another platform where they are flanked by a mosque to the west and a meeting hall to the east. The latter was included solely for the sake of architectural balance and reveals the rigor with which symmetry was implemented. From here, the mausoleum presides at an elevation 7.5 meters above an enormous chahar bagh with axial walkways and a raised pool at their point of intersection. The primary axis runs southward to a monumental gate that leads to a large forecourt (*jilau khana*), which served as a buffer between the mausoleum garden and the Taj Ganj, a residential and market area.

The use of white marble for an imperial Mughal tomb marked an aesthetic shift from the earlier red sandstone tombs of the emperors Humayun, Akbar, and Jahangir. At first, white was a color reserved for saint's tombs, such as that of Salim al-Din Chisti's marble mausoleum (built 1580–81) in the courtyard of Fatehpur-Sikri's congregational mosque, but it was subsequently used at the Tomb of I'timad al-Daula, built between 1622 and 1628 by the Empress Nur Jahan for her parents (Plate 21). In its use of white marble as well as in its decorative stone intarsia, insistence on garden representations, inclusion of a pleasure pavilion, and riverside location, the Tomb of I'timad al-Daula preceded many of the innovations seen soon afterward at the Taj Mahal.

Many of the new features that appeared in Mughal architectural and landscape vocabulary in this period can be traced to the taste of Nur Jahan (1577–1645) and her privileged position as not only the wife of Jahangir (r. 1605–27) from 1611 onward but also his agent in matters of culture and governance. Nur Jahan was an influential patron of art and literature. Highly educated and conversant in both Persian and Arabic, she sponsored and participated capably in poetry contests at court, had gourmet taste in cuisine, and introduced new textiles such as a lightweight cotton, a flowered muslin, and a silver-threaded brocade.[5] The intense interest in natural imagery that can be discerned in Mughal art and architecture in the second quarter of the seventeenth century was due in part to Nur Jahan, although it is often difficult to distinguish between her taste and that of her husband. It has been suggested that her love of flowers was due to her situation as a woman at court.[6] Barred from public events such as receptions in the Diwan-i 'Amm of the Agra Fort or public prayer in the congregational mosque, a typical noblewoman's spatial realm was limited to the *zenana* (women's quarters) and the private reception halls and gardens of the Fort. She would also enjoy excursions to the many privately owned garden estates that lined the banks of the Yamuna River, and indeed in the seventeenth century Nur Jahan, Mumtaz Mahal, and the princess Jahanara owned some of these. However, these gardens were not an exclusive province of women, for the countless miniatures showing Mughal princes enjoying feasts laid out on carpets with floral motifs set amidst gardens indicate that the interest in nature, flowers, and landscape was by no means a strictly gendered taste. The floral motifs that were popular in embroidery and textiles also appeared in wall reliefs and book illustration; nature imagery permeated both the private and public realm and was enjoyed by men and women equally. Nonetheless, in the specific patronage of Nur Jahan, we can trace an especially keen personal taste for gardens and garden imagery that appears first in arts such as textiles and manuscript painting, next in the empress's own architectural commissions, and finally in her stepson's imperial Taj Mahal complex.

The technique of intarsia (the inlay of colored stone) seen in the interior and exterior of the Tomb of I'timad al-Daula has both indigenous and European sources (see Fig. 50).[7] In buildings of Akbar's reign (1556–1605) such as Humayun's tomb and the so-called Jahangiri Mahal at the Agra Fort, red sandstone was inlaid with white marble for a crisp linear effect. At the same time, there was a South Asian artisanal tradition of wooden objects and furnishings inlaid with ivory or lustrous shell. By the seventeenth century, however, the intarsia technique erupted in a brilliant color spectrum that is more reminiscent of sixteenth-century Florentine *pietra dura*.[8] Such finely wrought works could well have traveled from Italy to the Mughal court, for Nur Jahan had a keen eye for European goods and was given art, books, and other objects from visiting ambassadors wishing to curry favor. Furthermore, from as early as the 1580s, the Jesuits had played an important intermediary role, bringing Flemish prints such as the Antwerp Polyglot Bible to the Mughal court.[9]

The repertoire of images in the wall ornament at the Tomb of I'timad al-Daula derives in part from Persian architecture, where scenes of flasks, drinking cups, vases, flowers, and cypress trees often decorated the walls of garden pavilions and palace halls such as the early seventeenth-century 'Ali Qapu of Isfahan (Fig. 77).¹⁰ Nur Jahan was probably an important agent in the transmission of Persian motifs to the Mughal court, for she was born to a Persian family and, along with her father, brother, and other ranking members of the royal court, probably expressed that cultural identity in the family's collection of furnishings and art. The I'timad al-Daula wall images are highly stylized, two-dimensional, and perfectly symmetrical with an occasional folded blade of a narcissus to suggest naturalism. But a decade or so later at the Taj Mahal, the floral ornament had become much more elaborate and had a sophisticated verisimilitude. On the Taj's white marble exterior walls, rendered in panels of carved relief, the flowers seem swollen with life, petals drooping, slightly asymmetrical (Fig. 78), while on the screen surrounding the cenotaphs in the tomb's dim interior, incised floral ornament represents the stages of a flower's cycle with a subtlety of hue and meticulous detail that is clearly the result of careful observation.

In the medium of painting, individuated flowers set within framed panels appeared in the first quarter of the seventeenth century during the reign of Jahangir. Many of these are precisely rendered botanical representations that showed the various stages of the flower, from bud to spent bloom. The fact that these pictures did not appear prior to 1610 suggests that a particular source—European prints—inspired the new painting subject.¹¹ Portuguese Jesuit missionaries to India and agents of the East India Company brought prints with religious themes as well as botanical herbals and *florilegia* as gifts, which were received with interest by the members of the Mughal court who often then commissioned Mughal painters to make copies.¹² It has also been suggested that Jahangir's love of flora, which was awakened as a result of his spring trip to Kashmir in 1620 when he saw an abundance

FIGURE 77.
The 'Ali Qapu, a Sa-
favid pavilion that
served as the portal
from Isfahan's May-
dan-i Shah into the
palace precinct, had
a music room on
its uppermost floor,
the walls and ceil-
ing of which were
pierced with *chini
khana* niches in
the shape of vases
and cups. (Abbas
Aminmansour)

FIGURE 78.
The exterior walls
of the Taj Mahal
are decorated with
marble reliefs
with naturalistic
representations of
flowers, as if there
were no distinction
between architec-
ture and garden.

of beautiful flowering bulbs, prompted a new taste for painted flower portraits and floral images on decorative media (Fig. 79). Indeed, he spoke of the flowers and their illustrations in the same breath: "The flowers seen in the summer pastures of Kashmir are beyond enumeration. Those drawn by Master Nadirul'asri Mansur the painter number more than a hundred."[13] Or, Nur Jahan herself may have been the reason for the sudden appearance of such floral imagery: her marriage to the emperor and the earliest Mughal botanical painting occurred within a year.

FIGURE 79. From the reign of the Mughal emperor Shah Jahan, circa 1650, this exquisite enameled box is covered with images of red blooms on slender green-leaved stalks. The flowers extend ingeniously from the central handle, a three-dimensional bud set atop four broad leaves. (Freer Gallery of Art, Smithsonian Institution, Washington, D.C.: Purchase, F1986.22ab)

Whatever the catalyst, a new genre of painting arose in the early seventeenth century that consisted of individual flowers accurately depicted with foliage and flowers complete with stamens and bracts in various stages of the plant's life cycle.

The taste for flowers that appeared so suddenly in painting existed earlier in textiles such as woven and especially embroidered silk and cotton textiles that included tailored garments (ironically, the evidence for this comes from the representation of textiles in manuscript painting).[14] Although these were repeating motifs rather than singular flower portraits, the role of the textile medium is worth noting. As one of the most used and frequently traded commodities in the pre-modern world, textiles played a critical role in the transfer of motifs within the Islamic world and between it and its European and East Asian trading partners. In textiles, as in painting, there was both Indian artisanal expertise as well as a willing ability to copy the European and particularly English fabrics that were bestowed as diplomatic gifts, such as the embroidered coats, gloves, scarves, and hangings commissioned by Sir Thomas Roe for the East India Trading Company. In 1617 he wrote of Indian artisans, "They imitate everything wee bring, and embroder now as well as wee."[15]

Once floral motifs were introduced as a thematic focus in textiles and paintings, they changed from a subordinate, stylized element in architectural mural ornament that alternated with geometrical abstraction to a markedly different display of exuberant naturalism. Such transfers of motifs from one medium to another were common in the Islamic world: for example, the *muqarnas* (stalactite vaulting) is a form of complex Islamic ornament that was variously realized in plaster, stone, wood, and ceramic tile and was rendered both three-dimensionally as well as inscribed on nearly flat surfaces. With respect to the flower motif, there is a strong visual similarity between the type of embroidery known as *chikan kari* (possibly of Persian origins), made of a white thread on a white or pale fabric, and the white marble carvings on the exterior of the Taj.[16] The presence of floral motifs on the walls of the Taj Mahal united the architecture with the landscape in much the same way that Mughal (and Safavid) pleasure pavilions brought the garden into the building by means of wall decoration, carpets, and cushions with floral ornament. Whether seated indoors or outside, a person was surrounded by a parade of flowers as well as flowing water channels and fountains that blurred the distinction between architecture and nature. Therefore, in addition to the architecture of the tomb of I'timad al-Daula and the embroideries beloved by Nur Jahan and other members of the court, the Mughal experience with pleasure gardens also explains the design of the Taj Mahal in its garden.

Unlike previous imperial Mughal tombs, the Taj Mahal does not stand at the heart of its chahar bagh where the principal axes intersect. Instead, it presides from an elevated platform at one end of the enclosure so that the garden stretches horizontally between tomb and monumental gate as an intermediary space between two powerfully vertical foci rather than a defining frame that envelops a central tomb. The position of the tomb lengthens the garden axis, subtly redefining the four-part plan as a bilateral composition that emphasizes a linear view. This stress on a dominant axis reflects the Mughal experience of building garden estates in the mountain vales of Kashmir, at the very north of their territory, where they sought retreat from the heat and aridity during the summer months. Around Lake Dal and in nearby valleys, the Mughals built some 777 estates, of which Akbar's Nasim Bagh was the first.[17] These magnificently situated garden estates were used as pleasant resorts for courtly parties and did not serve as permanent residences; instead, the court stayed at Hari Parbat, the official residence, and sallied forth by boat or traveled along the lake's shore road to spend the day at a chosen garden. Kashmir provided a cool alternative to the oppressive heat of the plains where Delhi and Agra were located, but the business of the empire necessarily accompanied the emperor in his retreat. Hence, although the gardens did not have sleeping quarters, those made for the emperor had formal public reception halls (*diwan-i 'amm*) where affairs of state could be conducted. They were invariably terraced on sloping ground with canals fed by snowmelt running through the central axis down to the lake.

Shalamar Bagh, built by Jahangir in 1619–20 and augmented by Shah Jahan around 1630, consisted of two stepped chahar baghs descending to a smaller entry enclosure (Fig. 80; see Sites). The emperor gave audiences on the lowest terrace seated on a throne in the Diwan-i 'Amm that straddled the central water channel, lined with poplar and plane trees.[18] The middle garden was reserved for semi-private use, while the uppermost terrace was reserved for the women of the zenana. The wide channel that ran through all three terraces not only united the gardens along a single axis but literally connected the majestic Himalayan

FIGURE 80.
A broad central channel runs down the middle of Shalamar Bagh, Kashmir, the imperial Mughal pleasure garden near Srinagar. Flowing from one level to the next, the channel ran through pavilions and over tiered chini khana niches. Although planted with turf and islands of flowers in the late twentieth century, a seventeenth-century description of another Kashmir garden mentioned one hundred varieties of flower in a single parterre.

mountains to Lake Dal through the intermediary of Shalamar. Shah Jahan's biographer wrote that a boat could pass directly from the lake into the grounds of Shalamar.[19] The water that ran through the stone-lined channels was produced by the runoff of melting snow from high above; but even more, the dynamic flow provided a drama in which the protagonists were water and landscape. The chahar bagh was used here not as a unitary plan generated from a single center that gave emphatic placement to a tomb or pavilion, but as a repeating module that formed a rectangle along a central linear axis. The shift from centralized square to linear axis offered possibilities for hierarchies of hydraulics, design, and particularly vision that the Mughals, with their keen perception of the power of architectural statesmanship, appreciated and subsequently replicated back in their capital cities of Lahore, Agra, and Delhi.

The Nishat Bagh, which was the work of Nur Jahan's powerful brother Asaf Khan in 1625, was similarly poised between the peaks and lake, with its gardens and channels descending downward as if they were natural terraces and mountain rivulets. It was divided into twelve terraces and was bisected by an axial watercourse that cascaded over a differently textured chadar at each change of level, imitating the churning turbulence of a mountain stream (Fig. 81; see Sites). As in the Shalamar Bagh, the narrative of the Nishat gardens was entirely about landscape: the sequence of terraces, channels, and chadars that stretched from the vertiginous snow-capped Himalayas to the silvery lake below reproduced in an orderly, rational fashion the most thrilling elements of the Kashmir landscape.

The Mughal gardens of Kashmir offered the kind of topographical variety, plant varieties, and visual excitement that the plains of north central India lacked. Furthermore, the mountains provided a steady source of water in the form of runoff so that an elaborate hydraulic scheme that included jets, chadars, large pools, and waterfalls could be installed. Indeed, the Kashmir garden of Achabal (first half of the seventeenth century) had enough water for not simply one but three rushing channels (see Sites). In this way a northern garden style was developed at Kashmir that relied on distinct seasonal shifts for its brilliant spring flowers (and fall crocus) and an intensely varied topography for its hydraulic drama and spectacular contrasts.

However, when Shah Jahan tried to bring the Kashmiri garden style back to his palaces in the plains, he had to devise substitute mechanisms to create the dynamic water play and visual spectacle. In 1641 at Lahore, he began another garden estate called Shalamar Bagh that, like its Kashmir namesake, was built in stepped terraces so that the whole formed an elongated series of chahar baghs (see Sites). Each of the three terraces was built about five meters above the next and water was prominently displayed. More than one hundred jets played in the wide pool on the central terrace, and water channels ran down the center of the four-part gardens that occupied the other terraces (Plate 22). But unlike Kashmir, Lahore lacked natural water pressure and steep slopes. Its water came from a canal that the emperor had built eight years earlier in 1633 to supply first the city and Fort, and eventually the Shalamar garden.[20] In the absence of mountains, the elevation necessary for stepped esplanades and water flow was achieved by exploiting and enhancing the slightly raised terrain along the riverbank.

This period of adaptation, from 1633 to 1641, coincided with the construction of the Taj Mahal, where similar aesthetic ambitions for the drama and hydraulic dynamism that were en-

FIGURE 81.
The garden of Nishat Bagh, Kashmir, built in 1625 near Srinagar, elaborated the four-part concept beyond recognition. Instead of multiple chahar baghs, there are stepped terraces that descend from the foot of the mountain to Lake Dal.

joyed in Kashmir met the topographic and hydraulic limitations that were encountered in Lahore. At the Taj, the natural landscape of rugged peaks was missing, as was the downward rushing water that such elevations produced. Hence, pools, channels, and fountains were supplied by an elaborate system that consisted of linked rehants (shafts with multiple buckets on chains) that lifted water from the river to an aqueduct along the complex's western wall that flowed into storage basins. From here, pulleys raised the water to elevated tanks from where it could be released into the gardens.[21] Instead of the stepped levels of the Shalamar, Nishat, or Achabal gardens, the Taj consists of a single four-part plan, but it is extended by a forecourt at one end and a raised platform with the mausoleum at the other so that, like the Kashmir gardens, the garden is lengthened along a dominant axis that connects land with water, in this case not a lake but a river.

The mausoleum is further distanced from the garden by its elevation on a terrace. From this raised position, a viewer can survey the garden on one side of the Taj or walk around the tomb to regard the river and its opposite bank. The pleasure gardens of Kashmir similarly used elevations to create prospects of verdant landscape and water; however, there were precedents for gardens with riverside pavilions much closer at hand. In the seventeenth century, Agra's Yamuna River was lined with garden estates, many of which were renovations of sites established by Babur in the mid-sixteenth century (Fig. 82). One of these was the Ram Bagh (Bagh-i Nur Afshan), an older garden remodeled in 1621 by Nur Jahan (Fig. 83).[22] The Bagh-i Jahanara, created by Mumtaz Mahal and remodeled in 1620 by Jahanara, was another.[23] These and other estates could be reached by either boat or road.

FIGURE 82.
The Mughals developed the lands along the Yamuna River in Agra, claiming many of the choicest locations for their pleasure gardens. (Terry Harkness)

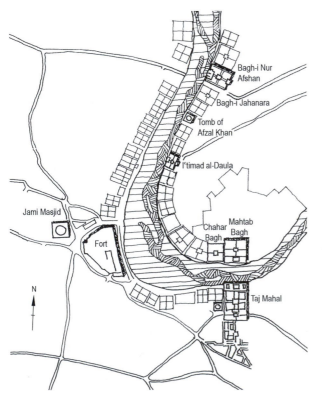

They were raised above the river by thick red sandstone retaining walls with chhatri-topped corner towers that permitted pleasant views onto the river and its lively boat traffic while at the same time providing a barrier sufficient to ensure visual privacy. Raised stone terraces along the river wall contained the principal pavilion buildings. The gardens themselves were situated at a lower level further inward, so that the water, which was lifted up from the river, filled the pool and channels on the stone terraces and then flowed over ornamental chadars to the lower garden level.

All the royal residential structures in the Mughal Forts in Agra and Delhi (and to a lesser extent, Lahore) had screened windows, projecting balconies, and rooftop cupolas that provided magnificent panoramas (Fig. 84). Within the Agra Fort enclosure, the Anguri Bagh (redesigned beginning in the early 1630s and completed January 1637), was positioned like the Ram Bagh: its three elegant pavilions stood on a high terrace along the palace's eastern wall (Fig.

86 and Plate 23). While the two smaller pavilions were private sleeping quarters and were separated from the Anguri Bagh by privacy walls, the largest and central of the three structures overlooked the four-part garden within the palace and also allowed panoramic views of the river through the partially screened windows of its outer walls.[24] Ebba Koch has showed that this type of waterfront garden, in which the pavilions were deliberately placed along the outer perimeter of the enclosure so that they offered both the panoramic view of river and the more contained, private view of the enclosed garden, was the model for the planning of the Taj Mahal and its garden.[25]

Although the actual planting and layout of the Taj garden beds have not been determined archaeologically, the stone-rimmed parterres seen today at the Taj also had precedents in earlier Agra gardens. The Taj beds are defined by red sandstone frames that form flower islands in the large expanses of turf (Fig. 85). There are more pronounced divisions made by paved borders in the shape of eight-pointed stars and elongated stars that run between the central water channel and the broad flanking walkways. These may have been filled with flowers. Eighteenth-century visitors to the garden described, in addition to cypress and orange trees, beds filled with carnations, red poppies, varieties of roses, and other flowers. By the British period, the records are more complete, but they also reflect a new garden taste.[26] Given the degree of British intervention in Mughal garden sites, and es-

pecially that of Lord Curzon himself (viceroy of India 1899–1905) at the Taj, it is often difficult to determine the originality of garden features. However, the parterres appear in nineteenth-century European paintings and prints of the Taj and similar parterres existed in other Mughal gardens in Agra. For instance, the quadrants of the Anguri Bagh were subdivided by even more ornate strips of stone that formed deep pockets penetrating approximately two meters into the ground (Fig. 86). More than mere surface tracery, the deep structure of the parterres is more

likely to be original fabric than a costly British rebuilding of an otherwise functioning garden.[27] Similar parterres are seen at the seventeenth-century Maunbari garden at the foot of the Amber Fort (Fig. 87). At the Lahore Fort, the Jahangiri Quadrangle has embedded stone paving articulating concentric rectangles that in the center frame a square pool with a fountain (Plate 24).

The inlaid stonework is unusual and seems to reflect an urge not to divide the space with neat garden beds but to embellish the ground surface with bold geometrical figures. In all of these, the stone framework of the parterres emphasizes the horizontal flatness of the garden surface so that flowers were organized in colorful masses that would have appeared as linearly defined swathes of color in an otherwise green field. The manuscript painting depicting Shah Jahan in the Nishat Bagh, discussed earlier (Plate 12), shows such segregation of plants, although they are disposed in plots that are square rather than ornately curvilinear. This is different from the traditional chahar bagh where the beds consisted of large quadrants within which flowers were planted in rows or scattered as if in a meadow.

The elaborately framed bed was a new phenomenon in Mughal India in the second quarter of the seventeenth century, and its appearance may be the result of international trade and artistic exchanges with Europe, such as Nur Jahan promoted. Indeed, a comparison can be drawn between the use of parterres in earlier French gardens such as Anet in Eure-et-Loir (1547) or the gardens of the Palais du Luxembourg in Paris (1615) and these Mughal examples.[28] The similarity is more than purely visual, because both societies were fascinated by textiles and the so-called decorative arts, and floral motifs that appeared first in cloth were soon applied to other media, including the garden. In Versailles (ca. 1657), the patterns of the *parterres de broderie* formed a lacy web and reflected designs used for knitted and printed fabric.[29] In the Mughal court, we have seen that Nur Jahan was an avid patron of both gardens and textile embroidery and printed patterns, some of which were made in India and others imported from Europe. While the theory remains hypothetical until the actual garden of the Taj has been studied archaeologically and its present quadri-

FIGURE 87.
Apparently afloat
in the lake made
by damming a
valley stream, the
Maunbari Garden
of Amber Fort is
comprised of mul-
tiple chahar baghs,
each organized in a
tight mesh of stone
parterres.

partite plan with curvilinear framing given an accurate date, one can speculate that new ideas in European garden style, such as the fancy scalloped parterre, may have arrived in the Mughal court hand in hand with other artistic techniques and motifs, such as pietra dura, narrative prints, and herbal manuals. Or, conversely, that the ornamental parterre was exported from India to the West along with the rich textiles and carpets that were so admired in Europe.[30] The chronology of the gardens is simply not clear enough to state categorically whether the idea of ornamental stone tracery, or the textile embroidery that inspired them, was of South Asian or European origin.

The design of the Taj reflected the experience of building earlier gardens along Agra's riverfront and in the mountains of Kashmir and may also have incorporated new ideas from Europe. However, it also responded specifically to the immediate landscape in ways that have been largely ignored by historians until the 1990s, when the Archaeological Survey of India and an archaeological team led by Elizabeth Moynihan undertook thorough investigations of the mysterious ruined garden on the Taj's opposite bank.[31] The site is the Mahtab Bagh, or Moonlight Garden, built between 1632 and 1643 while the Taj Mahal was also under construction (see Sites). Unfortunately, it was situated at the outward curve of the Yamuna River where the rising waters of the monsoon flood annually scoured the banks, overflowing disastrously in the fall of 1652, only a decade after its completion.[32] At some point in the seventeenth century it was abandoned altogether, perhaps because the effort to replant it after so many floods was recognized as futile, and its lovely fountains and pools were soon buried beneath several feet of silt.

The barely visible ruined walls of this garden gave rise to legends—recorded by European travelers from the seventeenth century to the present—that highlighted the Mughal patron's profound love, inconsolable grief, and megalomania in ways that satisfied the Western Orientalist desire to project excited emotions onto Eastern societies. Accordingly, the ruins were said to be the foundations of a planned twin tomb, the "Black Taj," from where the tomb of Shah Jahan would have gazed across the river to the gleaming white mausoleum of his beloved queen, Mumtaz Mahal. This romantic theme, however spurious, was recorded by the mid-seventeenth-century visitor Jean-Baptiste Tavernier, and it gained increasing popularity in later centuries.[33] The myth of the Black Taj may have endured in part because, while the Mahtab Bagh's ghostly ruins were visible from the north side of the Taj's terrace, hardly anyone actually went to the site (although a short distance away by boat, it cannot be reached by foot except through a circuitous route across a distant bridge).[34] As a result, for centuries visitors have projected a romantic narrative onto the "unattainable" Mahtab Bagh that echoes their own deeply passionate responses to the stunningly beautiful Taj.

The truth is that the Mahtab Bagh was not created to contain a tomb: it was a pleasure garden enjoyed for day outings, like the many other elite gardens that graced the banks of Agra's river throughout the Mughal era. However, it did have a visual kinship with the Taj, for the two complexes were built concurrently and seem to have been conceptualized in the same formal terms. The fact that the width of the Mahtab Bagh matches that of the Taj means that the rectangular plan of the Taj appears to bridge the river and achieve completion on the other side. Considered thus, the Taj occupies not one end of its own garden, but a central position between two gardens that are separated by a body of water, in much the same way that the two large chahar baghs at the Shalamar Bagh at Lahore were separated by a central terrace with a large pool. While the intervening river and the walls surrounding the Taj and the Mahtab Bagh prevented free movement between the two sites, they were united visually, for each was best seen from the elevated riverside terrace of the other.

The chhatris capping the low towers at either end of the Mahtab Bagh's riverfront walls provided roofed platforms where the garden's inhabitants could sit, gazing across the river, protected from direct sunlight yet cooled by the river's breezes. Like those within the Anguri Bagh's pavilion at the Fort, the people at the Mahtab Bagh could see the socially exclusive and carefully maintained grounds of the garden and, with a mere turn of the head, likewise regard the magnificent Taj and its silver reflection on the water's surface. The intercession of the river not only provided a suitable distance for mutual spectatorship, it also supplied a greater field of vision in which many of the imperial monuments of Agra were visually appreciated. The Agra Fort, for example, offers views of the opposite bank and the more distant Taj not only from the Khass Mahal pavilion of the Anguri Bagh but also from each one of the elite pavilions lining its river façade (Fig. 88). The palace pavilions, garden estates, and mausolea that lined both banks of the Yamuna River by the mid-seventeenth century all enjoyed long-range vistas up and down the river, each individual building providing a interior position for viewing outward—in the form of a window or chhatri–while at the same time serving as the destination for the vision generated from another pavilion, in a grand match of optical ping-pong. In this way, the river enhanced the display of highly valued real estate and social prominence as demonstrated in architectural patronage.[35]

The Taj Mahal was a funerary monument, but its gardens were characterized by worldly pleasure as well. For example, to mark the first anniversary of the death of Mumtaz Mahal, a commemoration ceremony was held in the gardens surrounding the tomb. Handsome temporary pavilions were erected and beautiful carpets were laid with platters of condiments, sweets, and other delectable foods. The feast was enjoyed by the nobles, dignitaries, and chief officers of the Mughal administration, led by Shah Jahan, and large sums were distributed to the poor of Agra.[36] Although this event, and the annual anniversary observances thereafter, were somber in purpose and were inaugurated by the reading of Qur'anic verses, the sight and consumption of the delicacies must have been delightful. Of course, there is nothing in the religious function of a funerary complex to preclude sensory pleasure: while the deceased savor succulent fruit and leisure beneath shady trees in paradise, the living are encouraged to dine and enjoy as well. The point is that, while the Taj's gardens were explicitly commemorative and redolent with eschatological connotation—a symbolic dimension emphasized by the mausoleum's Qur'anic inscriptions, which refer to the Day of Judgment, the fearsome greatness of God, and paradise—the gardens were also enjoyed as places for relaxation, set apart from the bustle of the markets just outside the tomb complex's gates, in much the same way as any of Agra's secular pleasure gardens. The distinctions between pleasure and tomb gardens were neither formal nor wholly functional.

At its simplest, the garden adopts the four-part plan as a way to facilitate irrigation and to express

FIGURE 88.
The Musamman Burj, Agra Fort, projects from the fort walls and rises well above the adjacent pavilions. The cupola's sublime panorama includes the Taj in the far distance.

fundamental concepts of rational order and territorial possession. Thus, the garden enables human patrons conceptually to both contain and imagine the landscape as a whole. But despite the enclosure walls and the artificiality of the water supply, plantings, and care bestowed on the garden, the landscape reasserts itself. The Taj's already enormous garden was subsumed within a much larger structure that included the river and the garden on the opposite bank, so that in addition to the great linear axis that was imposed from north to south, another more organic axis—the Yamuna River—ran east and west. Instead of forming a barrier, this river axis opened up possibilities for long-range views that extended beyond the discrete architectural entities of the Taj and the Mahtab Bagh, to address a continuously built and cultivated landscape. The union here of a commemorative garden, thoroughly imbued with paradisiac symbolism, with a garden intended for entertainment and ease, reveals the fluidity of garden meaning in this era.

11   Religion and Culture

The Adoption of Islamic Garden Culture by Non-Muslims

HE CLASSIC Islamic formal garden has distinctive characteristics that define it as Islamic, such as the cross-axial chahar bagh plan and ornamental elements such as the chadar and chini khana. To this can be added regional variations such as the pavilion opening to the garden through a portico of horseshoe arches in the Mediterranean (as in the Alhambra's Court of the Myrtles, see Plate 9, and Partal, see Fig. 45), the multicolumned talar pavilion in Iran (as in the Chihil Situn and the Palace of Mirrors in Isfahan, see Fig. 52), and the jali screen in South Asia (as in the Tomb of Jahanara in Delhi, see Fig. 75). Often these forms are associated with specific meanings: hence the chahar bagh plan is variously interpreted as a representation of the agricultural landscape or an earthly reflection of the four rivers of paradise, and the chadar represents a natural stream falling turbulently over a cataract. Gardens made by Muslim patrons using these forms are called Islamic, and they have an agreed upon set of meanings, although those meanings change along with the social practices and values of the patrons who employ them. The link between form and meaning is always a complicated matter, but it is simplified when form and meaning emerge from the same cultural and religious context. But how do we explain the meaning and social contextualization of gardens built by non-Muslims who employ a clearly "Islamic" set of forms?

Modern gardens such as the Viceroy's Palace gardens in New Delhi, designed by Sir Edwin Lutyens in the early twentieth century (see Sites), the Shangri La gardens made for Doris Duke near Honolulu, Hawai'i, in 1937–38 (Plate 25), and the 1987 Enid A. Haupt Garden at the Smithsonian in Washington, D.C. (see Sites) with its interpretation of an Islamic patio, are recognizably Islamic in their formal vocabulary, despite their modernist sensibilities. They are re-interpretations of Islamic architectural form, in each case by patrons and architects from a Western culture for whom Islam was a realm to be admired, exploited, and alternatively suppressed and collected. However, the adoption of Islamic art forms and techniques was not paralleled by a concomitant political acceptance—after all, Lutyens's design for the Viceroy's Palace was created at a time when India was subjugated to British colonial rule—nor did it reflect the adoption of other Islamic social practices or its religion. The borrowing was carefully researched and aesthetically successful, but it was largely formal, which begs the question of what occurred (and occurs) in the relationship between form and meaning when highly significant forms, such as the chahar bagh, were assimilated into cultures that did not embrace their original meanings.

This unequal shift in form and meaning was not purely a phenomenon of the twentieth century or the product of colonial relations that began more than a hundred years earlier. It occurs every time forms are exchanged between one culture and another: Islamic forms appeared in Byzantine palace gardens, mudéjar Spanish cloisters and palaces, Rajput India, and orientalizing fantasies such as the Royal Pavilion in Brighton (1803–32) and Frederic Edwin Church's Olana in Greendale-on-Hudson, New York (1870–91), just as Byzantine, Rajput, and modern European forms were assimilated into Islamic architectural vocabulary. In the Islamic world, the Rajput rulers' extensive patronage in South Asia offers many examples where Islamic forms were adopted, in some cases with the intention of displaying cultural affiliation with Mughal allies, and in others as a deliberate strategy of rivalry and resistance to Mughal hegemony. In both, Islamic forms that had been developed for Muslim patrons and a Muslim audience were now serving a very different clientele, begging the question of what those forms meant in their new non-Muslim context.

The previous chapter showed that the Mughals brought garden-making to a high art and enjoyed images of flowers and plants in a variety of media that extended the natural setting. Their Rajput contemporaries likewise built large palaces with gardened courtyards featuring pavilions, fountains, pools, sunken flower beds, and displays of flowering plants and trees both in the garden and on the walls of architectural structures. These can be seen at sites such as Udaipur, Orchha, Amber, and Dig, among others. At both Amber and Dig, the patrons embraced the four-part plan so that the palace's central garden appears thoroughly Mughal. The garden appears to have not only the dominant structure of an Islamic garden but also all of the meanings that the form expressed. However, the Rajput princes practiced Hinduism, and thus their adoption of Islamic forms could not have had the same kind of religious inflection as it did for Muslims—specifically references to paradise as promised to the faithful in the Qur'an.[1] What then was the meaning of a non-

FIGURE 89.
A mural painting of Ganesh, the Hindu god of new beginnings and successful outcomes, stands directly over the entrance to the Amber Fort's palatine quarters.

Muslim "Islamic" garden? The question is not merely terminological, for "Islamicate" already exists as a logical and useful alternative term;[2] rather, it asks the degree of attachment in the relationship between form and meaning. If the two are not inextricably bound to each other, then one of the historian's tasks must be to explore the meaning of a particular form in each of its historical moments and places.

The Amber Fort was built in the first half of the seventeenth century on a mountain above Jaipur (which did not yet exist) by the Rajput ruler Raja Man Singh (r. 1592–1615), one of the highest ranking members of the Mughal court. Rectangular in plan, it was built in successive stages, beginning with a large courtyard with high defensive walls at what is now the southwestern end of a much larger complex.[3] Mirza Raja Jai Singh I (r. 1623–67/8) extended it in 1623–28, building a handsome courtyard to serve as his own sumptuous quarters and beyond that a courtyard for public reception (see Sites). A monumental gate bearing an image of Ganesh, the elephant-headed god associated with auspicious beginnings and the removal of obstacles, marked the threshold between them (Fig. 89). A Hindu temple to Sila Devi stood in the western corner of a fourth, outermost courtyard, the Jaleb Chowk. However, while Hindu motifs announcing the patron's religious identity may have been explicit in the public reception court, in the raja's private courtyard Mughal architectural models were closely followed as a sign of political and cultural affiliation. The courtyard had an elaborated four-part garden plan with a central pool (Plate 26). Moreover, its position was elevated, for the palace as a whole stood on a hilltop above a stream that was dammed to create an artificial lake, following the typology of the classic Mughal waterfront garden at Agra and Lahore (the Delhi Fort was not yet constructed). The garden also used Mughal devices for the display of water: from the Sukh Nivas pavilion on the west side and the two-storied Jai Mandir with its glittering interiors of mirror mosaic on the east side of the garden, water poured down a chadar and over a panel of tiered niches (*chini khana*) to flow through channels of white marble toward the central pool that took the shape of an eight-pointed star (Fig. 90).

FIGURE 90. Water flows over the scalloped surface of a *chadar* in the Sukh Niwas pavilion of the Amber Fort, producing a cooling spray and a pleasing sound. The animation of water in the garden setting is the most visible sign of life.

The Islamic preference for privacy within the palace was respected while the exterior landscape was presented as a series of panoramic vistas. From the courtyard's Jai Mandir (comprised of the Jess Mandir on the lower floor and the Jas Mahal on the upper), palace residents could behold dramatic landscape views from screened windows that blocked the sunlight and heat yet allowed the passage of air. Looking outward from a chhatri atop the Jai Mandir's roof terrace, the palace residents could see magnificent mountains on the opposite side of the valley and, below, the elaborate parterres of the Maunbari Garden that projected into the artificially dammed lake (see Fig. 87). Despite its construction in three stepped terraces, this lower garden is strikingly planar with a network of low stone borders that define the garden beds. These were surely intended to be read from above, from the perspective of the Jai Mandir's belvedere. In other words, the Maunbari Garden was designed for a specific vantage point so that garden and belvedere, although separate structures, were united in a single visual field. The idea of a coherent visual field that unites architecture and landscape demonstrates the power of architecture to reach far beyond itself, and it was also a characteristic of Mughal architecture.

In the first half of the twentieth century, the historians Percy Brown and Hermann Goetz speculated that the use of the Mughal style at Amber and similar Rajput palaces was due to the presence of craftsmen trained previously by the Mughal Emperor Akbar. Giles Tillotson countered that such arguments emerge from the "insistence on the primacy of Indo-Islamic over Hindu styles" and urged instead an acknowledgment of the semi-auton-omous Rajput school of craft and architecture that existed alongside the Mughal styles.[4] These views differ with respect to the explanations they offer, yet both rely on a zeitgeist concept of architecture in which patrons and architects "contribute" to large architectural movements. Although architecture can be analyzed without ever referring to the individu-als who laid the brick and carved the sandstone, such an explanation masks the fact that elite buildings were constructed by traditionally trained yet diverse artisans and commis-sioned and used by people who wished to express personal preferences and complex po-litical affiliations, as well as to impress rival rulers, enemies, and clients (family members, dependents, and subjects of the lands they governed). If we adopt the perspective of the patrons and inhabitants of these buildings, we can look beyond the measurement of in-cremental stylistic changes in stone fabric and ornamental overlay and instead explore the meaning of those forms to the people who paid to have them built.

The garden at the Amber Fort used the same architectural vocabulary as gardens in the forts of Agra and Lahore, but the religion of the patrons indicates that the architecture was understood according to a different set of values. Because followers of Hinduism prac-ticed cremation rather than burial, they did not construct tombs and thus did not use the quadripartite garden form to evoke paradise. In Hindu cosmology, there is a continuum of life but no afterlife per se. Life is a repeated cycle of successive reincarnations until the spirit breaks through the world of the bodily sense and achieves a blissful state of nothing-ness. Thus, if there were any paradisiac meaning to a Rajput garden's use of the chahar bagh plan, it could only have been in the sense of a popular literary cliché stripped of specific theological reference.

However the realm of religion may have separated them, Hindus and Muslims could and did contribute equally to literature, art, and culture so that by the end of the sixteenth century, Mughal court culture was thoroughly hybridized.[5] The Rajput Kachhwaha dy-nasty of Amber served in high positions in the Mughal political administration—Raja Man Singh had been raised in the Mughal court and was one of Akbar's most trusted administrators[6]—and married their daughters into the Mughal house with the result that the two families had not only similar political ambitions but also a shared genealogy. The Kachhwahas were enmeshed with the Mughals to a degree that far exceeded any other Rajput dynasty, and it was probably in this sense of reflecting common cultural goals that the Islamic garden form acquired its most salient meaning for the Kachhwaha patrons in

FIGURE 91.
The Anand Mandal garden in front of the Rai Praveen pavilion in Orchha had several ornamental basins (foreground) and a grid of sunken cavities where plants and probably small trees were grown. Without trees to shade the extensive pavement, the radiant heat would have been unpleasant.

particular. Thus, when Mirza Raja Jai Singh adopted the chahar bagh at the Amber Fort, it was not a paradisiac symbol expressing the Islamic concept of life after death but a sign of his political affiliation with the Mughal ruling house.[7] This relationship was not one of subordination: rather, just as his political support was badly needed by the Mughals who saw no contradiction in forming strategic and personal alliances with powerful Rajput rulers, Mughal artistic forms were likewise appreciated and integrated into Raja Jai Singh's personal taste without any sense of incongruity.

South of Delhi was Orchha, founded as the capital city of the Bundela clan in 1531. The citadel stood on an island in the Betwa River, protected by this natural moat, a series of fortification walls beyond the citadel, and strategic alliances made with the Mughals. The greatest of the clan's architectural patrons was Bir Singh Deo (r. 1605–27), who built the last of the citadel's three major palaces, the so-called Jahangiri Mahal. At the foot of this palace on the north side was a residential pavilion, possibly built by Indramani (1672–75) for that patron's favorite, the poetess Rai Praveen (Fig. 91).[8] However, neither the pavilion nor the garden which it overlooks has been archaeologically studied, and it is quite likely that the garden complex was built at the same time as the Jahangiri Mahal itself, between 1610 and 1620.

The Rai Praveen complex was a walled enclosure with the principal pavilion—two-storied with rooftop chhatris and a basement—overlooking the Anand Mandal Bagh, a garden divided into two unequal portions. Although the river was not far away, there is no view of it from the pavilion or the Jahangiri Mahal. Water for the garden was obtained from three wells, one within the enclosure and two outside its walls. Due to the river's proximity, the water level is relatively high in Orchha, and these wells must have produced more than enough to irrigate the garden. Water conservation was also achieved by the use of a packed mortar surface that covered all but the actual planting beds of the garden. The beds were octagonal concavities that were deep enough for flowers and probably shrubs and small trees (but I was not able to determine if they had mortar floors or not). Water flowed to each through underground channels, and human movement was guided by raised pathways. The slightly elevated terrace in front of the pavilion was used for dancing.

West of the citadel and across the river, the Jujhar Singh Palace contained a similar garden. The palace was built by Jujhar Singh (1627–63), but the garden was laid out by Madhukar Singh (r. 1554–92) and finished or renovated by Bir Singh Deo in the early seventeenth century.[9] Overlooked by a two-story pavilion, the Palki Mahal, the Phul Bagh likewise had octagonal beds set within a hard surface and a system of pathways raised slightly above it. The fact that Bir Singh Deo was a common agent in the planning of both the Jahangiri Mahal and the Phul Bagh suggests that the Anand Mandal Bagh and Rai Praveen pavilion may date to his reign, rather than later.

Neither the gardens nor the rigidly symmetrical square palaces of Orchha evince Mughal architectural taste. Although Bir Singh Deo enjoyed amicable relations with Jahangir, this is reflected only in the name of his largest architectural work, not in its style. Clearly, for this clan of rulers, architectural works were an expression of autonomous Bundela identity and not a measure of their political investment in the Mughal empire. Therefore, unlike the Kachhwahas of Amber, their style of architecture and gardens did not reflect Mughal aesthetic values. This comparison between the Kachhwahas and the Bundelas suggests that Rajput architectural style was a simple and direct reflection of political alliance and dependence, which it was not. The powerful Kachhwahas may have served in Mughal imperial administration, but when they adopted a Mughal garden type for their principal palace it was not an indication of subordination to a dominant culture. Rather, it demonstrated that, at least by the early seventeenth century (and arguably already in the sixteenth century), such forms as the chahar bagh were available to everyone, regardless of religious affiliation.[10]

The political allegiances of the Mewar kingdom, ruled by the Rajput Sisodias, were quite different, and to the extent that their architecture and gardens shared a formal vocabulary with the Mughals, it was in a stridently competitive rather than cooperative spirit.[11]

FIGURE 92. The gridded garden beds in the middle of this early eighteenth-century Amar Vilas courtyard in the City Palace, Udaipur, are divided into polylobed pockets. The planting is far more disciplined than Mughal gardens of the previous century.

Of the Rajput clans, the Sisodias were one of the most successful in resisting Mughal hegemony, so much so that when the "damn Rana" (as Rana Amar Singh of Mewar was called in Jahangir's autobiography) finally submitted in 1614, Jahangir exclaimed, "Good news!" and wrote, "I turned my face in supplication to the divine court and knelt down in thanks."[12]

When the Sisodias had been forced by Akbar from the Chittorgarh Fort in 1567, they had selected Udaipur as their new capital. The site's rugged topography provided a natural defense, and water was supplied by damming a stream to form Lake Pichola. A great palace was built next to this lake on a rocky hilltop and extended and renovated by successive Sisodia rulers. At its topmost story, the City Palace opens to the sky in a gardened courtyard built by Amar Vilas (r. 1698–1710) and known by his name (Plate 17). On north side is the Badi Mahal pavilion with a large sunken tank in its floor that was used for bathing, a surrounding arcade of cusped arches, and outer walls pierced by projecting jharoka windows that enjoy magnificent vistas of the landscape, lake, and town at the palace's foot. On the south side of the Amar Vilas are the Badi Chatur Chowk, surrounded by pavilions with rooftop chhatris, and the stunning Peacock Court (Mor Chowk) with richly colored glass mosaics in high relief representing peacocks in a full display of plumage on the lower level, and a jharoka balcony projecting to the interior of the courtyard on the upper level flanked by images of trees and standing nobles.

The Amar Vilas courtyard consists of a symmetrical grid of twelve sunken garden beds arrayed around a central square pool (Figs. 92 and 93).[13] The rectangular beds are shaped by paved walkways that lead from the walkway running around the pool's perimeter to the raised pavement of the cusped arcade that surrounds the courtyard. Within the rectangular plots is a secondary grid of nine sunken polylobed cavities to which the actual plantings are restricted. Despite the limited size of the planting basins, some of them are planted with tall trees whose root structure must extend well below the surface and into the naturally elevated ground that supports this level of the palace.

A painting on cloth shows a formal reception hosted by Rama Sangram Singh II (r. 1710–34) in the Badi Mahal overlooking the Amar Vilas court peopled by his own courtiers, European visitors, musicians, and a large cat (possibly a chee-tah).[14] Although the size of the courtyard is exaggerated, the rendering of the rectangular plots containing sunken polylobed garden beds is well observed. Most of the beds surrounding the central pool are shown to contain trees; a white stone barrier fences off the south end of the courtyard; and slightly larger but similarly polylobed shapes surrounding the garden appear to be water basins.

This is not a garden that adheres to Mughal style. The preference at Orchha and Udaipur for a predominantly hard surface (hardscape) alleviated by small pockets of earth and vegetation is distinctly different from the traditional Mughal garden in which the paved paths do no more than delineate an otherwise permeable and cultivated earth. Yet the organization of the rectangular plots is reminiscent of a quadripartite chahar bagh plan; the emphasis on geometrical symmetry as well as the disciplined balance between vegetation and water are quintessential characteristics of Islamic gardens; and the panoramic view from this high courtyard to the lake below hearkens to the Mughal preference for elevated riverfront gardens. Rajput patrons such as the Sisodias of Udaipur clearly observed the garden practices of their Muslim and Rajput

FIGURE 93. On the Udaipur City Palace's topmost terrace, the Amar Vilas rises from natural rock foundations. At its center is a square pool, surrounded by twelve garden beds divided into nine scalloped cavities. The Badi Mahal projected from the northern walls, offering magnificent views of landscape and lake.

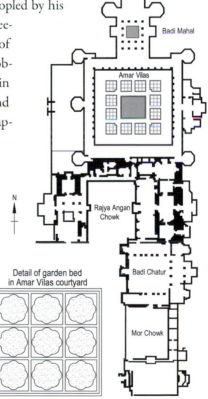

FIGURE 94.
The beds in the quadrants of the Anguri Bagh, Agra Fort, are not formed by stone borders laid upon the surface but are, in fact, deep cavities, as this excavation reveals.

neighbors, but—perhaps as a reflection of their hostile relations with the Mughals—they disdained slavish imitation and instead creatively manipulated the forms of the traditional Islamic garden in a way that made their patronage visibly distinct.

In the Rajput cities of Orchha and Udaipur, the main palaces are fortresslike and self-contained and very little of their interior space is given over to gardens (although in Udaipur, numerous other nondefensive and relatively open recreation palaces were constructed in and around the lake). Where gardens were created, they departed from the chahar bagh type of sunken quadrants of low vegetation traversed by linear walkways and, in Orchha, the Mughal predilection for distant views of water from framed windows. However, it was not just that the Rajputs borrowed from Mughal sources: there were lively exchanges in both directions and the Rajput style of planting in packed mortar cavities may in turn have influenced Mughal gardening. For example, at the Agra Fort the Anguri Bagh's chahar bagh is subdivided by elegant stone borders that form an undulating tracery (see Fig. 86). They are read by the viewer as a purely superficial articulation, but in January 2003 I was fortunate to see several of those beds entirely emptied of their contents (Fig. 94). It was apparent that the tracery capped a wall that extended approximately two meters to the depth of each bed, which was floored with packed mortar. The beds were fed by channels that flowed at a depth just below the tracery, less than a half meter below surface level.[15] Although the appearance of the gardens was dissimilar, with no emphasis on extensive hardscape surfaces at Agra, the technique of cultivating vegetation in contained beds was the same in both the Anguri Bagh and Orchha's Rai Praveen garden.

The Anguri Bagh was the work of Shah Jahan between 1628 and 1637; the Orchha gardens, although insecurely dated, are most likely the work of Bir Singh Deo between 1605 and 1627; and Udaipur belongs to end of the seventeenth century. The chronology is sketchy at best, and it is not clear whether the containment method of cultivation was developed first in a Rajput or Mughal context. Given that the laborers and architects who served the Mughals included both Muslims and Hindus and that these could move between architectural projects, such transfers of technique occurred constantly. Certainly in the seventeenth century there is evidence that the same artisans worked on both the Rajput and Mughal constructions, for in 1637 a royal decree mandated that all marble cutters cease work in Amber and move to Agra to serve the emperor.[16] Indeed, the Mughal adoption of India's local red sandstone and Indic forms such as serpentine brackets, the pot-and-vine motif, the chhatri, the *bangla* (curved) roof, and stepwells with angular flights of stairs for collecting and retrieving water has been documented in architectural studies. And similarly, in these pages we have observed the Hindu adoption of such typically Islamic forms as the chahar bagh garden and chadar, and the new function of the chhatri as a commemorative monument. The point here is to highlight the fact that when material and visual interactions occur with such frequency, the Muslim and Hindu contexts begin to look more and more alike until we can speak of a single South Asian visual culture characterized by a great many shared forms and habits, yet within which the boundaries of religious difference were observed, maintained, and for the most part tolerated.

Due to the loss of autonomy under colonial rule, the political conditions in South Asia changed radically from the eighteenth into the first half of the twentieth century, but nonetheless Islamic forms were again borrowed and used to express concepts and aspects of cultural identity that differed greatly from those of Islam. Now, in addition to Muslim and Hindu patrons creating Islamicate gardens, the British entered the scene, constructing their own versions of gardens that variously embraced and rejected Islamic forms. The expressive content of the garden was not only addressed to a new audience; it also could differentiate its Hindu or Muslim patron from that new set of European patrons through historical references to the Indian past.

The palace at Dig (or Deeg, northwest of Agra) was built in 1760 to adorn the new capital of the Jat kingdom of Bharatpur which had been established in the second quarter of the eighteenth century, a period of relative independence among Hindu and Muslim kingdoms marked by a burst of building activity.[17] This family had a long history of hostile relations with the Mughals—in one revolt they were reputed to have pillaged Akbar's tomb in Sikandra—during which the Mughals united with the Kachhwahas against other dynasties such as the Jats.[18] The Dig palace consists of a central garden block that extends between two artificial lakes, the square Rup Sagar on the east and the rectangular Gopal Sagar on the west. The garden is laid out as a chahar bagh with immense sunken quadrants that are formed by an axial walkway stretching from the residential Gopal Bhawan that commands the space from an elevated terrace at the west end, and the more ornamental Kesav Bhawan at the opposite end (Plate 16). The raised walkway that forms the cross axis joins the Nand Bhawan on the north side to the Kishan Bhawan on the south. The walkways flank broad channels with water jets, a magnificent form of dynamic hydraulic display developed earlier in the Mughal gardens in Kashmir. Not only does the water irrigate the gardens, it merges with architectural structures, running through and three-quarters of the way around a pavilion such as the Keshav Bhawan so that the latter functions both as a hall and an enlarged fountain. With the lakes at the east and west ends, augmented by additional garden pools and rooftop tanks, water was in ample supply. Indeed, water is a central theme of the Dig palace: the balconied pavilions not only stand at the water's edge but project onto its surface like the prows of ships (Fig. 95). The Sawan and Bhadon pavilions, flanking the Gopal Bhawan, were named for the seasons of the monsoon—a trope also seen in the Mughal's Delhi Fort (but learned from Indic models)—and their roofs were especially designed to resonate with the downpour.

The Gopal Bhawan is the grandest and most imposing of the pavilions. It stands on a terrace that is elongated by secondary quadripartite gardens to either side. The garden at the south end is overlooked by the graceful Suraj Bhawan which also overlooks a similar but more private chahar bagh on its opposite side. The Suraj Bhawan and its gardens en-

FIGURE 95.
The main axis of the
Dig Palace (built
largely 1756–68)
stretches between
two artificially
excavated lakes
and at either end,
pavilions project
over the water. The
Bhadon pavilion,
seen in the fore-
ground, and its twin
were named for
the seasons of the
monsoon—a theme
that ran throughout
this palace.

joyed greater privacy and smaller scale because it served as the women's quarters of the palace. The terrace of the pavilion is carved with chini khana niches which provide a spatially
textured backdrop to the jets of water spurting from marble basins. The ornament of this
pavilion—white marble with colored inlay—visually extends the garden theme so that not
only the beds but even the walls are vividly adorned with flowers and themes from nature
(Fig. 96). One can imagine carpets with floral motifs spread on the floor of the pavilion, art
and nature presented seamlessly as though there were no difference—indeed, for the audience in such a palace of meticulously designed gardens, there may have been none.

It is ironic that the Jats would have chosen a Mughal vocabulary for their principal
palace because their relationship with the Mughals had been hostile since a revolt at end
of seventeenth century and their seizure of Agra in the early eighteenth century.[19] Indeed,
Dig's mighty defensive walls with wide moats had been built to withstand Mughal on-
slaughts, and in the early nineteenth century they helped Dig withstand a British siege. But
in the second half of the eighteenth century, Mughal garden forms such as multiple chahar
baghs, chini khana, pools with jets, and pavilions overlooking landscape and lakes, were adopted not as an expression of contemporaneous political affiliation but as a quotation of an
already fading style. The Mughal Empire was in decline, replaced by an even more powerful British stranglehold on political and economic power, and yet the association with the
Mughal past served to convey an authority and a cultural prestige from a bygone era that
present political conditions could not provide. As at the Amber Fort, the Hindu character
of the Dig palace was by no means hidden: to the contrary, it was made explicit by the
dominance of the great tanks and the marble swing that straddled the central axis of the
garden.[20] Tanks were key elements in not only Islamic palaces but also Indic architecture
because bodies of water, whether natural or manmade, were regarded as sacred places associated with creation, regeneration, purity, and even the presence of the gods themselves.[21]
The swing was used in the popular Teej Festival and appeared in one of the love stories from

the great Sanskrit epic, the *Ramayana*, as a metaphor for the anticipation of the monsoon and erotic longing. The fact that a chahar bagh garden could become the setting for a popular Hindu narrative was emblematic of Indian culture in the eighteenth century and suggests that by this point, Islamicate forms such as the chahar bagh were not associated directly with Islam but had become thoroughly domesticated South Asian forms.

In contrast, some later palace patrons chose a European style that subsumed or denied the regional visual and botanical history of the Indian subcontinent. Such an example is the huge Lakshmi Vilas Palace in Baroda (Vadodara) (1878–ca. 1890), designed by the British architects Major Charles Mant and Robert Chisholm. The palace as a whole retains the traditional distinction between public, private, and zenana quarters, but it is surrounded by an extensive turf lawn that is reminiscent of a British park (Fig. 97), and inside, one of the courtyards resembles a Roman atrium with an oval pool surrounded by large-scale nude or classically draped sculptures.[22] The Jagatjit Palace in Kapurthala (the Punjab, finished 1908), designed by the Beaux-Arts architect M. Marcel, displayed a Mansard roof and classical ornament such as decorative urns and statuary.[23] The Sikh builder of this palace, Jagatjit Singh (1890–1947), was a europhile whose grandfather had sided with the British at the time of the mutiny in the mid-nineteenth century, and his "French chateau in the plains of the Punjab" satisfied his fantasy of being a latterday Louis XIV.[24] This palace embraced neither Mughal nor British models but instead adopted a distinctly European style as a bid to secure European status through emulation. Unlike the Jats of Dig, these later Indian princes no longer sought to affiliate themselves visibly with the Mughals because by then the Mughals had lost not only power but also prestige. The Mughals had declined to the extent that in 1803 the British General Gerard Lake had entered Delhi as conqueror and taken the Fort from the aged and blind emperor Shah Alam who was given a paltry stipend and reduced in rank to "King of Delhi." The bloody mutiny in 1857 on the part of younger Mughal claimants to the throne failed, and the last Mughal ruler died in exile in 1862. In 1877 Queen Victoria was declared Empress of India. From this point onward, many Indian princes began to express cultural prestige by adopting European signs of affluence and taste.

FIGURE 96.
The delicate marble inlay of colorful flowers at Suraj Bhawan, Dig Palace, emulated similar stone intarsia at the Taj Mahal more than a hundred years earlier.

FIGURE 97.
The architecture
of Lakshmi Vilas,
Baroda, built
between 1878
and 1890 by British
architects, makes
clear reference to
its Indian context,
but its English-style
landscape of turf
and statuary
does not.

In general, the British themselves preferred European to Indian forms in their architecture and landscape design. The selection of New Delhi as the new capital to replace Calcutta was announced in 1911, and the plan that was drawn up by Sir Edwin Lutyens and Sir Herbert Baker was intended to emulate great urban projects such as Paris and Washington, D.C. Just as the Champs-Elysées linked the three major nodes of the Louvre, Egyptian obelisk, and Arc de Triomphe, New Delhi's imperial avenue, today known as the Raj Path, ran from the Viceroy's residence to the Jaipur Column and culminated in the All India War Memorial Arch (begun in 1921). The Viceroy's residence (today the President's Palace, or Rashtrapati Bhawan) was intended to enunciate imperial power and authority by evoking European classicism, and yet since the shift from Calcutta to Delhi was a strategy intended to punish Calcutta for the uprising of 1905 and to woo disenchanted Muslims, the architecture and landscape vocabulary had to include recognizable and specific Indian references.[25] But for Lutyens, it was not a matter of "capturing Indian details and inserting their features, like hanging pictures on the wall."[26] He sought an integrated style, which was praised in 1931 as "a fusion of East and West . . . 'a double magnificence.'"[27]

The Viceroy's Palace contained an extensive designed landscape with a formal garden that was neither British nor Mughal but a modernist vision that responded to both traditions. The garden was designed by Sir Edwin Lutyens with W. R. Mustoe serving as the Director of Horticulture.[28] The palace stands on a low hill as a climax to the Raj Path, which runs through the new city. This axis reappears on the west side of the palace where it drives through and unites Mughal-style gardens, tennis courts, and a walled circular garden with a central pond and plantings in the European style (see Sites).

The Mughal garden was organized around a large central square of turf that provided an area for diplomatic receptions and parties where Europeans and a select list of Indian princes were served gin and tonic by uniformed Indian servants. Around this lawn was a geometric system of cultivated beds and broad water channels that were clearly inspired by the chahar bagh (Fig. 98). Lutyens had made a careful study of the gardens of Kashmir and the Agra and Delhi forts in preparation for the Viceroy's Palace commission,[29] and so not only in the plan but also in its details, the garden was designed to evoke the aesthetic of a Mughal garden. In some places the channels were spanned by flat slabs of stone, as seen in the Shalamar Bagh in Kashmir; the incised texture of the stonework over which water flowed recalled variously a traditional chadar as well as the variegated marble inlay lining the channel flowing from the terrace of the Anguri Bagh in Agra's Red Fort. At the intersections of the channels there were great fountains in which the Indic motif of the lotus was suggested by eighteen overlapping sandstone disks. At various points, the edges of the channels were stepped like the ghats lining the Ganges in Varanasi or the sacred tank of any Indic temple or sacred site. The overriding sense of the garden was modern and rational—even the trees encircling the central lawn were subordinated to severe pruning to produce perfectly spherical shapes—and yet it was achieved, like the architecture of the palace and attendant buildings, through the selective quotation of earlier Indian forms that, to the British, had appeared irrational and medieval.

This portion of the garden at the Viceroy's Palace is clearly a commentary or reinterpretation of a Mughal garden design; yet the attached tennis courts and lawn for cocktail parties asserted the taste of the colonial inhabitants for whom the gardens were made. In a bizarre functional twist, the lawn in the heart of the chahar bagh occupies the traditional position of the mausoleum in tomb complexes such as Humayun's tomb and garden, located nearby. The plan is similar, but the function and sociopolitical meaning could not have been more divergent. Yet, was the British colonial appropriation of Indian forms in New Delhi any different from the appropriation of Islamicate forms at the Dig Palace? And was the inclusion of a lawn for entertainment and cocktails here so very different from the kinds of public displays and private pleasures that occurred in the Shalamar Bagh in Kashmir?

The question returns us to the vexing problem of the extent to which a design vocabulary can be moved from one site to another and the extent to which the meaning is changed or lost in the process. Is garden-making sufficiently attached to a place that, even though the style may reflect the colonial conditions of the period, the mere fact of a garden's location in Delhi makes it part of South Asian heritage? Can material and visual forms such as the chadar and lotus motif be employed in new social contexts and still retain some or all of the meaning ascribed to them by the culture that produced them? If a person can don exotic garb without changing his or her

FIGURE 98. In the British colonial capital, New Delhi, Edwin Lutyens designed the Viceroy's Palace (now the Rashtrapati Bhawan) and its extensive gardens with specific references to South Asian architecture and garden design: abstract chadars and lotus-shaped fountains in a design characterized above all by symmetry and axiality. (Amita Sinha)

fundamental identity—and the British in India (and Europeans throughout the Middle East) loved to have their portraits painted thus—can a garden similarly be cloaked in exotic forms and still retain the identity of its maker?

The issue begs the question of patronage and place: a garden belongs to a particular place that derives its character from local flora, seasonal precipitation and climate conditions, and geological landforms that can be altered but not completely obliterated. The sense of place that one finds in a garden is the result of those conditions, and indeed Islamic gardens have long been explained by erudite scholars and popular writers as a response to the desert's aridity.[30] This perspective would demand that gardens such as Doris Duke's Shangri-La in Hawai'i and the portion of the Enid A. Haupt garden that is attached to the Sackler Gallery at the Smithsonian in Washington, D.C., be disqualified as Islamic gardens because they lack an elusive but fundamental feature that could define them as Islamic. An alternative point of view would assess garden meaning not in terms of place but rather the intentions of the patron, thus disqualifying the Mughal gardens of the Viceroy's Palace as well as the gardens of the Amber Fort and Dig Palace, since none of those were built by Muslims or patrons who wished to express Muslim beliefs. Or perhaps we can dispense with essentializing definitions that serve to limit meaning and assign the cultural positions that result invariably in an "us" and a "them," and instead discuss Islamic culture as a nearly worldwide phenomenon with architectural and landscape manifestations in a great many cities and places, some of which are not manifestly Islamic, and that are appreciated by patrons and audiences comprised of Muslims, both observant and not, and non-Muslims. With such a view, the question shifts from "Is a colonial British garden or a modern American garden Islamic?" to the more important question of what prompts us to pose such a query in the first place.

It may be self-serving for someone whose cultural formation occurred in the West to demand that Islamic gardens be viewed, not as a means of stabilizing a particularly Islamic cultural or Muslim identity, but as expressions of memory, place-making, humankind's position in the great cosmos, the imagination, rationality, political power, and the yearning for eternity. And yet, it is precisely by refusing to simplify these exquisitely beautiful, conceptually sophisticated, and diverse gardens to the level of a single meaning or identity that they can be permitted their full resonance.

If in the pages of this book, religion is not granted an omnipotent role in shaping the parameters of Islamic culture, it is because in societies where there was sufficient tolerance to allow minority (and sometimes majority) communities of Christians, Jews, Hindus, and Buddhists to flourish, religion alone is inadequate to explain artistic and intellectual achievement. Because some of the great Islamic gardens were not built by Muslims, an explanation for this diverse production and reception is needed. The Islamicate gardens of South Asia made by Rajput princes and Englishmen, as well as the mudéjar gardens of Spanish palaces and cloisters, and some highly respectable contemporary landscape design by British, French, and American architects for Muslim patrons in countries like Oman and Saudi Arabia, suggest that identity can be difficult to "place." Once the conversation is opened to include such sites and patrons, how can we talk about "the Islamic garden"? For the term and the perspective that it embodies, there is as much lost as is gained by the strategy of naming. Of course, it can be useful to insist on a simple yet clear identity when lobbying for the inclusion of Islamic studies in educational curricula or the inclusion of a few—lamentably few—major works of art and architecture in introductory surveys of art or landscape history. But the inevitable risk is that, in so doing, a few monuments or texts will be mistakenly viewed as sufficient to represent the breadth and complexity of Islamic history and civilization.

The presentation of Islamic gardens and landscape in this book has intentionally avoided the narratival structure in which gardens appear to emerge chronologically as a coherent body in a culturally unified field, changing only in response to specific catalysts such as invasions, innovations, or changes in dynasty. There is no single narrative to explain the thousands of connected events that comprise the histories of the Islamic societies that together constitute the Islamic world. Narrated histories that attempt to do this invariably fall into the trap of competing claims *within* Islam: for example, is the history of nineteenth-century Tunisia an Arab or a Turkish story? Is Mughal India an extension of Timurid Iran, does it emerge from the already well established sultanates of Delhi, or is it an acculturative mediation between Hindu Rajputs and new as well as old Muslims? How do we find evidence from everyday culture to counterbalance the narratives that the court chroniclers and biographers themselves insist upon, guided by political motivations to justify and exalt that are as complex and self-serving as the prejudices of modern-day historians?

Gardens and landscape are the result of ordinary decisions made on a relatively small scale. If in this book I often discuss garden-making from the perspective of wealthy patrons building for monumental sites, it is in large part because those are the gardens that survived or at least were described. Utilitarian waterworks, such as those in Umayyad Syria, and more ordinary gardens such as those at Fustat are included—even though there is little to be seen at those sites today—because they are as essential to the historical picture as the more elaborate, well-preserved, and visually stunning gardens of the elite. Instead of drawing a linear path from one great monument to the next, I have addressed the conceptualization of gardens, both tangible and fanciful, and the practical construction of gardens by means of an agricultural apparatus. Somewhere between the real and ideal, the spiritual and the worldly, and the quotidian and the extraordinary, lies not "the Islamic garden" but a limitless number of gardens built (or imagined) in Islamic societies to sustain the body, inspire the mind, express individual and social values, and represent identities. The gardens themselves are as diverse as the bodies, minds, values, and identities of the people who made and enjoyed them.

List of
Gardens and Sites

ARDEN SITES OF singular historical importance or unique character have entries here as well as representative landscape architecture types for which there are many examples (such as Ottoman cemeteries, Mughal garden estates in Kashmir, and nineteenth-century suburban mansions in Tunisia). The sites are listed geographically by region, from west to east, and within each of those categories they are listed alphabetically by city (or area) and site name. The list is not exhaustive; the intention is to provide an overview of the major sites and styles.

The short bibliography that follows each description gives sources in English where available as well as critical sources in other languages. It does not include primary texts such as chronicles, memoirs, and traveler's descriptions except where those are the only available sources. In general, the reader is urged to use the secondary sources listed for each garden site to find earlier treatments, archaeological reports, and primary sources. The most up-to-date publications can be located using the *Index Islamicus*, which exists in print and electronic format. In addition, the Web site www.archnet.org offers electronic access to quite a few of the articles on Islamic architecture and landscape design listed here.

Atasoy, Nurhan. *A Garden for the Sultan: Gardens and Flowers in the Ottoman Culture*. Istanbul: Aygaz, 2003. A unique survey of Ottoman Turkish gardens in English, based on hard-to find manuscript sources and Turkish secondary sources. Beautifully illustrated and wide-ranging in its treatment of sites and media.

Brookes, John. *Gardens of Paradise: The History and Design of the Great Islamic Gardens*. New York: New Amsterdam Books, 1987. An excellent survey of gardens from the designer's perspective; it is generally historically accurate, although it does not acknowledge its sources in citations. The book includes short treatments of Ottoman, Sicilian, and Egyptian gardens, which are often omitted from other surveys.

Conan, Michel, ed. *The Middle East Garden Traditions, Unity and Diversity: Questions, Methods, and Resources in a Multicultural Perspective*. Washington, D.C.: Dumbarton Oaks, 2007. A collection of regionally focused essays that represents current international scholarship on Islamic and earlier Middle Eastern gardens.

Crowe, Sylvia, Sheila Haywood, Susan Jellicoe, and Gordon Patterson. *The Gardens of Mughal India*. London: Thames and Hudson, 1972. A good early survey, particularly valuable for Kashmir, but now outdated.

Hussain, Mahmood, Abdul Rehman, and James L. Wescoat, Jr., eds. *The Mughal Garden*. Lahore: Ferozsons, 1996. An edited collection of papers representing the most recent research on Mughal gardens (a companion volume was edited by Wescoat and Wolschke-Bulmann; see below).

Khansari, Mehdi, M. Reza Moghtader, and Minouch Yavari. *The Persian Garden: Echoes of Paradise*. Washington, D.C.: Mage, 1998. Valuable for its colorful plans and plentiful photographs. It is particularly useful for the eighteenth- and nineteenth-century Persian gardens that are rarely discussed by other historians.

Lehrman, Jonas. *Earthly Paradise: Garden and Courtyard in Islam*. Berkeley: University of California Press, 1980. Written from the perspective of a designer. The descriptions and plans are good, but the emphasis often leans more toward present appearance than ascertaining the original historical condition of gardens.

MacDougall, Elisabeth, and Richard Ettinghausen, eds. *The Islamic Garden*. Washington, D.C.: Dumbarton Oaks, 1976. An important early collection of analytical essays on garden history and garden poetry, but now out of date.

Menjili-De Corny, Irène. *Jardins du Maroc*. Paris: Le Temps Apprivoisé, 1991. A well-illustrated introduction to many Moroccan sites that are discussed in no other source.

Moynihan, Elizabeth. *Paradise as a Garden in Persia and Mughal India*. New York: George Braziller, 1979. Extremely valuable for her eyewitness descriptions of gardens that other garden historians have ignored, although now out of date and lacking archaeological detail for some of the major gardens.

Petruccioli, Attilio, ed. *Gardens in the Time of the Great Muslim Empires*. Leiden: E. J. Brill, 1997. A collection of analytical essays by several authors; good for scholarly depth but not broad coverage.

Ruggles, D. Fairchild. *Gardens, Landscape, and Vision in the Palaces of Islamic Spain*. University Park: Pennsylvania State University Press, 2000. Focuses on Hispano-Islamic gardens in the larger context of an agricultural, political, and economic landscape, drawing from a wide base of medieval Arabic sources and hard-to-find archaeological reports.

Tabbaa, Yasser. "The Medieval Islamic Garden: Typology and Hydraulics." In *Garden History: Issues, Approaches, Methods*, ed. John Dixon Hunt, 303–30. Washington, D.C.: Dumbarton Oaks, 1989. This essay interprets garden symbolism in a comparative context in Islam.

Titley, Norah, and Frances Wood. *Oriental Gardens*. San Francisco: Chronicle Books, 1991. This study skims lightly over discussion of the actual sites, but it is an excellent source for manuscript and print representations of gardens, garden techniques, and plants.

Von Hantelman, Christa, and Dieter Zoern. *Gardens of Delight: The Great Islamic Gardens*. Cologne: DuMont Buchverlag, 2001. Good for photographs, plans, and short descriptions of the present state of gardens, but lacks historical analysis.

Wescoat, James L., Jr., and Joachim Wolschke-Bulmahn, eds. *Mughal Gardens: Sources, Places, Representations, and Prospects*. Washington, D.C.: Dumbarton Oaks, 1996. A collection of papers from a Dumbarton Oaks symposium representing the most recent research on Mughal gardens (a companion volume was edited by Hussain, Rehman, and Wescoat; see above).

Wilber, Donald. *Persian Gardens and Garden Pavilions*. 1962; reprint, Washington, D.C.: Dumbarton Oaks, 1979. Out of date, but an important early study.

Spain

CORDOBA

Great Mosque

Built by the Umayyad dynasty of emirs and caliphs beginning in 786 on the site of a Christian church, both the prayer hall and the courtyard of Cordoba's congregational mosque were expanded in the ninth and tenth centuries as the Muslim population grew. In 1236, the year Cordoba was conquered by Castile, the mosque was converted to a church, and in 1523 the architects of Charles V gutted the center of the prayer hall to insert a cathedral. In the eighth through eleventh centuries, the courtyard was unpaved and planted with fruit trees, probably citrus, and palms that were irrigated by cisterns fed by rainwater that poured from the parallel gables of the prayer hall roof and later by aqueduct. Although the courtyard has been only partially excavated, revealing the foundations of an earlier Visigothic church, it is quite likely that the original planting in the mosque would have been organized as a grid of trees connected by small surface channels incised in the earth. However, the condition of the irrigation channels today, lined with stone, is not original.

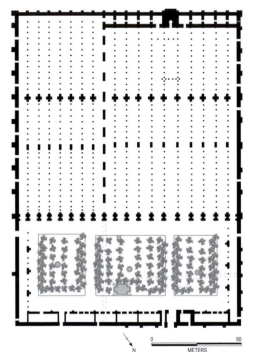

Great Mosque of Cordoba (Ruggles and Chodon)

BIBLIOGRAPHY

Castejón, Rafael. "El pavimento de la Mezquita de Córdoba." *Boletín de la Real Academia de Córdoba, de Ciencias, Bellas Letras y Nobles Artes*, 54 (1945): 327–30.

——. "Mas sobre el pavimento de la Mezquita." *Boletín de la Real Academia de Córdoba, de Ciencias, Bellas Letras y Nobles Artes* 55 (1946): 233–34.

Creswell, K. A. C. *Short Account of Early Muslim Architecture*, rev. by James Allan. Aldershot: Scolar Press, 1989.

Madinat al-Zahra'

A vast palace-city (1,506 m east to west) of ceremonial receptions halls, gardens, mosques, residences, baths, a mint, workshops, and barracks, Madinat al-Zahra' occupied three stepped terraces at the foot of a mountain from which water was brought by aqueducts to serve both the palace and nearby Cordoba. It was begun in 936 by the Umayyad caliph 'Abd al-Rahman III and was in full use a decade later. It was destroyed, as were so many of the other country estates surrounding Cordoba, in 1010–11 in a war over caliphal succession and legitimacy. It had at least three known gardens: (1) the small garden (or "Prince's Garden") on the uppermost terrace that was reserved for elite inhabitants of the palace, (2) a large quadripartite garden on the lowest terrace that has only partially been revealed through excavation, and east of this (3) a garden of equal dimensions and similar layout on the middle terrace, extending in front of the reception hall known as the Salon Rico.

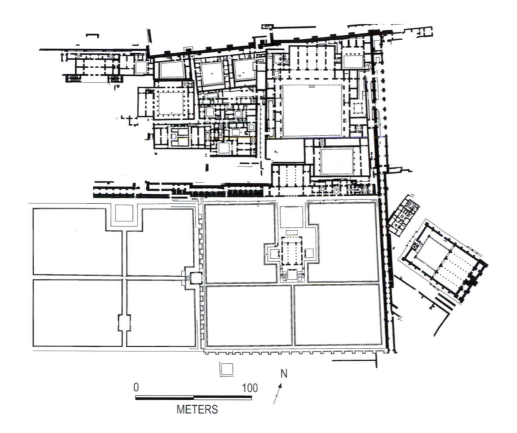

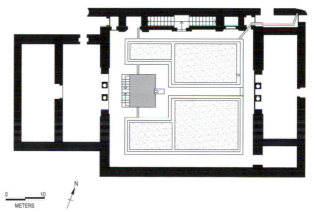

Madinat al-Zahra',
plan of upper levels
(Antonio Almagro),
left; Small Garden
(Almagro), below

In the center of the Salon Rico's garden stood a
pavilion surrounded by small rectangular pools of
water. The deeply sunken garden quadrants were
irrigated by channels that ran alongside the pavements marking the four-part plan.

BIBLIOGRAPHY

Cuadernos de Madinat al-Zahra' (Cordoba), various articles.
Hernández Giménez, Félix. *Madinat al-Zahra': Arquitectura
   y Decoración*. Granada: Patronato de la Alhambra, 1985.
Ruggles, D. Fairchild. *Gardens, Landscape, and Vision in the
   Palaces of Islamic Spain*. University Park: Pennsylvania
   State University Press, 2000.
Vallejo Triano, Antonio. "Madinat al-Zahra': The Triumph
   of the Islamic State." In Jerrilynn D. Dodds, ed., *Al-Andalus: The Art of Islamic Spain*, 27–39. New York:
   Metropolitian Museum of Art, 1992.

GRANADA

Alhambra

Built on the grounds of a palace that had occupied the top of Granada's Sabika hill in the
Zirid period (1013–90), the Alhambra seen today comprises numerous disparate garden

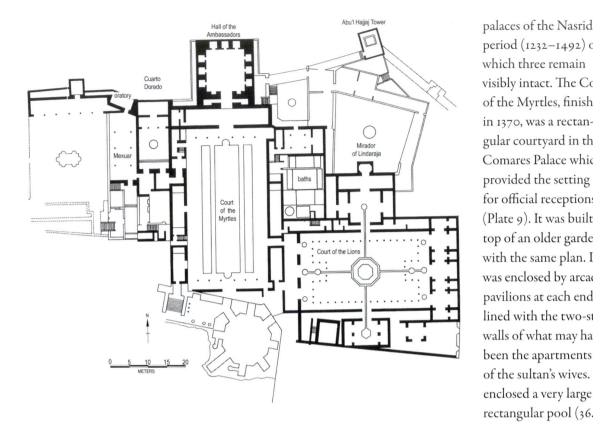

Alhambra, plan of precinct of Comares and Lions Palaces

palaces of the Nasrid period (1232–1492) of which three remain visibly intact. The Court of the Myrtles, finished in 1370, was a rectangular courtyard in the Comares Palace which provided the setting for official receptions (Plate 9). It was built on top of an older garden with the same plan. It was enclosed by arcaded pavilions at each end and lined with the two-story walls of what may have been the apartments of the sultan's wives. It enclosed a very large rectangular pool (36.6 m by 23.5 m) that was lined by water channels that irrigated the narrow beds on either side. A sixteenth-century observer noted orange trees and myrtles growing there. The pool's silvery surface reflected the imposing Comares Tower (containing the Hall of the Ambassadors), a mirror image that was animated by the two circular basins with vertical jets poised at each end of the pool.

The Partal Palace, built in 1302–8, may have been the model for the Court of the Myrtles. It, too, had a rectangular courtyard with a large rectangular pool, probably enclosed by high walls. At the north end, only the pavilion with the Torre de las Damas remains.

The Court of the Lions, built 1370–90 by Muhammad V, replaced an earlier garden. It consisted of a courtyard (28.5 by 15.7 m) with a chahar bagh of sunken quadrants (Plate 8). Although today these are shallow and have little vegetation, they were originally planted with orange trees and had a soil level about 80 centimeters below the pavement surface so that from a seated position, a person's view would skim the tops of the garden's flowers. In the middle of the garden, water gushed forth from a jet in a basin borne on the backs of twelve stone lions, which also spewed water into a channel that encircled the fountain. Four water channels originated in sunken basins in projecting kiosks or off-court halls and flowed down the walkways to this central point.

BIBLIOGRAPHY

Consejería de obras públicas y transportes de la Junta de Andalucía, Consejería de cultura de la Junta de Andalucía, et al. *Plan especial de protección y reforma interior de la Alhambra y Alijares*. Granada: Patronato de la Alhambra, 1986.

Dickie, James. "Palaces of the Alhambra." In Jerrilynn D. Dodds, ed., *Al-Andalus: The Art of Islamic Spain*, 135–51. New York: Metropolitan Museum of Art, 1992.

Fernández Puertas, Antonio. *The Alhambra I, From the Ninth Century to Yusuf I (1354)*. London: Saqi Books, 1997.

Grabar, Oleg. *The Alhambra*. 1978; reprint, Sebastapol, Calif.: Solipsist Press, 1992.

Jacobs, Michael. *The Alhambra*. New York: Rizzoli, 2000.

Orihuela Uzal, Antonio. *Casas y palacios nazaríes. Siglos XIII–XV*. Barcelona: El Legado Andalusí, 1996.

Pavón Maldonado, Basilio. *Estudios sobre la Alhambra. I: La Alcazaba, El Palacio de los Abencerrajes, Los accessos a la Casa Real Vieja, El Palacio de Comares, El Partal* (supplement to *Cuadernos de la Alhambra*). Granada: Patronato de la Alhambra y Generalife, 1975.

Ruggles, D. Fairchild. *Gardens, Landscape, and Vision in the Palaces of Islamic Spain*. University Park: Pennsylvania State University Press, 2000.

Generalife

The Generalife Palace was built on a hill across from the Alhambra by the Nasrid sultan Muhammad III (r. 1302–8); it was renovated by Isma'il in ca. 1319. Connected to the Alhambra by a protected passageway, the Generalife served the Nasrid rulers as a pleasurable escape characterized by gardens with gushing fountains and shady vegetation. Of its many gardens, today only two are original: the Acequía ("canal") Court and the stairway that rises through a grove of shady trees to the upper levels of the estate. (The ∪-shaped Garden of the Sultana was created in the sixteenth century.) The Acequía Court (48.7 by 12.8 m) took the form of an elongated rectangle nestled into a sloping ground. It was divided lengthwise by a single water channel that erupted at midpoint and at either end in marble basins set into the pavement (Plate 2). Of the two pavilions

Generalife
(Ruggles)

that enclosed the garden at either end, the northern one had five arches on its garden face and on the other face a projecting mirador with magnificent views of the snow-capped Sierra on the distant horizon.

Although today the Acequía Court is planted according to the modern taste for clumps of bright flowers, excavations in 1959 revealed its original appearance. It had quadrants recessed 70 centimeters below the Islamic-era pavement. These were planted with shallow-rooted plants so that the tops of the plants would probably just skim

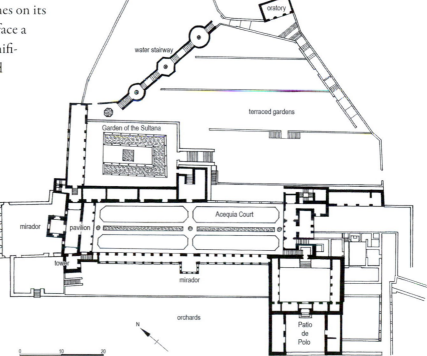

the level of the enframing pavements, while larger shrubs filled the corners. The west wall has seventeen blind arches today with a central salient mirador: these were formerly open and allowed multiple views onto the terraced orchards and vineyards that filled the valley separating the Generalife and Alhambra.

BIBLIOGRAPHY

Bermúdez Pareja, Jesús. "El Generalife después del incendio de 1958." *Cuadernos de la Alhambra* 1 (1965): 9–39.

Consejería de obras públicas y transportes de la Junta de Andalucía, Consejería de cultura de la Junta de Andalucía, et al. *Plan especial de protección y reforma interior de la Alhambra y Alijares*. Granada: Patronato de la Alhambra, 1986.

Orihuela Uzal, Antonio. *Casas y palacios nazaríes. Siglos XIII–XV*. Barcelona: El Legado Andalusí, 1996.

Pavón Maldonado, Basilio. *Estudios sobre la Alhambra. II* (supplement to *Cuadernos de la Alhambra*). Granada: Patronato de la Alhambra y Generalife, 1977.

Ruggles, D. Fairchild. *Gardens, Landscape, and Vision in the Palaces of Islamic Spain*. University Park: Pennsylvania State University Press, 2000.

Tito Rojo, José. "Permanencia y cambio en los jardines de la Granada morisca (1492–1571). Los jardines de los palacios nazaríes: La Alhambra y el Generalife." In Carmen Añón and José Luis Sancho, eds., *Jardín y Naturaleza en el reinado de Felipe II*, 363–79. Madrid: Sociedad Estatal para la Conmemoración de los Centenarios de Felipe II y Carlos V, 1998.

Vílchez Vílchez, Carlos. *El Generalife*. Granada: Proyecto Sur de Ediciones, 1991.

MONTEAGUDO

Castillejo

The smaller of two fortified hilltop castles near Murcia, the Castillejo appears to date to 1147–72, when Murcia was in its heyday under Muhammad ibn Mardanish. The residence (61 by 38 m) was centered around an open courtyard (33 by 18 m) which followed the plan of a *chahar bagh* with irrigated quadrants sunken 1.4 meters below the level of the pavements. Pools stood at the intersection of these axial walkways as well as at either end of the courtyard where they may have been capped by projecting kiosks (similar to the Court of the Lions at the Alhambra). The castle stood high above the surrounding landscape and

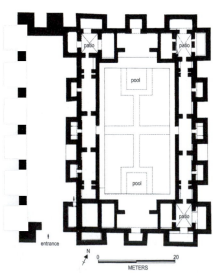

Castillejo of Monteagudo (Julio Navarro)

probably enjoyed panoramic views from its projecting salients. 14 meters to the west and 4–5 meters below the garden level, a second retaining wall with solid buttresses provided extra support for the foundations, and it may have supported a second terrace. Water was raised to the level of the courtyard gardens by means of a noria. Nothing remains of the original castle but its foundations, which were excavated in 1924–25.

BIBLIOGRAPHY

Navarro Palazón, Julio, and P. Jiménez Castillo. "El Castillejo de Monteagudo: Qasr Ibn Saʻd." In J. Navarro Palazón, ed., *Casas y Palacios de al-Andalus*, 63–103. Granada: El Legado Andalusí, 1995.

Ruggles, D. Fairchild. *Gardens, Landscape, and Vision in the Palaces of Islamic Spain*. University Park: Pennsylvania State University Press, 2000.

Torres Balbás, L. "Monteagudo y 'El Castillo,' en la Vega de Murcia." *Al-Andalus 2* (1934): 366–72.

Alcazar

The original Islamic palace was built
in Seville in the tenth century, but the
earliest surviving gardens date to the
eleventh through fourteenth centuries.
The four-part Patio del Crucero with its
long central channel was subsequently
buried beneath Gothic vaulting and infill
and a later garden superimposed on it;
only the original channel can be seen
today below ground. The second, the
Patio del Yeso, consisted of a rectangular
pool set in a small courtyard, two walls
of which preserve their original interlacing stucco tracery. The third, today
surrounded by government offices (the
Casa de Contratación), was a quadripartite courtyard (12.5 by 11 m) with deeply
sunken quadrants (approximately 2 m)

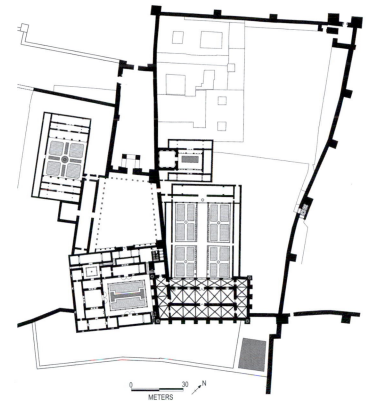

formed by cross-axial raised walkways (Plate 4). These paths,
the brick ornament of which may date to the fourteenth century,
carried water channels that met at the center of the garden in
a pool. At one end are the remains of three sunken beds from
an eleventh-century garden. Of the arcades at either end of
the courtyard, one had stucco interlace; today both have been
restored. The garden as it appears today is an interpretive version
of its fourteenth-century phase.

In the fourteenth century, the Alcazar was remodeled first by
Alfonso XI of Castile and Leon and second by his son, Pedro
I, in the mudéjar style. Mudéjar was not so much an imitation
of Islamic style and techniques as it was a continuation of it, for
although the patrons were Christian, the artisans were largely
Muslims employed for their skill in stucco, glazed ceramics, and
woodworking. Alfonso built (or rebuilt) the Hall of Justice next
to the Patio del Yeso soon after 1340. Pedro (r. 1350–69) built
much of what is seen today in the first floor of the Alcazar: the
Alcazar's courtyard façade (1364), Patio de Doncellas (Court of the Maidens), Hall of the
Ambassadors, Patio del León, Patio de las Muñecas (Court of the Dolls), and presumably some of the outlying gardens which were subsequently redesigned by later patrons.
Recently, excavations beneath the pavement of the Patio de Doncellas have revealed the

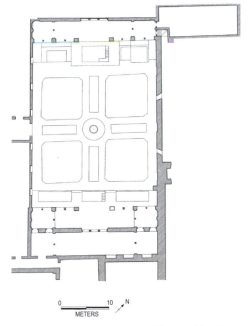

Alcazar of Seville
(Antonio Almagro),
top; Casa de
Contratación
(Antonio Almagro),
bottom

presence of an axially divided garden with two deeply sunken beds and a long rectangular pool, dating to Pedro's patronage.

BIBLIOGRAPHY

Almagro, Antonio. "El Patio del Crucero de los Reales Alcázares de Sevilla." *Al-Qantara* 20 (1999): 331–76.

——. "La Recuperación del Jardín Medieval del Patio de las Doncellas." *Apuntes del Alcázar de Sevilla* 6 (May 2005): 44–67.

Dickie, James. "The Islamic Garden in Spain." In *The Islamic Garden*, ed. Elisabeth B. MacDougall and Richard Ettinghausen, 89–105. Washington, D.C.: Dumbarton Oaks, 1976.

Hernández Núñez, Juan Carlos, and Alfredo J. Morales. *The Royal Palace of Seville*. London: Scala, 1999.

Manzano Martos, Rafael. "Casas y palacios en la Sevilla Almohade. Sus antecedentes hispánicos." In Julio Navarro Palazón, ed., *Casas y Palacios de al-Andalus*, 315–52. Granada: El Legado Andalusí, 1995.

Marín Fidalgo, Ana. *El Alcázar de Sevilla*. Seville: Ediciones Guadalquivir, 1990.

Ruggles, D. Fairchild. "The Alcazar of Pedro I in Seville." *Gesta* 43, no. 2 (2004): 87–98.

Tabales Rodríguez, Miguel Ángel. "El Patio de las Doncellas del Palacio de Pedro I de Castilla: Génesis y Transformación." *Apuntes del Alcázar de Sevilla* 6 (May 2005): 6–43.

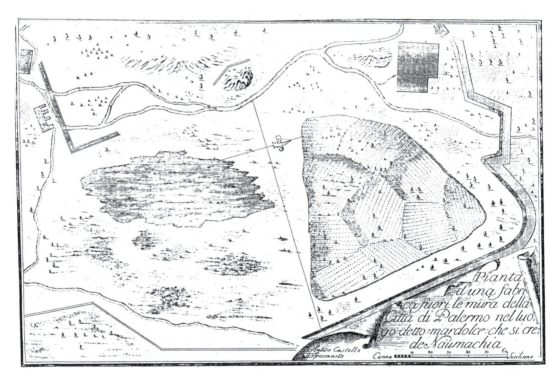

Favara Palace
(Andrea Pigonati, 1767)

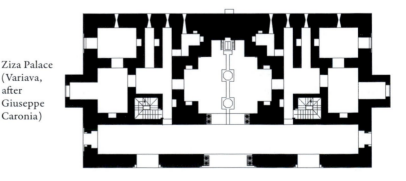

Ziza Palace
(Variava,
after
Giuseppe
Caronia)

Sicily

PALERMO

Favara Palace

The Favara was built in Palermo amidst what soon became a green belt of palaces and garden estates. Founded in the early eleventh century for an Arab governor, it was completely renovated to serve as the first suburban pleasure estate of the Norman king Roger II (1130–54). The name, which derives from the Arabic *fawwara*, or "fountain jet," is indicative of Norman syncretism, blending Byzantine administration, ceremonies, and art with Islamic law, taxation, terminology, art, and science. Hence, although this palace was the residence of a Christian ruler, it reflected a Mediterranean Islamic taste for a direct rapport between architecture and an exterior environment of gardens. Although only one wall of the palace survives today, the Favara formerly consisted of several structures surrounded by an artificial lake, in the center of which stood an irregular island. The lake may have been used for fishing or even boating, as occurred in the Qal'a Bani Hammad (Algeria), because iron rings for mooring were once visible. Water was plentiful in Sicily: it was brought to the palace by canal from the mountains to the west.

BIBLIOGRAPHY
Bellafiore, Giuseppe. *Architettura in Sicilia nelle età islamica e normanna (827–1194)*. Palermo: Arnoldo Lombardi Editore, 1990.
Braida, S. "Il castello di Favara." *Architetti di Sicilia* 5–6 (1965): 27–34.
Goldschmidt, A. "Die Favarades Königs Roger von Sizilien." *Jahrbuch der Kgl. Preuszischen Kunstsammlungen* 16, no. 3 (1895): 199–215.
Marçais, Georges. *L'Architecture musulmane d'occident*. Paris: Arts et Métiers Graphiques, 1954.

Ziza Palace

This palace, whose name derived from the Arabic *al-'aziza*, meaning "noble," was begun in 1166 by the Norman king William II (c. 1153–89); it was significantly renovated in 1636. The palace was a two-storied rectangular structure (32 by 23 m) that stood opposite a large pool in an enormous park. In the center of a sumptuous hall on the ground floor, opposite the entry, water poured from a niche in the wall, flowing down a marble chute (*salsabil*) into a channel that traversed the floor. To either side were stairs leading to a muqarnas-vaulted reception hall on the upper story. On the first floor, flanking the stairs were side chambers that opened directly to the extensive outdoor gardens. An Arabic inscription over the entry of the palace described its setting and its inhabitant: "Here, as oft as thou shalt wish, shalt thou see the loveliest possession of this kingdom, the most splendid of the world and of the seas. The mountains, their peaks flushed with the colour of narcissus. . . . Thou shalt see the great king of his century in his beautiful dwelling-place, a house of joy and splendour which suits him well. This is the earthly paradise that opens to the view; this king is the Musta'izz, this palace the 'Aziz" (Norwich, 601).

BIBLIOGRAPHY
Bellafiore, Giuseppe. *La Ziza di Palermo*. Palermo: S. F. Flaccovio, 1978.
Caronia, Giuseppe. *La Ziza di Palermo: Storia e restauro*. Palermo: Editori Laterza, c. 1982.

Marçais, Georges. *L'Architecture musulmane d'occident*. Paris: Arts et Métiers Graphiques, 1954.

Meier, Hans-Rudolf. ". . . 'das ird 'sche Paradies, das sich den Blicken öffnet': Die Gartenpaläste der Normannenkönige in Palermo." *Die Gartenkunst* 5, no. 1 (1994): 1–18.

Norwich, John Julius. *The Normans in Sicily*. 1970; London: Penguin, 1992.

Staacke, Ursula. *Un palazzo normano a Palermo. La Zisa*. Palermo: Ricerche et documenti, 1991.

Tabbaa, Yasser. "The 'Salsabil' and 'Shadirvan' in Medieval Islamic Courtyards." *Environmental Design: Journal of the Islamic Environmental Design Research Centre* 1 (1986): 34–37.

Morocco

FEZ

Dar al-Batha

This mansion was begun by Sultan Moulay Hassan and finished by his successor, 'Abd al-Aziz, in the Bou Jloud quarter of Fez where gardens had flourished for centuries. An inscription above the door to the audience hall states that the palace was finished in 1897. The house owes its trapezoidal plan to the exigencies of the preexisting urban context, but within this the large rectangular courtyard insists upon orthogonal symmetry. The main courtyard is surrounded by white walls pierced by horseshoe arched arcades. It is divided into a chahar bagh with large sunken

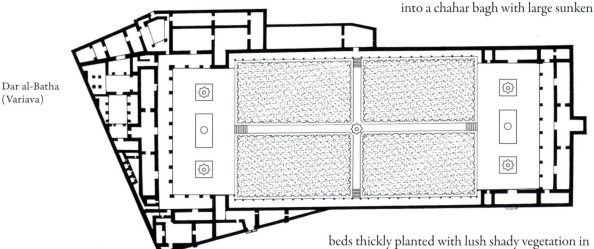

Dar al-Batha
(Variava)

beds thickly planted with lush shady vegetation in a traditional manner, which in the Maghreb is called a *riyad*. The beds are sunken 78 centimeters below the brick pavement of the cross-axial walkways, which themselves are sunken 34 centimeters below the paved terraces at each end of the courtyard. At the center of each of these terraces is a rectangular pool flanked by upright fountains set within tiled star-shaped recesses to catch the overflow. The walkways are lined with terra cotta and colorful *zellij* (mosaic) tile in complex geometrical patterns. Today the palace houses a museum of art and archaeology, and its gardens are still carefully tended. However, photographs and sketches from 1917, 1918, and 1932 show the garden planted with two rows of trees—including palm trees—stretching lengthwise through each side of the chahar bagh. Four cypresses surrounded the central fountain, as they still do.

BIBLIOGRAPHY

Cambazard-Amahan, Catherine. "Dar al-Batha." In Jacques Revault et al., eds., *Palais et Demeures de Fès, III—Époque Alawite (XIXeme-XXeme siècles)*. Paris: CNRS, 1992.

El Faïz, Mohammed, Manuel Gómez Anuarbe, and Teresa Portela Marques. *Jardins de Maroc, d'Espagne et du Portugal*. Madrid: Actes Sud and Fondation Telefónica Maroc, 2003.

Menjili-De Corny, Irène. *Jardins du Maroc*. Paris: Le Temps Apprivoisé, 1991.

Palace of Pasha 'Abd al-Kari

While in the twentieth century the elite families of Fez, Marrakesh, Rabat, and Tangier built homes outside the old medieval city walls, in the earlier period such houses were situated in the medina. The Palace of Pasha 'Abd al-Kari, also known as the Dar al-Aman, was such a mansion, built in the Fez medina in 1860. The palace, which serves as a private residence today, includes a large courtyard paved with colorful tile (*zellij*) that covers the raised star- and cross-shaped beds of vegetation and water basins (Plate 10). Irrigation runnels surround the shallow beds and the entire courtyard has an underground drainage network. While the plan expands upon the medieval love of geometry and order, the density of shapes and the subordination of vegetation to gleaming tile reflect a more modern taste.

BIBLIOGRAPHY

Von Hantelman, Christa, and Diert Zoern. *Gardens of Delight: The Great Islamic Gardens*. Cologne: DuMont Buchverlag, 2001.

Courtyard in the Palace of Pasha 'Abd al-Kari, Fez (Ruggles and Variava)

MARRAKESH

Agdal Basin and Gardens

Outside of Marrakesh, extending south from the Dar al-Makhzan and al-Badi' Palace, these gardens were created in the Almohad era (1130–1269) and still exist, although much altered. The term *agdal* refers to the type of garden: a vast expanse, sometimes walled, on the outskirts of an urban palace or city. There were agdals with huge manmade lakes in Meknes, Rabat, and all the palatine cities of Morocco. In Marrakesh, water was brought from the Atlas Mountains to fill two immense rectangular artificial reservoirs—the Dar al-Hana (west) and al-Kharsiya (east)—which then provided a steady source of water to irrigate the gardens and orchards in this agricultural zone encompassing more than 500 hectares. The Agdal Gardens were enclosed by 9 kilometers of wall and were contiguous with the city of Marrakesh itself. Each of the gardens was devoted to a single species, and those containing orange groves stood nearest the large basins because the trees, which did not naturally endure in desert climates, required lots of irrigation. The union of utilitarian function and aesthetic appeal, of agricultural production and recreation, is evident in the

Agdal Gardens
(after Menjili-De
Corny)

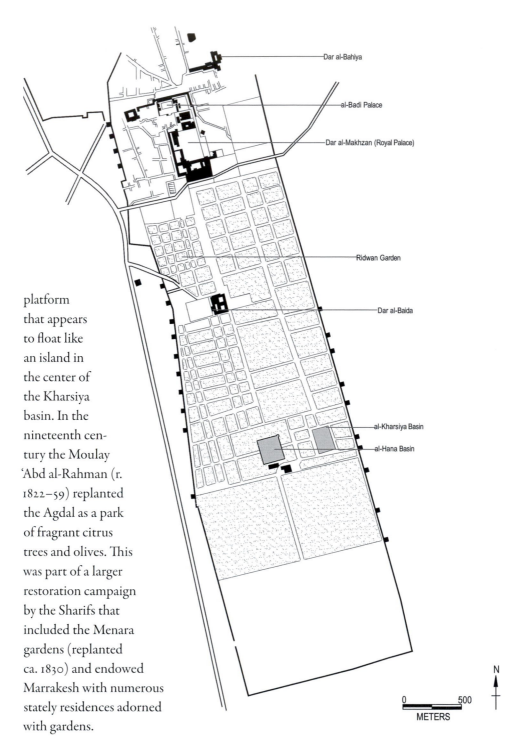

Dar al-Bahiya

al-Badi Palace

Dar al-Makhzan (Royal Palace)

Ridwan Garden

Dar al-Baida

al-Kharsiya Basin

al-Hana Basin

N

0   500
METERS

platform
that appears
to float like
an island in
the center of
the Kharsiya
basin. In the
nineteenth cen-
tury the Moulay
'Abd al-Rahman (r.
1822–59) replanted
the Agdal as a park
of fragrant citrus
trees and olives. This
was part of a larger
restoration campaign
by the Sharifs that
included the Menara
gardens (replanted
ca. 1830) and endowed
Marrakesh with numerous
stately residences adorned
with gardens.

BIBLIOGRAPHY

El Faïz, Mohammed. *Jardins de Marrakech*. Paris: Actes Sud, 2000.

———. *Les jardins historiques de Marrakech: Mémoire écologique d'une ville impériale*. Florence: EDIFIR, 1996.

Gallotti, Jean. *Moorish Houses and Gardens of Morocco*, 2 vols. New York: William Helburn, 1926, esp. vol. 2.

Menjili-De Corny, Irène. *Jardins du Maroc*. Paris: Le Temps Apprivoisé, 1991.

Al-Badiʿ Palace

Built in Marrakesh beginning in 1578 by the Saʿadian ruler Ahmad al-Mansur and destroyed in 1710, the Badiʿ Palace (the name means "marvelous") was huge with open courtyards containing sunken gardens and rectangular pools of water. The principal garden measured 135 by 110 meters and had an enormous pool running down the main axis. In its center, a square platform reached by walkways seemed afloat. Domed kiosks sheltering basins stood at either end of the pool, reminiscent of the Court of the Lions at the Alhambra (a stylistic reference that may have been made by Andalusian Muslim architects who fled to Morocco after 1492). These kiosks were flanked by smaller rectangular pools with raised water basins. One of these kiosks still stands: it had a door on each of the outer walls so that all three directions provided a view of shimmering water. The pools of water had a depth of about one meter, while the planted beds were sunken by approximately two and a half meters—low enough that the tops of the flowering shrubs and small trees formerly growing there would just reach the level of the paved walkways.

Al-Badiʿ Palace
(Variava after
von Hantelmann)

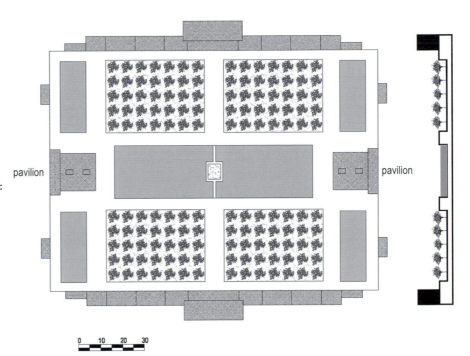

BIBLIOGRAPHY

El Faïz, Mohammed. *Jardins de Marrakech*. Paris: Actes Sud, 2000.

El Faïz, Mohammed, Manuel Gómez Anuarbe, and Teresa Portela Marques. *Jardins de Maroc, d'Espagne et du Portugal*. Madrid: Actes Sud and Fondation Telefónica Maroc, 2003.

Marçais, Georges. "Les jardins de l'Islam." In Marçais, *Mélanges d'histoire et d'archéologie de l'Occident musulman*, 2 vols. Algiers: Imprimerie officielle du Gouvernement général de l'Algérie, 1957. 1: 233–44.

Menjili-De Corny, Irène. *Jardins du Maroc*. Paris: Le Temps Apprivoisé, 1991.

Meunié, Jean. "Le grand Riad et les bâtiments saâdiens du Badiʿ à Marrakech." *Hespéris* 44 (1957): 129–34.

Torres Balbás, Leopoldo. *Artes almorávide y almohade*. Madrid: Consejo Superior de Investigaciones Científicas, 1955.

Von Hantelman, Christa, and Dieter Zoern. *Gardens of Delight: The Great Islamic Gardens*. Cologne: DuMont Buchverlag, 2001.

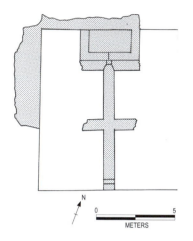

Kutubiya Garden
(Ruggles)

The Kutubiya

In 1952, an early twelfth-century garden was discovered partly beneath the present Kutubiya Mosque (built 1147–62 by Almohad rulers) in Marrakesh. The garden belonged to the palace of the Almoravid ruler 'Ali ibn Yusuf (1106–42) and consisted of a rectangular courtyard traversed by water channels that formed beds of vegetation. The palace and garden were apparently supplied by two cisterns in the present mosque's courtyard. Although the archaeological vestiges were minimal and cannot be seen today, the site is important because it is the earliest excavated four-part garden in Morocco and one of the earliest in the Islamic world.

BIBLIOGRAPHY

Meunié, Jacques, Henri Terrasse, and Gaston Deverdun. *Recherches Archéologiques à Marrakech*. Paris: Institut des hautes études marocaines, 1952.

RABAT

Chella Necropolis

Built largely between 1310 and 1334 to serve as a cemetery for the Merinid rulers of Morocco, Chella stands outside of Rabat on the remains of the Roman town of Sala Colonia. A gate in the western corner marks the entrance into the irregular five-sided large enclosure (the longest side of which measures 300 m). The landscape slopes from here past ancient ruins and Merinid graves until one reaches a rectangular enclosure (44 by 25 m) containing the royal tombs, two mosques, and a zawiya. The courtyard of the Mosque of Abu Yusuf Ya'qub (1258–86) serves as the antechamber to the complex. It leads on the southwest side to a ruined area with the stump of a minaret. The northeast side leads to the zawiya built by Abu'l Hassan which has a tiled minaret (14.1 m high), latrines, and an open courtyard formerly surrounded by an arcade of marble columns (Plate 20). Behind this, residential cells lined the walls in two stories. A rectangular tiled pool with marble scalloped basins at either end occupied the center of the court, and a prayer hall stood at the eastern end. South of this area is an enclosed area of gravestones, of which only that of the queen Shams al-Dawla can be identified. The grave of her husband, Abu'l Has-

Chella
Necropolis, Site
(top) and Zawiya
(bottom)
(Ruggles and
Variava)

san, is located in a richly decorated tomb structure in the southern corner of the complex. Basset and Lévi-Provençal examined the vestiges of paved walkways and proposed that this area was gardened.

BIBLIOGRAPHY

Basset, Henri, and E. Lévi-Provençal. "Chella: Une nécropole mérinid." *Hespéris* 2 (1922): 1–92, 255–316, 385–425.

Menjili-De Corny, Irène. *Jardins du Maroc*. Paris: Le Temps Apprivoisé, 1991.

Parker, Richard. *A Practical Guide to Islamic Monuments in Morocco*. Charlottesville, Va.: Baraka Press, 1981.

Algeria

QAL'A BANI HAMMAD

Dar al-Bahr

The Qal'a was a fortified palatine city built by various members of the Hammadid dynasty between 1007 and 1105 in what is today Algeria. Situated at an altitude of 1,418 meters in the peaks of the central Maghreb, the city and the agricultural

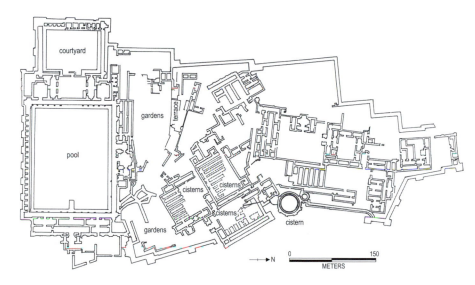

Qal'a Bani Hammad, Lake Palace (after L. de Beylié, 1909)

lands along the plains below it were well supplied with water from the mountains. The Qal'a included a mosque and four residential complexes, the largest of which was the Dar al-Bahr (Lake Palace), so named for its rectangular pool (67 by 47 m). The courtyard's monumental entrance on the east side and the portico that surrounded the pool suggest that it was a handsome arena for spectacle. The pool was large enough for boats, which could have been launched from the sloping ramp at the pool's east end, and medieval authors described nautical entertainments staged there. At a higher level in the palace, there was an area of gardens and at an even higher elevation a terrace probably had delightful views of both the gardens and the artificial lake. Gardens were clearly sites of pleasure and display: although archaeologists have not explored the gardens, they have discovered several decorative fountains with lion motifs.

BIBLIOGRAPHY

Beylié, L. de. *La Kalaa des Beni-Hammad: Une capitale berbère de l'Afrique du Nord au XIe*. Paris: E. Leroux, 1909.

Blanchet, Paul. "Description des Monuments de la Kalaa des Bani Hammad." *Nouvelles archives des missions scientifiques* 17 (ca. 1887): 1–21.

Golvin, Lucien. *Recherches archéologiques à la Qal'a des Banu Hammad*. Paris: Maisonneuve et Larose, 1953.

Ruggles, D. Fairchild. "Vision and Power at the Qala Bani Hammad in Islamic North Africa." *Journal of Garden History* 14 (1994): 28–41.

Tunisia

KAIROUAN

Aghlabid Basins

These basins were part of a larger hydraulic catchment system built just outside the walls of Kairouan. Round, polygonal and of various sizes, several still remain. The largest of

them was built by the Aghlabid ruler Ahmad ibn Muhammad (r. 856–63). It was a huge, forty-eight-sided polygon (128 m diameter) that, according to al-Bakri in the eleventh century, had an octagonal tower topped by an open-sided, domed kiosk. The foundations of this partially survive, measuring only 2.85 meters, and Marçais suggests that if such a pavilion was built there, its floor may have been extended by corbelled supports. Next to this tank is a smaller, seventeen-sided basin (37.4 m diameter), and these together decant into a vaulted cistern. The water was brought here from the mountains 36 kilometers to the west.

Aghlabid basins
(Ruggles)

Kairouan was a large and important city under Aghlabid rule (800–909) and was first capital of the Fatimids (909–21). Such extensive waterworks were necessary to sustain not only the inhabitants but the agriculture and gardens that flourished here.

BIBLIOGRAPHY

Marçais, Georges. *L'Architecture musulmane d'occident*. Paris: Arts et Métiers Graphiques, 1954.
Solignac, Marcel. "Recherches sur les installations hydrauliques de Kairouan et des steppes tunisiennes du VIIe au XIe siècle." *Annales de l'Institut des Études Orientales de l'Université d'Alger* (1953): 60–170.

MANOUBA

Burj al-Kabir

Manouba, about 10 kilometers west of Tunis, was a suburban area of recreation estates developed sometime in the seventeenth century by the beys who ruled Tunisia in the name of the Ottomans. However, only those constructions from the nineteenth-century onward remain. One of these is the Burj al-Kabir (also known as the Qasr al-Ward), built by the bey Hamuda Pasha (r. 1790–1814), in a mixed European and Maghrebi style, probably as an escape from the more official Bardo Palace. The palace consisted of four courtyards: an outer access court with an allée of cypresses, and inner entrance court with an impressive flight of stairs leading into the principal halls, a side court, and a large courtyard surrounded by a colonnade. Originally a tank of water occupied the center of the court, but this was later filled in to make a small garden. The apartments on the second story looked inward to this courtyard while also enjoying views on the other side toward the surrounding gardens. The views were enhanced on three sides of the palace by projecting salients with windows. The plantings of the gardens are unknown, but they were formerly adorned by an elegantly ornamented pavilion that was subsequently moved to the Belvedere Park in Tunis where it is known as the Belvedere Qubba.

BIBLIOGRAPHY

Revault, Jacques. *Palais, demeures et maisons de plaisance à Tunis et ses environs: Du XVIe au XIXe siècle.* Aix-en-Provence: Édisud, 1984.

——. *Palais et résidences d'été de la région de Tunis (XVIe–XIXe siècles).* Paris: Éditions du Centre National de la Recherche Scientifique, 1974.

Saladin, Henri. *Tunis et Kairouan.* Paris: H. Laurens, 1908.

Burj Qubbat al-Nas

In Manouba, quite near the Burj al-Kabir, was another vast estate built between 1790 and 1814 with a similar plan and setting. The Burj Qubbat al-Nas consisted of successive courtyards beginning with an entry court planted with trees with a large flight of stone steps leading into the palace proper. This was separated into two portions; the first and northernmost was a series of domed and groin-vaulted halls with a small courtyard on the upper story, and salient halls with windows that provided excellent views toward the surrounding orchard. The second part was a large open court taken up by a rectangular pool (approximately 25 by 20 m). An annex at the south end had a noria and a well which supplied the pool with water. Entirely walled, this served as a private garden for the women. Projecting entrances on the middle of the east and west sides led into a larger walled enclosure where aromatic citrus trees, pomegranates, and figs grew, irrigated with water raised by noria from wells on the east and south sides. The surrounding lands would have been planted with olive groves and utilitarian crops.

BIBLIOGRAPHY

Revault, Jacques. *Palais, demeures et maisons de plaisance à Tunis et ses environs: Du XVIe au XIXe siècle .* Aix-en-Provence: Édisud, 1984.

——. *Palais et résidences d'été de la région de Tunis (XVIe–XIXe siècles).* Paris: Éditions du Centre National de la Recherche Scientifique, 1974.

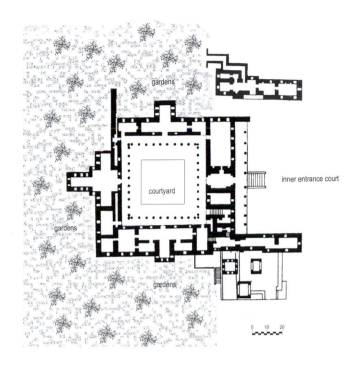

Burj al-Kabir, Manouba (Ruggles and Variava)

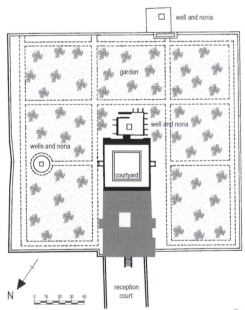

Burj al-Nas, Manouba (Ruggles and Variava, after J. Revault)

Egypt

CAIRO

Azhar Park

Opened in 2005 after fifteen years of planning, the Azhar Park occupies 31 hectares atop the Darassa Hills near the Citadel of Cairo. It is a magnificent site that evokes historic Islamic gardens in its powerful geometries, sunken garden beds, Mamluk-style polychromatic stonework, axial water channels, and playing fountains, all interpreted in a subdued modern design (Plate 27). The composition is organized by an axis that stretches from a hilltop restaurant with panoramic views at the northeast end, descending through six chahar baghs to a central crossing where water jets spring directly from the stone pavement, along a lengthy promenade to a juncture where the axis shifts and begins a slight rise through a formal garden (with a perpendicular axial path that leads to smaller sunken gardens with raised fountains), culminating in a café that projects into an artificial lake. Surrounding this highly rectilinear core and contrasting with it are curvilinear paths that lead to a children's playground, kiosks, and various lookouts from where the surrounding city can be surveyed.

The park is part of a larger urban redevelopment scheme addressing the needs of the surrounding low-income community. It also includes an archaeology project that has revealed the historic Ayyubid walls extending for more than a kilometer and that were buried in some places by 45 meters of debris. The design and implementation of the park demanded extensive regrading and the construction of a reservoir system and plant nurseries. It was sponsored by the Aga Khan Trust for Culture in association with the Cairo Governorate. The master plan is by Sasaki Associates; the landscape architects were Maher Stino and Laila Elmasry Stino of Sites International; the architects of the hilltop restaurant and the main entrance pavilion were Rami El Dahan and Soheir Farid; and the architects of the lakeside café were Serge Santelli and Karine Martin.

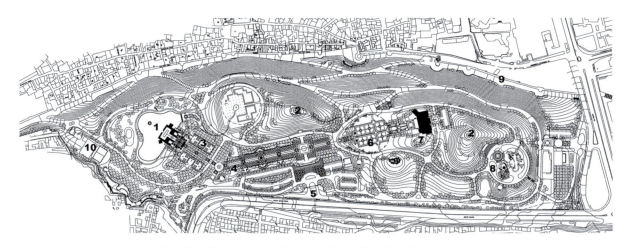

Azhar Park (Aga Khan Trust for Culture): 1) Lakeside café, 2) Lookout points, 3) Sunken gardens,
4) Palm processional walk, 5) Main entrance, 6) Formal garden, 7) Restaurant, 8) Children's play area,
9) Ayyubid wall promenade, 10) Neighborhood recreation fields

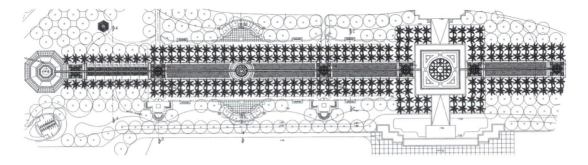

BIBLIOGRAPHY
Bianca, Stefano, and Philip Jodidio, eds. *Cairo: Revitalising a Historic Metropolis.* Turin: Aga Khan Trust for Culture and Umberto Allemandi, 2004; see especially Cameron Rashti, "The Development of Azhar Park," 149–63.

Azhar Park, Palm Processional Walk (Aga Khan Trust for Culture)

Ezbekiyah Gardens

The area in Cairo known as the Ezbekiyah has a long history. In the Mamluk era, it grew as a quarter around the lake that was filled by the Nasiri Canal at the annual flooding of the Nile. That seasonal event was celebrated by festivities with music, and colorfully festooned boats were launched in the lake. The area's architectural development expanded and receded according to the economic fortunes of Cairo. In 1485 the Amir Azbak min Tutuh endowed the lake as a waqf, transforming it from an abandoned marsh by excavating it anew, building a paved walkway around its perimeter, and erecting a handsome palace on the southeastern shore. When the French invaded Cairo (1798–1801), they settled around the Ezbekiyah, which had been recently rebuilt after a 1776 fire. They redesigned the quarter with broad straight streets, restored the Nasiri Canal's bridge, and planted trees along the streets and edges of the lake. After the French, the Ottoman governor Muhammad 'Ali (r. 1805–45) decided to modernize Cairo by filling in its canals and unhygienic ponds (which stank in the season of the water's recession), including the Ezbekiyah. It became a public park with three intersecting tree-lined promenades, an encircling canal for drainage during flood season, and a girdle of trees that included many tropical exotics. With restaurants, cafés, European-style hotels such as the Hotel d'Orient and Shepheard's, and cultural institutions such as a theater and the Thomas Cook Agency, the quarter had a distinctly European flavor and was a center for entertainment.

When the Khedive Isma'il went to the Paris Exposition

Ezbekiyah gardens in the third quarter of the nineteenth century (G. Delchevalerie, 1872); Key: 1) photographer, 2) European café, 3) restaurant, 4) lagoon, 5) Oriental Café, 6) shooting booth, 7) ice cream café and grotto, 8) belvedere, 9) Greek café, 10) tobacconist, 11) music kiosk, 12) bar, 13) lemonade stand

Universelle in 1867, he returned with a new vision of what Cairo and the Ezbekiyah would become. Under his director of public works, 'Ali Mubarak, the Ezbekiyah was given an octagonal shape, reduced acreage, winding paths, and a small pond, becoming a French-style park much like the Parc Monceau of Paris. He hired the French Barillet Deschamps to supervise the landscape and the German botanist Schweinfurth to import trees, shrubs, and flowering plants. The park was walled, lit by gas lamps with colored glass, and entry was restricted to those who could pay the price of admission.

BIBLIOGRAPHY

Abu-Lughod, Janet. *Cairo: 1001 Years of the City Victorious*. Princeton: Princeton University Press, 1971.

Behrens-Abouseif, Doris. *Azbakkiyya and Its Environs from Azbak to Isma'il, 1476–1879* (Supplément aux Annales Islamologiques, Cahiers no. 6). Cairo: Institut Français d'Archéologie Orientale, 1985.

Clerget, Marcel. *Le Caire: Étude de géographie urbaine et d'histoire économique*, 2 vols. Cairo: Imprimerie E. & R. Schindler, 1934.

Mostyn, Trevor. *Cairo, La Belle Epoque 1869–1952*. London: Quartet Books, 1989.

Tagher, Jeanette. "Le jardin de l'Ezbékieh." *Cahiers d'Histoire Égyptienne* 5–6 (1951): 413–21.

Fustat Houses

The city of Fustat (now part of Cairo) from the mid-ninth to the late twelfth centuries was a densely built, important urban center in which thirty-nine small residences have been excavated and studied, reflecting the ordinary dwelling of an average family. A typical Fustat house had an irregular perimeter due to being wedged into the labyrinthine network of streets, but the central courtyard was orderly and symmetrical with one or more porticoed iwans looking onto it as well as a host of peripheral rooms. Some houses had more than one courtyard. Water was piped through the courts and basins from a private reservoir inside the exterior walls of the house; there were interior latrines from which waste water was flushed away to a sewage canal. The larger courtyards

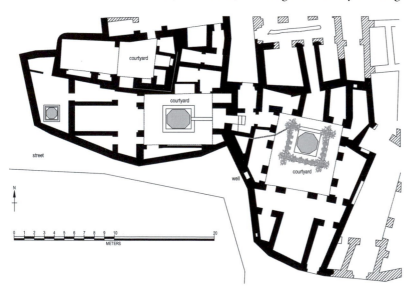

Fustat House (after Baghat and Gabriel)

had simple rectangular basins or more ornamental ones and plots for gardens. Archaeologists have found pits to confirm the presence of shrubs and perhaps low trees. Indeed, the plans give the impression that the graceful inclusion of limited amounts of vegetation was not unlike the urban mansions of the eighteenth and nineteenth century.

Archaeologists have found stairways and wall flues for waste water, indicating that houses had either true upper stories or rooftop terraces. When Nasiri Khusrau visited Fustat in 1046, he saw a prosperous city of multistoried houses and learned of one with a roof garden complete with flowers and orange and banana trees, irrigated by water raised by an animal-driven wheel.

BIBLIOGRAPHY

Bahgat, Aly, and Albert Gabriel. *Fouilles d'al-Foustat*. Paris: E. de Boccard, 1921.

Ostrasz, Antoni A. "The Archaeological Material for the Study of the Domestic Architecture at Fustat." *Africana Bulletin* 26 (1977): 57–87.

Scanlon, George. "Housing and Sanitation: Some Aspects of Medieval Egyptian Life." In A. H. Hourani and S. M. Stern, eds., *The Islamic City*, 185–94. Philadelphia: University of Pennsylvania Press, 1970.

——. Multiple articles in the *Journal of the American Research Center in Egypt*, 1966–84.

Turkey

ALANYA

Hasbahçe

This estate was the largest of a series of pleasure residences built in the region of Alanya, on Turkey's southern coast. The Saljuq rulers conquered the area in 1221 and adopted the area as a winter resort. The estates that they built were devoted to gardens and agriculture and placed their patrons in close proximity to wooded hills with good hunting. The Hasbahçe (Royal Garden) was the largest of the enclosures (5.1 hectares). It had one Saljuq-era pavilion and at least five other structures, all standing on high ground. Some of these were two-storied with windows, and one can imagine that from these airy chambers the prospects of the hilly scenery surrounding the estate would have been delightful. The gardens were fed by a natural spring from which water was collected and stored in a cistern at a lower level. The site also had a large open tank with many channels leading into what was presumably an extensive irrigation system. The discovery of a late Roman aqueduct and canalization nearby indicates that it was also cultivated in that era.

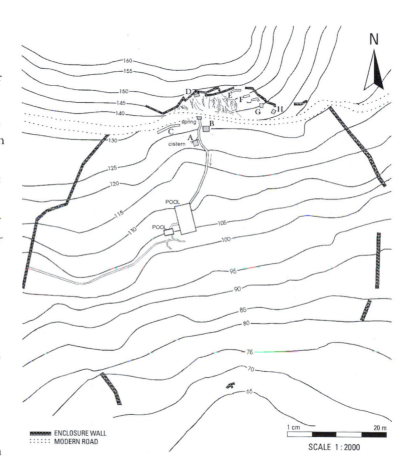

Hasbahçe, Alanya
(Scott Redford)

BIBLIOGRAPHY

Redford, Scott. *Landscape and the State in Medieval Anatolia: Seljuk Gardens and Pavilions of Alanya.* Oxford: Archaeopress, 2000.

——. "Seljuk Pavilions and Enclosures in and Around Alanya." *Arastirma Sonuçlari Toplantisi* 14 (Ankara, 1997): 453–67.

Bosphorus Kiosks

Not only the Ottoman sultan but also the elite nonimperial families built waterside palaces and residences not far from Istanbul along the Bosphorus that on one side enjoyed a river view and on the other had a garden (*bahçe*) sloping upward with the natural contours of the peninsula's terrain. A manuscript illustration from 1738–39 shows both banks of the Bosphorus lined with walled gardens, dotted with towers, and with entries on land and via waterside docks. The gardens were planted with tall shady trees, smaller citrus trees, box-hedges, and beds of flowers that, especially during the Tulip Era (*lala devre*) of 1703–30, contained masses of rare and exotic tulips. The larger palaces imitated the multi-courtyard organization of the Topkapı while the smaller houses had, at the least, a pavilion consisting either of a simple roofed shelter or an enclosed tiled room surrounded by a broad porch, perhaps covered with jasmine or honeysuckle vines. In the sixteenth century, these were stone pavilions with domes; by the seventeenth century, the preference changed to wooden kiosks (*yalıs*). Today, the oldest surviving yali is at the former Amcazade estate, built in 1699 at Andolu Hisari on the Asian side of the Bosphorus (the harem, kitchen, bath, and other buildings no longer exist).

Bosphorus kiosks
(Deniz Calis)

BIBLIOGRAPHY

Artan, Tulay. "Architecture as a Theater of Life: Profile of the Eighteenth-Century Bosphorus." Ph.D. diss. MIT, 1989.

Atasoy, Nurhan. *A Garden for the Sultan: Gardens and Flowers in the Ottoman Culture*. Istanbul: Aygaz, 2002.

Çelebi, Evliya. *Narrative of Travels*, trans. J. von Hammer. London, 1834.

Esin, Emil. "An Eighteenth-Century 'Yali' Viewed in the Line of Development of Related Forms in Turkic Architecture." In *Atti del Secondo Congresso Internationale di Arte Turca*. Naples, 1965.

Necipoğlu, Gulru. "The Suburban Landscape of Sixteenth-Century Istanbul." In Attilio Petruccioli, ed., *Gardens in the Time of the Great Muslim Empires*, 32–71. Leiden: Brill, 1997.

Titley, Norah and Frances Wood. *Oriental Gardens*. San Francisco: Chronicle Books, 1991.

Fenerbahçe

Formerly the site of a Byzantine villa estate in Constantinople, the estate was adapted to serve the Ottoman rulers soon after the conquest of the city (now Istanbul) in 1453. The Fenerbahçe, or Lighthouse Kiosk, was the favorite of Suleyman II and his wife Hurrem Sultan (Roxelana), and in 1562 the sultan remodeled the Byzantine lighthouse and commissioned Mimar Sinan to build a residential palace. In addition to this residence, there were baths, dormitories for the gardeners, a mosque, a small pavilion, and a belvedere tower. The French visitor G.-J. Grelot in 1680 described it thus: "At the end of a split of land ten miles wide which extends into the sea at Kadıköy, there is a large lighthouse . . . [and] a beautiful imperial mansion known as Fener Köşkü. Like almost all the other mansions, this is a square building surrounded by covered galleries with many columns. It stands in a beautiful, well-laid out garden where there are orderly paths and well-tended flowerbeds. However, other Imperial gardens are only a disorderly mixture of trees." A 1711 painting shows a kiosk surrounded by cypress trees and having an open-air porch containing a sunken pool.

Fenerbahçe (Cornelius Loos, National Museum, Sweden)

BIBLIOGRAPHY

Aktepe, Munir. "Istanbul Fenerbahçesi Hakkında Bazı Bilgiler." *Edebiyat Fakültesi Tarih Dergisi* 32 (1979): 349–72.

Atasoy, Nurhan. *A Garden for the Sultan: Gardens and Flowers in the Ottoman Culture*. Istanbul: Aygaz, 2002.

Necipoğlu, Gulru. "The Suburban Landscape of Sixteenth-Century Istanbul." In Attilio Petruccioli, ed., *Gardens in the Time of the Great Muslim Empires*, 32–71. Leiden: Brill, 1997.

Karabali Garden

This garden, which no longer exists, was built by an Ottoman official in the early sixteenth century (prior to 1514) in Kabataş, not far from the Topkapı Palace on the Bosphorus's European side of Istanbul. An unusual example of an Ottoman experiment with the chahar bagh form, it was an oval with intersecting axial paths that were sufficiently broad for the passage of three horses, according to an observer in 1581. The entire garden was surrounded by a thick double row of cypress trees, and the axial paths were lined with alternating cypresses and rosemary shrubs. One of the quadrants was subdivided into smaller beds; another quadrant had pavilions, a marble pool and a fountain; and a third contained a dormitory for the gardeners who tended the estate.

Karabali Garden in Kabataş, Istanbul (Salomon Schweigger, 1608)

A drawing and description of the garden made between 1578 and 1581 by an Austrian diplomat shows its layout. He managed to gain entrance to the garden by bribing the gardeners.

BIBLIOGRAPHY

Atasoy, Nurhan. *A Garden for the Sultan: Gardens and Flowers in the Ottoman Culture*. Istanbul: Aygaz, 2002.

Necipoğlu, Gulru. "The Suburban Landscape of Sixteenth-Century Istanbul." In Attilio Petruccioli, ed., *Gardens in the Time of the Great Muslim Empires*, 32–71. Leiden: Brill, 1997.

Suleymaniye Cemetery

Ottoman charitable foundations (*kulliyes*) typically had a large mosque with an attached cemetery for the founder's tomb (*turbe*). Beyond the *qibla* wall of his mosque in Istanbul, the tomb of Sultan Suleyman II (d. 1566) was a double-shell domed octagon with an entrance porch on the eastern face. Family members were buried in sarcophagi next to him

Suleymaniye
Cemetery (Ruggles)

in the same tomb or, later, they were interred in simpler graves in the same enclosed cemetery next to the mosque. Only Suleyman's wife Hurrem (d. 1558) also had the status of a free-standing mausoleum, although it is smaller than his. The area surrounding the tomb was gradually filled with graves consisting of horizontal marble slabs with headstones inscribed with the deceased's name, death date, a verse from the Qur'an, and often a carved floral relief. Some of the slabs had polylobed apertures for a plant, while others consisted of slightly raised, boxed marble enclosures, the interior of which served as a small garden bed. Most of the graves at the Suleymaniye date to the late nineteenth and twentieth centuries, and certainly the specific planting of predominantly brilliantly colorful, sweet-smelling roses is of quite recent date. However, the fact that many of the slabs have holes for a single vine or provide space for a cultivated plot indicates that planting was intended and that the graves were imagined as miniature gardens. The flowers were more than tokens of care and commemoration bestowed upon the deceased; blooming anew each year, they were symbols of eternal life.

The cemetery at the Suleymaniye is not unique, although it is particularly well tended. Large cemeteries on the edge of urban centers and funerary gardens attached to mosques were ubiquitous in Istanbul and other Ottoman cities.

BIBLIOGRAPHY
Dickie, James. "Garden and Cemetery in Sinan's Istanbul." *Environmental Design: Journal of the Islamic Environmental Design Research Centre* (*Sinan and the Urban Vision*), nos. 1–2 (1987): 70–85.
Goodwin, Godfrey. "Gardens of the Dead in Ottoman Times." *Muqarnas* 5 (1988): 61–69.
———. *A History of Ottoman Architecture*. London: Thames and Hudson, 1971.

Topkapı Saray

The Topkapı Saray was the Ottoman palace and seat of government, built in Istanbul at the tip of the peninsula surrounded by the Golden Horn, Sea of Marmara, and the Bosphorus beginning in 1455. As early as the fifteenth century, an observer described large handsome gardens around the palace with a variety of fruit trees and plants in orchards and meadows, copiously supplied by cold fresh water. Built by different patrons over a period of more than four hundred years, these gardens took the form of semi-natural parks arrayed in the outer enclosure that surrounded the three courtyards of the inner palace, as well as more formally planned gardens adjacent to paved terraces and pavilions with rectangular pools. Unlike the Safavid and Mughal patrons who preferred the tight

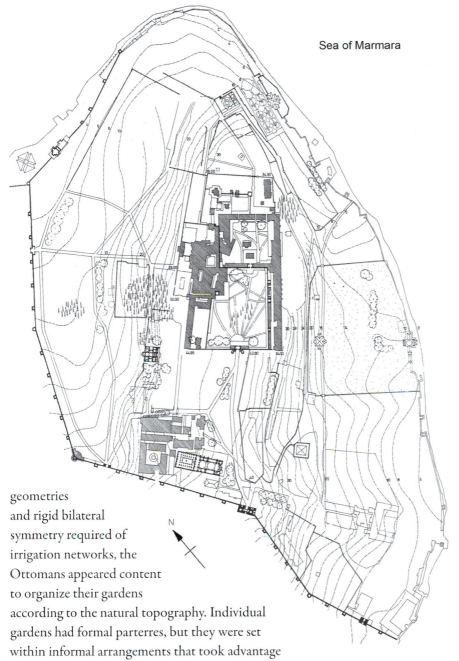

Sea of Marmara

N

Topkapı Saray
(after Eldem and
Akozan)

geometries
and rigid bilateral
symmetry required of
irrigation networks, the
Ottomans appeared content
to organize their gardens
according to the natural topography. Individual
gardens had formal parterres, but they were set
within informal arrangements that took advantage
of the naturally hilly terrain to provide broad views of varied landscapes. The Ottoman
emphasis, therefore, was on the naturalism of the setting rather than strictly imposed
artificial designs and linear organization of water canalization.

Suleyman the Magnificent (1520–66) loved his gardens of flowering bulbs, roses, and
cypresses and employed 2,500 gardeners to tend them. Ahmet III was another of the
Topkapı's most keen garden patrons: he planted a tulip garden in the Fourth Court just
outside the Circumcision Room for the private enjoyment of himself and his immediate
entourage. In addition to the living gardens, the theme of nature was extended in the

ornament of the Topkapı's architecture: tilework, wall paintings, and textiles depicted tulips, carnations, the blossoms of fruit trees, and singing birds.

BIBLIOGRAPHY

Atasoy, Nurhan. *A Garden for the Sultan: Gardens and Flowers in the Ottoman Culture.* Istanbul: Aygaz, 2002.

Eldem, Sedad H., and Feridun Akozan. *Topkapı Sarayı bir Mimari Araştırma.* Istanbul: Millî Eğitim Basımevi, 1982.

Goodwin, Geoffrey. *A History of Ottoman Architecture.* London: Thames and Hudson, 1971.

Necipoğlu, Gulru. *Architecture, Ceremonial, and Power: The Topkapı Palace in the Fifteenth and Sixteenth Centuries.* Cambridge, Mass.: MIT Press, 1991.

Titley, Norah, and Frances Wood. *Oriental Gardens.* San Francisco: Chronicle Books, 1991.

Uskudar Saray

This large rambling imperial estate (also known as the Kavak Palace) stood on the Bosphorus shore of Istanbul across from the Topkapı Palace, from where it was easily reached by boat. It was built with three enclosed gardens in the 1550s by Suleyman I and was expanded and received new buildings during the course of the next century by Selim II, Murad III, Ahmet I, and Murad IV. The sultan and his family used it as a pleasurable escape from the formality and constrictive spaces of the imperial palace, and its extensive grounds allowed many pursuits such as riding, hunting, and the launching of miniature boats in broad pools. It was demolished in the late eighteenth century, but contemporary sources mentioned a main palace and multiple pavilions, with latticed passageways, pools, fountains, terraces, belvedere towers with gilded domes, and a jasmine-covered balustrade. A variety of

Uskudar Saray (Choiseul-Gouffier, 1892)

trees such as cypress, pine, plane, and cherry were planted there according to historical descriptions, but a seventeenth-century observer wrote that mostly vegetables grew in the garden beds and that there were no formal garden plots.

BIBLIOGRAPHY

Atasoy, Nurhan. *A Garden for the Sultan: Gardens and Flowers in the Ottoman Culture.*, Istanbul: Aygaz, 2002.

Necipoğlu, Gulru. "The Suburban Landscape of Sixteenth-Century Istanbul." In Attilio Petruccioli, ed., *Gardens in the Time of the Great Muslim Empires*, 32–71. Leiden: Brill, 1997.

Yıldız Saray

On an elevated site overlooking the Bosphorus, in Istanbul, on land used for hunting by Ottoman sultans since the early sixteenth century, Sultan Selim (r. 1789–1807) built a summer palace with a rococo fountain for his mother, Mihrişah. At mid-century, these structures were demolished and a new pavilion was built for the Valide Sultan, Bezmialem. When Sultan Abdul Hamid II (r. 1876–1909) ascended the throne, he transferred the court from the Dolmabahçe Palace to the Yıldız Saray, which remained the seat of imperial government throughout his reign. The succession of pavilions and administrative halls set within a succession of courtyards with monumental gates resembles the planning of the Topkapı Palace. There were ten acres of gardens at the palace. These included both formal walled gardens and parkland, large pools and a small artificial canal, fountains and pavilions set within the gardens as well as poised at the water's edge. In the private garden, next to the harem quarters, there is an elongated artificial lake with a central island adorned by a small kiosk. At the south end of the garden, the three-storied Cihannuma (Scenic) Kiosk had views of not only the garden within but also outside the palace precinct to the Sea of Marmara and the Bosphorus.

Yıldız Palace
(Ruggles and
Variava)

BIBLIOGRAPHY

Bilgin, Bulent. *Geçmişte Yıldız Sarayı/Only Yesterday at Yıldız Sarayı*. Istanbul: Yıldız Sarayı Vakfı, 1988.

MANISA

Manisa Saray

This palace of eight acres, no longer in its original state, housed a succession of Ottoman princes who, as was customary until the seventeenth century, were sent to gubernatorial posts such as Manisa in order to train to lead as emperor. Hence the palace was grand and reflected imperial privilege. A double-page manuscript painting from 1595 shows the palace and surrounding buildings, including a cemetery in the lower right with a variety of trees and a stream spanned by a bridge. Within the palace, several courtyards are depicted. On the left is the rectangular harem courtyard with a prominent central fountain surrounded by colonnades. As this

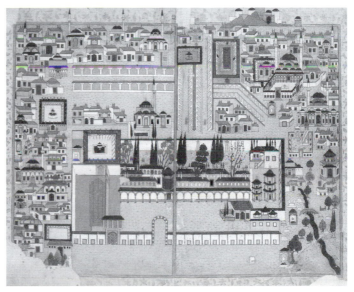

Manisa Saray
(Topkapı Museum)

would not have been seen by the artists, it is schematic and probably does not reflect the actual harem courtyard. The large courtyard in the foreground has a small fenced area with two cypress trees and flowers. The courtyard behind this has several buildings, a large tree awash with pink blooms, two other deciduous trees, and many tall cypresses. The informal placement of the vegetation was typical of Ottoman landscape planning.

BIBLIOGRAPHY

Atasoy, Nurhan. *A Garden for the Sultan: Gardens and Flowers in the Ottoman Culture*. Istanbul: Aygaz, 2002.

Syria and Region

AL-RUSAFA

After the Umayyads (661–750) took over the Byzantine city of Rusafa in northern Syria, the caliph Hisham (724–43) built a palace outside the walls that included a garden or orchard enclosed by walls of mud brick (although archaeologists are not sure that these walls belong to the same period as the garden itself). The archaeologists who excavated the garden in the late 1980s found a square stone pavilion in the garden's center. The pavilion was surrounded by an arcade and had an opening on each side from which three steps ran down to the garden. Extending away from the steps on the west side was a slightly elevated rubble and lime walkway, and it is possible that similar walkways once existed on the other three sides, thus forming the earliest discovered *chahar bagh* garden plan.

This Syrian Rusafa may have been the model for a garden-palace with the same name built by 'Abd al-Rahman I, Hisham's grandson, outside of Cordoba in the second half of the eighth century. If so, it would explain how the four-part cross-axial plan was transmitted from the eastern Mediterranean to the Iberian peninsula.

Al-Rusafa
(after Thilo Ulbert)

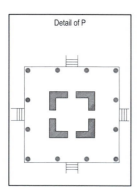

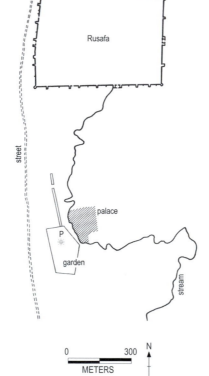

BIBLIOGRAPHY

Otto-Dorn, Katharina. "Grabung im Ummayadischen Rusafah." *Ars Orientalis* 2 (1957): 119–33. (N.B. This is not the same site identified as the Umayyad Rusafa by Ulbert, see below.)

Ruggles, D. Fairchild. "Il giardini con pianta a croce nel Mediterraneo Islamic." In Attilio Petruccioli, ed., *Il giardino islamico: Architettura, natura, paesaggio*, 143–54. Milan: Electa, 1993. German edition: "Der als Achsenkreuz angelegte islamische Garten des Mittelmeerraums und seine Bedeutung." In *Der islamische Garten: Architektur. Natur. Landschaft*. Stuttgart: Deutsche Verlag-Anstalt, 1994.

Ulbert, Thilo. "Ein Umaiyadischer Pavillion in Resafa-Rusafat Hisam." *Damaszener Mitteilungen* 7 (1993): 213–31.

DAMASCUS

Palace al-Azem

Built in the neighborhood of the Great Mosque in Damascus beginning in 1749 by As'ad Pasha al-Azem, the al-Azem Palace (5,500 square m) was built using spolia from older houses in Damascus. Hence, it has the appearance of greater age. It was severely damaged in 1924 and restored in mid-century, winning an Aga Khan Award for Architecture in 1981–83.

Like the elite houses of the period, it is divided between the public reception area (*saramlik*) and the large, open paved courtyard that comprises its domestic heart (*haramlik*), with baths in the northeast corner of the latter. The domestic courtyard (25 by 25 m) has a large rectangular pool at the north end which is connected by a channel to a raised fountain at the other; there are beds for flowers and trees—oranges are planted there today—reserved in its handsomely paved marble floors. Surrounding the courtyard are iwans and recessed chambers that provide shade and cushioned seating so that the residents could enjoy the brilliant colors, pleasing sounds, and fragrant scents of the garden without subjecting themselves to the sun's heat.

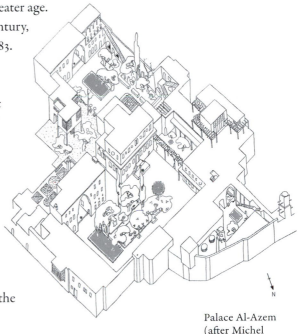

Palace Al-Azem
(after Michel
Écochard, 1935)

BIBLIOGRAPHY

Cantacuzino, Sherban. "Azem Palace." In S. Cantacuzino, ed., *Architecture in Continuity*, 164–69. New York: Aperture, 1985.

Écochard, Michel. "Le Palais Azem de Damas." *Gazette des Beaux-Arts*, 6th ser., 13 (1935): 231–41.

Maury, Bernard. "La Maison damascène au XVIIIe siècle et au début du XIXe siècle." In *Habitat traditionnel dans les pays musulmans autour de la Méditerranée (Aix-en-Provence, 6–8 juin 1984)*, 3 vols. 1:1–42. Cairo: Institut français d'archéologie orientale, ca. 1988–91.

Houses of the Eighteenth–Nineteenth Centuries

When the American George William Curtis went to Damascus in 1852 he visited a Jewish merchant's house and described a central marble reservoir with fountains, huge pots of flowers arranged along the walls and next to the reservoir, and roses and lemon and orange trees. He exclaimed, "Each Damascus house is a paradise" (Keenan, 91). These mansions of the Ottoman period (1517–1920) housed many generations of the same family and were organized in multiple stories around one or more courtyards, which could be added as the family expanded. However, in the nineteenth century the congestion of the old city limited architectural expansion to the extent that families began to build new mansions outside the city walls in suburbs such as the Sarouja Quarter.

Generally, these Ottoman-era houses were divided between an outer public courtyard (*saramlik*) and an inner domestic courtyard (*haramlik*). The plan here shows the eighteenth-century Bayt Siba'i, which was organized around two courtyards (it is now owned by the Syrian government and used as a museum).

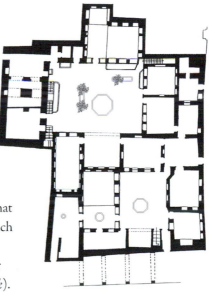

Bayt Siba'i,
Damascus
(after Bridget
Keenan)

BIBLIOGRAPHY
Keenan, Brigid. *Damascus: Hidden Treasures of the Old City*. New York: Thames and Hudson, 2000.
Moaz, Abd al-Razzaq. "Domestic Architecture, Notables and Power: A Neighborhood in Late Ottoman Damascus: An Introduction." In *Art turc/Turkish Art (Tenth International Congress of Turkish Art, Geneva, 17–23 September 1995)*, 489–95. Geneva: Fondation Max van Berchem, 1999.
Sack, Dorothée. *Damaskus: Entwicklung und Struktur einer orientalisch-islamischen Stadt*. Mainz: P. von Zabern, 1989.

KHIRBAT AL-MAFJAR

Built about 739–43 by the Umayyad heir apparent, two kilometers north of Jericho, Khirbat al-Mafjar consisted of a handsomely ornamented palace that included a mosque and a huge, sumptuously appointed bathhall that also doubled as a reception hall. Dominating the forecourt that led to the palace and baths was a large roofed square fountain (approximately 16 m each side) that received water from an artificial reservoir outside the walls. This water flowed from the 'Ain al-Sultan spring two kilometers to the southwest and two smaller springs four kilometers to the northwest. Traces of two portions of above-ground aqueducts, one of which spanned the wadi in three arched tiers, are still visible. On the east side of the palace there was an additional enclosure used for agriculture or pasturage. Khirbat al-Mafjar exploited natural sources of water, using it for limited but effective irrigation. Although it did not have any identifiable formal gardens, it was a dramatic example of landscape transformation, arising from the desert like a verdant oasis.

BIBLIOGRAPHY
Baer, Eva. "Khirbat al-Mafjar." In *Encyclopaedia of Islam*, 2nd ed., 5: 10–17. Leiden: E. J. Brill, 1986.
Creswell, K. A. C. *A Short Account of Early Muslim Architecture*, rev. James Allan. Aldershot: Scolar Press, 1989.
Hamilton, R. W. *Khirbat al Mafjar: An Arabian Mansion in the Jordan Valley*. Oxford: Clarendon Press, 1959.

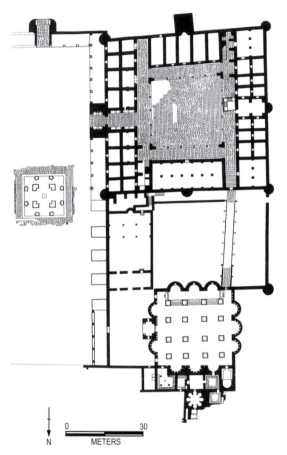

Khirbat al-Mafjar
(after R. W.
Hamilton)

QASR AL-HAYR EAST

Qasr al-Hayr East (al-Sharqi) was an estate built by Umayyad patrons in the years 700–730 in the desert about 100 km northeast of Palmyra (Syria). Its outer walls enclosed a caravanserai, large residence with an open courtyard, and a bathhouse clustered at the north end. The enclosed area was an irregular shape 6.6 km long and 2.2 km wide, with a

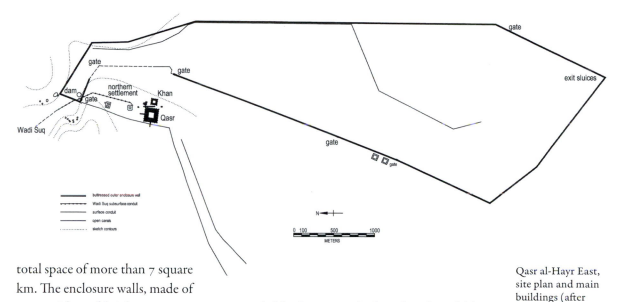

Qasr al-Hayr East,
site plan and main
buildings (after
Grabar et al.)

total space of more than 7 square
km. The enclosure walls, made of
stone with mud-brick upper courses, were probably about 3.5 m high and easily scalable;
their purpose was clearly not to repel attackers but to trap the seasonal rains inside. These
rains poured down in a broad stream bed (wadi) from the ridge of hills, the Jabal Bishri,
to the north and caused flash floods. But large sluices at the north and south ends of
the enclosure admitted water in manageable quantities and kept it there to soak the soil.
Archaeologists found an olive press, vats, and heaps of olive pits indicating that olive and
perhaps other fruit trees were cultivated here, the agricultural production complemented
by animal husbandry outside the walls.

BIBLIOGRAPHY

Creswell, K. A. C. *A Short Account of Early Muslim Architecture*, rev. James Allan. Aldershot: Scolar Press,
     1989.
Gabriel, Albert. "Kasr el-Heir." *Syria* 8 (1927): 302–29.
Grabar, Oleg. "Qasr al-Hayr Ash-Sharqi." In *The Oxford Encyclopedia of Archaeology in the Near East*, 5 vols.
     4: 379–80. New York: Oxford University Press, 1997.
Grabar, Oleg, R. Holod, J. Knustad, and W. Trousdale. *City in the Desert: Qasr al-Hayr East*. Cambridge,
     Mass.: Harvard University Press, 1978.
Seyrig, Henri. "Antiquités syriennes: Les jardins de Kasr el-Heir." *Syria* 12 (1931): 316–18.

Oman

MUSCAT

Sultan Qaboos University

In Al-Khod, a short distance from Muscat, a modern university campus for 5,000 students was built from 1981 to 1986. The plan of Sultan Qaboos University, by the British
architectural firm YRM International in consultation with the landscape firm Brian

Clouston International, combines Beaux-Arts principles of clarity, openness, and apsidal spaces with the linear garden effect of Isfahan's Chahar Bagh Avenue. Its broad central axis begins west of the mosque: here the student center is located as well as the Arts and Business Colleges with gardens with square pools and fountains. The axis proceeds eastward to central campus where the most important university buildings are arrayed, linked by lightly sketched arcades to create permeable courtyards. Off this axis are the individual and group residences for faculty, staff, and students, each with gardens designed to adapt to the arid climate of the desert. At the female student residence (shown here), there is a garden with a broad walkway that descends in gently sloping terraces carrying a single water channel (fed by a natural wadi). At changes in ground level, pedestrians descend steps and the channel cascades over stylized chadars made of brick tiers set in a sawtooth pattern. The green vegetation is confined to small beds that alternate with areas of softly contoured rocks, indicating the attention paid to water conservation and xeriscaping.

The built forms are geometrically spare, modern, and white; yet the primacy of the garden and the inclusion of forms such as ornamental screens, arcades, and fountains reflect traditional Islamic principles of architecture and landscape design.

BIBLIOGRAPHY
Damluji, Salma Samar. *The Architecture of Oman*. Reading, U.K.: Garnet Publishing, 1998.
"Sultan Qaboos University." *Mimar* (Architecture in Development) 37 (1990): 46–49.

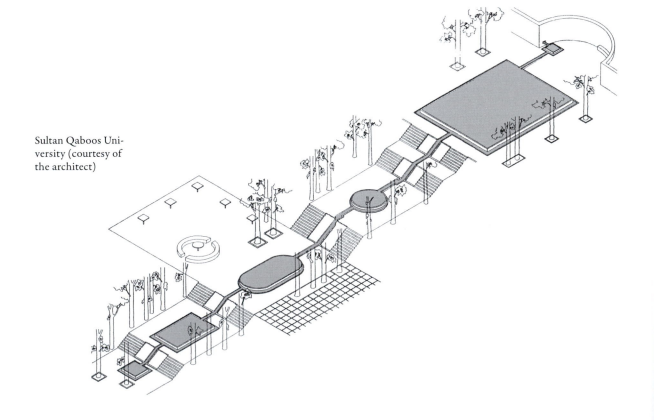

Sultan Qaboos University (courtesy of the architect)

Iraq

SAMARRA

Balkuwara Palace

Al-Mutawakkil, in addition to his own palace, Dar al-Khilafa, also constructed magnificent residences for his sons, among them Balkuwara built for al-Muʻtazz (r. 866–869) at the southernmost end of Samarra. As at the Dar al-Khilafa, the entire palace exploited natural topography so that from highest point—the throne room—there was a seemingly endless view of the surrounding plains. The palace proper, which stood within a huge outer enclosure (1,171 m on each side), contained small and monumental halls and courtyards, some of which may have been gardened. The southwest façade opened toward the Tigris with a courtyard, walled on three sides, that sat on a bluff 15 meters above the river. This space was axially aligned with the throne room and adjoined it via a three-iwan portal that was richly decorated with mosaic, mother-of-pearl, painted and gilded wood, and colored glass windows. The courtyard had a water basin in its center and was presumably gardened. River traffic arrived at this end of the palace; at the northeast end there was a monumental portal that opened onto one of three interior courtyards. The archaeologist Ernst Herzfeld saw evidence of water in these courtyards and, in the two largest, observed that cross-axial visual axes were created by the entrances on the center of each side. He speculated that these courtyards consisted of gardens on four-part plans with fountains at the intersection of the defining axes. However, the evidence for this has been challenged by later archaeologists who examined Herzfeld's field notes, and Alastair Northedge's plan (reproduced here) shows garden courtyards divided bilaterally. Herzfeld may have been imposing his conception of what a palace courtyard *should* be onto an environment where the chahar bagh plan was not yet standard.

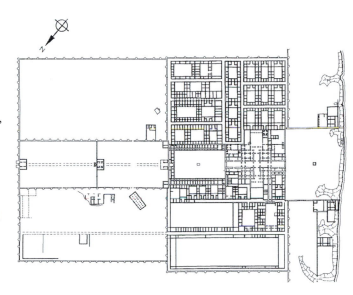

Balkuwara Palace, Samarra (Alastair Northedge)

BIBLIOGRAPHY

Creswell, K. A. C. *A Short Account of Early Muslim Architecture*, rev. by James Allan. Aldershot: Scolar Press, 1989. Contains a summary of Ernst Herzfeld's preliminary report (below).

Herzfeld, Ernst. *Erster vorläufiger Bericht über die Ausgrabungen von Samarra*. Berlin, 1912.

Northedge, Alastair. "The Palaces of the Abbasids at Samarra." In Chase Robinson, ed., *A Medieval Islamic City Reconsidered: An Interdisciplinary Approach to Samarra,* 29–67. Oxford: Oxford University Press, 2001.

Dar al-Khilafa

Also known as the Jawsaq al-Khaqani, this palace was built in 836 at the northern end of Samarra, a new development founded along the banks of the Tigris River by the

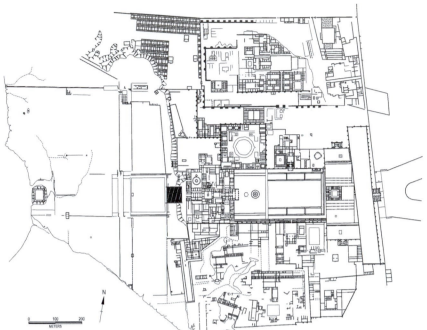

Abbasid caliph al-Muʻtasim (r. 833–842) who had begun to feel confined by the rigid, circular plan of Baghdad. From a slightly raised bluff, the palace overlooked the river from its west side. Its principal entrance was a large three-iwan portal (the so-called Bab al-ʻAmma), 12 meters high, atop a high terrace, reached by an enormous flight of steps, 60 meters wide and 17 meters high. The portal had a second story from which either the palace guards or the royal inhabitants could

Dar al-Khilafa, Samarra (Alastair Northedge)

have surveyed the surrounding landscape. Indeed, because of its height, the entire terrace had a panoramic view, overlooking a large square pool with a pavilion, gardens, and a channel that led from the pool to a raised pavilion poised along the riverbank some 300 meters away. Hence, the palace commanded not only a huge expanse of walled space, but also the landscape surrounding it and on the opposite bank of the river.

Entering through the great portal into the palace complex, the visitor passed through a series of halls into a square courtyard with a fountain in its center and further along the central axis, to the throne room. These are not all of the same date but were built successively over the course of more than fifty years. Beyond lay the great esplanade (350 by 180 m) which had water channels and two fountains and thus could have been gardened. On its east side, the palace again opened up to the surrounding landscape. Along much of the façade, there was a long polo ground with a two-story pavilion from which spectators could watch the sports in the arena below or, on the opposite side, look further afield to an immense elliptical track (5 km long) that was either a racetrack or a hunting preserve.

BIBLIOGRAPHY
Creswell, K. A. C. *A Short Account of Early Muslim Architecture*, rev. by James Allan. Aldershot: Scolar Press, 1989. Contains a summary of Ernst Herzfeld's work (below).
Hammudi, Khalid Khalil. "Qasr al-khalifa al-Muʻtasim fi Samarra." *Sumer* 38 (1982): 168–205.
Herzfeld, Ernst. "Mitteilungen über die Arbeiten der zweiten Kampagne von Samarra." *Der Islam* 5 (1915): 196–204.
Northedge, Alastair. "Creswell, Herzfeld, and Samarra." *Muqarnas* 8 (1991): 74–93.
——. "An Interpretation of the Palace of the Caliph at Samarra." *Ars Orientalis* 23 (1993): 143–70.
——. "The Palaces of the Abbasids at Samarra." In Chase Robinson, ed., *A Medieval Islamic City Reconsidered: An Interdisciplinary Approach to Samarra,* 29–67. Oxford: Oxford University Press, 2001.
Viollet, Henri. "Description du palais de al-Moutasim à Samara," and "Fouilles à Samara." *Mémoires de l'Académie des Inscriptions et Belles-lettres,* ser. 1, vol. 12, pt. 2 (1909, 1911): 567–94, 685–717.

Iran

ISFAHAN

Bagh-i Bulbul and the Hesht Behesht

The Bagh-i Bulbul ("Garden of the Nightingale") was the largest of the gardens along the Chahar Bagh Avenue in Isfahan in the Safavid period, and is the only one that remains today. It was built in 1670 by Shah Suleyman I, renovated in the Qajar period

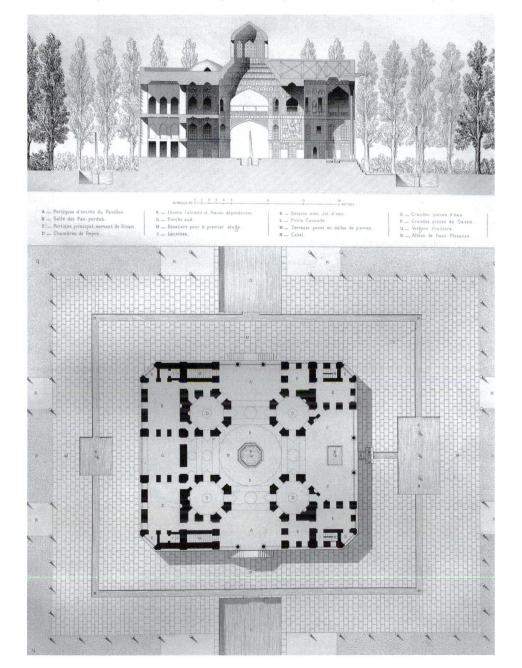

Hesht Behesht and the Bagh-i Bulbul (Pascal Coste, 1867)

A — Portiques d'entrée du Pavillon.
B — Salle des Pas-perdus.
C — Portique principal servant de Divan.
D — Chambres de Repos.

E — Divers Cabinets et Pièces dépendantes.
G — Porche sud.
H — Escaliers pour le premier étage.
I — Latrines.

K — Bassins avec Jet-d'eau.
L — Petite Cascade.
M — Terrasse pavée en dalles de pierres.
N — Canal.

O — Grandes pièces d'eau.
P — Grandes pièces de Gazon.
Q — Vergers fruitiers.
R — Allées de haut-Platanes.

(1779–1924), and restored in the 1970s. Of its plantings, nothing remains. But its broad axial watercourses (7.6 m wide) still converge on the octagonally planned Hesht Behesht ("Eight Paradises") pavilion that rises on an elevated platform about two-thirds of the way down the garden's central axis (Plate 18). An 1867 engraving shows a magnificent muqarnas-domed interior with a lantern above corresponding to a fountain at floor level. From here as well as the broad porches, the garden could be regarded with enjoyment. Indeed, the theme of nature and gardens permeated the painted and tile ornament of the hall, and the water that emerged in the pavilion's center to flow over chadars seemed to bind the inside and outside together as one continuous environment.

BIBLIOGRAPHY
Blake, Stephen. *Half the World: The Social Architecture of Safavid Isfahan, 1590–1722*. Costa Mesa, Calif.: Mazda, 1999.
Brookes, John. *Gardens of Paradise: History and Design of the Great Islamic Gardens*. London: Weidenfeld and Nicolson, 1987.
Golombek, Lisa. "From Tamerlane to the Taj Mahal." In A. Daneshvari, ed., *Essays in Islamic Art and Architecture in Honor of Katharina Otto-Dorn*, 43–50. Malibu, Calif.: Undena, 1981.
Golombek, Lisa, and Renata Holod. "Preliminary Report on the Isfahan City Project." In *Akten VII. Internationalen Kongresses für Iranische Kunst und Archäologie (Munich, 1976)*, 578–90. Berlin: D. Reimer, 1979.
Holod, Renata, ed. *Iranian Studies* (special issue: Proceedings of The Isfahan Colloquium) 7 (1974).
Honarfar, L. *Historical Monuments of Isfahan*, 3rd ed. Isfahan: Emami Press, 1964.

Chahar Bagh Avenue

When Shah 'Abbas I (1587–1629) moved the Safavid capital to Isfahan in 1598, he commenced a major transformation of the city that included a new *maydan* (public plaza) with a palace precinct on its west side that led to a long avenue called the Chahar Bagh. Lined with plane trees and enclosed gardens with romantic names like Bagh-i Guldasta (Garden of Flowers) and Bagh-i Bulbul (Garden of the Nightingale), the avenue presented a coherent façade of gates and pavilion-portals that belied the individuality of the spaces laid out within. The 50-meter-wide avenue had a central watercourse flanked by smaller channels that flowed over chadars in slightly descending levels from the Jahan Nama pavilion at its northern end, down to the Ziyandeh River and the Allah Wardi Khan Bridge. On the opposite bank, the Chahar Bagh continued uphill to a vast imperial estate called the Hazar Jarib (1596, destroyed in 1722) which consisted of twelve terraces, each raised approximately 2 meters above the next. This estate in turn was connected by a tree-lined avenue to the extensive Farahabad gardens to the west.

BIBLIOGRAPHY
Alemi, Mahvash. "The Royal Gardens of the Safavid Period: Types and Models." In Attilio Petruccioli, ed., *Gardens in the Time of the Great Muslim Empires*, 72–96. Leiden: E. J. Brill, 1997.
Ameli, Abdulah J., A. Montazer, and S. Ayvazian. "Repères sur l'évolution urbaine d'Ispahan." In Darab Diba, P. Revault, and S. Santelli, eds., *Maisons d'Ispahan*, 23–43. Paris: Maisonneuve & Larose, 2001.
Blake, Stephen. *Half the World: The Social Architecture of Safavid Isfahan, 1590–1722*. Costa Mesa, Calif.: Mazda, 1999.
Pinder-Wilson, Ralph. "The Persian Garden: *Bagh* and *Chahar Bagh*." In Elisabeth MacDougall and Richard Ettinghausen, eds., *The Islamic Garden*, 71–85. Washington, D.C.: Dumbarton Oaks, 1976.
Wilber, Donald. *Persian Gardens and Garden Pavilions*. 1962; reprint, Washington, D.C.: Dumbarton Oaks, 1979.

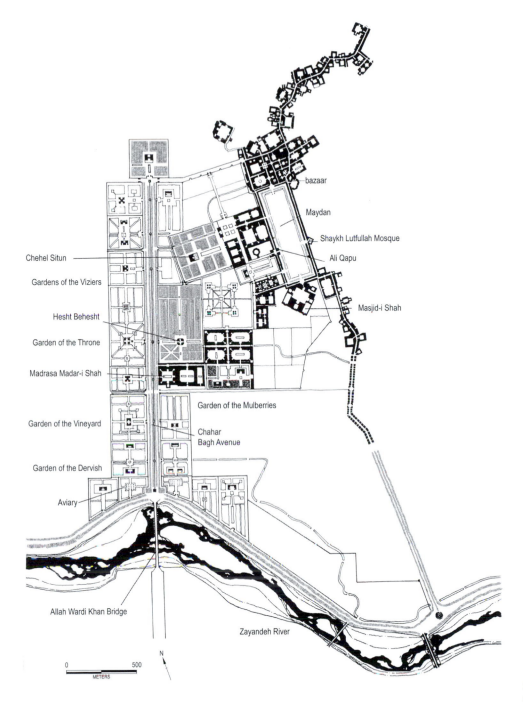

bazaar

Maydan

Shaykh Lutfullah Mosque

Chehel Situn

Ali Qapu

Gardens of the Viziers

Masjid-i Shah

Hesht Behesht

Garden of the Throne

Madrasa Madar-i Shah

Garden of the Mulberries

Garden of the Vineyard

Chahar
Bagh Avenue

Garden of the Dervish

Aviary

Allah Wardi Khan Bridge

Zayandeh River

N

0   500
METERS

Isfahan and
the Chahar Bagh
Avenue
(after N. Ardalan
and L. Bakhtiar)

Chihil Situn
(Pascal Coste, 1867)

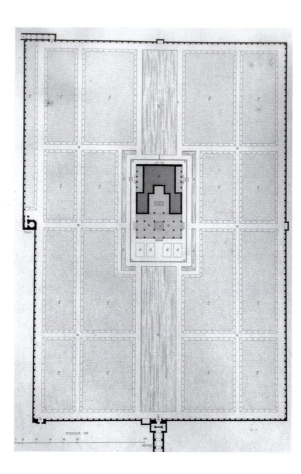

Bagh-i Fin, Kashan
(Variava)

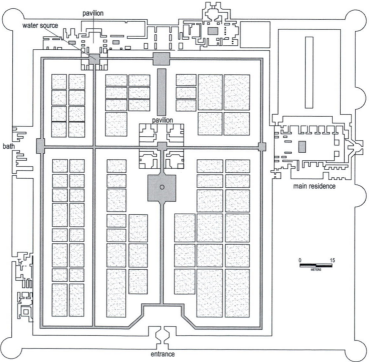

GARDENS AND SITES

Chihil Situn

Finished 1647 by the Safavid Shah 'Abbas II, the Chihil Situn was a reception hall within a fifteen-acre garden (90 m on a side) that belonged to the larger array of royal gardens between Isfahan's palace precinct and the Chahar Bagh Avenue. The hall burned in 1706 and was rebuilt within a year by Shah Sultan Husain. In the garden, there were three walkways lined with trees that led to the hall. The name means "Forty Columns," a reference to the twenty wooden supports that form the *talar* porch and their reflection, which effectively replicates them, in the long rectangular pool that extends from the eastern façade of the pavilion. The talar nearly doubles the length of the pavilion: an 1840 engraving gives a sense of the spatial permeability achieved by the pavilion's open interior and lofty porch. The pavilion's cedar columns correspond to the trees in the garden and the distant minarets; the water of the rectangular basin set within the heart of the pavilion reappears as the spouting fountains of the talar and ultimately in the channels and broad pools in the garden. Finally, the theme of a garden parterre filled with colorful blooms would have been introduced to the architectural interior in the form of rich carpets depicting flowers and chahar bagh layouts on the pavilion's floor. Elsewhere on its grounds, the garden formerly had four smaller pavilions.

BIBLIOGRAPHY

Blake, Stephen. *Half the World: The Social Architecture of Safavid Isfahan, 1590–1722*. Costa Mesa, Calif.: Mazda, 1999.
Brookes, John. *Gardens of Paradise: History and Design of the Great Islamic Gardens*. London: Weidenfeld and Nicolson, 1987.
Holod, Renata, ed. *Iranian Studies* (special issue: Proceedings of The Isfahan Colloquium) 7 (1974).
Wilber, Donald. *Persian Gardens and Garden Pavilions*. 1962; reprint, Washington, D.C.: Dumbarton Oaks, 1979.

KASHAN

Bagh-i Fin

The Bagh-i Fin is a six-acre estate built about 1587 by the Safavid Shah 'Abbas I near Kashan. Restored in 1797–1834 by the Qajar Fath 'Ali Shah and made a national monument in 1935, it now reflects both Safavid and Qajar taste. The garden is organized as a chahar bagh with a pavilion at the intersection of the principal axes. This pavilion faces the main house in one direction and in the other a smaller pavilion with a talar porch. It faces a large pool on its south side and, on the north side, overlooks a broad channel that runs to various subsidiary buildings along the north wall, which is slightly elevated. Accentuated by the luminous blue faience tile lining the channels, water is everywhere present in the garden: it defines the principal axes of the plan, encircles the garden, and runs through the central pavilion (Plate 1). It runs down small cascades (chadars) and jets upward in fountains. A secondary water axis runs along the southwest side, leading to another nineteenth-century pavilion and basin (called the Howz Jushan) that marks the water's point of entry into the garden.

The waterworks and dense shady plantings of fruit, willow, and ancient cypress trees are a dramatic contrast to the desert setting of the Bagh-i Fin estate. The water is drawn by qanat from the Karkas mountains to the south and is stored in a reservoir about a mile from the garden. It not only supplies the estate gardens but surrounding orchards as well.

BIBLIOGRAPHY

Brookes, John. *Gardens of Paradise: History and Design of the Great Islamic Gardens*. London: Weidenfeld and Nicolson, 1987.

Khansari, Mehdi, M. Reza Moghtader, and Minouch Yavari. *The Persian Garden: Echoes of Paradise*. Washington, D.C.: Mage, 1998.

Moynihan, Elizabeth. *Paradise as a Garden in Persia and Mughal India*. New York: George Braziller, 1979.

Wilber, Donald. *Persian Gardens and Garden Pavilions*. 1962; reprint, Washington, D.C.: Dumbarton Oaks, 1979.

SHIRAZ

Bagh-i Takht

Nestled in a high valley, the city of Shiraz was famed for its lovely gardens in the Timurid period and later, and many eighteenth-century gardens survive partially today. These include the Bagh-i Jahan Numa (of much earlier origins), Bagh-i Arg, the qanat–fed Bagh-i Dilgusha (built by the local Zand dynasty in 1750–79), Bagh-i Nazar, Haft Tan (third quar-

Bagh-i Takht, Shiraz (Variava), below left; Shah-Gul Garden, Tabriz (Chodon), below right

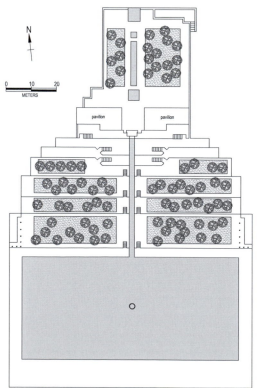

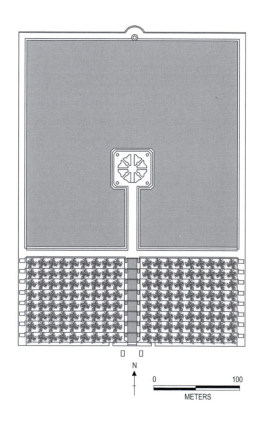

ter of the eighteenth century), Narangistan (built by the Qavam family in the 1870s), Bagh-i Eram (1824), and Bagh-i Takht. The latter, founded in the mid-seventeenth century as the Bagh-i Firdaus, was apparently renamed and probably rebuilt in 1789 by Muhammad Shah. It consisted of seven garden terraces tumbling steeply from a hill, the geometry of the traditional chahar bagh adapted to suit the natural mountainous topography. At the summit, a large residential pavilion (*'imarat*) stood at the edge of a garden called the Bagh-i Khalvat from where it overlooked the lower terraces through a talar porch. The water, which came from the river, flowed from here through a central channel that bisected the terraces until it culminated in an enormous rectangular pool on the lowest one. Contemporary accounts describe regattas of miniature boats held in such pools. A *bagh-i takht* was in fact a common name and a stock type; the Safavid and Qajar patrons had a penchant for naming and modeling their estates after Timurid originals.

BIBLIOGRAPHY

Arianpour, Ali-Reza. *Bagh-ha ye, Tarikhy-e Shiraz* (in Persian). Tehran: Farhang-Sara, 1986 (1365 H.).

Brookes, John. *Gardens of Paradise: History and Design of the Great Islamic Gardens.* London: Weidenfeld and Nicolson, 1987.

Khansari, Mehdi, M. Reza Moghtader, and Minouch Yavari. *The Persian Garden: Echoes of Paradise.* Washington, D.C.: Mage, 1998.

Moynihan, Elizabeth. *Paradise as a Garden in Persia and Mughal India.* New York: George Braziller, 1979.

Wilber, Donald. *Persian Gardens and Garden Pavilions.* 1962; reprint, Washington, D.C.: Dumbarton Oaks, 1979.

TABRIZ

Shah-Gul Garden

The Qajar period (1779–1924) saw the building of many country estates by the ruling dynasty and wealthy families of Iran, and Tabriz was a popular place for such residences. The Shah-Gul ("Royal Basin"), one of the few still remaining in Tabriz, was built in 1785 or possibly earlier. Its central feature is a square lake (approximately 11 acres) created by a raised embankment at the north end. It is surrounded by rows of fruit trees with seven stepped terraces rising from it on the south side. In the middle of the lake, a modern pavilion stands on an eighteenth-century platform, reached by a causeway running south. The water comes from a spring and flows downward in five channels with cascades.

BIBLIOGRAPHY

Brookes, John. *Gardens of Paradise: History and Design of the Great Islamic Gardens.* London: Weidenfeld and Nicolson, 1987.

Khansari, Mehdi, M. Reza Moghtader, and Minouch Yavari. *The Persian Garden: Echoes of Paradise.* Washington, D.C.: Mage, 1998.

Wilber, Donald. *Persian Gardens and Garden Pavilions.* 1962; reprint, Washington, D.C.: Dumbarton Oaks, 1979.

Central Asia

HERAT

Shrine of 'Abdallah Ansari

The shrine was built in 1425 in Gazur Gah about 5 kilometers from Herat by the Timurid ruler to commemorate the remains of Khvajah 'Abd Allah Ansari (d. 1089). Because of the saint's importance, the shrine was expanded and altered many times subsequently. The mausoleum consisted of a raised plinth open to the sky (a *hazira*) with a balustrade and framed by an iwan. To the west there was a pavilion (*namakdan*) that stood in a walled garden, probably dating to the seventeenth century and the era of Safavid patronage. The shrine was situated at the foot of mountains and about two kilometers from a river; the garden was watered by canals built in 1451–69. One of the more interesting features of the shrine is two groups of seventeenth-century paintings: one group shows trees, foliage, pavilions, and palaces, while the other shows a hilly landscape with clusters of dwellings.

BIBLIOGRAPHY
Golombek, Lisa. *The Timurid Shrine of Gazur Gah*. Toronto: Royal Ontario Museum, 1969.

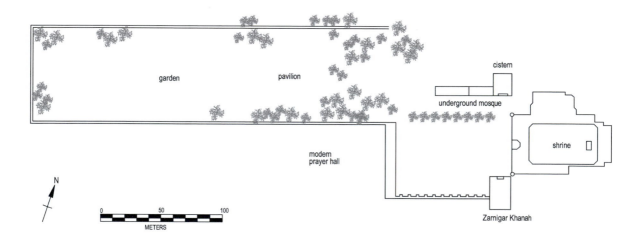

Shrine of 'Abdallah Ansari (after Lisa Golombek)

Bagh-i Kalan, Istalif (Ratish Nanda)

Bagh-i Kalan

Outside the small village of Istalif about twenty miles north-northwest of Kabul, Babur bought a site called the Bagh-i Kalan ("Big Garden") in 1504–5. There he planted vineyards and made a terraced garden, straightening the course of a natural stream to do so. When Elizabeth Moynihan visited the site in the 1970s, she saw this terrace and its watercourse, still surrounded by aged plane trees (chenars) encircled by raised, earthen, grass-covered platforms.

A few miles below Istalif, Babur admired an attractive spring surrounded by plane, oak, and Judas trees. In his memoirs he wrote that he had the spring lined with stone and plaster, "such that the four sides would form straight, symmetrical benches overlooking the entire grove of Judas trees. When the trees blossom, no place in the world equals it" (*Baburnama*, 137).

BIBLIOGRAPHY

Babur, Zahir al-Din. *The Baburnama: Memoirs of Babur, Prince and Emperor*, ed. and trans. Wheeler Thackston. Washington, D.C.: Freer Gallery of Art and Arthur M. Sackler Gallery of Art; New York: Oxford University Press, 1996.

Moynihan, Elizabeth. *Paradise as a Garden in Persia and Mughal India*. New York: George Braziller, 1979.

KABUL

Bagh-i Babur

When Babur died in 1530, he was temporarily buried in Agra; his body was removed to Kabul sometime between 1539 and 1544 where it was interred in a garden setting. His open-air tomb in Kabul does not survive, but in 1832 Charles Masson described it as "an enclosure of white marble, curiously and elegantly carved" and made a drawing of it using a camera lucida (see Fig. 74). In the reign of Shah Jahan (1628–57), the garden was described as having fifteen stepped terraces with Babur's grave located on the fourteenth. A water channel emerged on the twelfth terrace and flowed down to the other levels. Shah Jahan rebuilt this channel, added three big pools, and eventually added a headstone at Babur's tomb, a small mosque (completed 1645–46), and caravanserai. He also buried Babur's

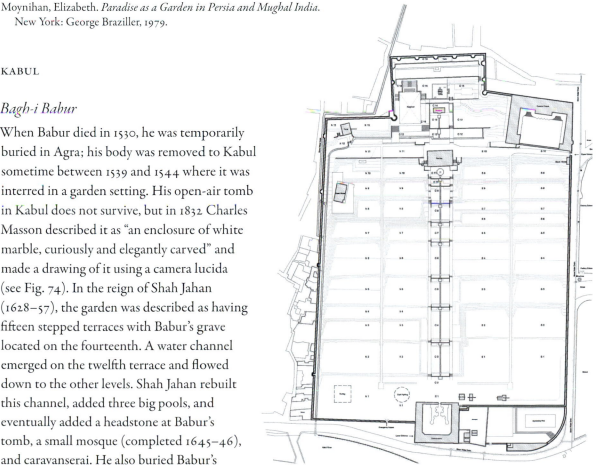

Bagh-i Babur
(Aga Khan Trust
for Culture, 1842)

grandaughter, Ruqaiya Sultan Begum (d. 1626), on the fifteenth level and enclosed her tomb with a marble jali screen three yards high, a style that can be seen today in Mughal tombs in the Nizam-ud-Din *dargah* (Sufi shrine complex) area in Delhi.

Between 2002 and 2006 the Aga Khan Trust for Culture excavated and restored the architecture, gardens, and waterworks. In addition to its commemorative function, the site is a popular park for Kabul residents.

BIBLIOGRAPHY

Frank-Vogt, Ute, K. Bartle, and Th. Urban. "Bagh-e Babur, Kabul: Excavating a Mughal Garden." In Ute Frank-Vogt and Hans-Joachim Weisshaar, eds., *South Asian Archaeology*. Proceedings of the Seventeenth International Conference of the European Association of South Asian Archaeologists, 7–11 July 2003, Bonn. 541–57. Aachen: Linden Soft, 2005.

Masson, Charles. *Narrative of Various Journeys in Balochistan, Afghanistan, and the Panjab,* 3 vols. London, 1842. See volume 2 on Kabul.

Moynihan, Elizabeth. *Paradise as a Garden in Persia and Mughal India.* New York: George Braziller, 1979.

———. "'But What a Happiness to Have Known Babur!'" In James L. Wescoat, Jr., and Joachim Wolschke-Bulmahn, eds., *Mughal Gardens: Sources, Places, Representations, and Prospects,* 95–126. Washington, D.C.: Dumbarton Oaks, 1996.

Nanda, Ratish, and Jolyon Leslie. "Rehabilitating the Garden of Babur and Its Surroundings in Kabul." In Aga Khan Historic Cities Programme, *Urban Conservation and Area Development in Afghanistan,* 21–41. Geneva: Aga Khan Trust for Culture, 2007. www.akdn.org/hcsp/afghanistan/Afghanistan%20Brochure.pdf.

Parpagliolo, M. T. S. *Kabul: The Bagh-i Babur.* Rome: Instituto Italiano per il Medio e l'Estremo Oriente, 1972.

Zajadacz-Hastenrath, Salome. "A Note on Babur's Lost Funerary Enclosure at Kabul." *Muqarnas* 14 (1997): 135–42.

LASHKARI BAZAR

Palaces

The Ghaznavids built this sprawling fortified and palatine complex near Bust (Afghanistan) in the eleventh and twelfth centuries. The Ghurids partially burned it, and either they or the Ghaznavids rebuilt it around 1150. It was burned again by the Mongols in 1221 and lay in ruins thereafter. In 1949–51 it was excavated by archaeologists looking for architectural layout and wall paintings, rather than gardens. However, in its three main palaces at least one of the several large courtyards appears to have been gardened: the Center Palace overlooked a large, square, unpaved enclosure that was subsequently extended westward to expand the area. In its midst an elevated cruciform pavilion with outward looking iwans was surely meant for viewing the surrounding garden. The Lashkari Bazar was a suburban pleasure palace where the Ghaznavids could escape Bust's urban and mercantile bustle, and views of nature were part of the attraction. The North Palace stood on a raised bluff above the Helman River plain, providing the privileged inhabitant of the richly decorated throne room with long-distance views of landscape. Along the river to the south of the palace, there were smaller manor houses that may also have enjoyed elevated views of their surroundings.

BIBLIOGRAPHY

Bosworth, C. E. "Lashkar-i Bazar." In *Encyclopedia of Islam*, 2nd ed. 5: 690–92. Leiden: E.J. Brill, 1986.

Schlumberger, Daniel. *Lashkari Bazar: Une résidence royale ghaznévide et ghoride. 1a L'architecture*, 2 vols. in 3. Paris: Diffusion de Boccard, 1978.

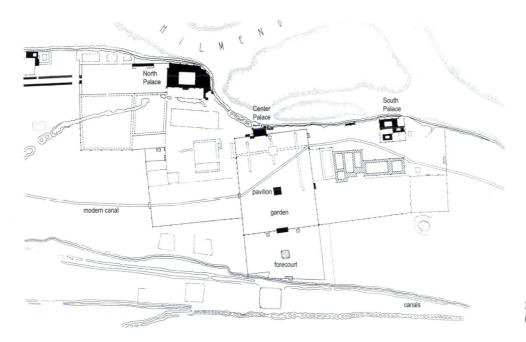

Lashkari Bazar
(after Schlumberger)

MERV

Tomb of Sultan Sanjar

The domed tomb of the Saljuq sultan Muʿizz
al-Din Sanjar, built in 1157 in Merv, although
in lonely ruins today, may once have stood in
a chahar bagh. A description made in 1879–81
by an English visitor to the site described the
tomb's position as occupying the intersection of
"two great causeways running respectively north
and south and east and west," and surrounded
by graves and small tombs. The same observer
drew a plan that clearly shows the tomb in
the center of a four-part enclosure. While the
presence of vegetation is entirely conjectural,
the model of so many later tomb gardens with
domed mausoleums set amidst quadripartite
gardens suggests that this may have been an
early experiment with the plan.

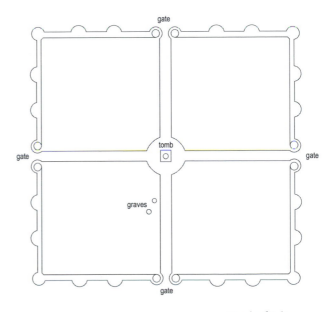

Tomb of Sultan
Sanjar (O'Donovan)

BIBLIOGRAPHY

Bulatov, M. S. "The Tomb of Sultan Sanjar." *Architectural Heritage* 17 (in Russian). Moscow, 1964.
O'Donovan, Edmond. *The Merv Oasis*, 2 vols. London, 1882.
Ruggles, D. Fairchild. "Humayun's Tomb and Garden: Typologies and Visual Order." In Attilio Petruccioli,
ed., *Gardens in the Time of the Great Muslim Empires*, 173–86. Leiden: E. J. Brill, 1997.

Pakistan

LAHORE

Lahore Fort

Built upon older remains by the Mughal Emperor Akbar in 1566, the Lahore Fort was almost entirely rebuilt by Jahangir and Shah Jahan in the seventeenth century. It stands on the river Ravi's left bank in the northwest corner of Lahore's old walled city. As in the Agra and Delhi Forts, handsome pavilions overlooking interior gardens were built along the north perimeter of the Fort: the Shah Burj with its exquisitely carved sunken basin, the twin projecting towers called the Kala Burj and the Lal Burj, the Shah Jahan Quadrangle, and finally the enclosed garden known today as Jahangir's Quadrangle (Plate 24). That courtyard (112.5 by 73.8 m) was finished by the emperor in 1620. On the courtyard's north side, the Khawabgah held his personal sleeping quarters fronted by a hall giving onto the garden. The layout of the Jahangir Quadrangle is unusual, for instead of a quadripartite organization, as seen in both the garden of the Shah Jahan Quadrangle and the Shah Burj's courtyard, the plan consists of concentric rectangles articulated in sandstone pavement, with a fountain at the center. The effect is like a flat maze. How it would have looked with plantings, and whether the nested beds formed by the pavements would have accentuated the plan, is unknown.

The Lahore Fort is a World Heritage Site, and even before this was protected since 1927 by the Ancient Monuments Protection Act. However, due to British interventions in the nineteenth century and decades of neglect thereafter, the original relationship of its architecture and landscape is uncertain.

Lahore Fort
(Mir, Hussain,
and Wescoat)

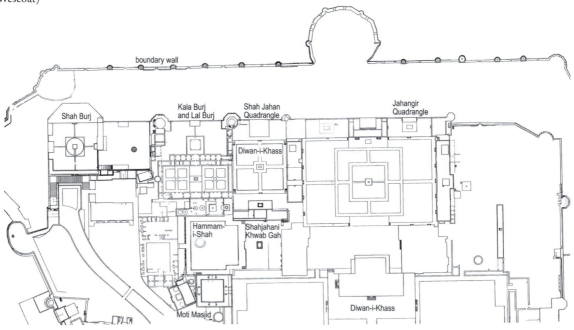

BIBLIOGRAPHY

Baksh, Nur. "Historical Notes on the Lahore Fort and Its Buildings." *Annual Report of the Archaeological Survey of India, 1902–03.* Calcutta, 1904.

Crowe, Sylvia, S. Haywood, S. Jellicoe, and G. Patterson. *The Gardens of Mughal India.* London: Thames and Hudson, 1972.

Dar, Saifur Rehman. *Historical Gardens of Lahore.* Lahore: Aziz Publishers, 1982.

Khokhar, Masood-ul-Hassan. "Conservation of Lahore Fort Gardens." In Mahmood Hussain, Abdul Rehman, and James L. Wescoat, Jr., eds., *The Mughal Garden,* 129–32. Lahore: Ferozsons, 1996.

Latif, Syed Muhammad. *Lahore: Its History, Architectural Remains, and Antiquities.* Lahore, 1892.

Mir, Muhammad Naeem, Mahmood Hussain, and James L. Wescoat, Jr. *Mughal Gardens in Lahore: History and Documentation.* Lahore: Department of Architecture, University of Engineering and Technology, 1996.

Hiran Minar

Hiran Minar, in Sheikhupura, near Lahore (Pakistan) is a Mughal hunting park set amidst scrub forest. It had no formal gardens and was not intended for long-term residence but allowed royal visitors to enjoy the semi-wild environment and indulge in the popular pastime of game hunting.

At its heart is an enormous square tank (approximately 229 by 273 m) with an octagonal pavilion in its center that dates to the reign of Shah Jahan. A long walkway with its own gate connects this lake pavilion to the edge of the tank where a 30-meter high minaret (from where this photograph was taken) was built in 1606 by Jahangir to mark the grave of a pet antelope. The tower was inscribed with a eulogy. On the sides of the tank, brick ramps slope into the water to facilitate access for the animals and waterfowl that the hunters sought. The tank was supplied by an ingenious means of water collection: at its corners were square structures that drew water from underground.

Hiran Minar (James L. Wescoat, Jr.)

BIBLIOGRAPHY

"Gardens of the Mughal Empire." www.mughalgardens.org. Smithsonian Productions.

Khan, Ahmad Nabi. "Conservation of the Hiran Minar and Baradari at Sheikhpura," *Pakistan Archaeology* 6 (1969).

Rabbani, Ahmad. "Hiran Munara at Shekhupura." In S. M. Abdullah, ed., *Armughan-e 'Ilmi, Professor Muhammad Shafi' Presentation Volume.* Lahore, 1955.

Wescoat, James L., Jr., Michael Brand, and Muhammad Naeen Mir. "The Shahdara Gardens of Lahore: Site Documentation and Spatial Analysis." *Pakistan Archaeology* 25 (1993): 333–66.

Tombs of Jahangir, Asaf Khan, and Nur Jahan

Outside of Lahore in the Shahdara gardens, the tomb for the Emperor Jahangir was probably built by his son, Shah Jahan, although there is some evidence for the Empress Nur Jahan as the patron. The simple mausoleum (built 1627–37) departs from the tradition of earlier imperial mausolea with monumental domes, for it consists simply of a cenotaph

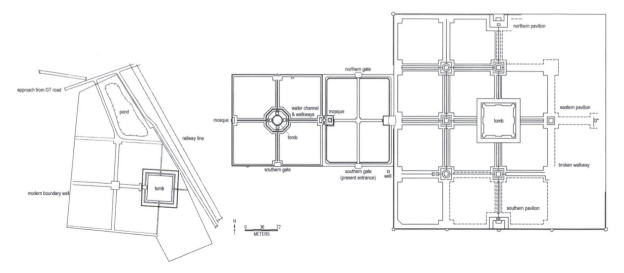

Tombs of Jahangir, Asaf Khan, and Nur Jahan (after Mir, Hussain, and Wescoat)

on a broad platform (*chabutra*), open to the sky above it, its corners marked by minarets. The cenotaph was originally surrounded by a marble screen which is missing today. The platform (84 m square) stands in a 55–acre chahar bagh, subdivided into sixteen units, which is preceded by a forecourt (*chawk-i jilau khana*) with a mosque. In this outer court, visitors would formerly dismount and leave their weapons when entering the tomb precinct. As is the case with so many Mughal tomb gardens, the plantings today are not original, but an eighteenth-century painting on cloth (in the Royal Asiatic Society, London) shows trees lining the principal walkways dividing densely planted quadrants. Eight wells just outside the garden enclosure supplied the water which was lifted up to aqueducts that ran on top of the walls and flowed into the eight fountain basins and channels that marked the garden's subdivisions.

West of this tomb garden was the tomb of Asaf Khan, Jahangir's *wakil* (the highest Mughal administrative office) and the brother of Nur Jahan. He was buried about 1641 in a domed mausoleum set within a chahar bagh that was one quarter the size of Jahangir's.

The tomb of Nur Jahan (d. 1645) was situated adjacent to Asaf Khan's tomb garden and had the same dimensions. It was a platform type with a cenotaph surrounded by a marble screen (now missing). Formerly, it would have stood in a chahar bagh, although the original garden was destroyed in the late nineteenth century when the British ran a railway line through it. The present garden was created by the Archaeological Survey of India in 1911.

BIBLIOGRAPHY

Asher, Catherine. *Architecture of Mughal India*. New Cambridge History of India, 1: 4. Cambridge: Cambridge University Press, 1995.

Brand, Michael. "The Shahdara Gardens of Lahore." In James L. Wescoat, Jr., and Joachim Wolschke-Bulmahn, eds., *Mughal Gardens: Sources, Places, Representations, and Prospects*, 188–211. Washington, D.C.: Dumbarton Oaks, 1996.

Hussain, Mahmood, Abdul Rehman, and James L. Wescoat, Jr., eds. *The Mughal Garden*. Lahore: Ferozsons, 1996.

Koch, Ebba. *Mughal Architecture*. Munich: Prestel-Verlag, 1991.

Mashmud, Muhammad Khalid. "The Mausoleum of the Emperor Jahangir." *Arts of Asia* 13 (1983): 57–66.

Thompson, J. P. "The Tomb of Jahangir." *Journal of the Punjab Historical Society* 1 (1911): 31–46.

Shalamar Bagh

The riverside site for this garden near Lahore was selected in 1641 for the Mughal Emperor Shah Jahan and the garden itself was begun soon after. It was modeled after the Shalamar Bagh of Kashmir. However, unlike the mountainous topography of Kashmir, Lahore was flat and lacked naturally rushing torrents to animate the garden. Instead, water was brought by canal to the south end of the complex and raised by waterwheels to cisterns poised above the gardens. The architects took advantage of a raised bluff overlooking the Ravi River, northeast of Lahore city, stepping the gardens in three great terraces just sufficiently to allow water to flow through a central canal. At the south end the highest terrace, reserved for the women of the court, consisted of a quadripartite garden with the four arms of its axes terminating at the Aramgah, the empress's residence (Begum Ki Khawab Gah), the Jharoka-i Daulat Khana-i-khas-o-'amm, and at the juncture with the middle terrace, the pavilion known as the Aiwan (Plate 22). The Aiwan looks across the middle terrace's enormous rectangular pool (61 m wide) to the handsome Sawan Bhadon, a white marble pavilion surrounded by chini khana panels. The lowest terrace mirrored the layout of the uppermost, and in both the chahar bagh was subdivided into sixteen plots. Despite the natural conditions of the site, water is ever present in the Shalamar Bagh, flowing under platforms (including the marble throne), through pavilions (*baradaris*), over textured chadars and chini khana, and in fountain jets set in channels and elegant scalloped basins. It sustained lush plantings that included orange, lime, pomegranate, and cedar trees.

Shalamar replaced the Lahore Fort as the emperor's preferred place of residence. Furthermore, it served as a magnet that attracted development to its suburban vicinity, reconfiguring the settlement patterns in that region.

Shalamar Bagh, Lahore (Mir, Hussain, and Wescoat)

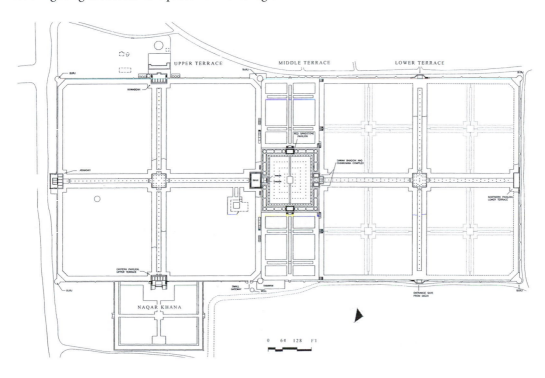

BIBLIOGRAPHY

Crowe, Sylvia, S. Haywood, S. Jellicoe, and G. Patterson. *The Gardens of Mughal India*. London: Thames and Hudson, 1972.

Kausar, Sajjad, M. Brand, and James L. Wescoat, Jr. *Shalamar Garden Lahore: Landscape, Form and Meaning*. Islamabad: Department of Archaeology and Museums, Ministry of Culture, Pakistan, 1990.

Wescoat, James L., Jr. "Lahore." In *The Grove Dictionary of Art Online*. Oxford University Press. www.groveart.com (accessed 19 July 2007).

India

AGRA

Tomb of I'timad al-Daula

The Empress Nur Jahan built this tomb in Agra between 1622 and 1628 for her father, the prime minister Mirza Giyas Beg (d. 1622), called I'timad al-Daula ("Pillar of the Empire"), and her mother, Asmat Begum, who died a few months previously. While the mausoleum adheres to the typical hesht behesht plan, its second story is realized with a canopy-roofed rectangular aedicule rather than the monumental double-shell dome of imperial Mughal tombs (Plate 21). It stands at the center of a chahar bagh (165 m square) that could be entered through a large gate on the land side to the east or by a boat landing and red sandstone riverside pavilion on the west side. This multi-windowed pavilion together with the chhatri-topped towers placed at the corners of the garden provided pleasant views of the curving Yamuna River and the more than thirty gardens lining its banks. The theme of pleasure gardens and nature permeates the iconography of the site, for the white marble floors and walls of the pavilion and the tomb were variously painted or inlaid with semi-precious stone representing scrolling vines, fruit and cypress trees, flowers in vases, and drinking vessels—the very accoutrements that Nur Jahan and her entourage might have used at a picnic in this garden. While the images in stone are stylized and rigidly symmetrical, the wall paintings on the interior of the tomb are more naturalistic and reflect, perhaps, a fascination with the contemporary European botanical treatises and prints that were in circulation in the Mughal court. In particular, red poppies and red lilies—literary symbols of death and suffering—abound (Koch, *Complete Taj*, 51).

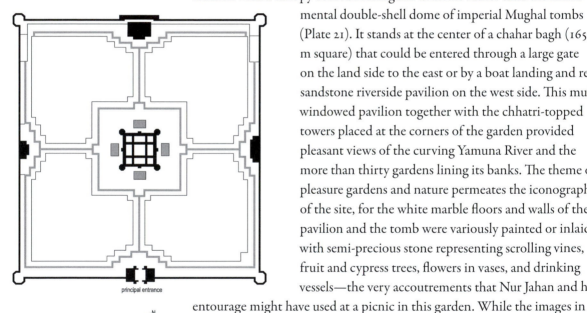

riverfront facade

principal entrance

0 5 10 20 50

N

Tomb of I'timad al-Daula (Ruggles and Variava)

BIBLIOGRAPHY

Asher, Catherine. *Architecture of Mughal India*. New Cambridge History of India, 1:4. Cambridge: Cambridge University Press, 1995.

Brown, Percy. *Indian Architecture (Islamic Period)*. Rev. ed. 1944, reprint, Bombay: D. B. Taraporevala, 1981.

Crowe, Sylvia, S. Haywood, S. Jellicoe, and G. Patterson. *The Gardens of Mughal India*. London: Thames and Hudson, 1972.

Koch, Ebba. *The Complete Taj and Riverfront Gardens of Agra*. London: Thames and Hudson, 2006.

———. *Shah Jahan and Orpheus*. Graz: Akademische Druck- und Verlagsanstalt, 1988.

Okada, Amina, and Jean-Louis Nou. *Un Joyau de l'Inde Moghole: Le mausolée d'I'timâd ud-Daulah*. Milan: 5 Continents Éditions, 2003. Good photographs but incorrect plans.

Mahtab Bagh

The Mahtab Bagh ("moonlight garden") is a recently excavated imperial pleasure garden of 9.7 hectares (24 acres) that stands across from the Taj on the Yamuna River in Agra. Its dimensions and layout clearly indicate that it was designed as a visual extension of the Taj, and it appears to have been built in conjunction with that project between 1632 and 1643. In the late seventeenth century, when its origins were already forgotten, its barely discernible traces gave rise to the mistaken identification of the site as the "black Taj," a tomb purportedly intended for Shah Jahan himself.

An octagonal lotus-shaped sandstone pool occupied the Mahtab Bagh's river edge, complementing the position of the Taj on the opposite bank. Similarly, the red sandstone wall that defined the riverfront of the Mahtab Bagh was marked at each end by graceful chhatris that correspond to a similar wall with chhatris across the river. At the foot of both these walls, there were riverside landings for access by boat. The visual axis of the central water channel that flows through the Taj is continued across the river in the watercourse that drops from the large octagonal pool (17.3 m on each side) into a lotus-shaped basin and flows from there to the chahar bagh's central square pool (6.9 m each side) and axial arms. The water came from a cistern and river-charged wells in the southwest corner of the garden. Severe flooding of the Yamuna in 1652 or a bit earlier erased much of the surface of the garden, so that its original plantings and form remain somewhat speculative.

BIBLIOGRAPHY
Moynihan, Elizabeth, ed. *The Moonlight Garden: New Discoveries at the Taj Mahal*. Washington, D.C.: Arthur M. Sackler Gallery; Seattle: University of Washington Press, 2000.

Ram Bagh

This is the modern name of the Bagh-i Nur Afshan ("light-scattering garden"), finished for the Mughal Empress Nur Jahan sometime before March 1621 along the east bank of the Yamuna River in Agra. It probably replaced an earlier garden of Babur's period. The garden is a chahar bagh (340 by 227 m) defined by water channels and walkways; however, unlike previous gardens, there is no central pavilion. Instead there is a broad terrace (136 by 96 m) on the garden's river side with

Ram Bagh
(Chodon)

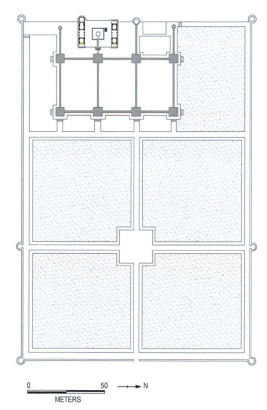

0   50   → N
METERS

two contraposed pavilions. The oblong pavilions, which consist of three verandas alternating with two enclosed chambers, flank a rectangular water pool. The terrace was elevated, since water lifted from the river to its level could then be released into the garden beds at the lower level. Ebba Koch also notes that while the raised terrace allowed the garden's residents to approach the edge for excellent views of the river, it nonetheless formed a visual barrier that shielded them from public view. An eighteenth-century map of Agra's riverscape shows this barrier effect and a variety of mature trees growing in the garden.

The disposition of the pavilions on a raised terrace overlooking the river may have had Persian origins, since such an arrangement is described in the *Irshad al-zira'a*. Nur Jahan, who was Persian, is a logical agent of transmission of the type. Once introduced among the Mughals, it soon became a standard type for not only pleasure gardens but palaces and eventually tomb enclosures as well.

BIBLIOGRAPHY

Koch, Ebba. *The Complete Taj and Riverfront Gardens of Agra*. London: Thames and Hudson, 2006.

——. "The Mughal Waterfront Garden." In Attilio Petruccioli, ed., *Gardens in the Time of the Great Muslim Empires*, 140–60. Leiden: E. J. Brill, 1997.

——. "Notes on the Painted and Sculptured Decoration of Nur Jahan's Pavilions in the Ram Bagh (Bagh-i Nur Afshan) at Agra." In Robert Skelton et al., eds., *Facets of Indian Art*, 51–65. London: Victoria and Albert Museum, 1986.

Red Fort

The Red Fort was rebuilt by the Mughals between 1564 and the 1570s from Lodi-period foundations; the massive walls, imposing gates, and the so-called Jahangiri Mahal (the zenana quarters) date to this period. However, most of the other halls that lined the river façade were the work of Shah Jahan in the period 1628–37. Among the gardens that were attached to these, the Anguri Bagh ("grape garden") still remains. The Machchi Bhawan ("fish house"), although often identified by modern historians as a garden, was a courtyard enclosed by arcaded wings where the emperor could observe his horses and hunting animals from the terrace of the Daulat Khana-i Khass (now called the Diwan-i Khass).

The Anguri Bagh was similarly overlooked by the trio of pavilions called the Khass Mahal, consisting of the central Aramgah flanked by the *bangla*-roofed sleeping chamber of the emperor on the north side and to the south, for symmetry, the apartment of his daughter Jahanara. The garden was a classic chahar bagh with a raised pool at the intersection of the defining axial walkways of white marble. From the elegant lotus-shaped pool on the Aramgah's terrace, water poured over a chini khana panel into a basin from where it flowed to the rest of the garden (Plate 23). The garden's four quadrants were further articulated with ornate parterres formed by red sandstone dividing walls that recent excavations have revealed extended to an extraordinary depth of approximately six feet.

BIBLIOGRAPHY

Ashraf Husain, Muhammad. *An Historical Guide to the Agra Fort*. Delhi: Manager of Publications, 1937.

Baksh, Nur. "The Agra Fort and Its Buildings." *Annual Report of the Archaeological Survey of India, 1903–04*. Calcutta, 1906.

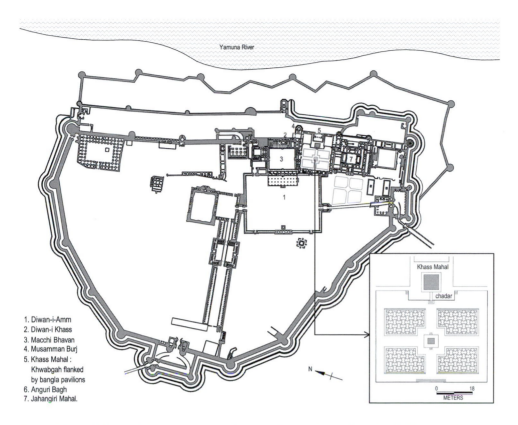

Yamuna River

1. Diwan-i-Amm
2. Diwan-i Khass
3. Macchi Bhavan
4. Musamman Burj
5. Khass Mahal :
   Khwabgah flanked
   by bangla pavilions
6. Anguri Bagh
7. Jahangiri Mahal.

Khass Mahal

chadar

N

0   18
METERS

Crowe, Sylvia, S. Haywood, S. Jellicoe, and G. Patterson. *The Gardens of Mughal India.* London: Thames and Hudson, 1972.

Koch, Ebba. *The Complete Taj and the Riverfront Gardens of Agra.* London: Thames and Hudson, 2006.

——. *Mughal Architecture.* Munich: Prestel-Verlag, 1991.

——. "Mughal Palace Gardens from Babur to Shah Jahan (1526–1648)." *Muqarnas* 14 (1997): 143–65.

——. "The Mughal Waterfront Garden." In Attilio Petruccioli, ed., *Gardens in the Time of the Great Muslim Empires: Theory and Design*, 140–60. Leiden: E. J. Brill, 1997.

Agra Fort and Anguri Bagh (inset) (Ruggles and Variava)

Taj Mahal

Standing on the banks of the Yamuna River in Agra, the Taj Mahal was built by the Mughal Emperor Shah Jahan from 1632 to 1643 for his wife, Mumtaz Mahal. The monumental white marble tomb on a raised plinth dominates the garden from the north end. It is flanked by a mosque on the west side and on the east side, a symmetrically placed meeting hall. The garden is a classic chahar bagh with a raised pool at the meeting of the four arms of the north-south and east-west axial walkways. The mausoleum stands not in the center, as in previous imperial and subimperial tombs, but at one end on an elevated terrace, like the pavilions ranging the riverfront of the Agra Fort. To the south, the central axis is further lengthened by a huge gate dividing the chahar bagh from a large forecourt which itself is preceded by the Taj Ganj, a bazaar and residential area for tomb staff and traders who served the seventeenth-century visitors to the complex.

Water was drawn from the river in successive rehants (a bullock-driven version of the rope-and-pulley mechanism), filling a storage tank outside the west wall of the complex,

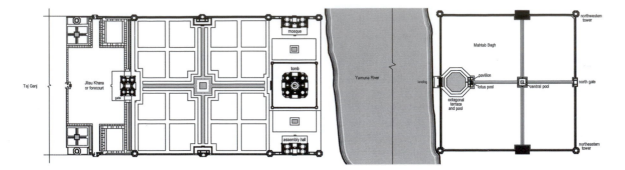

Taj Mahal and
Mahtab Bagh
(Chodon, after
Elizabeth
Moynihan)

from where it was released as needed to the grounds of the garden. Additionally, a tower in the southwest corner of the terrace contained a deep well. With other demands on the river, the hydraulic resources for the Taj are now considerably diminished. The vegetation today suffers from this lack and reflects British colonial taste from the year 1903 when the garden was replanted; but in 1663 the visitor Bernier described pavements raised by "eight French feet" above beds with flowers and shady trees.

BIBLIOGRAPHY

Begley, Wayne. "The Garden of the Taj Mahal: A Case Study of Mughal Architectural Planning and Symbolism." In James L. Wescoat, Jr., and Joachim Wolschke-Bulmahn, eds., *Mughal Gardens: Sources, Places, Representations, and Prospects*, 213–31. Washington, D.C.: Dumbarton Oaks, 1996.

Begley, Wayne E. and Z. A. Desai. *Taj Mahal: The Illumined Tomb: An Anthology of Seventeenth-Century Mughal and European Documentary Sources*. Seattle: University of Washington Press, 1990.

Koch, Ebba. *The Complete Taj and the Riverfront Gardens of Agra*. London: Thames and Hudson, 2006.

Moynihan, Elizabeth. *Paradise as a Garden in Persia and Mughal India*. New York: George Braziller, 1979.

Moynihan, Elizabeth, ed. *The Moonlight Garden: New Discoveries at the Taj Mahal*. Washington, D.C.: Arthur M. Sackler Gallery; Seattle: University of Washington Press, 2000.

Nath, Ram. *The Immortal Taj, The Evolution of the Tomb in Mughal Architecture*. Bombay: D. B. Taraporevala, 1972.

Pal, Pratapaditya, and Janice Leoshko, eds. *Romance of the Taj Mahal*. Los Angeles: Los Angeles County Museum of Art; London: Thames and Hudson, 1989.

AMBER

Amber Fort

The fort and the palace within it were built in Amber at the beginning of the seventeenth century by the Kachhwahas, a prominent Rajput family. (It stands about 14 km above Jaipur, which was not founded until 1727). Subsequently, Mirza Raja Jai Singh I (r. 1623–68) added two courtyards, one of which contained a lovely garden with an elaboration of a chahar bagh concept: the hexagonal geometry of sunken beds was defined by narrow channels of white marble that met at a star-shaped pool in the garden center (Plate 26). On the east and west sides stood two luxuriously ornamented halls, the Jai Mandir and Sukh Nivas. From the latter, water poured over a scalloped chadar into the channels of the garden, while the Jai Mandir had a terrace from which water cascaded over a panel of chini khana niches. This pavilion had a second story called the Jas Mandir with a rooftop terrace and kiosk that enjoyed far-reaching views of the mountains and valley, where a stream was dammed to

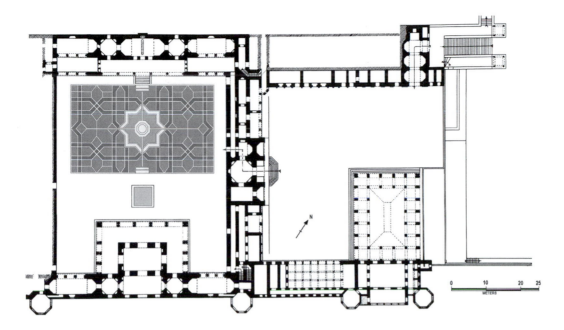

Amber Fort
(Ruggles
and Variava)

create an artificial lake, following the typology of the classic Mughal waterfront garden. On the edge of this lake was built the Maunbari garden, an artificial platform with a garden of three terraces divided into an ornate system of parterres. The smallest and topmost terrace followed the plan of a chahar bagh with a scalloped basin at its center. Water was raised from the lake by a system of staggered rehants (similar to the Taj Mahal). There were no trees, ensuring visual clarity when the garden was viewed from the palace quarters above.

BIBLIOGRAPHY
Michell, George, and Antonio Martinelli. *The Royal Palaces of India*. New York: Thames and Hudson, 1994.
Moynihan, Elizabeth. *Paradise as a Garden in Persia and Mughal India*. New York: George Braziller, 1979.
Reuther, Oskar. *Indische Paläste und Wohnhäuser*. Berlin: L. Preiss, 1925.
Ruggles, D. Fairchild. "The Framed Landscape in Islamic Spain and Mughal India." In Brian Day, ed., *The Garden: Myth, Meaning, and Metaphor*, 21–50. Working Papers in the Humanities 12. Windsor: University of Windsor, 2003.
———. "Gardens." In Frederick Asher, ed., *Art of India: Prehistory to the Present*, 258–70. S.l.: Encyclopaedia Britannica, 2003.
Tillotson, G. H. R. *The Rajput Palaces: The Development of an Architectural Style, 1450–1750*. New Haven: Yale University Press, 1987.

Jaigarh Fort

Poised on a rugged peak of the Aravilies Mountains high above the Amber Fort and fortified by thick walls, Jaigarh was built a half a century later in various phases to provide defense for the Amber Fort as well as to serve as a residence for the same family of Rajput patrons. It is three kilometers from north to south and about one kilometer wide. The palace quarters were located at the north end and contained residences and courtyards such as the large Laxmi Vilas, the smaller adjoining Lalit Mandir, the zenana in the Vilas Mandir, and the Aram Mandir overlooking a large garden. This square garden

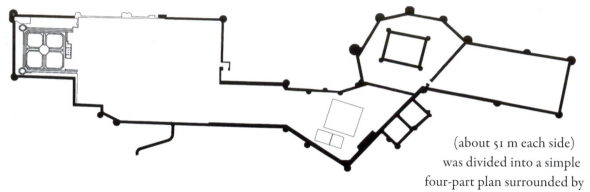

Jaigarh Fort
(Ruggles and
Variava)

(about 51 m each side)
was divided into a simple
four-part plan surrounded by
high defensive walls of red sandstone with sloping ramps in each corner for access to
the encircling upper story. In many of the courts and halls, screened windows and raised
parapets allowed dramatic views of the landscape of mountains and deep valleys as well
as Amber itself. The triple-arched opening on the north side of the Aram Mandir's
garden was enlarged in the twentieth century, probably to enhance the inhabitants'
enjoyment of the view of the Sagar Lake below. The artificially dammed lake supplied
some of the water to the palace, carried in bags by elephants to a tank on the west side of
the Fort as well as via humans passing water pots. Water was also carried by canal from a
catchment area four kilometers to the north.

BIBLIOGRAPHY
Khangarot, R. S., and P. S. Nathawat. *Jaigarh: The Invincible Fort of Amber*. Jaipur: RBSA Publishers, 1990.
Ruggles, D. Fairchild. "The Framed Landscape in Islamic Spain and Mughal India." In Brian Day, ed., *The
Garden: Myth, Meaning, and Metaphor,* 21–50. Working Papers in the Humanities 12. Windsor: Univer-
sity of Windsor, 2003.
——. "Gardens." In Frederick Asher, ed., *Art of India: Prehistory to the Present*, 258–70. S.l., Encyclopaedia
Britannica, 2003.

BIJAPUR

Ibrahim Rauza

On Bijapur's west side, Ibrahim II of the Adil Shah dynasty completed a complex in
1626 to house the graves of his wife, himself, and various family members. A domed
tomb and domed mosque face each other across a tank of water on a raised platform
(120 by 50 m) that stands within a square enclosure (137.2 m each side). The platform
and its architecture stand within a walled garden (maintained as turf today) that
enhances the meaning of both mosque and mausoleum. For the latter, the garden is a
visual metaphor for the paradise to come, and indeed an inscription over the doorway
announces: "Heaven stood astonished at the elevation of this building, and it might be
said, when its head rose from the earth that another heaven was erected. The garden of
paradise has borrowed its beauty from this garden." The mosque addressed the garden
in a different manner, for from its side walls projected balconies that offered views onto
the verdant surroundings.

BIBLIOGRAPHY
Alfieri, Bianca Maria. *Islamic Architecture of the Indian Subcontinent*. London: Laurence King, 2000.
Brown, Percy. *Indian Architecture (Islamic Period)*. Rev. ed. 1944; reprint, Bombay: D. B. Taraporevala, 1981.
Cousens, Henry. *Bijapur and Its Architectural Remains*. Bombay: Archaeological Survey of India (vol. 37), 1916; reprint, New Delhi, 1976.

DELHI

Bagh-i Jud (Lodi Gardens)

When New Delhi was created as the new British capital in the first quarter of the twentieth century, the British redesigned major portions of the older areas nearby. One such area, which had several fifteenth-century Lodi tombs and mosques, was restyled as an English park of approximately one hundred acres, known today variously as the Jor Bagh or simply the Lodi Gardens. While the principal architectural works—the four octagonal domed tombs of the Lodi dynasts (1450–1526)—were preserved in relatively good condition, their context changed radically when the cemetery became a place for public gathering and leisure. The free-standing tombs thus became garden follies and acquired new meaning as focal points in an otherwise picturesque landscape of rolling green lawns, groves of trees, stands of bamboo, and winding pathways bordered by bright annual flowers. In the 1970s, the New Delhi Municipal Committee undertook a renovation of the park based on plans by Garrett Eckbo and J. A. Stein. Their installation of modern metal and concrete lights and planters was sharply criticized as unsuitable for a funerary complex of significant historicity; however, it is unclear to what period of history the park "belongs."

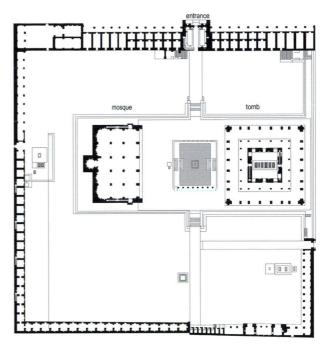

Ibrahim Rauza complex (Chodon after Christopher Tadgell)

Bagh-i Jud (Lodi Gardens)

BIBLIOGRAPHY
INTACH. "Lodi Gardens" (map). New Delhi: Indian National Trust for Art and Cultural Heritage (INTACH), Heritage Education and Communication Service, n.d.
Lang, Jon, Madhavi Desai, and Miki Desai. *Architecture and Independence: The Search for Identity—India, 1880–1980*. Delhi: Oxford University Press, 1997.
Singh, Patwant. "The Tragedy of the Lodi Tombs." *Design* 15 (April 1971): 15–26.
Spear, T. G. P. *Delhi, Its Monuments and History*, 2nd rev. ed., updated by Narayani Gupta and Laura Sykes. Delhi: Oxford University Press, 1994.

Hauz Khas

This madrasa-mausoleum complex in Delhi was built adjacent to an enormous reservoir dating from the Khalji sultanate (1296–1316). It was enlarged by the Tughluq ruler Firoz Shah beginning in 1352 when he built the handsome two-storied madrasa (teaching college) that rose above the southeast corner of the complex. A huge flight of steps wrapped itself around the inside corner of the enclosure wall and led from the madrasa down to the reservoir. This reservoir filled seasonally with monsoon water which it stored for much of the rest of the year. Such grand architectural and irrigation projects were typical of Firoz Shah (r. 1351–88), who proclaimed that he had a God-given love of architectural patronage and that, as well as constructing mosques, madrasas, and religious hostels, he dug canals and planted trees.

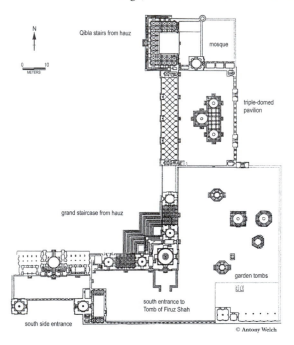

Hauz Khas
(Anthony Welch)

The precinct of his madrasa was walled and gardened with hyacinths, roses, tulips, and a multitude of varied fruit trees. It was embellished with pavilions including, eventually, Firoz Shah's own tomb. In his era and today, the elevated grounds provide pleasing and panoramic landscape views and they provide a popular yet tranquil escape from Delhi's summer heat. At the northern end of the complex stood a mosque with five mihrabs. The open grillwork of three of the mihrabs was distinctly unusual, for the screens not only allow light and cooling breezes into the prayer hall but also permit a limited view through the qibla wall to the reservoir and its verdant rim of vegetation. Furthermore, the main mihrab projects from the outer wall and serves as a portal, each side of which has a flight of steps leading down to the reservoir below. That a mihrab should have such functional flexibility as both a door and a window is a rare phenomenon.

BIBLIOGRAPHY
Rani, Abha. *Tughluq Architecture of Delhi*. Varanasi: Bharati Prakashan, 1991.
Welch, Anthony. "Gardens That Babur Did Not Like: Landscape, Water, and Architecture for the Sultans of Delhi." In James Wescoat, Jr., and Joachim Wolschke-Bulmahn, eds., *Mughal Gardens: Sources, Places, Representations, and Prospects*, 59–93. Washington, D.C.: Dumbarton Oaks, 1996.
——. "Hydraulic Architecture in Medieval India: The Tughluqs." *Environmental Design* 2 (1985): 74–81.
——. "A Medieval Center of Learning in India: The Hauz Khas Madrasa in Delhi." *Muqarnas* 13 (1996): 165–90.

Tomb of Humayun

This tomb was erected in Delhi for the Emperor Humayun (r. 1530–39 and 1555–56), probably by his widow, Hajji Begum, in either 1565 or 1569. The first imperial Mughal tomb, it followed Timurid models of a tall double-shell dome rising from a hesht behesht plan on a raised plinth (6.5 m above ground level) that itself was raised one meter above the level of the surrounding walkways (Plate 3). The mausoleum stood at the center of a huge chahar bagh, 12 hectares (30 acres) enclosed by a wall 6 meters high. Each quadrant of the four-part plan was subdivided into nine units, articulated by broad walkways with water channels that expanded to square pools at their points of intersection. There were great gates on the center of the west and south walls, and these were complemented on the north and east walls by pavilions for the sake of symmetry. There were numerous other tombs and residences just outside these walls, such as the Tomb and Mosque of 'Isa Khan (1547–48). The Tomb of the Barber was apparently added to the southeast quadrant of the chahar bagh in about 1590.

The restoration of the garden and its hydraulic infrastructure were completed in 2003 by the collaborative efforts of the Archaeological Survey of India and the Aga Khan Trust for Culture under the aegis of the National Culture Fund.

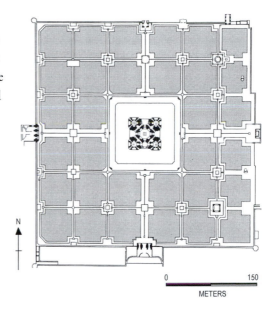

Tomb of Humayun
(Chodon, after ASI)

BIBLIOGRAPHY
Aga Khan Trust for Culture Web site: www.akdn.org/agency/aktc_humayun.html1#objectives.
Archaeological Survey of India. *Humayun's Tomb and Adjacent Monuments*. New Delhi: ASI, 2002 (revised from the original 1946 ASI publication by S. A. A. Naqvi).
Lowry, Glenn. "Humayun's Tomb: Form, Function, and Meaning in Early Mughal Architecture." *Muqarnas* 4 (1987): 133–48.
Ruggles, D. Fairchild. "Humayun's Tomb and Garden: Typologies and Visual Order." In Attilio Petruccioli, ed., *Gardens in the Time of the Great Muslim Empires*, 173–86. Leiden: Brill, 1997.

Rashtrapati Bhawan (Viceroy's Palace) "Mughal" Gardens

In 1931 the British inaugurated New Delhi as the new colonial capital of India. A Tripartite Planning Committee had been formed in 1912 to plan the layout of the new city, and that committee chose Sir Edwin Lutyens and Sir Herbert Baker to design it. For the centerpiece of the new city, Lutyens built the Viceroy's House (today appropriately renamed the Rashtrapati Bhawan, or President's Palace) on the Raisina Hill and the extensive gardens on its west side. W. R. Mustoe served as the director of horticulture for the project, supervising a staff of 418.

The 15-acre garden, which was but a small portion of the 250-acre grounds, had three parts united along a long central axis that was generated from the architectural axis of the palace and New Delhi's principal artery, the King's Way (now Raj Path). The first part had a geometrical plan reminiscent of a chahar bagh, although its center, where a tomb might stand in a Mughal garden, consisted of an island of turf used for outdoor receptions. Lutyens had studied the Mughal gardens of Kashmir, Agra, and Delhi and reinterpreted Mughal and Indic elements in this colonial setting: orthogonal channels spanned by flat slab bridges, textured surfaces that were modernist interpretations of a chadar, and fountains made of eighteen overlapping sandstone disks to suggest lotus pads. Along the watercourses, steps led down to the water, like ghats along a sacred tank or river. The

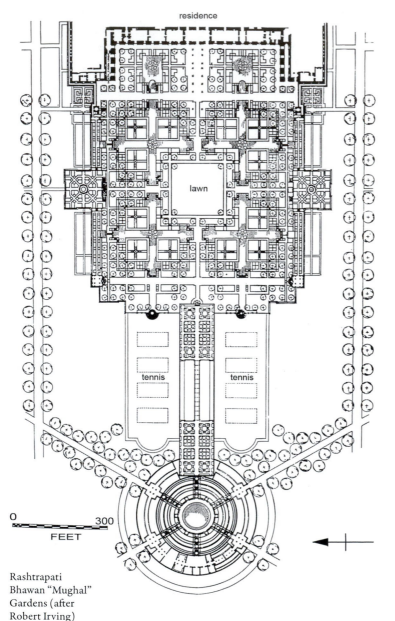

residence

lawn

tennis   tennis

0 ——————— 300
FEET

Rashtrapati
Bhawan "Mughal"
Gardens (after
Robert Irving)

plantings were similarly subordinated
to geometry: even the trees were carefully pruned to form solid volumes
that contrasted with the flatness of
the ground plane.

The central portion of the garden
consisted of tennis courts flanking a
sandstone pergola that marked the
central axis. The axis terminated in
a walled circular perennial garden.
Steps led up into the garden gate, and
then descended into the garden's
three concentric terraces. In contrast
to the first garden, this one evoked
an English garden and surely satisfied
the occasional nostalgia of the British
inhabitants.

BIBLIOGRAPHY
Irving, R. G. *Indian Summer: Lutyens,
    Baker and Imperial Delhi*. New Haven:
    Yale University Press, 1981.
Metcalf, Thomas. *An Imperial Vision: Indian
    Architecture and Britain's Raj*. Berkeley:
    University of California Press, 1989.
Prasad, H. Y. Sharada. *Rashtrapati Bhavan:
    The Story of the President's House*. New
    Delhi: Publication Division, Ministry of
    Information and Broadcasting in
    association with National Institute of
    Design for Rashtrapati Bhavan, 1992.
Volwahsen, Andreas. *Imperial Delhi:
    The British Capital of the Indian Empire*.
    Munich: Prestel, 2002.

Red Fort

This fort, built in Shahjahanabad by Shah Jahan beginning in 1639, was intended to
improve upon and regularize the planning and architectural splendor of the older Agra
Fort. Its enclosure walls form a slightly irregular octagon 2.4 kilometers in circumference.
They rise 18 meters above ground on the river side, and they rise above a broad moat
(22.5 m wide) on the land side which was formerly filled with water and stocked with fish.
An earthquake in 1719, battles in 1759, and the British neglect of the fort after the Mutiny
of 1857 caused serious damage to the buildings and the overall plan, so that today the only
portion that retains a sense of the original is the string of riverfront pavilions including
the Mumtaz Mahal, the Rang Mahal, the hammam, and the Moti Mahal that together

constituted the more private quarters of the complex. Running through these was an ornamental canal, the Nahr-i Behesht ("stream of paradise") which was brought from a canal drawing from the Jumna at a sufficiently high point about 10 kilometers upstream. It entered the fort through a carved marble chadar in the Shah Burj pavilion.

Of the many gardens that formerly complemented the pavilions, there remains the eastern half of the Hayat Bakhsh, extending between the Moti Mahal on the riverfront, the symmetrical pavilions named Sawan (the first month of the Indian rainy season) and Bhadon (the second month of the rainy season) to the north and south, and the Mahtab Bagh on the western side, which was lamentably replaced by military barracks in the modern era. Observers described grass with jonquils and roses shaded by fruited trees, including oranges, in a large chahar bagh with a huge square tank in its center decorated with 161 jets. The Zafar Mahal that stands in the middle of the tank presently is a nineteenth-century addition of Bahadur Shah II. The garden that one sees today is largely reconstruction made on the basis of excavations carried out in 1904–5.

Delhi Fort (Gordon Sanderson, 1936)

BIBLIOGRAPHY

Andrews, Peter A. "Mahall. Vi." In *Encyclopaedia of Islam,* 2nd ed. 5: 1214–20. Leiden: E. J. Brill, 1986.

Crowe, Sylvia, S. Haywood, S. Jellicoe, and G. Patterson. *The Gardens of Mughal India.* London: Thames and Hudson, 1972.

Mukherji, Anisha S. *The Red Fort of Shahjahanabad.* Delhi: Oxford University Press, 2003.

Sanderson, Gordon, with Maulvi Shuaib. *A Guide to the Buildings and Gardens: Delhi Fort.* 4th ed. 1936; reprint, Delhi: Asian Educational Services, 2000.

Tomb of Safdar Jang

Safdar Jang (r. 1739–54) was a Nawab (governor) of Awadh (Oudh) in the period when the Mughal empire had shrunk to Delhi (ruled by Nasir al-Din Muhammad Shah) and the few provinces such as Awadh that did not claim independence. The shi'a Nawabs (1722–1856) built more than six hundred monuments. Safdar Jang's son built the tomb and garden for him in Delhi after Safdar Jang's death in 1754, the pink and white stone platform pierced with regular iwans, and simple chahar bagh plan evoking the first imperial Mughal tomb of Humayun. The garden measures over 300 square meters and is a four-part plan subdivided into smaller quadrants with a large gate piercing its eastern wall.

The tomb's nostalgia for earlier Mughal prototypes was embraced by other rulers of Awadh. For example the tomb of Shuja' al-Daula (1775), popularly called the Gulabari, and that of his wife (just after 1816), both in Faizabad, continue the by now antiquated tradition of tall domed mausolea set within four-part gardens.

BIBLIOGRAPHY

Asher, Catherine. *Architecture of Mughal India*. New Cambridge History of India, 1: 4. Cambridge: Cambridge University Press, 1995.

Sharma, Y. D. *Delhi and Its Neighbourhood*. New Delhi: Archaeological Survey of India, 1990.

Tandon, B. "The Architecture of the Nawabs of Avadh, 1722–1856." In Robert Skelton et al., eds., *Facets of Indian Art*, 66–75. London: Victoria and Albert Museum, 1986.

Tomb of Safdar
Jang (Ruggles)

DHOLPUR

Bagh-i Nilufar

One of the very few Islamic gardens to have ever been excavated, the Bagh-i Nilufar (Lotus Garden) was built by Babur, founder of the Mughal Empire, between 1527 and 1530 at Dholpur. From an outcrop of fine-grained sandstone, he made a broad platform from which terraces descended to a garden. The site included a stepwell that supplied water to the garden by a raised aqueduct (almost 83 m in length) and a distribution pool, bathhouse, Timurid-style pavilion, and various enclosed gardens with large and small pools, all linked by a water channel (18 cm wide and 5–8 cm deep) incised in the rock surface and pouring over small chadars as it fell from one terrace to the next. The garden takes its name from the sequentially linked basins, developing from the lotus's tight bud to full swollen bloom and finally the spent stage of withering petals. The full bloom stage was the largest basin: it stood on the lowest of the stone terraces at the center of intersecting water channels. From here, the water flowed to a lower gardened level that took the form of a chahar bagh. Because the water was lifted from a deep well, pressure was minimal and the display of water was limited to small cascades and basins rather than the fountain jets seen at later Mughal gardens.

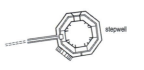

Bagh-i Nilufar
(after Elizabeth
Moynihan)

BIBLIOGRAPHY

Moynihan, Elizabeth. "The Lotus Garden Palace of Zahir al-Din Muhammad Babur." *Muqarnas* 5 (1988): 135–52.

———. "'But What a Happiness to Have Known Babur!'" In James L. Wescoat, Jr., and Joachim Wolschke-Bulmahn, eds., *Mughal Gardens: Sources, Places, Representations, and Prospects*, 95–126. Washington, D.C.: Dumbarton Oaks, 1996.

DIG

Dig Palace

Built by Jat patrons near Bharatpur in the eighteenth century, the oldest portion of the Dig (or Deeg) Palace is called the Purana Mahal; it was built on the southern end and dates to 1722–30. But the majority of the palace was built by the rulers Surajmal (r. 1756–63) and Jawahirsingh (1764–68). Traditional Mughal garden typology is combined here with a water palace (*jal-mahal*). The main grounds consist of a symmetrical chahar bagh with deeply sunken beds that extends between two artificially constructed reservoirs, the Rup Sagar and Gopal Sagar (Plate 16). The Nand Bhawan and Kishan Bhawan pavilions command the north and south termini of the arms of the axes defining this garden; along the principal east-west axis the Gopal Bhawan (90 by 18 m) and Kesav Bhawan pavilions project into and even onto the reservoirs, providing delightful views of landscape and water. The terrace in front of the Gopal Bhawan is taken up by shallow tanks with fountain jets. There are smaller chahar baghs at either end of the Gopal Bhawan—those on the west side served as the zenana—and several additional, although derelict, gardens in the southwest corner of the complex. In the terrace center, overlooking the principal gar-

Dig Palace (after M.C. Joshi, ASI)

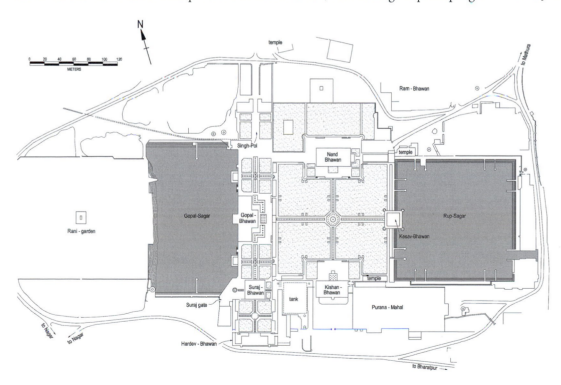

den, a marble arch (*hindola*) dated 1630–31 carries a swing that was taken from an earlier palace. This swing is an allusion to the *Ramayana*'s theme of desire and anticipation, not only in the sense of longing for the beloved, but also for the monsoon rains, and indeed the roofs of the pavilions, named for the monsoon months, resonate in the downpour.

BIBLIOGRAPHY
Begde, Prabhakar. *Forts and Palaces of India*. New Delhi: Sagar Publications, 1982.
Joshi, M. C. *Dig.* 3rd ed. New Delhi: Archaeological Survey of India, 1982.
Michell, George, and Antonio Martinelli. *The Royal Palaces of India*. New York: Thames and Hudson, 1994.
Tillotson, G. H. R. *The Rajput Palaces: The Development of an Architectural Style 1450–1750*. New Haven: Yale University Press, 1987.

FATEHPUR-SIKRI

Zenana Garden

This royal palace city and shrine complex was founded in 1571 by the Mughal Emperor Akbar at the home of his spiritual advisor, Salim ad-Din Chisti, 38 kilometers east of the Mughal capital, Agra. Eleven kilometers of fortified wall enclose the site which rises on a natural sandstone ridge that is visible from a considerable distance. Along the northwest perimeter, the city had an artificial reservoir that was tapped by wells. In one, water was lifted up to the palace via a man-powered treadmill to a succession of holding tanks and an aqueduct that was passed through building walls and traversed gardens. It filled a roofed cistern in the zenana (women's quarters) from where it was released as needed for the nearby baths and the small stepped garden, north of Jodh Bai's palace. This garden consisted of two stepped levels (one 27 by 28.4 m, and the other 37 by 19 m) bisected by a central water channel that flowed beneath diminutive chhatris. Few other original gardens can be discerned in the complex today, but the omnipresence of water channels incised in the stone pavements indicates that water was transported—at great effort—throughout the palace to fill basins and tanks such as the Anup Talao's square sunken pool and probably to irrigate gardens as may have existed just east of the Pachisi courtyard or in the courtyard of the Diwan-i 'Amm.

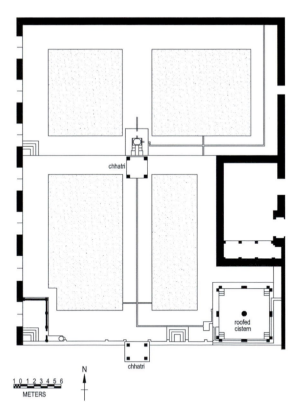

Zenana garden, Fatehpur-Sikri (after Ebba Koch)

BIBLIOGRAPHY
Archaeological Survey of India. *Fatehpur Sikri*. New Delhi: ASI, 2002.
Brand, Michael and Glenn Lowry, eds. *Fatehpur-Sikri: A Sourcebook*. Cambridge, Mass.: Aga Khan Program for Islamic Architecture at Harvard and the Massachusetts Institute of Technology, 1985.

Koch, Ebba. "Mughal Palace Gardens from Babur to Shah Jahan (1526–1648)." *Muqarnas* 14 (1997): 143–65.
Marg. Special issue on Fatehpur-Sikri, 38, no. 2 (1986).
Rizvi, S. A. A., and Vincent Flynn. *Fatehpur-Sikri*. Bombay: D. B. Taraporevala Sons, 1975.
Smith, Edmund W. *The Moghul Architecture of Fathpur-Sikri*, 4 vols. 1894–98; reprint, Delhi: Caxton Publications, 1985.

KASHMIR

Achabal Bagh

Located in the same river valley as Srinagar, but 50 kilometers south, Achabal Bagh was built by Nur Jahan, wife of the Mughal Emperor Jahangir, sometime soon after 1620 and refashioned by Shah Jahan's daughter, Jahanara, in 1634–40. The primary axis is a broad channel that runs down from the source, a sacred spring at the foot of a hill, in a striking waterfall at the elevated northern end of the garden, expanding into rectangular pools with a grid of spraying fountains. Two parallel narrower channels run along either side. In the Mughal era, the water force was so intense that excess was carried off by underground channels. The garden's four stepped terraces adapt to the sloping skirt of the mountainside. According to Attilio Petruccioli, "Monumentality is not achieved by the heroic scale, but by mastering the force of the natural elements" (p. 69).

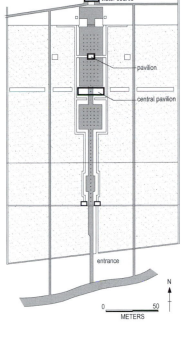

Achabal Bagh, Kashmir (Chodon, after Jonas Lehrman)

BIBLIOGRAPHY
Brookes, John. *Gardens of Paradise: History and Design of the Great Islamic Gardens*. London: Weidenfeld and Nicolson, 1987.
Crowe, Sylvia, S. Haywood, S. Jellicoe, and G. Patterson. *The Gardens of Mughal India*. London: Thames and Hudson, 1972.
Petruccioli, Attilio. "Gardens and Religious Topography in Kashmir." In *Environmental Design* 1–2 (1991): 64–73.

Nishat Bagh

Nishat Bagh, the "garden of delight," was the work of Asaf Khan, the elder brother of the Mughal Empress Nur Jahan, in 1625 in Srinagar and is widely regarded as the finest of the Kashmir gardens. Like Shalamar Bagh, it enjoys a magnificent setting between vertiginous, snow-capped mountains and the calm Lake Dal below, but its plan is more sophisticated. Its original plan had twelve levels corresponding to the signs of the zodiac (the lowest portion has been erased by a modern road). These descended from the topmost terrace, the zenana, which was set apart from the rest by a six-meter-high wall of blind arches with octagonal pavilions marking each end and providing views across the lower gardens to the lake and its distant shore. A broad watercourse runs down the central axis

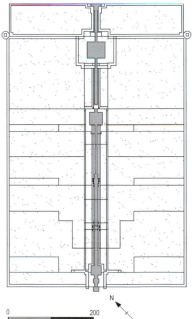

Nishat Bagh, Kashmir (Chodon, after Jonas Lehrman)

of the garden and at each change of level, it pours over a differently textured chadar. The dynamism of the water as it splashes boisterously in fountain jets and cascades contrasts pleasantly with the serene horizonality of the lake.

BIBLIOGRAPHY

Brookes, John. *Gardens of Paradise: History and Design of the Great Islamic Gardens*. London: Weidenfeld and Nicolson, 1987.

Crowe, Sylvia, S. Haywood, S. Jellicoe, and G. Patterson. *The Gardens of Mughal India*. London: Thames and Hudson, 1972.

Lehrman, Jonas. *Earthly Paradise: Garden and Courtyard in Islam*. Berkeley: University of California Press, 1980.

Villiers-Stuart, Constance Mary. *Gardens of the Great Mughals*. London: A&C Black, 1913.

Shalamar Bagh

One of many gardens built in the reign of the Mughal Emperor Jahangir, who loved the dramatic landscape of Kashmir (1,500 m above sea level), Shalamar (near the city of Srinagar) consisted of two great four-part gardened terraces with a smaller entry court at lake level. The older and upper gardens, called the Bagh-i Fayz Bakhsh, were built by Jahangir in 1619–20, while the later lower Bagh-i Farah Bakhsh was the addition of Shah Jahan around 1630, advised by the Empress Nur Jahan. The uppermost garden served as the zenana and had a pavilion of black marble set within a square pool. The middle terrace had a more public function including an audience hall, while the lowest and most public level had the Diwan-i 'Amm, a hall of public audience.

The mountains form a stunning backdrop to the garden and provide a constant torrent of water that not only pours vigorously down the successive levels but also powers fountain jets and, formerly, supplied the baths of the second terrace. A central channel (6 m wide) runs straight through the three terraces, with a cross-axial channel on the uppermost level. The watercourse swells to form pools in the center of the two chahar baghs, and at the entrance at the bottom of the garden it disappears below ground level to reemerge on the other side as a canal that flows to Lake Dal. On each terrace, a pavilion stands in the center of the pool or straddles the water channel, and all along the channel there are broad stepping stones, bridged walkways, and platforms (*chabutra*s) that seem to invite one to step into the water. As for the original planting at the site, the visitor François Bernier described turf and poplar trees in 1665. Manuscript paintings of other imperial Kashmiri gardens show plots filled with colorful flowers.

BIBLIOGRAPHY

Brookes, John. *Gardens of Paradise: History and Design of the Great Islamic Gardens*. London: Weidenfeld and Nicolson, 1987.

Crowe, Sylvia, S. Haywood, S. Jellicoe, and G. Patterson. *The Gardens of Mughal India*. London: Thames and Hudson, 1972.

Moynihan, Elizabeth. *Paradise as a Garden in Persia and Mughal India*. New York: George Braziller, 1979.

Petruccioli, Attilio. "Gardens and Religious Topography in Kashmir." *Environmental Design*, 1–2 (1991): 64–73.

Villiers-Stuart, Constance Mary. *Gardens of the Great Mughals*. London: A&C Black, 1913.

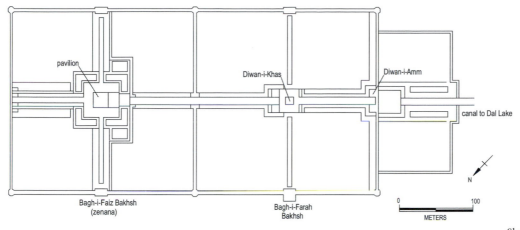

pavilion

Diwan-i-Khas

Diwan-i-Amm

canal to Dal Lake

N

Bagh-i-Faiz Bakhsh
(zenana)

Bagh-i-Farah
Bakhsh

0   100
METERS

Shalamar Bagh,
Kashmir (Ruggles
and Variava)

Verinag

Verinag is built at a sacred site at the Banihal pass on the
way to Kashmir, at the source of the Bihar River, amidst
a pine forest. The water in the garden flows from a deep
spring-fed octagonal pool that is surrounded by an arcade
and overlooked by a domed pavilion. From there it courses
in a straight, 330-meter long, stone-lined channel that
divides the enclosed garden symmetrically. Although much
simpler than the other Mughal gardens in Kashmir, Verinag
is similarly set in a dramatic landscape between mountains
and a body of water, in this case a stream. It was built in
1609, according to an inscription containing the following
praise: "this canal is like the canal of Paradise; this cascade
is the glory of Kashmir." The octagonal pool was built by
Jahangir just before his ascension to the throne in 1605,
according to Shah Jahan's biographer. The garden was a
favorite of Shah Jahan, who called it Shahabad and developed it further by adding pavilions, baths, tanks, chadars,
and fountains.

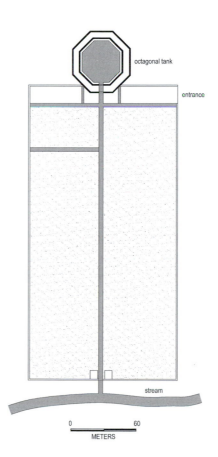

octagonal tank

entrance

stream

0   60
METERS

Verinag, Kashmir
(Chodon, after
Jonas Lehrman)

BIBLIOGRAPHY
Alfieri, Bianca Maria. *Islamic Architecture of the Indian Subcontinent.*
    London: Laurence King, 2000.
Brookes, John. *Gardens of Paradise: History and Design of the Great
    Islamic Gardens.* London: Weidenfeld and Nicolson, 1987.
Crowe, Sylvia, S. Haywood, S. Jellicoe, and G. Patterson. *The Gardens
    of Mughal India.* London: Thames and Hudson, 1972.
'Inayat Khan, *The Shah Jahan Nama of 'Inayat Khan,* ed. and trans. W.
    E. Begley and Z. A. Desai. Oxford: Oxford University Press, 1990.
Petruccioli, Attilio. "Gardens and Religious Topography in Kashmir."
    Environmental Design 1–2 (1991): 64–73.

Palaces

Mandu, the fortified capital of the Sultans of Malwa from 1405 to 1436, occupied an isolated plateau in central India. In its northwest corner, the palace complex included a maydan, mosque, and two artificial lakes: the Munj Talao and the Kapur Talao. Poised between these, the Jahaz Mahal ("Ship Palace," so named for its long narrow form, 121.9 m long, 15.2 m wide, and 9.7 m tall) was a handsome hall built by the Khalji ruler Ghiyas al-Din (r. 1469–1500). Inside and to the south end of the hall there was a cistern that supplied the baths; water was also lifted by pulley to the lower of the rooftop terraces where it flowed through scrolling water channels to fill deep pools whose recessed and stepped levels suggest that bathers would sit partially immersed in them. These scallop-edged basins bear a resemblance to ornamental basins in fourteenth- and fifteenth-century Egyptian Mamluk houses, but there are also much older ornamental lotus tanks in Polonnarva, Sri Lanka. On the roof, reached by broad steps that ran up the southern end of the building's exterior, airy pavilions offered charming views of the surrounding landscape and two lakes which in turn were encircled by wells, baths, and handsome pavilions such as the Jal Mahal (on the northwest corner of the Munj Talao), and a "floating" platform in the midst of the Kapur Talao.

On the southern edge of the city, the so-called Baz Bahadur Palace, built in 1509–10 by Sultan Nasir Shah and augmented in 1534–61 by Sher Shah's governor, similarly was poised next to an artificial lake. Water was lifted from the northern end of this lake, the Rewa Kund, to the Baz Bahadur Palace where it filled an ornamented cistern in an open court and watered a garden to the north. The palace has a rooftop terrace with pavilions that offer magnificent views down to the Nimar Plains that surround Mandu. On a high ridge south of this palace, equally sweeping panoramas can be seen from the group of buildings known as Rupmati's pavilions.

Palace Precinct, Mandu (after George Michell), right; Baz Bahadur Palace (Ruggles), far right

Hathi Pol

Dilwar Khan's Mosque

Hindola Mahal

Palace of Gada Shah

Lal Mahal

Jahaz Mahal

0   150

N

Whether the palaces gaze inward to gardens or outward beyond the city walls, Mandu is compelling for the way that the architecture exploits the views of natural landscape and palatine gardens. Long after the city's political importance faded, it was a favorite resort of the Mughals, who built there the Nil-Kanth Palace, among others.

BIBLIOGRAPHY

Alfieri, Bianca M. *Islamic Architecture of the Indian Subcontinent*. London: Laurence King, 2000.

Brand, Michael. "Mughal Ritual in Pre-Mughal Cities: The Case of Jahangir in Mandu." *Environmental Design*, 1–2 (1991): 8–17.

Goetz, H. "An Irruption of Gothic Style Forms into Indo-Islamic Architecture." *Artibus Asiae* 22 (1959): 53–58.

Patil, D. R. *Mandu*. New Delhi: Archaeological Survey of India, 1992.

Yazdani, Ghulam. *Mandu: The City of Joy*. Oxford, 1929.

NAGAUR

Ahhichatragarh Fort

Nagaur, northeast of Jodhpur in central Rajasthan, had its origins in the twelfth century and was a sultanate stronghold from the thirteenth to the sixteenth century. It was controlled by the powerful Khalji and Tughluq dynasties from Delhi and was independent under Rajput rule thereafter. Annexed by the Mughals in 1556–57, it was then governed by Muslim and later Rajput governors.

The hilltop Ahhichatragarh Fort lies in the southwest part of the old city, an irregular shape enclosed by massive rubble defense walls faced with stone. At its center is a walled palatine complex in sandstone, consisting of a temple, mosque (1631–32), main palace, rani's palace, zenana, bathhouse, polo ground, and many smaller halls with pools, pavilions, and gardens. The largest garden—probably semi-utilitarian—lies on the east side of the main palace. Approximately 70 by 80 meters, it is geometrically divided into rectangular beds, walled, and encircled by an aqueduct that runs within the enclosure walls. At the south end (to the right in this image) an enormous pool with island pavilion dates to the second half of the sixteenth century, but most of the rest

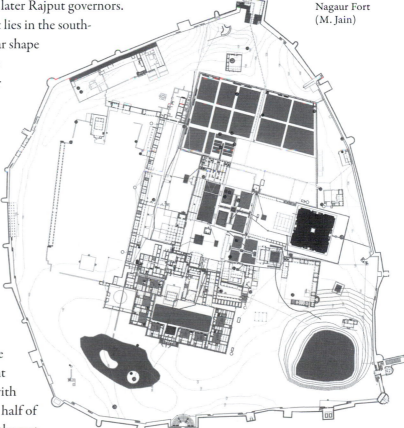

Nagaur Fort
(M. Jain)

of the palace dates to the seventeenth century or after. The fort lies in an extremely arid desert landscape with only seasonal precipitation. A connected system of large reservoirs, stepwells, and a moat collected the water that was then mechanically raised to the palace halls and distributed by an aqueduct. The rooftop terraces that surrounded the various courtyards also served to catch and funnel water into the pools from which the gardens were irrigated. Considerable areas of the fort were given over to enclosed or open gardens, verdant and irrigated. These included two chahar baghs. In the one opposite the main palace, two quadrants were filled with concavities (like Orchha's Anand Mandal) that may have been planted with low shrubs or flooded and planted with lotus.

BIBLIOGRAPHY

Goetz, H. "The Nagaur School of Rajput Painting." *Artibus Asiae* 12 (1949): 89–98.

Jain, Minakshi, and Kulbhushan Jain. *The Fort of Nagaur.* Jodhpur: Mehrangarh Museum Trust; Ahmedabad: CEPT School of Architecture, 1993.

Shokoohy, Mehrdad, and Natalie Shokoohy. *Nagaur: Sultanate and Early Mughal History and Architecture of the District of Nagaur, India.* Royal Asiatic Society Monographs, 28. London: Royal Asiatic Society, 1993.

ORCHHA

Anand Mandal Bagh

Orchha, the capital of the Rajput state of Bundelkhand in the sixteenth and seventeenth century, has a handsome citadel that stands on an island in the middle of the Betwa River. The citadel includes three palaces, one of which is the Jahangiri Mahal, built between 1610 and 1619 by Bir Singh Deo (r. 1605–27), a contemporary and ally of Jahangir. On its northern side it has a view of the Rai Praveen pavilion and its garden, called the Anand Mandal Bagh. The garden served as the residence of Rai Praveen, the consort of Indramani (r. 1672–75), but it is unclear whether it was built entirely by that patron or existed already in some form in the time of Bir Deo Singh, having been built in conjunction with the palace.

Anand Mandal Bagh, Orchha (Ruggles)

At the south end of the garden stands a two-story stone and brick pavilion that overlooks a walled asymmetrically planned garden with a much smaller single-story pavilion opposite. In front of the former, there is a terrace below which is a basement with a broad pool that could hold water to a depth of about a half meter. The garden is divided in two halves by a gated wall. On both sides, there are raised walkways and sunken water basins. The garden had one well outside its walls and two within, and water could be lifted by waterwheel from these into underground earthen channels as well as surface conduits that are still in evidence. Unlike Mughal gardens, where the preference is for broad quadrants of flower-filled parterres, the Rai Praveen ground is paved with packed mortar punctuated by an even grid of deep octagonal basins. With the cessation of irrigation little grows there today and the ubiquitous paved surface is hot and visually unappealing. But if the pits were deep enough, plants or low trees could have flourished with the effect of a shady orchard, as is partially evident today.

The Amar Vilas courtyard in the City Palace at Udaipur had a similar system and, filled with vegetation, gives a sense of the original planting.

BIBLIOGRAPHY

Begde, Prabhakar V. *Forts and Palaces of India*. New Delhi: Sagar Publications, 1982.

Joffee, Jennifer, and D. Fairchild Ruggles. "Rajput Gardens and Landscapes." In Michel Conan, ed., *The Middle East Garden Traditions, Unity and Diversity: Questions, Methods, and Resources in a Multicultural Perspective*, 269–85. Washington, D.C.: Dumbarton Oaks, 2007.

Michell, George, and Antonio Martinelli. *The Royal Palaces of India*. New York: Thames and Hudson, 1994.

Singh, A. P., and Shiv Pal Singh. *Monuments of Orchha*. Delhi: Agam Kala Prakashan, 1991.

SIKANDRA

Tomb of Akbar

This enormous tomb was completed by the Mughal Emperor Jahangir in Sikandra, a short distance from Agra, between 1612 and 1614. The architecturally enigmatic mausoleum (105 m each side), stands in the center of a simple chahar bagh that a contemporary source called Behishtabad ("Abode of Paradise"). Virtually nothing is known about the plantings of this garden. The four-part plan was formed by the intersection of north-south and east-west walkways traversed by water channels. Although the chahar bagh derives from Timurid prototypes, the tomb's unusual five-tier structure rejects such associations and embraces pre-Mughal palatine architecture such as the pre-Mughal Kimlasa Fort's fifteenth-century Nagina Mahal and the sixteenth-century Panch Mahal of Fatehpur-Sikri.

The entrance is a monumental gate on the south side, matched for the sake of symmetry by blind gates on the other three enclosure walls. On the gate's south (outer) face, an inscribed poem compares the garden to paradise and its buildings to the divine throne. Its final stanza reads: "These are the gardens of Eden, enter them and live forever."

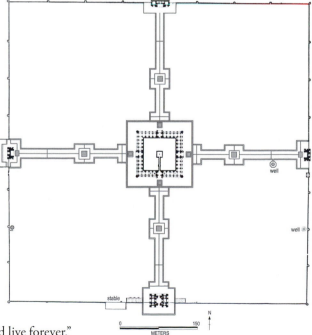

Tomb of Akbar (Chodon, after Edmund Smith, 1909)

BIBLIOGRAPHY

Asher, Catherine. *Architecture of Mughal India*. New Cambridge History of India, I: 4. Cambridge: Cambridge University Press, 1995.

Smith, Edmund. *Akbar's Tomb, Sikandrah near Agra, Described and Illustrated*. ASI New Imperial Series, no. 35. Allahabad: Superintendent Government Press, United Provinces, 1909.

UDAIPUR

City Palace

The City Palace was founded in the mid-sixteenth century by the Rajput ruler Udai Singh II when the Sisodia dynasty shifted its capital to Udaipur. It was built in successive levels on a natural rise along the banks of Lake Pichola. Its principal garden is the courtyard built by Amar Vilas (r. 1698–1710), which although situated on the palace's topmost terrace, sits directly on bedrock. The garden takes the form of a rectangular grid of twelve squares, demarcated by narrow bands of pavement set within a larger expanse of the stone pavement (Plate 17). Set within each square is a smaller grid of nine sunken polylobed cavities planted with flowers and small trees, the canopies of which provide pleasant shade. The garden is surrounded by a portico that leads to halls with windows that, on one side, gaze toward the lake and the island palaces where the rulers of Udaipur could sojourn to escape the affairs of the city.

BIBLIOGRAPHY

Joffee, Jennifer, and D. Fairchild Ruggles. "Rajput Gardens and Landscapes." In Michel Conan, ed. *The Middle East Garden Traditions, Unity and Diversity: Questions, Methods, and Resources in a Multicultural Perspective*, 269–85. Washington, D.C.: Dumbarton Oaks, 2007.

Michell, George, and Antonio Martinelli. *The Royal Palaces of India*. New York: Thames and Hudson, 1994.

Tillotson, G. H. R. *The Rajput Palaces: The Development of an Architectural Style, 1450–1750*. New Haven: Yale University Press, 1987.

United States

HONOLULU, HAWAIʻI

Shangri La

This Islamic-inspired estate on the Hawaiʻian island of Oʻahu was built in 1937–38 by the firm Wyeth & King, for the heiress Doris Duke (1912–93), who, advised by Arthur Upham Pope, filled it with installations of Islamic art including ceramics, tile, textiles, and glass and metal objects. The architecture blends Hawaiʻian and Islamic elements in a modern reinterpretion that included technologically ingenious devices such as an electrically powered retractable glass wall and a diving board with a hydraulic lift. The house faces the Pacific Ocean and rises above the rocks and surf on a high wall of local lava. The complex is organized in a series of L-shapes and consists of two principal buildings: the residence and the playhouse with an intervening swimming pool. The residence centers on a courtyard with an arcade of inlaid wooden Isfahan-style columns that wraps around a small sunken garden, pool, and water jet (Plate 25): the effect is of a grove of slender trees. The retractable glass wall and sliding jali screens, together with arcades and porches, create a flexible relationship between interior architecture and exterior landscape.

Date palms and banyan trees are planted throughout the estate. One terrace is given over to a Mughal-style garden with a central channel with water jets, flanked by brick pavement and sunken garden beds with parterres outlined in white stone. The water enters the channel from a stepped landing at one end of the garden and pours over a chini khana panel that could be lit with electric candles. Water for the swimming pool cascades from a raised terrace with pool and a vigorous jet flowing downward over textured chadars. This watercourse is flanked by stairs and raised beds with trees.

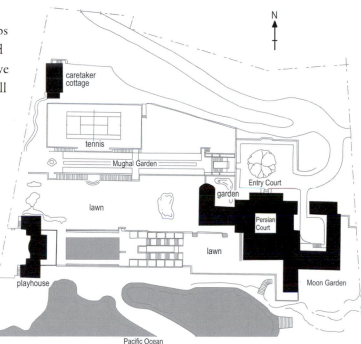

Shangri-La, Honolulu (Variava, after Doris Duke Charitable Foundation)

BIBLIOGRAPHY
Littlefield, Sharon, with Introduction by Carol Bier. *Doris Duke's Shangri La*. Honolulu: Honolulu Academy of Arts, 2002.
Rochlin, Margy. "Her Own Shangri La." *Town and Country*, July 2007: 88–97, 117.

WASHINGTON, D.C.

Enid A. Haupt Garden

Opened in 1987 and named for its patron, this four-acre garden occupies the space between the Smithsonian Arts and Industries Building, the Freer Gallery of Art, and the underground twins: the Arthur M. Sackler Gallery of Asian Art and the National Museum of African Art. Indeed, it is planted on the roof of the latter. The architect Jean Paul Carlihan designed the gardens to reflect the art housed in the collections in the museums, so that there are two large moongates of pink granite in the Asian portion nearest the Sackler and the Freer and a modern interpretation of an Islamic garden, called the Fountains Garden, near the Museum of African Art. The octagonal Fountains Garden centers on a quadripartite courtyard where the quadrants are raised above the pavement, rather

Fountains Garden at the Smithsonian (Thaisa Way)

than sunken as is more typical in historic Islamic gardens. In the center of the court, a water jet recessed below a grill shoots water upward in a manner reminiscent of the water stairway at the Generalife (Granada). The north side of the garden (seen here) has a chadar with water splashing down a sloping scalloped granite surface into a pool below. The water flows in channels incised in the stone walls, pausing at regular intervals to fill shallow basins. This visual axis terminates on the other side of the courtyard at a series of low steps that lead to one of the museum's windows, centered beneath a dome to give the effect of a garden pavilion.

BIBLIOGRAPHY
Kernan, Michael. "Turning a New Leaf." *Smithsonian*, August 2000.
Smithsonian. www.gardens.si.edu/horticulture/gardens/Haupt/enid.htm.

Glossary

agdal – (Maghreb) an extensive cultivated area of fields and gardens

aiwan – (South Asia) any hypostyle construction (corresponds to Persian *talar*)

bagçe – (Turkish). See *bagh*

bagh – garden

bangla – (South Asia) type of curved roof, probably derived from Bengali prototypes

baradari – (South Asia) a rectangular pavilion open on each side through arches or colonnades

baraka – literally "blessing"; refers to the aura of sanctity that emanates from a Muslim saint's tomb

bustan – (Arabic) garden

caravanserai – inn

chabutra – (South Asia) a raised platform

chadar – a water chute with three-dimensional texture such as scalloping

chahar bagh – literally, "four gardens"; used by historians to designate quadripartite gardens in a cross-axial arrangement, but used more loosely in premodern texts to designate any garden of multiple beds

chawk. See *chowk*

chhatri – (South Asia) literally, "umbrella"; a small, domed, open-air kiosk, either free-standing or added as an architectural element to a larger structure

chini khana – literally, "China cabinet"; a panel of niches used in interiors as shelving but in the garden used as the backdrop for water cascades, sometimes filled with oil lamps or flowers

chowk – (South Asia) an open courtyard or public plaza

dargah – various meanings: in South Asia, it can designate a Sufi shrine complex or the imperial court itself

diwan – various meanings: administrative or reception hall; an administrative office; a raised platform for sitting; or a collected body of poetic, literary or legal work

eyvan – (Persian). See *iwan*

ghat – (South Asia) a stepped embankment to a river or tank

hammam – bathhouse

haramlik – (Turkish) the private quarters of a large mansion

harem (or *haram*) – sanctuary; the private quarters of a house; the women's quarters (see also *zenana*)

hayr – a cultivated or gardened enclosure

hazira – an enclosure screen surrounding an unroofed tomb

hesht behesht – literally, "eight paradises"; architecturally, refers to an octagonally shaped plan with eight bays rotated around a central bay

hindola – (South Asia) marble arch

'imarat – (*imaret,* Turkish) literally, a large building; architecturally, can refer to a soup kitchen

iwan – (*eyvan,* Persian) large niche, usually barrel-vaulted, open on one side; (South Asia, *aiwan*) any hypostyle construction

jali – (South Asia) ornamental stone screen, equivalent to a *mashribiyya jal-mahal* – (South Asia) water palace

janna – paradise; also garden

jharoka – (South Asia) projecting window or balconied oriel used in South Asia for official appearances of the sovereign

kulliye – (Turkish) a charitable architectural complex usually comprised of a mosque, *madrasa*, and other institutions such as a library, hospital, Qur'an school, and soup kitchen

madina – (or *medina*) walled and gated city

madrasa – (*medrese,* Turkish) theological college

mahal – hall, pavilion, or palace

martyrium – (Latin) monument marking the site of the martyrdom, grave, or relics of a Christian saint

masjid – mosque

maydan – (or *maidan*) public or semi-public plaza

mazar – literally, a "visiting place"; a sanctuary or shrine

mihrab – niche designating the *qibla* wall of a mosque and thus the direction of prayer

mina'i – ceramic with stain and overglaze painting

mirador – from the Spanish "mirar"; a designated place for viewing, a belvedere

mudéjar – (Iberia) Muslims living under Christian rule, or the arts and architecture of those artisans and their descendants

muqarnas – suspended ornamental vaulting, also called "stalactite" vaults; usually concave and arched but sometimes rendered as flat niches

namakdan – (Persian) pavilion

nivas – (South Asia) a small palace

noria – (or *na'ura*) waterwheel that lifts water with dippers attached to the wheel's frame (compare with *saqiya*)

oratory – small prayer hall for individual use

pietra dura – (or *pietre dure*) (Italian) an intarsia technique using hard polished colored stone inlaid like mosaic

qanat – an underground water canal

qasr – a fortified residence

qibla – literally meaning "the direction toward" and used architecturally to refer to the wall in the mosque closest to Mecca and thus toward which prayer is directed

qubba – a cupola or domed structure

rawda – cemetery garden; can also refer to the tomb itself

riyad – (Maghreb) an interior courtyard garden

saqiya – literally, a water channel; in architecture, refers to a waterwheel that lifts water from deep source using dippers attached to a chain rotated by the movement of the wheel (compare with *noria*)

saramlik – (Turkish) the public reception area of a large mansion

talao – (South Asia) water tank or artificial lake

talar – (Persian) porch with tall wooden columns

turbe – (Turkish) tomb

wadi – seasonal stream

waqf – (*vakf,* Turkish) a perpetual charitable endowment to support architectural establishments and social services

yalı – (Turkish) wooden kiosk or residential pavilion

zawiya – (*zaviye,* Turkish) monastery-retreat for prayer and contemplation

zellij – (Maghreb) glazed tile, cut and assembled like mosaic

zenana – (South Asia) women's quarters, harem

Notes

PREFACE

1. Witness a passage written in 1976 with the title "The Persian Garden Under Islam," in which the author describes the allure of the gardens of paradise promised to the faithful in the Qur'an: "To highly-sexed people living in hot and arid lands, the appeal of these pledged gardens of delight contributed considerably to the strength of Islam; with the provision of wine it would have been irresistible." Wilfrid Blunt, "The Persian Garden Under Islam," *Apollo* 103, nos. 170–72 (1976): 302.

CHAPTER 1. PLACE AND MEMORY IN LANDSCAPE HISTORY

1. *Baburnama*, ed. and trans. Wheeler Thackston (New York: Oxford University Press, 1996), p. 332.

2. Ibn Battuta, *The Travels of Ibn Battuta*, trans. H. A. R. Gibb, 3 vols. (Cambridge: Hakluyt Society, 1958–71).

3. Donald Wilber, *Persian Gardens and Garden Pavilions* (Washington, D.C.: Dumbarton Oaks, 1979), p. 17.

4. William Hanaway, Jr., "Paradise on Earth: The Terrestrial Garden in Persian Literature," in Elisabeth MacDougall and Richard Ettinghausen, eds., *The Islamic Garden* (Washington, D.C.: Dumbarton Oaks, 1976), p. 51.

5. D. Fairchild Ruggles, *Gardens, Landscape, and Vision in the Palaces of Islamic Spain* (University Park: Penn State University Press, 2001), chapters 4 and 5.

6. Ruggles, *Gardens, Landscape, and Vision*, ch. 8; and Ruggles, "The Eye of Sovereignty: Poetry and Vision in the Alhambra's Lindaraja Mirador," *Gesta* 36 (1997): 182–91.

7. As an example of such a study, see James L. Wescoat, Jr., and Gilbert White, *Water for Life: Water Management and Environmental Policy* (Cambridge: Cambridge University Press, 2003).

8. On this topic, see D. Fairchild Ruggles, "Making Vision Manifest: Frame, Screen, and View in Islamic Culture," in Dianne Harris and D. F. Ruggles, eds., *Sites Unseen: Landscape and Vision* (Pittsburgh: University of Pittsburgh Press, 2007), pp. 131–56.

9. Nur al-Din Jahangir, *The Jahangirnama: Memoirs of Jahangir, Emperor of India*, ed. and trans. Wheeler Thackston (Washington, D.C.: Freer Gallery of Art, 1999), pp. 332–33.

10. For a discussion of sacred place and time and theories of memory, see Jonathan Z. Smith, *To Take Place: Toward a Theory of Ritual* (Chicago: University of Chicago Press, 1987), pp. 24–35.

11. Imru al-Qays, *Mu'allaqa,* this translation adapted from that of A. J. Arberry, *The Seven Odes* (London: George Allen & Unwin, 1957), p. 61.

12. Ruggles, *Gardens, Landscape, and Vision*, pp. 136–37.

13. Frances Robinson, *Islam and Muslim History in South Asia* (New Delhi: Oxford University Press, 2000), p. 39, citing Akbar Ahmad; D. Fairchild Ruggles, "Arabic Poetry and Architectural Memory in al-Andalus," *Ars Orientalis* 23 (1993): 171–78.

14. Oleg Grabar, *The Formation of Islamic Art*, rev. ed. (New Haven: Yale University Press, 1987), pp. 46–64; Grabar, *The Shape of the Holy: Early Islamic Jerusalem* (Princeton: Princeton University Press, 1996).

15. Godfrey Goodwin, *A History of Ottoman Architecture* (New York: Thames and Hudson, 1971), pp. 102, 121 ff.

16. Mahvash Alemi, "Royal Gardens of the Safavid Period: Types and Models," in Attilio Petruccioli, ed., *Gardens in the Time of the Great Muslim Empires* (Leiden: E. J. Brill, 1997), pp. 72–96.

17. R. D. McChesney, "Some Observations on 'Garden' and Its Meaning in the Property Transactions of the Juybari Family in Bukhara, 1544–77," in Attilio Petruccioli, ed., *Gardens in the Time of the Great Muslim Empires* (Leiden: E. J. Brill, 1997), pp. 97–109.

18. Wilber, *Persian Gardens,* pp. 28–29.

19. Ibn Arabshah, *Tamerlane or Timur the Great Amir*, trans. J. H. Saunders (London: Luzac, 1936), p. 310.

20. Clavijo, *Embassy to Tamerlane, 1403–1406*, trans. Guy le Strange (New York: Harper & Brothers, 1928), pp. 287–88.

21. *Baburnama*, trans. Thackston, p. 360.

22. Adapted from Wilber, *Persian Gardens*, p. 18.

23. Ruggles, *Gardens, Landscape, and Vision*, p. 137.

24. Paula Sanders, *Ritual, Politics, and the City in Fatimid Cairo* (Albany: State University of New York Press, 1994).

CHAPTER 2. MAKING THE DESERT BLOOM

1. On the suitability of the Syrian landscape and climate for agriculture, see Georges Tchalenko, *Villages Antiques de la*

Syrie du Nord: Le Massif du Bélus à l'Époque Romaine, 2 vols. (Paris: Paul Geuthner, 1953), 2: 64–72.

2. John Brookes, *Gardens of Paradise* (New York: New Amsterdam Books, 1987), pp. 214–17.

3. A. Ventura Villanueva, *El abastecimiento de agua a la Córdoba romana. I. El Acueducto de Valdepuentes* (Cordoba: University of Cordoba, 1993). On the hydraulic infrastructure of Madinat al-Zahra', see Antonio Vallejo Triano, "Madinat al-Zahra', capital y sede del Califato omeya andalusí," in *El Esplendor de los Omeyas cordobeses* (Granada: Fundación Andalusí, 2001), pp. 386–97.

4. K. A. C. Creswell, *A Short Account of Early Muslim Architecture*, rev. by James Allan (Cairo: American University in Cairo Press, 1989), pp. 118–22; Jean Sauvaget, "Les ruines omeyyades du Djebel Seis," *Syria* 20 (1939): 239–56.

5. Creswell, *Short Account*, pp. 135–46; Oleg Grabar, "Umayyad 'Palace' and Abbasid 'Revolution,'" *Studia Islamica* 18 (1962): 18; D. Schlumberger, "Les fouilles de Qasr el-Heir el-Gharbi (1936–1939)," *Syria* 20 (1939): 195–238, 324–73.

6. For the excavation, survey, and analysis of this site, see Oleg Grabar, R. Holod, J. Knustad, and W. Trousdale, *City in the Desert: Qasr al-Hayr East* (Cambridge, Mass.: Harvard University Press, 1978).

7. Creswell, *Short Account*, pp. 149–62.

8. Creswell, *Short Account*, p. 180; R. W. Hamilton, *Khirbat al-Mafjar: An Arabian Mansion in the Jordan Valley* (Oxford: Clarendon Press, 1959).

9. The Valens Aqueduct still stands today; the panoramic view of it, drawn in 1559 by Melchior Lorichs, shows its descent from high ground to the lower ground of Istanbul's peninsula as well as the way that the Roman aqueduct was integrated into urban fabric and served major mosque complexes in the Ottoman imperial era. Cyril Mango and Stephan Yerasimos, *Melchior Lorichs' Panorama of Istanbul, 1559* (Bern: Ertug & Kocabiyik, 1999), facsimile edition.

10. Ventura Villanueva, *El abastecimiento de agua a la Córdoba romana,* passim.

11. Torres Balbás calls it a *noria*, in the general sense of any waterwheel, but given the height, a chain wheel (saqiya) is most likely ("Monteagudo y 'El Castillejo,' en la Vega de Murcia," *Al-Andalus* 2 [1934]: 366–72, and *Artes almorávide y almohade* [Madrid: Consejo Superior de Investigaciones Científicas, 1955], p. 17).

12. Karl Butzer, *Early Hydraulic Civilization in Egypt* (Chicago: University of Chicago Press, 1976), pp. 39–56.

13. Thorkild Schiøler, *Roman and Islamic Water-Lifting Wheels* (Denmark: Odense University Press, 1971).

14. Henri Goblot, *Les Qanats: Une technique d'acquisition de l'eau* (Paris: Mouton, 1979), pp. 59–73.

15. Rainfall evaporates at a rate of 20 percent (Brookes, *Gardens of Paradise*, p. 215).

16. Thomas Glick, *Islamic and Christian Spain in the Early Middle Ages* (Princeton: Princeton University Press, 1979), pp. 68–76.

17. Karl Wittfogel, *Oriental Depotism* (New Haven: Yale University Press, 1957), argued that large-scale water management led to centralized leadership and despotism, and claimed that arid climates such as the Middle East were natural spawning grounds for tyranny.

18. Eva Hunt and Robert C. Hunt, "Irrigation, Conflict, and Politics: A Mexican Case," in Theodore E. Downing and McGuire Gibson, eds., *Irrigation's Impact on Society* (Tucson: University of Arizona Press, 1974), pp. 129–57.

19. Husam Qawam El-Samarraie, *Agriculture in Iraq During the Third Century, A.H.* (Beirut: Librairie du Liban, 1972), p. 105, citing Qudama b. Ja'far (864–932), *Kitab al-kharaj* (ms. Koprolulu Library, mo. 1076, fol. 100b).

20. Abu Bakr Ahmad ibn Wahshiyya, *Kitab al-filaha al-nabatiyya* (ms. Istanbul, Vallyudin Barazid Library, no. 2485; Oxford Bodleian Library, nos. Hunt 340, Hunt 326; Beyazid, no. 4064); Abu'l-wafa al-Buzjani, *Kitab al-hawli li'l a'mal al-sultaniyya wa rusum al-hisab al-diwaniyya* (ms. Paris, Bibliothèque Nationale, no. arabe 2462); Ya'qub b. Ibrahim Abu Yusuf, *Kitab al-kharaj* (Cairo: 1352/1933); discussed in El-Samarraie, *Agriculture in Iraq*, passim.

21. Abu Yusuf, *Kitab al-kharaj*, cited in El-Samarraie, *Agriculture in Iraq*, p. 42.

22. Al-Ya'qubi, *Les Pays*, ed. and trans. G. Wiet (Cairo: Imprimerie de l'Institut Français d'Archéologie Orientale, 1937), p. 251 (Arabic) and 35 (French trans.).

23. J. M. Rogers, "Samarra: A Study in Medieval Town Planning," in Albert Hourani and S. M. Stern, eds., *The Islamic City* (Philadelphia: University of Pennsylvania Press, 1970), p. 139.

24. Rogers, "Samarra," p. 134, citing al-Ya'qubi.

25. Rogers, "Samarra," p. 140.

26. George T. Scanlon, "Housing and Sanitation," in Albert Hourani and S. M. Stern, eds., *The Islamic City*, p. 188; see also André Raymond, "Les porteurs d'eau du Caire," *Bulletin de l'Institut Français d'Archéologie Orientale* 57 (1958): 183–202.

27. Tchalenko, *Villages Antiques de la Syrie du Nord*; A. Reifenburg, *The Struggle Between the Desert and the Sown: The Rise and Fall of Agriculture in the Levant* (Jerusalem: Jewish Agency, 1955); Grabar, "Umayyad 'Palace' and Abbasid 'Revolution,'" pp. 5–18.

28. Grabar, "Umayyad 'Palace' and Abbasid 'Revolution,'" pp. 5–18.

29. Ernst Herzfeld, *Erster vorläufiger Bericht über die Ausgrabungen von Samarra* (Berlin, 1912), and Herzfeld, "Mitteilungen über die Arbeiten der zweiten Kampagne von Samarra," *Der Islam* 5 (1914): 196–204, excerpted and trans. by Creswell (with Herzfeld's review and approval), *Early Muslim Architecture*, 2: 232–42, 265–70. See also Henri Viollet, "Description du palais de al-Moutasim à Samara" and "Fouilles à Samara," *Mémoires de l'Académie des Inscriptions et Belles-Lettres*, ser. I, vol. 12, part 2 (1909 and 1911): 567–94, 685–717. For a complete bibliography, see Alastair Northedge, "An Interpretation of the Palace of the Caliph at Samarra," *Ars Orientalis* 23 (1993): 143–70.

30. Al-Buhturi, *Diwan al-Buhturi* (Cairo, 1911), II: 124, cited in Qasim al-Samarrai, "The Abbasid Gardens in Baghdad and Samarra (7th–12th Centuries)," in Leslie Tjon Sie Fat and

Erik de Jong, eds., *The Authentic Garden* (Leiden: Clusius Foundation, 1991).

CHAPTER 3. THE SCIENCE OF GARDENING

1. Claude Cahen, "Notes pour une histoire de l'agriculture dans les pays musulmans médiévaux: Coup d'oeil sur la littérature agronomique musulmane hors d'Espagne," *Journal of the Economic and Social History of the Orient* 14 (1971): 67.

2. For a discussion of Andalusian botanical calendars and treatises, see Ruggles, *Gardens, Landscape and Vision*, pp. 19–21; Yemeni calendars are discussed in Daniel Varisco, *Medieval Agriculture and Islamic Science: The Almanac of a Yemeni Sultan* (Seattle: University of Washington Press, 1994), and Varisco, "Agriculture in Rasulid Zabid," *Journal of Semitic Studies, Supplement 14. Studies on Arabia in Honour of Professor G. Rex Smith,* ed. J. F. Healey and V. Porter (Oxford: Oxford University Press, 2002), pp. 323–51.

3. Varisco, *Medieval Agriculture and Islamic Science*, p. 7.

4. R. Dozy, ed., *Le Calendrier de Cordoue*, new ed. in Arabic and Latin with French trans. by Charles Pellat (Leiden: E. J. Brill, 1961). See also E. Lévi-Provençal, *Histoire de l'Espagne Musulmane*, 3 vols. (Paris: Maisonneuve, 1950–53), 3: 239–43; Julio Samsó, "La tradición clásica en los calendarios agrícolas hispanoárabes y norteafricanos," in *Actas del II Congreso para el Estudio de la Cultura en el Mediterráneo Occidental (1975)* (Barcelona, 1978), pp. 177–86; and Angel C. López, "Vida y obra del famoso polígrafo cordobés del siglo X, 'Arib Ibn Sa'id," in E. García Sánchez, ed., *Ciencias de la Naturaleza en al-Andalus: textos y estudios*, 2 vols. (Granada, 1990), 1: 317–47.

5. Daniel Varisco notes that the use of a solar schedule in the Yemen was based on practical and local observations, not the adoption of the Christian calendar. He discusses the copy of the *Milh* treatise by al-Malik al-Ashraf Yusuf that was edited by 'Abd al-Rahim Jazm in "The State of Agriculture in Late Thirteenth-Century Rasulid Yemen," paper prepared for the "Storia e cultura dello Yemen in età islamica, con particolare riferimento al periodo Rasulide," Accademia Nazionale dei Lincei, Rome (October 30–31, 2003). I am grateful to Professor Varisco for allowing me to read the paper prior to its publication.

6. Charles Pellat, *Cinq Calendriers Égyptiens* (Textes arabes et études islamiques, XXVI) (Cairo: Institut Français d'Archéologie Orientale du Caire, 1986), p. xxiii.

7. In addition to the works cited in note 4, see Pellat, *Cinq Calendriers Égyptiens*; Ibn Qutayba, *Kitab al-Anwa'*, ed. Hamidullah and Pellat (Hyderabad, 1956); José Vázquez Ruíz, "Un calendario anónimo granadino del siglo XV," *Revista del Instituto de Estudios Islámicos en Madrid* 9–10 (1961–62): 23–64; and Julio Samsó, "Un calendrier tunisien d'origine andalouse?" *Cahiers de Tunisie* 24 (1978): 65–82.

8. There appears to be some overlap between the Yemeni and Egyptian texts. See David King's review of Charles Pellat, *Cinq Calendriers Égyptiens* (1986) in *Journal of the American Research Center in Egypt* 25 (1988): 252–53; on the Yemeni calendars, see Varisco, *Medieval Agriculture and Islamic Science*.

9. This manuscript is now in the collection of the J. Pierpont Morgan Library of New York; some of its illustrations are reproduced in Kurt Weitzmann, "The Greek Sources of Islamic Scientific Illustrations," in G. Miles, ed., *Archaeologica Orientalia in Memoriam Ernst Herzfeld* (Locust Valley, N.Y.: J. J. Augustin, 1952), plate XXXIV. On the Dioscorides and its translations, see C. E. Dubler, *La "materia medica" de Dioscórides*, 6 vols. (Barcelona: Tipografía Emporium, 1953), 1: 47–48.

10. Expiración García Sánchez, "Agriculture in Muslim Spain," in *The Legacy of Muslim Spain*, ed. S. K. Jayyusi (Leiden: E. J. Brill, 1992), pp. 987–99.

11. Johannes Pedersen, *The Arabic Book*, trans. Geoffrey French (Princeton: Princeton University Press, 1984), pp. 20–36.

12. Ruggles, *Gardens, Landscape, and Vision*, pp. 17–18.

13. Al-Maqqari, *History of the Mohammedan Dynasties in Spain*, trans. Pascual de Gayangos, 2 vols. (London: Oriental Translation Fund, 1840–43), 2: 120; Renata Holod, "Luxury Arts of the Caliphal Period," in Jerrilynn D. Dodds, ed., *Al-Andalus: The Art of Islamic Spain* (New York: Metropolitan Museum of Art, 1992), pp. 41–47; Manuela Cortés García, "Ziryab, la música y la elegancia palatina," in *El Esplendor de los Omeyas cordobeses, Estudios* (Granada: Fundación El Legado Andalusí, 2001), pp. 240–43.

14. El-Samarraie, *Agriculture in Iraq*, citing Ibn Wahshiyya, *Kitab al-filaha al-nabatiyya*.

15. Varisco, *Medieval Agriculture and Islamic Science*, pp. 156–57.

16. For a more extensive discussion of agricultural manuals, see Ruggles, *Gardens, Landscape, and Vision*, pp. 21–29.

17. This work has been published in a critical edition by Toufic Fahd, *L'agriculture nabatéenne, traduction en arabe attribuée à Abu Bakr Ahmad b. Ali al-Kasdani connu sous le nom d'Ibn Wasiyya (IV/Xe siècle)*, 2 vols. (Damascus: Institut Français de Damas, 1993–95). For a critical study see Jaakko Hämeen-Anttila, *The Last Pagans of Iraq: Ibn Wahshiyya and his Nabatean Agriculture* (Leiden-Boston: Brill, 2006). El-Samarraie, for his 1972 study, *Agriculture in Iraq*, made full use of Ibn Wahshiyya (see Ch. 2, note 20).

18. Hämeen-Anttila, *Last Pagans of Iraq*, p. 241.

19. Hämeen-Anttila, *Last Pagans of Iraq*, p. 282.

20. López, "Vida y obra," pp. 317–47.

21. According to a brief reference by G. S. Colin in 1965 ("Filaha: Muslim West," *Encyclopaedia of Islam*, new ed., 12 vols., 2: 901–2), Abulcasis' agricultural manual was discovered some years earlier by Henri Pérès, who intended to publish it; however, nothing further has appeared. See also García Sánchez, "Agriculture in Muslim Spain," pp. 987–99.

22. Ibn Bassal, *Libro de agricultura*, trans. J. M. Millas Vallicrosa and M. Aziman (Tetuan: Instituto Muley el-Hasan, 1955); for a discussion of the plant lists, see J. Esteban Hernández Bermejo and E. García Sánchez, "Economic Botany and Eth-

nobotany in Al-Andalus (Iberian Peninsula: Tenth-Fifteenth Centuries), an Unknown Heritage of Mankind," *Economic Botany* 52 (1998): 15–26.

23. See Varisco, *Medieval Agriculture and Islamic Science*, and a valuable summary presented by Varisco in "The State of Agriculture in Late Thirteenth-Century Rasulid Yemen."

24. Abu'l-Khayr, *Kitab al-Filaha ou le livre de la culture*, extracts trans. A. Cherbonneau and ed. Henri Pérès (Algiers: Editions Carbonel, 1946).

25. Margareta Tengberg, "Research into the Origins of Date Palm Domestication," in *The Date Palm: From Traditional Resource to Green Wealth* (Abu Dhabi: Emirates Center for Strategic Studies and Research, 2003), pp. 51–62.

26. Abu'l-Khayr, *Kitab al-filaha*, pp. 16, 22.

27. Ibn Wafid translated by José Millás Vallicrosa, "La traducción castellana del *Tratado de agricultura* de Ibn Wafid," *Al-Andalus* 8 (1943): 309.

28. Ibn Wafid in Millás Vallicrosa, "La traducción castellana," p. 304. My thanks to Professor Richard Kagan for his help in translating this passage many years ago.

29. R. B. Serjeant and Husayn 'Abdullah al-'Amri, "A Yemeni Agricultural Poem," in *Studia Arabica et Islamica* (festschrift for Ihsan 'Abbas), ed. Wadad al-Qadi (Beirut: American University of Beirut, 1981).

30. Daniel Varisco, "A Royal Crop Register from Rasulid Yemen," *Journal of the Economic and Social History of the Orient* 34 (1991): 1–22.

31. Henri Bresc, "Les jardins de Palerme (1290–1460)," *Mélanges de l'Ecole Française de Rome* 84 (1972): 55–127.

32. Ziva Vesel, "Les traits d'agriculture en Iran," *Studia Iranica* 15 (1986): 99–108.

33. Ruggles, *Gardens, Landscape, and Vision*, ch. 2.

34. Al-Ya'qubi, *Les Pays*, trans. Wiet, p. 56.

35. Al-Maqqari (citing Abu 'Abdullah al-Yaquri), *History*, ed. and trans. Gayangos, 1: 62–63.

36. Al-Maqqari, *History*, ed. and trans. Gayangos, 2: 170; al-Nuwayri, *Historia de los musulmanes de España y Africa*, ed. and trans. M. Gaspar Remiro (Granada, 1917), p. 57.

37. Clavijo, *Embassy to Tamerlane*, trans. Guy Le Strange, p. 288.

38. Jahangir, *The Jahangirnama*, ed. and trans. Thackston, p. 332.

39. From al-Muhassin ibn 'Ali al-Tanukhi, *The Table-Talk of a Mesopotamian Judge, Being the First Part of the Nishwar al-Muhadarah or Jami' al-Tawarikh of Abu 'Ali al-Muhassin al-Tanukhi*, ed. and trans. D. S. Margoliouth (London: Royal Asiatic Society, 1921–22), pp. 146 (144 of ms. numbering) and 160 (157 of ms.).

40. Jahangir, *The Jahangirnama*, ed. and trans. Thackston, pp. 332–33.

41. Maria Subtelny, "A Medieval Persian Agricultural Manual in Context: The *Irshad al-Zira'a* in Late Timurid and Early Safavid Khorasan," *Studia Iranica* 22 (1993): 167–217.

42. On these see Jerrilynn D. Dodds, "Ahmad Ibn Baso," in *Macmillan Encyclopedia of Architects*, 4 vols. (New York: Free

Press, 1982), 1: 38, and María Jesús Rubiera Mata, *La arquitectura en la literatura árabe* (Madrid: Editora Nacional, 1981), pp. 139–40. The gardens of Seville are discussed in Ruggles, *Gardens, Landscape, and Vision*, pp. 141–47.

43. Wayne Begley, "Ghiyas, Mirak Mirza," in *Macmillan Encyclopedia of Architects*, 2: 194. The information and conclusions in this paragraph are summarized from Maria Subtelny, "Mirak-i Sayyid Ghiyas and the Timurid Tradition of Landscape Architecture," *Studia Iranica* 24 (1995): 19–54.

CHAPTER 4. ORGANIZING THE EARTH

1. Robert D. McChesney, "Some Observations on 'Garden' and Its Meanings in the Property Transactions of the Juybari Family in Bukhara, 1544–77," in Attilio Petruccioli, ed., *Gardens in the Time of the Great Muslim Empires* (Leiden: Brill, 1997), pp. 97–109.

2. David Stronach, "Parterres and Stone Watercourses at Pasargadae: Notes on the Achaemenid Contribution to Garden Design," *Journal of Garden History* 14 (1994): 3–12, and Stronach, "The Royal Garden at Pasargadae: Evolution and Legacy," in L. vanden Berghe and L. De Meyer, eds., *Archaeologia Iranica et Orientalis. Miscellanea in Honorem Louis Vanden Berghe* (Ghent: Peeters Presse, 1989), pp. 475–502.

3. Wilhemina Jashemski, *The Gardens of Pompeii,* vol. 1 (New York: Caratzas Brothers, 1979), pp. 45–47 (Tiburtinus) and p. 201 (Foro Boario); also Jashemski, "Town and Country Gardens at Pompeii and Other Vesuvian Sites," in William Kelso and Rachel Most, eds., *Earth Patterns* (Charlottesville: University Press of Virginia, 1990), pp. 213–25.

4. A. G. McKay, *Houses, Villas and Palaces in the Roman World* (Ithaca: Cornell University Press, 1975), p. 61.

5. Sites with garden murals include Pompeii (see Jashemski, *The Gardens of Pompeii*), as well as Masad, Fishbourne (England), and Herod's palace in Jerusalem.

6. Thilo Ulbert, "Ein umaiyadischer Pavillon in Resafa-Rusafat Hisam," *Damaszener Mitteilungen*, 7 (1993): 213–31. Although only three sets of steps were revealed, Ulbert believed that there had been steps on the fourth side as well.

7. The best treatment of this subject is Andrew Watson, *Agricultural Innovation in the Early Islamic World* (Cambridge: Cambridge University Press, 1983), and "The Arab Agricultural Revolution and Its Diffusion, 711–1100," *Journal of Economic History* 34 (1974): 8–35. See also Hernández Bermejo and García Sánchez, "Economic Botany and Ethnobotany in Al-Andalus," 15–26.

8. For a more complete explanation of the four-part plan both in the sense of multiple garden beds divided by walkways as well as the visual partitioning of space via perceived axes, see Ruggles, "Il giardini con pianta a croce nel Mediterraneo islamico," in Attilio Petruccioli, ed., *Il giardino islamico: Architettura, natura, paesaggio* (Milan: Electa, 1993), pp. 143–54.

9. Aly Bahgat and Albert Gabriel, *Fouilles d'al-Foustat* (Paris, 1921); Antoni A. Ostrasz, "The Archaeological Material for the Study of the Domestic Architecture at Fustat," *Africana Bulletin* 26

(1977): 57–87; George Scanlon in various issues of the *Journal of the American Research Center in Egypt*, 1966–1984, and "Housing and Sanitation: Some Aspects of Medieval Egyptian Life," in A. H. Hourani and S. M. Stern, eds., *The Islamic City* (Philadelphia: University of Pennsylvania Press, 1970), pp. 185–94.

10. The site was excavated under the direction of Herzfeld and the preliminary publication report appeared in translation in K. A. C. Creswell, *Early Muslim Architecture*, 2: 265–70. For a discussion of the problems encountered by Herzfeld, as well as those incurred later by the lack of published excavation reports, see Alastair Northedge, "Creswell, Herzfeld and Samarra," *Muqarnas* 8 (1991): 74–93.

11. Alastair Northedge, personal communication. A more correct plan of Balkuwara is shown in the Sites section.

12. The garden was excavated by F. Hernández Giménez in the 1950s, and a decade later its plan was published by B. Pavón Maldonado in *Al-Andalus* 33 (1968): 21.

13. Ruggles, *Gardens, Landscape, and Vision*, pp. 73–85.

14. Ruggles, *Gardens, Landscape, and Vision*, pp. 101–3, and Ruggles, "The Gardens of the Alhambra and the Concept of the Garden in Islamic Spain," in Jerrilynn D. Dodds, ed., *Al-Andalus: The Arts of Islamic Spain* (New York: Metropolitan Museum of Art, 1991), pp. 162–71.

15. The garden has recently been published as an architectural study, with no information regarding the actual excavation: Manuel Vigil Escalera, *El jardín musulmán de la antigua Casa de Contratación de Sevilla. Intervención arquitectónica*, 2 vols. (Seville: Junta de Andalucía, Consejería de obras públicas y transportes, 1992).

16. The Seville Alcazar is a confusing mixture of superimposed layers of garden and architecture. The quadrants in El Crucero owe some, but not all, of their unusual depth to a subsequent layer that was added here, sometime after the Christian conquest.

17. See the entire issue of *Apuntes del Alcazar de Sevilla* 6 (May 2005), especially articles by Miguel Angel Tabales Rodríguez and Antonio Almagro; for discussion of the possible dating and visual strategy of this garden, see D. F. Ruggles, "The Alcazar of Seville and Mudéjar Architecture," *Gesta* 43 (2005): 87–98.

18. Jacques Meunié, Henri Terrasse, and Gaston Deverdun, *Recherches archéologiques à Marrakech* (Paris, 1952).

19. L. Torres Balbás, "Patios de crucero," *Al-Andalus* 23 (1958): 171–92; Ruggles, *Gardens, Landscape, and Vision*, pp. 160–62.

CHAPTER 5. TREES AND PLANTS

1. See Kathryn Gleason and Naomi Miller, eds., *The Archaeology of Garden and Field* (Philadephia: University of Pennsylvania Press, 1994). George Rapp, Jr., and Christopher L. Hill, *Geoarchaeology: The Earth Science Approach to Archaeological Interpretation* (New Haven: Yale University Press, 1998).

2. Jashemski, *The Gardens of Pompeii*; W. Jashemski and E. MacDougall, eds., *Ancient Roman Gardens* (Washington, D.C.: Dumbarton Oaks, 1981); W. Jashemski and Frederick Meyer, eds., *The Natural History of Pompeii* (Cambridge: Cambridge University Press, 2002).

3. Ruggles, *Gardens, Landscape, and Vision*, pp. 135–38.

4. Abu'l-Khayr, *Kitab al-filaha*, trans. Cherboneau, pp. 14–15.

5. García Sánchez, "Agriculture in Muslim Spain," pp. 987–99.

6. E. Martín-Consuegra, J. L. Ubera, and E. Hernández-Bermejo, "Palynology of the Historical Period at the Madinat al-Zahra Archaeological Site, Spain," *Journal of Archaeological Science* 23 (1996): 249–61, and a much longer and more detailed treatment of the same subject, E. Martín-Consuegra, F. Hernández-Bermejo, and J. L. Ubera, *Palinología y botánica histórica del complejo arqueológico de Madinat al-Zahra* (Monografías del Jardín Botánico de Córdoba 8) (Cordoba, 2000).

7. Martín-Consuegra, Hernández-Bermejo, and Ubera, *Palinología y botánica histórica*, p. 16.

8. Martín-Consuegra, Ubera, and Hernández-Bermejo, "Palynology of the Historical Period at the Madinat al-Zahra Archaeological Site, Spain," p. 260.

9. Jesús Bermúdez Pareja, "El Generalife después del incendio de 1958," *Cuadernos de la Alhambra* 1 (1965): 9–39.

10. Andres Navagero, *Viaje por España (1524–1526)*, Spanish trans. Antonio Fabie (Madrid: Turner, 1983), p. 47.

11. Navagero, *Viaje por España (1524–1526)*, p. 48.

12. Reported by James Dickie, "The Islamic Garden in Spain," in MacDougall and Ettinghausen, eds., *The Islamic Garden*, p. 100.

13. For a lengthy description of the Court of the Lions and other gardens at the Alhambra, see Ruggles, *Gardens, Landscape, and Vision*, chapter 8.

14. M. T. Shephard-Parpagliolo, *Kabul: The Bagh-i Babur* (Rome: Instituto Italiano per il Medio e l'Estremo Oriente, 1972); on the recent excavations and restorations, see Ute Franke-Vogt et al., "Bagh-e Babur, Kabul: Excavations in a Mughal Garden," in Ute Franke-Vogt and Hans-Joachim Weisshaar, eds., *South Asian Archaeology 2003: Proceedings of the Seventeenth International Conference of the European Association of South Asian Archaeologists (7–11 July, 2003, Bonn)* (Aachen: LindenSoft, 2005), pp. 539–55.

15. Elizabeth Moynihan, "The Lotus Garden Palace of Zahir al-Din Muhammad Babur," *Muqarnas* 5 (1988): 135–52; and "'But What a Happiness to Have Known Babur!'" in James L. Wescoat, Jr., and Joachim Wolschke-Bulmahn, eds., *Mughal Gardens: Sources, Places, Representations, and Prospects* (Washington, D.C.: Dumbarton Oaks, 1996), pp. 95–126.

16. Personal communication, Ratish Nanda (January 2006).

17. David Lentz, "Botanical Symbolism and Function at the Mahtab Bagh," in Elizabeth Moynihan, ed., *The Moonlight Garden: New Discoveries at the Taj Mahal* (Washington, D.C.: Arthur M. Sackler Gallery; Seattle: University of Washington Press, 2000), pp. 43–57.

18. Andrew Wilson, "Water Supply in Ancient Carthage," in J. T. Peña et al., *Carthage Papers* (*Journal of Roman Archaeology*, Supplementary series 28) (Portsmouth, R.I.: 1998), pp.

65–102. See also A. T. Hodge, *Roman Aqueducts and Water Supply* (London: Duckworth, 1992), and B. D. Shaw, "The Noblest Monuments and the Smallest Things: Wells, Walls and Aqueducts in the Making of Roman Africa," in A. T. Hodge, ed., *Future Currents in Aqueduct Studies* (Leeds: F. Cairns, 1991), pp. 63–91.

19. Al-Bakri, *Description de l'Afrique septentrionale*, trans. De Slane, 2nd ed. (Algiers, 1911–12), p. 59 (Arabic p. 26).

20. Marcel Solignac, "Recherches sur les installations hydrauliques de Kairouan et des steppes tunisiennes du VIIe au XIe siècle (J.-C.)," *Annales de l'Institut d'Etudes orientales, Alger* 11 (1953): 60–170. This study is summarized in Georges Marçais, *L'Architecture musulmane d'occident* (Paris: Arts et Métiers Graphiques, 1954), pp. 36–39.

21. Al-Maqqari (quoting al-Shaqundi), *History of the Mohammedan Dynasties in Spain*, trans. Gayangos, 1: 41.

22. The ornamental crocus is enjoyed as an early spring flower in American gardens, but the saffron crocus (*crocus sativus L.*) is a fall-blooming variety. 'Inayat Khan, *The Shah Jahan Nama*, ed. W. E. Begley and Z. A. Desai (Delhi: Oxford University Press, 1990), p. 136; Hernández-Bermejo and Garciá-Sánchez, "Economic Botany and Ethnobotany in Al-Andalus," p. 21.

23. Anna Pavord, *The Tulip* (New York: Bloomsbury, 1999), pp. 28–31. See also D. Yildiz, "Tulips in Ottoman Turkish Culture and Art," in Michiel Roding and Hans Theunissen, eds., *The Tulip: A Symbol of Two Nations* (Utrecht: M. Th. Houtsma Stichting; Istanbul: Turco-Dutch Friendship Association, 1993).

24. Pavord, *The Tulip*, p. 36, citing Ahmed Refik, *Eski: Istanbul manzaralari, 1553–1839* (Istanbul, 1931).

25. William Hanaway, "Paradise on Earth: The Terrestrial Garden in Persian Literature," in MacDougall and Ettinghausen, eds., *The Islamic Garden*, pp. 43–67.

26. Translated in Hanaway, "Paradise on Earth," p. 53.

27. A. R. Nykl, *Hispano-Arabic Poetry* (Baltimore: J. H. Furst, 1946), p. 149; R. Dozy, ed., *Scriptorum Arabum Loci de Abbadidis, nunc primum editi*, 3 vols. (1846; reprint Hildesheim: George Olms Verlag, 1992) I, p. 145; III, p. 25.

28. Ibn Sa'id, in al-Maqqari, *Analectes sur l'histoire et la littérature des arabes d'Espagne*, ed. R. Dozy et al., 2 vols. in 3 (Leiden: E. J. Brill, 1855–61; reprint London: Oriental Press, 1967), 1: 383–84; trans. in R. Blachère, "Un pionnier de la culture arabe orientale en Espagne au Xe siècle: Sa'id de Bagdad," *Hespéris* 10 (1930): 30.

29. Al-Ya'qubi, *Les Pays*, trans. Wiet, pp. 263–64 (p. 56 in translation).

30. *History of Mehmed the Conqueror by Kritovoulos,* trans. Charles Riggs (Princeton: Princeton University Press, 1954), pp. 22, 118, 14, 208.

31. Jahangir, *The Jahangirnama*, ed. and trans. Wheeler Thackston (Washington, D.C.: Freer Gallery of Art, New York: Oxford University Press, 1999), p. 332. Akbar also noticed rooftop tulips in 1589 (Norah Titley, *Plants and Gardens in Persian, Mughal and Turkish Art* [London: British Library, 1979], p. 25), and Shah Jahan also described it ('Inayat Khan, *Shah Jahan Nama*, p. 125). The practice continues today.

32. 'Inayat Khan, *Shah Jahan Nama*, pp. 124–38.

33. Ibn Zaydun, *Diwan*, ed. Kamil Kilani and A. R. Khalifa (Cairo: 1351/1932), p. 168. Of course the science of artificial pollination was known since the ninth-century B.C.E. when Assyrian wall reliefs depicted the fertilization of date palms.

34. Miguel Asín Palacios, *Glosario de voces romances, registradas por un botánico anónimo hispano-musulman (siglos XI–XII)* (Madrid: Consejo Superior de Investigaciones Científicas, 1943), pp. xxx–xxxi.

35. François Bernier, *Travels in the Mogul Empire AD 1656–1668*, trans. Archibald Constable, 2nd rev. ed. Vincent A. Smith (Delhi: Low Price Publications, 1989), p. 397.

36. Ibn Luyun, *Ibn Luyun: Tratado de Agricultura*, ed. and trans. Joaquina Eguaras Ibáñez (Granada: Patronato de la Alhambra, 1975), pp. 183–84.

37. Ibn Luyun, *Tratado de agricultura*, (Arabic), pp. 171–75; trans. Dickie, "The Islamic Garden in Spain," p. 94. For similar instructions by Ibn Bassal, see Ruggles, *Gardens, Landscape, and Vision*, p. 26.

38. Maria Subtelny, "Agriculture and the Timurid *Chaharbagh*: The Evidence from a Medieval Persian Agricultural Manual," in Attilio Petruccioli, ed., *Gardens in the Time of the Great Muslim Empires* (Leiden: E. J. Brill, 1997), pp. 110–28; Jürgen Jakobi, "Agriculture Between Literary Tradition and Firsthand Experience: The *Irshad al-zira'a* of Qasim b. Yusuf Abu Nasri Haravi," in Lisa Golombek and Maria Subtelny, eds., *Timurid Art and Culture* (Leiden: E. J. Brill, 1992), pp. 201–8; and Mahvash Alemi, "Il giardino persiano: tipi e modelli," in Attilio Petruccioli, ed., *Il giardino islamico: Architettura, natura, paesaggio* (Milan: Electa, 1994), pp. 39–62.

39. Subtelny, "Agriculture and the Timurid *Chaharbagh*," p. 113.

40. My reconstruction based on the translation is slightly different from that reconstruction offered in Subtelny, "Agriculture and the Timurid *Chaharbagh*," p. 128. Hers omits a row of irises; this discrepancy may be due to the difference of working from the original text, as she is, as opposed to using the translation, which I have done.

41. Gauvin Bailey, "The Sweet-smelling Notebook: An Unpublished Mughal Source on Garden Design," in Attilio Petruccioli, ed., *Gardens in the Time of the Great Muslim Empires* (Leiden: E. J. Brill, 1997), pp. 129–39.

CHAPTER 6. REPRESENTATIONS
OF GARDENS AND LANDSCAPE

1. Esin Atil, *Kalila wa Dimna: Fables from a Fourteenth-Century Arabic Manuscript* (Washington, D.C.: Smithsonian Institution Press, 1981), pp. 9–10.

2. Bernard O'Kane, *Early Persian Painting* (London: I. B. Tauris, 2003), p. 281.

3. Oleg Grabar, *The Illustrations of the Maqamat* (Chicago: University of Chicago Press, 1984).

4. Richard Ettinghausen, *Arab Painting*, 2nd ed. (New York: Rizzoli, 1977), pp. 83–86.

5. A. R. Nykl, *Historia de los amores de Bayad y Riyad* (New York: Hispanic Society, 1941). Recent scholarship leans toward a thirteenth-century date; see Sabiha Khemir, entry 82, in Dodds, ed., *Al-Andalus: The Art of Islamic Spain*, pp. 312–13, and Cynthia Robinson, "The Lover, His Lady, Her Lady, and a Thirteenth-Century Celestina," in Oleg Grabar and Cynthia Robinson, eds., *Islamic Art and Literature* (Princeton: Markus Wiener, 2001), p. 81, note 6.

6. This image is illustrated in R. Ettinghausen, O. Grabar, and M. Jenkins-Madina, *Islamic Art and Architecture, 650–1250*, Pelican History of Art (New Haven: Yale University Press, 2001), p. 287, fig. 474.

7. For a discussion of this manuscript and actual gardens of the period of the manuscript, see Ruggles, *Gardens, Landscape, and Vision*, esp. pp. 195–97.

8. Eleanor Sims, *Peerless Images: Persian Painting and Its Sources* (New Haven: Yale University Press, 2002), p. 45.

9. On Il-khanid painting see Robert Hillenbrand, "The Arts of the Book in Ilkhanid Iran," pp. 135–67, and Linda Komaroff, "The Transmission and Dissemination of a New Visual Language," pp. 169–95, in Linda Komaroff and Stefano Carboni, eds., *The Legacy of Genghis Khan: Courtly Art and Culture in Western Asia, 1256–1353* (New York: Metropolitan Museum of Art; New Haven: Yale University Press, 2002).

10. Zaynuddin Wasifi of Herat, quoted in Maria Subtelny, "The Poetic Circle at the Court of the Timurid Sultan Husain Baiqara, and Its Political Significance," Ph.D. diss., Harvard University, 1979, p. 208; cited in Thomas Lentz and Glenn Lowry, *Timur and the Princely Vision* (Los Angeles: Los Angeles County Museum of Art; Washington, D.C.: Arthur M. Sackler Gallery, 1989), p. 290.

11. Sheila Blair and Jonathan Bloom, *The Art and Architecture of Islam, 1250–1800* (New Haven: Yale University Press, 1994), p. 173.

12. Blair and Bloom, *The Art and Architecture of Islam, 1250-1800*, pp. 173, 232.

13. Sylvia Crowe, Sheila Haywood, Susan Jellicoe, and Gordon Patterson, *The Gardens of Mughal India* (New York: Thames and Hudson, 1972).

14. Ellen Smart, "Graphic Evidence for Mughal Architectural Plans," *Art and Archaeology Research Papers* (December 1974): 22–23.

15. James L. Wescoat, Jr., "Picturing an Early Mughal Garden," *Asian Art 2* (1989): 59–79; Wheeler Thackston, "Translator's Preface," in *The Baburnama*, ed. and trans. W. Thackston (Washington, D.C.: Freer Gallery of Art; New York: Oxford University Press, 1996), especially pp. 9–15.

16. Titley, *Plants and Gardens*, p. 7.

17. A pergola with vines is depicted in a seventeenth-century album painting, reproduced in Franz Taeschner, *Alt-Stambuler Hof- und Volksleben* (Hanover, 1925), fig. 41; and in Gulru Necipoğlu, "The Suburban Landscape of Sixteenth-Century Istanbul as a Mirror of Classical Ottoman Garden Culture," in Attilio Petruccioli, ed., *Gardens in the Time of the Great Muslim Empires* (Leiden: E. J. Brill, 1997), p. 68, fig. 17.

18. Ibn Battuta, *Travels in Asia and Africa, 1325–1354*, trans H. A. R. Gibb (1929; abridged version, New Delhi: Manohar, 2001), p. 114. François Bernier, *Travels in the Mogul Empire, AD 1656–1668*, trans. Archibald Constable, 2nd rev. ed. Vincent A. Smith (Delhi: Low Price Publications, 1989), p. 397.

19. Stuart Cary Welch, *Persian Painting: Five Royal Safavid Manuscripts of the Sixteenth Century* (New York: George Braziller, 1976), p. 116. For a study devoted to the *Haft awrang*, see Marianna Shreve Simpson, *Sultan Ibrahim Mirza's "Haft Awrang": A Princely Manuscript from Sixteenth-Century Iran* (New Haven: Yale University Press, 1997).

20. Norah Titley shows another kind of tree watered in such an oversize pot (*Plants and Gardens*, p. 54).

CHAPTER 7. IMAGINARY GARDENS

1. See W. Montgomery Watt, "Iram," in *Encyclopaedia of Islam*, 2nd ed. III (1975): 1270; and Edgar Weber, "La ville de cuivre, une ville d'al-Andalus," *Sharq al-Andalus* 6 (1989): 43–81. These and similar stories of mythical and fantastic palaces are discussed in Rubiera Mata, *La arquitectura en la literatura árabe*, pp. 45–68. See also Finbarr Flood, *The Great Mosque of Damascus* (Leiden: Brill, 2001), pp. 34–35.

2. *The Book of the Thousand Nights and a Night*, trans. and ed. Richard Burton (n.p.: The Burton Club, 1885), IV: 116.

3. *The Book of the Thousand Nights and a Night*, trans. and ed. Burton, IV: 116–17.

4. On the genesis of this tale in Ibn Habib's, *Kitab al-ta'rikh*, (*Kitab al-Tar'rij [La historia])*, ed. Jorge Aguadé (Madrid: Consejo Superior de Investigaciones Científicas, 1991), see Janina Safran, "From Alien Terrain to the Abode of Islam: Landscapes in the Conquest of Al-Andalus," in John Howe and Michael Wolfe, eds., *Inventing Medieval Landscapes* (Gainesville: University Press of Florida, 2002), pp. 136–49, and Safran, *The Second Umayyad Caliphate* (Cambridge, Mass.: Center for Middle Eastern Studies and Harvard University Press, 2000), pp. 141–62. Weber, "La ville de cuivre."

5. *The Book of the Thousand Nights and a Night*, trans. and ed. Burton, VI:102. The story can also be found in Abu Hamid al-Garnati (flourished in al-Andalus in the early twelfth century), *Tuhfat al-albad*, ed. Gabriel Ferrand, in *Journal Asiatique*, 207 (1925): 1–148, 193–304 (but see especially pp. 55–60).

6. *The Book of the Thousand Nights and a Night*, trans. and ed. Burton, VI: 112.

7. *The Book of the Thousand Nights and a Night*, trans. and ed. Burton, VI: 112.

8. For example, this story also appears in al-Nuwayri, *Nihayat al-arab* (Cairo, 1943), XIV: 100, 121–22; it is discussed in Rubiera Mata, *La architectura en la literatura árabe*, pp. 45–51.

9. For discussion of the Toledo pavilion, see Ruggles, *Gardens, Landscape, and Vision*, 147–48.

10. *Al-Qur'an*, trans. Ahmed Ali (Princeton: Princeton University Press, 1988).

11. The Muslim vision of paradise can be compared with Byzantine precedents: *Revelation* 21:10–21 describes heavenly Jerusalem as having twelve gates and high walls of jasper and gold garnished with pearls, sapphires, emeralds, topaz, and other precious stones, the street was of gold that was like transparent glass. For elaboration of paradisiac imagery and citation of sources, see Flood, *The Great Mosque of Damascus*, chapter 2.

12. Julie Scott Meisami, "Palaces and Paradises: Palace Description in Medieval Persian Poetry," in O. Grabar and C. Robinson, eds., *Islamic Art and Literature* (Princeton: Markus Wiener, 2001), pp. 21–54.

13. 'Abd al-Vasi' Jabali (d. after 1145–46), *Diwan*, ed. Zabih Allah Asafa (Tehran: Danishgah-i Tihran, 1960), pp. 153–54; trans. in Meisami, "Palaces and Paradises," p. 38.

14. Al-Khatib al-Baghdadi, *Ta'rikh Baghdad*, (Cairo) I: 100–104; Spanish trans. in Rubiera Mata, *La arquitectura en la literatura árabe*, pp. 69–74. Cairo similarly had a pavilion that seemed to float in a pond with orange trees, reached by a copper bridge (Maqrizi, *Kitab al-khitat* I: 487).

15. Janina Safran offers a sophisticated explanation for the story of the Copper City in Ibn Habib's *Kitab al-ta'rikh*; see Safran, "From Alien Terrain to the Abode of Islam," pp. 136–49, and Safran, *The Second Umayyad Caliphate*, pp. 143–50.

16. The scene is illustrated in a copy of the *Shahnama* made for Sultan-Ali Mirza in Iran, 1493–4 (now in the Vever Collection, Arthur Sackler Gallery). It is reproduced in Glenn Lowry and Susan Nemazee, *A Jeweler's Eye: Islamic Arts of the Book from the Vever Collection* (Washington, D.C.: Sackler Gallery, 1988), pp. 98–99.

17. A. Littlewood, "Gardens of the Palace," in Henry Maguire, ed., *Byzantine Court Culture from 829 to 1204* (Washington, D.C.: Dumbarton Oaks, 1997), p. 32.

18. Maqrizi, *Kitab al-khitat*, II: 108–9; Rubiera Mata, *La arquitectura*, pp. 84–85; Doris Behrens-Abouseif, "Gardens in Islamic Egypt," *Der Islam* 69, no. 2 (1992): 302–12.

19. Gustave von Grunebaum, "The Response to Nature in Arabic Poetry," *Journal of Near Eastern Studies* 4 (1945): 137–51.

20. Al-Maqqari, *Analectes*, 1: 349.

21. For a discussion of Madinat al-Zahira and zoomorphic fountains, see Ruggles, *Gardens, Landscape, and Vision*, pp. 123–28.

22. Zoja Pavloskis, *Man in an Artificial Landscape: The Marvels of Civilization in Imperial Roman Literature* (Leiden: Brill, 1973), pp. 50–51, gives the example of lion fountains in a fifth-century bathhouse.

23. Erica C. Dodd, "On a Bronze Rabbit from Fatimid Egypt," *Kunst des Orients* 8 (1972): 60–76; Priscilla Soucek, entry 28, in Christine V. Bornstein and P. Soucek, *The Meeting of Two Worlds: The Crusades and the Mediterranean Context* (Ann Arbor: Michigan Museum of Art, 1981), p. 52. The Metropolitan Museum of Art in New York has a Fatimid-era drawing of a remarkably similar leaping hare; it is reproduced in Ettinghausen, Grabar, and Jenkins-Madina, *Islamic Art*, p. 212, fig. 343; also see Basil Gray, "A Fatimid Drawing," *British Museum Quarterly* 12 (1938): 91–96.

24. Marilyn Jenkins, "Al-Andalus: Crucible of the Mediterranean," in Metropolitan Museum of Art, *The Art of Medieval Spain, A.D. 500–1200* (New York: Metropolitan Museum of Art, 1993), pp. 73–84.

25. See Ruggles, *Gardens, Landscape, and Vision*, pp. 164–66, for a summary of the theories proposed by Frederick Bargebuhr (*The Alhambra* [Berlin, 1968]) and Raymond Scheindlin ("El poema de Ibn Gabirol y la fuente del Patio de los Leones," *Cuadernos de la Alhambra* 29–30 [1993–94]: 185–89).

26. On these fountain fragments see Jenkins, "Al-Andalus: Crucible of the Mediterranean," pp. 73–84; and Ruggles, *Gardens, Landscape, and Vision*, pp. 209–11.

27. Banu Musa bin Shakir, *The Book of Ingenious Devices* (*Kitab al-hiyal*), trans. Donald Hill (Dordrecht: D. Reidel, 1979); Ahmad Y. al-Hassan, ed., *Kitab al-hiyal: The Book of Ingenious Devices* (Aleppo: University of Aleppo, 1981).

28. Flood, *The Great Mosque of Damascus*, pp. 114–38; Donald Hill, *Arabic Water-Clocks* (Sources and Studies in the History of Arabic-Islamic Science, History of Technology Series, 4) (Aleppo: University of Aleppo, 1981), pp. 69–88; and Donald Hill, *On the Construction of Water-Clocks* (*Kitab arshimidas fi 'amal al-binkamat*) (Turner and Devereaux Occasional Papers, 4) (London, 1976), pp. 6–9, 30–33.

29. For al-Jaziri, see A K. Coomaraswamy, *The Treatise of al-Jazari* (Boston, 1924), and al-Jaziri, *The Book of Ingenious Mechanical Devices,* trans. and ed. Donald Hill (Dordrecht: D. Reidel, 1974); on ancient and medieval automata in general, see Lynn White, Jr., *Medieval Technology and Social Change* (Oxford: Clarendon Press, 1962).

30. Al-Jaziri, *The Book of Ingenious Mechanical Devices*, trans. Hill, p. 16.

31. Al-Jaziri, *The Book of Ingenious Mechanical Devices*, trans. Hill, pp. 153–55.

32. Charles Barber, "Reading the Garden in Byzantium: Nature and Sexuality," *Byzantine and Modern Greek Studies* 16 (1992): 1–19.

33. Ruy Gonzalez de Clavijo, *Embajada a Tamorlán*, ed. F. López Estrada (Madrid, 1943), nos. 194.34–195.17.

34. *Baburnama*, trans. Thackston, p. 237.

35. Nurhan Atasoy, *A Garden for the Sultan* (Istanbul: Aygaz, 2002), pp. 42–44.

36. The floats were large that they were preceded by men with ladders, hatchets, and poles, ready to remove any obstacles in the way of the procession, according to Esin Atıl, *Levni and the Surname: The Story of an Eighteenth-Century Ottoman Festival* (Istanbul: Koçbank, 1999), pp. 132–37.

37. Sayyid Ahmad, *Atharu-s-Sanadid* cited in Gordon Sanderson and M. Shuaib, *A Guide to the Buildings and Gardens: Delhi Fort,* 4th ed. (1936; reprint, Delhi: Asian Educational Services, 2000), p. 31.

38. N. Manucci, *Storia do Mogor by Niccolao Manucci*, trans. W. Irvine (London: John Murray, 1907), I: 184, cited in Sanderson and Shuaib, *A Guide to the Buildings and Gardens: Delhi Fort*, p. 29.

39. Wayne Begley and Z.A. Desai, *Taj Mahal: The Illumined Tomb: An Anthology of Seventeenth-Century Mughal and*

European Documentary Sources (Cambridge, Mass.: The Aga Khan Program for Islamic Architecture, 1989), p. 83; also cited in Ebba Koch, *Mughal Architecture* (Munich, 1991; reprint Oxford: Oxford University Press, 2002), p. 95.

40. On garden carpets, see the entire issue of *Hali* 5 (1982–83).

41. On the ornament of Persian palaces, see Yves Porter and Arthur Thévenart, *Palaces and Gardens of Persia* (Paris: Flammarion, 2003), esp. pp. 153–234.

42. In addition to this steel etched apple, a pear and a gourd are reproduced in the museum catalogue *Images of Paradise in Islamic Art*, ed. Sheila Blair and Jonathan Bloom (Hanover: Hood Museum of Art, 1991), p. 104.

43. *Al-Qur'an*, trans. Ahmed Ali.

CHAPTER 8. THE GARDEN AS PARADISE

1. *Al-Qur'an*, trans. Ahmed Ali.

2. Oleg Grabar signaled this within the context of iconography in general when he wrote that "the symbolic or iconographic use of the Qur'an in Islamic art nearly always *followed* the development of a symbolic or iconographic need. Symbols, signs, or meanings were discovered in the Qur'an but, at least as far as the arts are concerned, do not actively derive from it." Grabar, "Symbols and Signs in Islamic Architecture," in Renata Holod and D. Rostorfer, ed., *Architecture and Community* (Millerton, N.Y.: Aperture, 1983), p. 29. See also Terry Allen, "Imagining Paradise in Islamic Art" (Sebastopol, Calif.: Solipsist Press, 1993), http://sonic.net/~tallen/palmtree/ip.html.

3. *Al-Qur'an*, trans. Ahmed Ali. Although Adam's spouse is unnamed, the early tenth-century commentator Tabari supplied the name of Hawa (Eve) in his explanations of this Qur'anic passage and the creation story, drawing his information from the Bible and Jewish theologians (Tabari, I: 458–89, 513–14). For a discussion of the Qur'anic exegesis, see Mahmoud Ayoub, *The Qur'an and Its Interpreters* (Albany: State University of New York Press, 1984).

4. Two introductory books on Islamic science are Ahmad al-Hassan and Donald Hill, *Islamic Technology: An Illustrated History* (Cambridge: Cambridge University Press, 1986), and Howard R. Turner, *Science in Medieval Islam* (Austin: University of Texas Press, 1995).

5. The meaning of the plantings in the courtyard of the Mosque of Cordoba is briefly mentioned in Ruggles, *Gardens, Landscape, and Vision*, p. 216.

6. These are listed in K. A. C. Creswell, *Early Muslim Architecture*, 2 vols. (Oxford: Oxford University Press, 1932–40), and in Creswell, *Short Account*.

7. Ibn Ghalib, *Kitab farhat al-anfus fi-akhbar al-andalus*, ed. Lutfi 'Abd al-Badi' in *Majallat Ma'had al-makhtutat al-'arabiya*, vol. 1 (Cairo, 1955), p. 298; trans. Joaquín Vallvé Bermejo, "La descripción de Córdoba de Ibn Galib," in *Homenaje a Pedro Sainz Rodríguez*, 3 vols. (Madrid: Fundación Universitaria Española, 1986), III, p. 672.

8. Creswell, *Short Account*, pp. 299–300.

9. I examined the roof in October 2004 in the company of the cathedral's archaeologist Pedro Marfil and observed that between the gables that run from the courtyard façade to the qibla wall, there are very deep runnels lined with lead.

10. Gayangos, *History*, 1: 226. The event was celebrated in a verse by the tenth-century poet Ibn Shuhayd (A. R. Nykl, *Hispano-Arabic Poetry*, p. 43).

11. Ibn 'Idhari, *Histoire de l'Afrique du Nord et de l'Espagne musulmane intitulée kitab al-bayan al-mughrib*, ed. E. Lévi-Provençal and G. S. Colin, 2 vols. (Leiden: E. J. Brill, 1948–51), 2: 240; trans. E. Fagnan, *Histoire de l'Afrique et de l'Espagne*, 2 vols. (Algiers, 1901–4), 2: 396.

12. See drawing by G. Ruiz Cabrero, p. 138, in Manuel Nieto Cumplido and Carlos Luca de Tena y Alvear, *La Mezquita de Córdoba: planos y dibujos* (Cordoba: Colegio oficial de arquitectas de Andalucia occidental, 1992).

13. The prayer hall's floor consisted of beaten earth coated with hard plaster. Even as late as 1557, instructions were given for sprinkling the building's floor, indicating that those parts which the Christian patrons had not paved with brick were still earthen. Rafael Castejón, "El pavimento de la Mezquita de Córdoba," *Boletín de la Real Academia de Córdoba, de Ciencias, Bellas Letras y Nobles Artes* 54 (1945): 327–30.

14. Abu'l Asbagh 'Isa Ibn Sahl Ibn 'Abd Allah al-'Asadi al-Kawatibi came from an Arab family that had lived in al-Andalus since the Muslim conquest. He was born in a village near Jaen in 1022 and died in 1093, probably in Granada. He began his career as a qadi in Jaen and Baeza (Cordoba province), moving around 1051 to Cordoba, which was the provincial capital of the Banu Jawhar governors. He later rose to the higher post of qadi for the taifa rulers of Jaen, Baeza, Cordoba, Granada, Tangier, Ceuta, and Meknes. See introduction to Thami Azemmouri, "Les *Nawazil* d'Ibn Sahl, section relative à l'*Ihtisab*," *Hespéris-Tamuda* 14 (1973): 7–108.

15. He collected more than six hundred of these decisions in the work known variously as the *Nawazil* or al-*Ahkam al-kubra*, which he intended should provide a model of juridical practice for judges and jurisconsults. Dr. Christian Müller kindly steered me toward the published versions of Ibn Sahl, which are those of Thami Azemmouri, "Les *Nawazil* d'Ibn Sahl," and M. Khallaf, *Watha'iq fi shu'un al-'umran fi'l-Andalus* (Cairo, 1983). For an analysis of Ibn Sahl's singular importance, see C. Müller, "Judging with God's Law on Earth: Judicial Powers of the *Qadi al-jama'a* of Cordoba in the Fifth/Eleventh Century," *Islamic Law and Society* 7, no. 2 (2000): 159–86.

16. Azemmouri, "Les *Nawazil* d'Ibn Sahl," p. 24 (Arabic text). The word *amsar* (cities) refers specifically to the early garrison towns of Kufa, Basra, and Fustat. The word that I have read as *muezzin* appears as *mudawwana* in Azemmouri's edition and may be a typographical error. A *shubha* in Islamic law is something that is an illicit action but resembles a licit action. I am grateful to David Powers, my former colleague in the Department of Near Eastern Studies at Cornell University, for his corrections to my translation of this passage and help in identifying the legal authorities cited therein.

17. Ibn Sahl in Azemmouri, "Les *Nawazil* d'Ibn Sahl," p. 24.

18. Castejón, "El pavimento de la Mezquita de Córdoba," p. 329.

19. Gaston Wiet, *Catalogue général du Musée de l'Art Islamique du Caire: Inscriptions historiques sur Pierre* (Cairo: Imprimerie de l'Institut Français d'Archéologie Orientale, 1971), p. 36, cited in Bernard O'Kane, "The Arboreal Aesthetic: Landscape, Painting and Architecture from Mongol Iran to Mamluk Egypt," in Bernard O'Kane, ed., *Iconography of Islamic Art: Studies in Honor of Robert Hillenbrand* (Cairo: American University in Cairo Press, 2005), p. 249, note 55.

20. Ibn Battuta, *Travels*, trans. Gibb (1958-71): 2: 345, cited in O'Kane, "The Arboreal Aesthetic," p. 249, note 55.

21. Ibn Battuta, *Travels in Asia and Africa, 1325–1354*, trans. H. A. R. Gibb (New Delhi: Manohar, 2001), p. 314.

22. Alfonso Jiménez Martín, "El Patio de los Naranjos y la Giralda," in *La Catedral de Sevilla* (Seville: Ediciones Guadalquivir, 1984), pp. 83–132. However, Jiménez states that the rows of orange trees connected by inlaid channels seen in the courtyard today were installed by Félix Hernández in the mid-twentieth century (p. 92).

23. The cathedral was built in stages between 1402–1507. Stephen Brindle, "Seville, IV: Buildings, Cathedral," in *The Grove Dictionary of Art Online* (Oxford University Press, accessed 3 April 2007) *http://www.groveart.com*.

24. Regarding Damascus, Jean Sauvaget, "Le plan antique de Damas," *Syria* 26 (1949): 354–55; regarding Aleppo, Ibn al-Shihnah, *"Les perles choisies" d'Ibn ach-Chihna*, ed. Jean Sauvaget (Beirut, 1933), p. 56; regarding Fustat, Ibn 'Abd al-Hakam, *Futuh Misr wa akhbaruha*, translated in Robert Hoyland, *Seeing Islam as Others Saw It: A Survey and Evaluation of Christian, Jewish and Zoroastrian Writings on Early Islam* (Princeton: Darwin Press, 1997), p. 563; regarding 'Amr and Cairo, al-Maqrizi, *Kitab al-khitat*, iv, 6. This information on the possible garden context of Syrian mosques is drawn from J. Pedersen, "Masdjid," in the *Encyclopaedia of Islam*, rev. ed. (electronic), and Flood, *The Great Mosque of Damascus*, chapter 5.

25. Hans-Caspar Graf von Bothmer, "Archittekturbilder im Koran—eine Prachthandschrift der Umayyadenzeit aus dem Yemen," *Pantheon* 45 (1987): 4–20.

26. Henry Maguire, "Imperial Gardens and the Rhetoric of Renewal," in Paul Magdaline, ed., *New Constantines* (Aldershot: Variorum, 1994), pp. 181–98; Littlewood, "Gardens of the Palaces," pp. 13–38.

27. On the ideological relationship between the Great Mosque of Cordoba and the Umayyad Mosque of Damascus, see K. A. C. Creswell, *Early Muslim Architecture*, 2: 138–61; and Manuel Ocaña Jiménez, "La Basílica de San Vicente y la Gran Mezquita de Córdoba: nuevo examen de los textos," *Al-Andalus* 7 (1942): 347–66. The ideology of that relationship is critiqued in D. F. Ruggles, "Mothers of a Hybrid Dynasty: Race, Genealogy, and Acculturation in al-Andalus," *Journal of Medieval and Early Modern Studies*, 34 (2004): 65–94.

28. Ibn Zabala, cited in J. Sauvaget, *La Mosquée Omeyyade de Médine* (Paris: Vanoest, 1947), pp. 26, 81. This translation is from Myriam Rosen-Ayalon, *The Early Islamic Monuments of al-Haram al-Sharif: An Iconographic Study* (Jerusalem: Hebrew University, 1989), p. 49. The date for Ibn Zabala is supplied by Klaus Brisch, "Observation on the Iconography of the Mosaics in the Great Mosque at Damascus," in Priscilla Soucek, ed., *Content and Context of Visual Arts in the Islamic World* (University Park: Penn State University Press, 1988), p. 18.

29. Miriam Rosen-Ayalon and Klaus Brisch have both interpreted the mosaics as paradisiac in theme. Rosen-Ayalon, *The Early Islamic Monuments*, and Brisch, "Observations on the Iconography," pp. 13–20. See also Flood, *The Great Mosque of Damascus*, esp. pp. 31–34.

30. Regarding the windows, see Dickie, "Granada: A Case Study of Arab Urbanism in Muslim Spain," in S. K. Jayyusi, ed., *The Legacy of Muslim Spain*, pp. 100–101; for the inscriptions see Darío Cabanelas Rodríguez, "La Madraza árabe de Granada y su suerte en época cristiana," *Cuadernos de la Alhambra* 24 (1988): 29–54.

31. Torres Balbás, "El Oratorio y la casa de Astasio de Bracamonte en el Partal de la Alhambra," *Al-Andalus* 10 (1945): 440–49. The adjoining Casa de Astasio de Bracamonte was a later addition to its south side.

32. *Al-Qur'an*, trans. Ahmed Ali.

33. Ibn Battuta, *Travels*, p. 315.

34. Rachel Arié, "Une métropole hispanomusulmane au Bas Moyen Age: Grenade nasride," *Les Cahiers de Tunisie* 34, nos. 137–38 (Tunis), (1986): 66–67.

35. Olivia Constable, *Trade and Traders in Muslim Spain* (Cambridge: Cambridge University Press, 1994), pp. 141–42, 211.

36. Jan Pieper, "Arboreal Art and Architecture in India," *Art and Archaeology Research Papers* (*AARP*) 12 (Dec. 1977): 47–54; Amita Sinha, "The Cosmic Tree in Buddhist Landscapes," *Geographical Review of India* 63, no. 1 (2001): 1–15; Sankar Sen Gupta, ed., *Tree Symbol Worship in India* (Calcutta: India Publications, 1965).

37. Amita Sinha, "Nature in Hindu Art, Architecture, and Landscape," *Landscape Research* 20 (1995): 3–10.

38. Muhammad Siraju-l-Islam, "The Lodi Phase of Indo-Islamic Architecture," Ph.D. diss., Freie Universität, Berlin, 1960, pp. 28–51.

39. Ruggles, "Making Vision Manifest." pp. 143–56. The delicate stone traceries of the screens here and elsewhere are fragile and many have been lost to willful destruction and looting.

40. Gulru Necipoğlu, "Anatolia and the Ottoman Legacy," in Martin Frishman and Hasan-Uddin Khan, eds., *The Mosque* (London: Thames and Hudson, 1994), p. 154.

41. Necipoğlu, "Anatolia and the Ottoman Legacy," p. 154, n. 12.

42. For a discussion of plantings and illustrations, see Maurice M. Cerasi, "Open Space, Water and Trees in Ottoman Urban Culture in the XVIIIth–XIXth Centuries," *Environmental Design* 2 (1985): 36–49.

43. Godfrey Goodwin, *A History of Ottoman Architecture* (New York: Thames and Hudson, 1971), p. 358, citing C.

Pertusier, *Promenades pittoresques dans Constantinople et sur les rives du Bosphore* (Paris, 1815), p. 187.

CHAPTER 9. THE HERE AND HEREAFTER

1. Gabrielle d'Henry, "Scafati (Salerno): Monumento funerario," *Bollettino d'Arte* ser. 4, v. 49 (1964): 368–69.

2. Thomas Leisten, "Between Orthodoxy and Exegesis: Some Aspects of Attitudes in the Shari'a Toward Funerary Architecture," *Muqarnas* 7 (1990): 18, citing Abu al-Hasan 'Ali al-Shabushti, *Kitab al-diyarat*, ed. J. 'Awwad (Baghdad, 1366/1866), p. 299.

3. Terry Allen, "The Tombs of the 'Abbasid Caliphs in Baghdad," *Bulletin of the School of Oriental and African Studies* 46 (1983): 421–31.

4. On Byzantine tombs, see Philip Grierson, "The Tombs and Obits of the Byzantine Emperors (337–1042)," *Dumbarton Oaks Papers* 16 (1962): 3–63; on late Roman mausolea, see Mark J. Johnson, "Late Imperial Mausolea," Ph.D. diss., Princeton University, 1986; my thanks to Robert Ousterhout for directing me to these sources and for his reflections on the transmission of the mausoleum type from Roman and Byzantine usage to Islam.

5. A brief summary of the large bibliography and interpretations of the Dome of the Rock's historical and modern meanings can be found in Ettinghausen, Grabar, and Jenkins-Madina, *Islamic Art and Architecture*, pp. 15, 305 notes 3–5.

6. Jane I. Smith and Yvonne Y. Haddad, *The Islamic Understanding of Death and Resurrection* (Albany: State University of New York Press, 1981), pp. 183–91.

7. Oleg Grabar, "The Earliest Islamic Commemorative Structures. Notes and Documents," *Ars Orientalis* 6 (1966): 7–46, and Grabar, "The Islamic Dome, Some Considerations," *Journal of the Society of Architectural Historians* 22 (1963): 191–98.

8. Robert Hillenbrand, *Islamic Architecture: Form, Function and Meaning* (New York: Columbia University Press, 1994), pp. 278–80.

9. Ruggles, *Gardens, Landscape, and Vision*, p. 131.

10. Basilio Pavón Maldonado, *Estudios sobre la Alhambra. I: La Alcazaba, El Palacio de los Abencerrajes, Los accesos a la Casa Vieja, El Palacio de Comares, El Partal* (Granada: Patronato de la Alhambra y Generalife, 1975), pp. 87–88; see also several articles on the restoration of this area, in *Cuadernos de la Alhambra* 36 (2000).

11. Al-Maqrizi, *Khitat* (Cairo, 1853), 2: 459–60, trans. in Jonathan Bloom, "The Mosque of the Qarafa in Cairo," *Muqarnas* 4 (1987): 7.

12. Henri Basset, and E. Lévi-Provençal, "Chella: Une nécropole mérinide," *Hespéris* 2 (1922): 1–92, 255–316, 385–425.

13. G. Salmon, "Marabouts de Tanger," *Archives Marocaines* 2 (1905): 115–26. This shrine is discussed in Susan G. Miller, "Finding Order in the Moroccan City: The *Hubus* of the Great Mosque of Tangier as an Agent of Urban Change," *Muqarnas* 22 (2005): 265–83.

14. Barbara Brend, *Islamic Art* (Cambridge, Mass.: Harvard University Press, 1991), pp. 191–92.

15. Ibn Shuhayd, *El-Diwan de Ibn Shuhayd al-Andalus, 382–426 H = 992–1035 C., Texto y Traducción*, ed. and trans. James Dickie (Cordoba: Real Academia de Córdoba, 1975), pp. 59–60.

16. Ibn Khaqan (d. 1134/529), *Qala'id*, p. 153, trans. James Dickie, "The Islamic Garden in Spain," pp. 92–93.

17. Ibn Khaqan, trans. Dickie, "The Islamic Garden in Spain," pp. 92–93.

18. A more detailed analysis of the transformation from pleasure pavilion to mausoleum is given in Ruggles, *Gardens, Landscape, and Vision*, pp. 130–32.

19. For examples see Abbas Daneshvari, *Medieval Tomb Towers of Iran: An Iconographical Study* (Lexington, Ky.: Mazda, 1986); Mary Burkett, "Tomb Towers and Inscriptions in Iran," *Oriental Art* 11 (1965): 101–6.

20. O'Donovan's description and the Sultan Sanjar tomb are discussed in the context of the development of tombs in chahar bagh settings in D. F. Ruggles, "Humayun's Tomb and Garden: Typologies and Visual Order," in Attilio Petruccioli, ed., *Gardens in the Time of the Great Muslim Empires* (Leiden: E. J. Brill, 1997), pp. 173–86.

21. W. H. Siddiq, "The Discovery of Architectural Remains of a Pre-Mughal Garden at New Delhi," in B. M. Pande and B. D. Chattopadhyaya, eds., *Archaeology and History: Essays in Memory of Shri A. Gosh* (Delhi: Agam Kala Prakasham, 1987), 2: 573–77; Anthony Welch, "Gardens That Babur Did Not Like: Landscape, Water, and Architecture for the Sultans of Delhi," in James Wescoat, Jr., and Joachim Wolschke-Bulmahn, eds., *Mughal Gardens: Sources, Places, Representations, and Prospects* (Washington, D.C.: Dumbarton Oaks, 1996), pp. 59–93.

22. Lisa Golombek, *The Timurid Shrine at Gazur Gah* (Toronto: Royal Ontario Museum, 1969).

23. Discussions of sultanate gardens can be found in the various publications of Anthony Welch, such as "Gardens That Babur Did Not Like," pp. 59–93; "Hydraulic Architecture in Medieval India: The Tughluqs," *Environmental Design* (1985): 74–81; and "A Medieval Center of Learning in India: the Hauz Khas Madrasa in Delhi," *Muqarnas* 13 (1996): 165–90.

24. Catherine Asher, "The Mausoleum of Sher Shah Suri," *Artibus Asiae* 39, nos. 3–4 (1977): 273–98.

25. Glenn Lowry, "Humayun's Tomb: Form, Function, and Meaning in Early Mughal Architecture," *Muqarnas* 4 (1987): 133–48.

26. Catherine Asher, *Architecture of Mughal India,* New Cambridge History of India, I:4 (Cambridge: Cambridge University Press, 1995), p. 37.

27. Koch, *Mughal Architecture*, p. 74.

28. Michael Brand, "Orthodoxy, Innovation, and Revival: Considerations of the Past in Imperial Mughal Tomb Architecture," *Muqarnas* 10 (1993): 323–34.

29. Edmund W. Smith, *Akbar's Tomb, Sikandrah* (Archaeological Survey of India, New Imperial Series 35) (Allahabad, 1909), pp. 34–35. The poem is reprinted in John Hoag, *Islamic Architecture* (New York: Rizzoli, 1987), p. 181.

30. Wayne Begley and Z. A. Desai, *Taj Mahal: The Illumined Tomb*.

31. Ram Nath, *The Immortal Taj Mahal: The Evolution of the Tomb in Mughal Architecture* (Bombay: D. B. Taraporevala, 1972), p. 86.

32. Brookes, *Gardens of Paradise*, p. 143.

33. Gulbadan Begum, *The History of Humayun*, trans. Annette Beveridge (1901; reprint, Delhi, 1972), pp. 110–11.

34. Qazwini, *Padshahnama*, trans. and quoted in Annette Beveridge, trans., *Babur-nama (Memoirs of Babur)* (1922; reprint, Delhi, 1979), p. lxxx; see also Salome Zajadacz-Hastenrath, "A Note on Babur's Lost Funerary Enclosure at Kabul," *Muqarnas* 14 (1997): 135–42.

35. Asher, *Architecture of Mughal India*, pp. 252–61.

36. Stephen Carr, *Archaeology and Monumental Remains of Delhi* (Simla, 1876), pp. 108–9; reprinted in H. K. Kaul, *Historic Delhi: An Anthology* (New Delhi: Oxford University Press, 1985), pp. 284–86.

37. Asher, *Architecture of Mughal India*, pp. 265–66.

38. Asher, *Architecture of Mughal India*, p. 260; the words are from Saqi Must'ad Khan, *Ma'asir-i 'Alamgiri*, trans. Sir Jadunath Sarkar (Calcutta: Royal Society of Bengal, 1947), pp. 309–10, quoted in Brand, "Orthodoxy, Innovation, and Revival," p. 331. Brand also reproduces a photograph of Aurangzeb's grave on p. 332.

CHAPTER 10. A GARDEN IN LANDSCAPE:
THE TAJ MAHAL AND ITS PRECURSORS

1. Wayne Begley, "The Myth of the Taj Mahal and a New Theory of Its Symbolic Meaning," *Art Bulletin* 61 (1979): 7–37; Ram Nath, *The Immortal Taj Mahal*, pp. 76 ff.; Michael Brand, "Orthodoxy, Innovation, and Revival," pp. 329–30, 332.

2. On the historians' treatment of the Taj as the culmination of this series, see Brand, "Orthodoxy, Innovation, and Revival," pp. 323–34.

3. On the Taj and these riverside gardens see Ebba Koch, *The Complete Taj Mahal and the Riverfront Gardens of Agra* (London: Thames and Hudson, 2006), pp. 18–20.

4. Bianca Maria Alfieri, *Islamic Architecture of the Indian Subcontinent* (London: Laurence King, 2000), p. 254.

5. Ellison Banks Findly, *Nur Jahan: Empress of Mughal India* (New York: Oxford University Press, 1993), pp. 220–22; see also Chandra Pant, *Nur Jahan and Her Family* (Allahabad: Dan Dewal Publishing, 1978).

6. Ellison Banks Findly, "Nur Jahan's Embroidery Trade and Flowers of the Taj Mahal," *Asian Art and Culture* (Spring–Summer 1996): 7–25.

7. For a discussion of intarsia and *pietra dura* in Mughal tombs, see Ebba Koch, "Pietre Dure and Other Artistic Contacts Between the Court of the Mughals and that of the Medici," *Marg* 39, no. 1 (s.d.): 30–56; and Koch, *Mughal Architecture*, especially pp. 75, 98, 101.

8. Vincent A. Smith, *A History of Fine Art in India and Ceylon*, 2nd ed. rev. by K. de B. Codrington (Oxford: Clarendon Press, 1930), pp. 174–75; Findly, *Nur Jahan*, p. 231.

9. Ebba Koch, *Shah Jahan and Orpheus* (Graz: Akademie Druck-u. Verlagsanstalt, 1988), p. 8; and Koch, "Pietre Dure and Other Artistic Contacts Between the Court of the Mughals and That of the Medici," p. 52.

10. Asher, *Architecture of Mughal India*, p. 132.

11. The earliest such image in a painting of a red blossom by Mansur, ca. 1610 (in the Habib Ganj Library, Aligarh), according to Vivien Rich, "Mughal Floral Painting and Its European Sources," *Oriental Art* n.s. 33 (1987): 183.

12. Rich, "Mughal Floral Painting and Its European Sources," pp. 183–89; on gifts, see Findly, "Nur Jahan's Embroidery Trade," pp. 7–25.

13. Jahangir, *The Jahangirnama: Memoirs of Jahangir, Emperor of India*, ed. and trans. Thackston, pp. 332–33; Robert Skelton, "A Decorative Motif in Mughal Art," in Pratapaditya Pal, ed., *Aspects of Indian Art* (Leiden: E. J. Brill, 1972), pp. 147–52.

14. Veronica Murphy argues that plant motifs occurred first in textiles and were transferred from that medium to other forms of art (*The Origins of the Mughal Flowering Plant Motif* [London: Indar Pasricha Fine Arts, 1987]).

15. Murphy, *The Origins of the Mughal Flowering Plant Motif*, p. 3.

16. Findly, "Nur Jahan's Embroidery Trade," p. 23.

17. Susan Jellicoe, "The Development of the Mughal Garden," in MacDougall and Ettinghausen, eds., *The Islamic Garden*, p. 115, citing *Imperial Gazetteer of India* 15 (Oxford: Clarendon Press, 1908): 93.

18. 'Inayat Khan, *Shah Jahan Nama*, p. 126.

19. 'Inayat Khan, *Shah Jahan Nama*, p. 126.

20. Sajjad Kausar, M. Brand, and J. Wescoat, *Shalamar Garden Lahore: Landscape, Form and Meaning* (Islamabad: Dept. of Archaeology and Museums, Ministry of Culture, Pakistan, 1990).

21. Koch, *The Complete Taj Mahal*, p. 208; James L. Wescoat, Jr., "Waterworks and Landscape Design at the Mahtab Bagh," in Elizabeth Moynihan, *The Moonlight Garden: New Discoveries at the Taj Mahal* (Washington, D.C.: Arthur M. Sackler Gallery; Seattle: University of Washington Press, 2000), pp. 59–78.

22. Ebba Koch, "The Mughal Waterfront Garden," in Attilio Petruccioli, ed., *Gardens in the Time of the Great Muslim Empires*, pp. 140–60; and Koch, *The Complete Taj Mahal*, pp. 37–40.

23. Ebba Koch, "The Zahara Bagh (Bagh-i Jahanara) at Agra," *Environmental Design* 2 (1986): 30–37; Koch, *The Complete Taj Mahal*, pp. 41–42.

24. Nur Baksh, "The Agra Fort and Its Buildings," *Annual Report of the Archaeological Survey of India, 1903–04* (Calcutta, 1906), pp. 180–81. The question of screening is historically problematic because windows that appear open today may have once had screens that were removed during the British colonial era. On the visual effect of screens, see Ruggles, "Making Vision Manifest: Frame, Screen, and View in Islamic Culture," in D. Harris and D. Ruggles, eds., *Sites Unseen: Landscape and Vision* (University Park: Pennsylvania State University Press, 2007), pp. 131–58.

25. Koch, "The Mughal Waterfront Garden," and Koch, *The Complete Taj*, passim.

26. Koch, *The Complete Taj*, pp. 138–39.

27. In January 2003 I saw these under excavation in the company of James and Florrie Wescoat. The latter observed that the sunken beds seemed more appropriate for a water garden, because the extreme depth of the parterres' cement walls was unnecessary for plants, which need a soil depth of no more than a meter. Furthermore, while there were apertures for water at the height of the beds, there was no evidence of drainage at floor level, indicating that of the cavities would not have drained easily. But our examination was regrettably brief, and if floor drains were present, it is possible that we simply missed them.

28. On the use of the parterre, see Denis Lambin, "Garden, §VIII, 4(ii): France, c. 1550–c. 1800," *The Grove Dictionary of Art Online* (Oxford University Press, accessed April 20, 2004, *http://www.groveart.com.*); W. H. Adams, *The French Garden, 1500–1800* (New York: Braziller, 1979); and K. Woodbridge, *Princely Gardens: The Origins and Development of the French Formal Style* (London: Rizzoli, 1986).

29. Chandra Mukerji, *Territorial Ambitions and the Gardens of Versailles* (Cambridge: Cambridge University Press, 1997), pp. 124–35.

30. Mukerji locates the source for French and Italian garden parterres in "the Oriental carpets, textiles, or other design patterns that were being brought through trade and print from Asia to Europe by the sixteenth century" (*Territorial Ambitions*, p. 124).

31. Moynihan, ed., *The Moonlight Garden*.

32. This is recorded in a letter written by the future emperor Aurangzeb in December of that year, translated by Wheeler Thackston in Moynihan, *Moonlight Garden*, p. 28.

33. Jean-Baptiste Tavernier, *Tavernier's Travels in India*, trans. and ed. V. Ball (London, 1889). For the web of myths attached to the Taj from the seventeenth through the twentieth centuries, see Pratapaditya Pal and Janice Leoshko, eds., *Romance of the Taj Mahal* (Los Angeles: Los Angeles County Museum of Art; London: Thames and Hudson, 1989), and Begley, "The Myth of the Taj Mahal and a New Theory of Its Symbolic Meaning."

34. Unlike the active boat traffic on the Ganges at Varanasi (Benares), the Yamuna River at Agra is seldom used for urban transportation anymore. The river's upstream waters have been siphoned off for industry and irrigation projects to such an extent that, except in flood season, the great Yamuna has been reduced to a paltry trickle.

35. Amita Sinha and D. Fairchild Ruggles, "The Yamuna Riverfront, India: A Comparative Study of Islamic and Hindu Traditions in Cultural Landscapes," *Landscape Journal* 23, no. 2 (2004): 141–52.

36. 'Inayat Khan, *Shah Jahan Nama*, pp. 83–84; the twelfth anniversary ceremony is described pp. 299–30.

CHAPTER 11. RELIGION AND CULTURE

1. Like the terms Muslim and Islamic (discussed in the Preface), "Hindu" is similarly complex in its use to describe, variously, religion, culture, and people. Indeed, it is more complicated because, while the term Muslim refers to a clearly defined group of adherents to the faith of Islam, united by the singular Qur'an and the Prophet, Hinduism refers to a collection of diverse traditions in which gods such as Shiva and Kali have well established cults next to a proliferation of local, spontaneous, and tribal cults. While such cult distinctions are beyond the scope of this study, I have tried throughout to distinguish between "Hindu" as a term referring to religious and philosophical belief, and Indic (or South Asian) as a term to refer to South Asian, non-Muslim culture. For a historiography of the Western view of Hinduism and Hindu art, see Catherine Asher and Thomas Metcalf, "Introduction," in Asher and Metcalf, eds., *Perceptions of South Asia's Visual Past* (New Delhi: Oxford & IBH Publishing, 1994), esp. pp. 1–5; also P. J. Marshall, ed. *The British Discovery of Hinduism in the Eighteenth Century* (Cambridge: Cambridge University Press, 1970). I am grateful to Professor Ajay Sinha for his patient explanation of these important nuances in meaning some years ago.

2. Marshall Hodgson, "The Role of Islam in World History," in Edmund Burke III, ed., *Rethinking World History* (Cambridge: Cambridge University Press, 1993), pp. 97–125; Phillip Wagoner, "Sultan Among Hindu Kings: Dress: Titles, and the Islamicization of Hindu Culture at Vijayanagara," *Journal of Asian Studies* 55, no. 4 (1996): 851–80.

3. On the Amber Fort, see Oskar Reuther, *Indische Paläste und Wohnhäuser* (Berlin: L. Preiss, 1925), and G. H. R. Tillotson, *The Rajput Palaces* (New Haven: Yale University Press, 1987). On its gardens, see Ruggles, "Gardens," in Frederick Asher, ed., *Art of India* (Chicago: Encyclopaedia Britannica, 2003), pp. 258–70, and "The Framed Landscape in Islamic Spain and Mughal India," in Brian Day, ed., *The Garden: Myth, Meaning, and Metaphor* (Working Papers in the Humanities, 12) (Windsor, Ontario: University of Windsor, 2003), pp. 21–50.

4. Tillotson, *Rajput Palaces*, p. 98; Percy Brown, *Indian Architecture (Islamic Period)* (reprint, Bombay: D. B. Taraporevala, 1981).

5. On the political strategy of the Mughal inclusion of certain Rajput families, particularly the Kachhwahas, in Mughal imperial service, see John Richards, *The Mughal Empire* (*The New Cambridge History of India,* 1.5) (Cambridge: Cambridge University Press, 1995), pp. 20–24; and Francis Taft, "Honor and Alliance: Reconsidering Mughal-Rajput Marriages," in Karine Schomer, Joan L. Erdman, Deryck O. Lodnick, and Lloyd I. Rudolph, eds., *The Idea of Rajasthan: Explorations in Regional Identity,* 2 vols. (New Delhi: Manohar and the American Institute of Indian Studies, 1994), 2: 217–41.

6. On Raja Man Singh's service to the Mughal court, see Catherine Asher, "Sub-Imperial Patronage: The Architecture of Raja Man Singh," in Barbara Stoler Miller, ed., *The Powers of Art: Patronage in Indian Culture* (Delhi: Oxford University Press, 1992), pp. 183–201; and Catherine Asher, "Sub-Imperial Palaces: Power and Authority in Mughal India," *Ars Orientalis* 23 (1994): 284–85.

7. D. Fairchild Ruggles, "What's Religion Got to Do With It? A Skeptical Look at the Symbolism of Islamic and Rajput Gardens," *DAK: The Newsletter of the American Institute of Indian Studies* 4 (Autumn, 2000): 1, 5–8.

8. A. P. Singh and Shiv Pal Singh, *Monuments of Orchha* (Delhi: Agam Kala Prakashan, 1991), pp. 32–33.

9. Singh and Singh, *Monuments of Orchha*, pp. 44–45.

10. The *chhatri* is a similar case of architectural hybridity. Although Hindus did not bury the dead or commemorate places of burial, they did adopt the chhatri (an indigenous Indic form) to serve as memorials for the deceased, and the road from Amber toward Delhi is lined with twenty-seven standing chhatris commemorating deceased members of the Kachhwaha family.

11. The argument that the Sisodias employed Islamicate forms as an expression of anti-Mughal rivalry is a central thesis of the doctoral dissertation of Jennifer Joffee, "Art, Architecture, and Politics in Mewar, 1628–1710," Ph.D. diss., University of Minnesota, 2005. Rajput patronage of the Udaipur and Pichola lake palaces is discussed in Jennifer Joffee and D. F. Ruggles, "Rajput Gardens and Landscapes," in preparation for Michel Conan, ed., *The Middle East Garden Traditions* (Washington, D.C.: Dumbarton Oaks, 2007), pp. 269–85.

12. Jahangir, *The Jahangirnama*, ed. and trans. Thackston, p. 8, note 28, and pp. 164–65.

13. Tillotson, *Rajput Palaces*, pp. 109–12; George Michell and Antonio Martinelli, *The Royal Palaces of India* (London: Thames and Hudson, 1994), pp. 158–61.

14. This painting and others representing the Sisodian palaces of Udaipur can be found in Andrew Topsfield, *The City Palace Museum, Udaipur: Paintings of Mewar Court Life* (Ahmedabad: Mapin Publishing, 1990), and Topsfield, "City Palace and Lake Palaces: Architecture and Court Life in Udaipur Painting," in Giles (G.H.R.) Tillotson, ed., *Stones in the Sand: The Architecture of Rajasthan* (Mumbai: Marg Publications, 2001), pp. 54–67.

15. My companions were James L. Wescoat, Jr., Florrie Wescoat, and students from the University of Illinois, Urbana-Champaign. When we examined the beds, we were surprised not to find apertures for drainage at the bottom of the cavity. Clearly such a containment system of gardening would have facilitated flood irrigation by preventing the water from leaching into the subsoil. But conversely, during monsoon season, the absence of drainage could have caused the roots of the plants to rot.

16. Asher, *Architecture of Mughal India*, p. 246. That year, in addition to ongoing work at the Taj Mahal, two new projects were begun: a great assembly plaza in front of the Agra Fort and the congregational mosque ('Inayat Khan, *The Shah Jahan Nama*, pp. 205–6).

17. Prabhakar V. Begde, *Forts and Palaces of India* (New Delhi: Sagar Publications, 1982), pp. 128–31; M. C. Joshi, *Dig*, 3rd ed. (New Delhi: Archaeological Survey of India, 1982).

18. Richards, *The Mughal Empire*, pp. 250–52; on the looting of Akbar's tomb, he cites the contemporary witness N. Manucci, *Storia do Mogor or Mogul India,* 2: 320.

19. C. Bayly, "Delhi and Other Cities in North India During the 'Twilight,'" in R. E. Frykenberg, ed., *Delhi Through the Ages: Essays in Urban History, Culture, and Society* (Delhi: Oxford University Press, 1986), pp. 232–33.

20. Asher, *Architecture of Mughal India*, pp. 317–18.

21. Amita Sinha, "Nature in Hindu Art, Architecture and Landscape," 4–5; Sinha and Ruggles, "The Yamuna Riverfront, India," 141–51; and S. Bhardwaj, *Hindu Places of Pilgrimage in India* (Berkeley: University of California Press, 1973).

22. Thomas Metcalf, *An Imperial Vision: Indian Architecture and Britain's Raj* (Berkeley: University of California Press, 1989), pp. 113–18; Michell, *The Royal Palaces of India*, pp. 200–201, 220.

23. Metcalf, *An Imperial Vision*, p. 119; Michell, *The Royal Palaces of India*, pp. 208–9, 222.

24. Metcalf, *An Imperial Vision*, p. 120.

25. Andreas Volwahsen, *Imperial Delhi* (Munich: Prestel, 2002), p. 100.

26. Metcalf, *An Imperial Vision*, p. 231.

27. Philip Davies, *Splendours of the Raj: British Architecture in India, 1660–1947* (Harmondsworth: Penguin, 1987), citing Robert Byron in *Country Life*.

28. On the design on New Delhi see Robert Irving, *Indian Summer: Lutyens, Baker, and Imperial Delhi* (New Haven: Yale University Press, 1981), and Volwahsen, *Imperial Delhi*.

29. Volwahsen, *Imperial Delhi*, pp. 124–29.

30. Thus Derek Clifford calls the Islamic garden "an illusory oasis of delights. . . a garden of shade and sherbet, of fountains and houris, of all that the desert had denied him," in *A History of Garden Design,* rev. ed. (New York: Frederick A. Praeger, 1966), p. 48. James Dickie states that "The Arab love of gardens stems from the fear and antipathy which the Oriental has always felt for nature in its hostile aspect of the desert which signified for him death, aridity, and the resort of ogres and evil spirits," in "The Hispano-Arabic Garden: Its Philosophy and Function," *Bulletin of the School of Oriental and Asian Studies* 31 (1968): 237. Frederick Bargebuhr refers to the Arab as "the son of the arid peninsula" in *The Alhambra*, p. 235. Richard Ettinghausen wrote that the Islamic garden was a response to the ecological condition of the barren desert and was created "as a higher form of relief from this formless and hostile environment" in his "Introduction," in MacDougall and Ettinghausen, eds., *The Islamic Garden*, p. 7.

Bibliography

It can be difficult to distinguish between first name, pati-
onymic, and *Kunya* in premodern Arabic and Persian; these
are listed exactly as they appear in the chapters and references
of this book, disregarding the Western category of "last name."

Abd al-Vasiʻ Jabal. *Diwan*. Ed. Zabih Allah Asafa. Tehran:
    Danishgah-i Tihran, 1960.

Abuʼl Fazl. *Akbarnama*, trans. Henry Beveridge, 3 vols. Cal-
    cutta, 1897–1921.

Abu Hamid al-Garnati. *Tuhfat al-albad*. Ed. Gabriel Ferrand.
    Journal Asiatique 207 (1925): 1–148, 193–304.

Abuʼl Khayr. *Kitab al-Filaha ou le livre de la culture*. Extracts
    trans. A. Cherbonneau and ed. Henri Pérès. Algiers: Edi-
    tions Carbonel, 1946.

Abu-Lughod, Janet. *Cairo: 1001 Years of the City Victorious*.
    Princeton: Princeton University Press, 1971.

Adams, William H. *The French Garden, 1500–1800*. New York:
    Braziller, 1979.

Aga Khan Trust for Culture. *AKTC – Afghanistan Newsletter*,
    July 2006. Web site www.akdn.org/hcsp/afghanistan/
    hcspafghanistan_0706.pdf.

Aga Khan Trust for Culture Web site: www.akdn.org/agency/
    aktc_humayun.html1#objectives

Aktepe, Munir. "Istanbul Fenerbahçesi Hakkında Bazı Bilgiler."
    Edebiyat Fakultesi Tarih Dergisi 32 (1979): 349–72.

Alemi, Mahvash. "Il giardino persiano: tipi e modelli." In *Il
    giardino islamico: Architettura, natura, paesaggio*, ed. Attilio
    Petruccioli, 39–62. Milan: Electa, 1994.

——. "Royal Gardens of the Safavid Period: Types and Models."
    In *Gardens in the Time of the Great Muslim Empires*, ed.
    Attilio Petruccioli, 72–96. Leiden: E. J. Brill, 1997.

Alfieri, Bianca Maria. *Islamic Architecture of the Indian Subcon-
    tinent*. London: Laurence King, 2000.

Allen, Terry. "Imagining Paradise in Islamic Art." Sebastopol,
    Calif.: Solipsist Press, 1993, http://sonic.net/~tallen.palm-
    tree/ip.html.

——. "The Tombs of the ʻAbbasid Caliphs in Baghdad." *Bulletin
    of the School of Oriental and African Studies* 46 (1983): 421–31.

Almagro, Antonio. "El Patio del Crucero de los Reales Al-
    cázares de Sevilla." *Al-Qantara* 20 (1999): 331–76.

——. "La Recuperación del Jardín Medieval del Patio de las Don-
    cellas." *Apuntes del Alcázar de Sevilla* 6 (May 2005): 44–67.

Ameli, Abdullah J., A. Montazer, and S. Ayvazian. "Repères sur
    l'évolution urbaine d'Ispahan." In Darab Diba, P. Revault,
    and S. Santelli, eds., *Maisons d'Ispahan*, 23–43. Paris: Mai-
    sonneuve & Larose, 2001.

Andrews, Peter A. "Mahall. Vi." In *Encyclopaedia of Islam*, new
    ed. 5: 1214–1220.

Arberry, A. J. *The Seven Odes*. London: George Allen & Unwin,
    1957. Leiden: E. J. Brill, 1986.

Archaeological Survey of India. *Fatehpur Sikri*. New Delhi:
    Archaeological Survey of India (ASI), 2002.

——. *Humayun's Tomb and Adjacent Monuments*. New Delhi:
    ASI, 2002 (revised from the original 1946 ASI publication
    by S.A.A. Naqvi.)

Arianpour, Ali-Reza. *Bagh-ha ye, Tarikhy-e Shiraz* (in Persian).
    Tehran: Farhang-Sara, 1986 (1365 H.).

Arié, Rachel. "Une métropole hispanomusulmane au Bas
    Moyen Age: Grenade nasride." *Les Cahiers de Tunisie* 34:
    137–38 (Tunis) (1986): 47–67.

Artan, Tulay. "Architecture as a Theater of Life: Profile of
    the Eighteenth-Century Bosphorus." Ph.D. diss., MIT,
    1989.

Asher, Catherine. *Architecture of Mughal India*. (*New Cam-
    bridge History of India*, I: 4). Cambridge: Cambridge
    University Press, 1995.

——. "The Mausoleum of Sher Shah Suri." *Artibus Asiae* 39,
    nos. 3–4 (1977): 273–98.

——. "Sub-Imperial Palaces: Power and Authority in Mughal
    India." *Ars Orientalis* 23 (1994): 284–85.

——. "Sub-Imperial Patronage: The Architecture of Raja Man
    Singh." In *The Powers of Art: Patronage in Indian Culture*,
    ed. Barbara Stoler Miller, 183–201. Delhi: Oxford Univer-
    sity Press, 1992.

Asher, Catherine, and Thomas Metcalf. "Introduction." In
    Perceptions of South Asia's Visual Past, ed. Asher and Metcalf,
    1–12. New Delhi: Oxford & IBH Publishing, 1994.

Ashraf Husain, Muhammad. *An Historical Guide to the Agra
    Fort*. Delhi: Manager of Publications, 1937.

Asín Palacios, Miguel. *Glosario de voces romances, registradas
    por un botánico anónimo hispano-musulman (siglos XI-XII)*.
    Madrid: Consejo Superior de Investigaciones Científicas,
    1943.

Atasoy, Nurhan. *A Garden for the Sultan: Gardens and Flowers
    in the Ottoman Culture*. Istanbul: Aygaz, 2002.

Atil, Esin. *Kalila wa Dimna: Fables from a Fourteenth-Century Arabic Manuscript*. Washington, D.C.: Smithsonian Institution Press, 1981.

———. *Levni and the Surname: The Story of an Eighteenth-Century Ottoman Festival*. Istanbul: Koçbank, 1999.

Ayoub, Mahmoud. *The Qur'an and Its Interpreters*. Albany: State University of New York Press, 1984.

Azemmouri, Thami. "Les *Nawazil* d'Ibn Sahl, section relative à l'*Ihtisab*." *Hespéris-Tamuda* 14 (1973): 7–108.

Babur, Zahir al-Din. *Baburnama: Memoirs of Babur, Prince and Emperor*. Ed. and trans. Wheeler Thackston. New York: Oxford University Press; Washington, D.C.: Freer Gallery of Art, 1996.

———. *Babur-nama (Memoirs of Babur)*. Trans. Annette Beveridge. 1922; reprint, Delhi: Oriental Books Reprint, 1979.

Baer, Eva. "Khirbat al-Mafjar." In *Encyclopaedia of Islam*, new ed., 5: 10–17. Leiden: E. J. Brill, 1986.

Bahgat, Aly, and Albert Gabriel. *Fouilles d'al-Foustat*. Paris: E. de Boccard, 1921.

Bailey, Gauvin. "The Sweet-smelling Notebook: An Unpublished Mughal Source on Garden Design." In Attilio Petruccioli, ed., *Gardens in the Time of the Great Muslim Empires*, 129–39. Leiden: E. J. Brill, 1997.

al-Bakri. *Description de l'Afrique septentrionale*. Trans. De Slane. 2nd ed. Algiers, 1911–12.

Baksh, Nur. "The Agra Fort and Its Buildings." *Annual Report of the Archaeological Survey of India, 1903–04*, 180–81. Calcutta, 1906.

———. "Historical Notes on the Lahore Fort and Its Buildings." *Annual Report of the Archaeological Survey of India, 1902–03*. Calcutta, 1904.

Bannerji, S. K. "Shah Jehan's Monuments in Agra." *Journal of United Provinces Historical Society* 17 (1944): 55–70.

———. "Shah Jehan's Monuments in Delhi and Ajmer." *Journal of United Provinces Historical Society* 19 (1946): 148–62.

Banu Musa bin Shakir. *The Book of Ingenious Devices (Kitab al-hiyal)*. Trans. Donald Hill. Dordrecht: D. Reidel, 1979.

Barber, Charles. "Reading the Garden in Byzantium: Nature and Sexuality." *Byzantine and Modern Greek Studies* 16 (1992): 1–19.

Bargebuhr, Frederick P. *The Alhambra: A Cycle of Studies on the Eleventh Century in Moorish Spain*. Berlin: De Gruyter, 1968.

Basset, Henri, and E. Lévi-Provençal. "Chella: Une nécropole mérinide." *Hespéris* 2 (1922): 1–92, 255–316, 385–425.

Bayly, C. "Delhi and Other Cities in North India During the 'Twilight.'" In R. E. Frykenberg, ed., *Delhi Through the Ages: Essays in Urban History, Culture, and Society*, 232–33. Delhi: Oxford University Press, 1986.

Begde, Prabhakar V. *Forts and Palaces of India*. New Delhi: Sagar Publications, 1982.

Begley, Wayne. "The Garden of the Taj Mahal: A Case Study of Mughal Architectural Planning and Symbolism." In James L. Wescoat, Jr., and Joachim Wolschke-Bulmahn, eds., *Mughal Gardens: Sources, Places, Representations, and Prospects*, 213–31. Washington, D.C.: Dumbarton Oaks, 1996.

———. "Ghiyas, Mirak Mirza." In *Macmillan Encyclopedia of Architects*. 4 vols., 2: 194. New York: Free Press, 1982.

———. "The Myth of the Taj Mahal and a New Theory of Its Symbolic Meaning." *Art Bulletin* 61 (1979): 7–37.

Begley, Wayne, and Z. A. Desai. *Taj Mahal: The Illumined Tomb: An Anthology of Seventeenth-Century Mughal and European Documentary Sources*. Cambridge, Mass.: Aga Khan Program for Islamic Architecture, 1989.

Behrens-Abouseif, Doris. *Azbakkiyya and Its Environs from Azbak to Isma'il, 1476–1879* (Supplément aux Annales Islamologiques, Cahiers no. 6). Cairo: Institut Français d'Archéologie Orientale, 1985.

———. "Gardens in Islamic Egypt." *Der Islam* 69, no. 2 (1992): 302–12.

Bellafiore, Giuseppe. *Architettura in Sicilia nelle età islamica e normanna (827–1194)*. Palermo: Arnoldo Lombardi Editore, 1990.

———. *La Ziza di Palermo*. Palermo: S. F. Flaccovio, 1978.

Bermúdez Pareja, Jesús. "El Generalife después del incendio de 1958." *Cuadernos de la Alhambra* I (1965): 9–39.

Bernier, François. *Travels in the Mogul Empire AD 1656–1668*. Trans. Archibald Constable, 2nd revision ed. by Vincent A. Smith. Delhi: Low Price Publications, 1989.

Beveridge, Annette. *See* Babur

Beylié, L. de. *La Kalaa des Beni-Hammad: Une capitale berbère de l'Afrique du Nord au IXe*. Paris: E. Leroux, 1909.

Bhardwaj, S. *Hindu Places of Pilgrimage in India*. Berkeley: University of California Press, 1973.

Bianca, Stefano, and Philip Jodidio, eds. *Cairo: Revitalising a Historic Metropolis*. Turin: Aga Khan Trust for Culture and Umberto Allemandi, 2004.

Bilgin, Bulent. *Geçmişte Yıldız Sarayı/Only Yesterday at Yıldız Sarayı*. Istanbul: Yıldız Sarayı Vakfı, 1988.

Blachère, Régis. "Un pionnier de la culture arabe orientale en Espagne au Xe siècle: Sa'id de Bagdad." *Hespéris* 10 (1930): 15–36.

Blair, Sheila, and Jonathan Bloom. *The Art and Architecture of Islam, 1250–1800*. New Haven: Yale University Press, 1994.

———, eds. *Images of Paradise in Islamic Art*. Hanover, N.H.: Hood Museum of Art, 1991.

Blake, Stephen. *Half the World: The Social Architecture of Safavid Isfahan, 1590–1722*. Costa Mesa, Calif.: Mazda, 1999.

Blanchet, Paul. "Description des monuments de la Kalaa des Beni Hammad." *Nouvelles archives des missions scientifiques* 17 (ca. 1897): 1–21.

Bloom, Jonathan. "The Mosque of the Qarafa in Cairo." *Muqarnas* 4 (1987): 7–20.

Blunt, Wilfrid. "The Persian Garden Under Islam." *Apollo* 103, nos. 170–72 (1976): 302–6.

The Book of the Thousand Nights and a Night. *See* Burton, Richard

Bornstein, Christine V., and Priscilla Soucek. *The Meeting of Two Worlds: The Crusades and the Mediterranean Context*. Ann Arbor: Michigan Museum of Art, 1981.

Bosworth, C. E. "Lashkar-i Bazar." In *Encyclopaedia of Islam*, new ed. 5: 690–92.

Braida, S. "Il castello di Favara." *Architetti di Sicilia* 5–6 (1965): 27–34.

Brand, Michael. "Mughal Ritual in Pre-Mughal Cities: The Case of Jahangir in Mandu." *Environmental Design*, 1–2 (1991): 8–17.

——. "Orthodoxy, Innovation, and Revival: Considerations of the Past in Imperial Mughal Tomb Architecture." *Muqarnas* 10 (1993): 323–34.

——. "The Shahdara Gardens of Lahore." In James L. Wescoat, Jr., and Joachim Wolschke-Bulmahn, eds., *Mughal Gardens: Sources, Places, Representations, and Prospects*, 188–211. Washington, D.C.: Dumbarton Oaks, 1996.

——. *See also* Kavsar, Brand, and Wescoat.

Brand, Michael, and Glenn Lowry. *Fatehpur-Sikri*. Bombay: Marg Publications, 1987.

Brand, Michael, and Glenn Lowry, eds. *Fatehpur-Sikri: A Sourcebook*. Cambridge, Mass.: Aga Khan Program for Islamic Architecture at Harvard and the Massachusetts Institute of Technology, 1985.

Brend, Barbara. *Islamic Art*. Cambridge, Mass.: Harvard University Press, 1991.

Bresc, Henri. "Les jardins de Palerme (1290–1460)." *Mélanges de l'École Française de Rome* 84 (1972): 55–127.

Brindle, Stephen. "Seville, IV: Buildings, Cathedral." In *The Grove Dictionary of Art Online* (Oxford University Press, accessed 19 April 2004). *www.groveart.com*.

Brisch, Klaus. "Observation on the Iconography of the Mosaics in the Great Mosque at Damascus." In Priscilla Soucek, ed., *Content and Context of Visual Arts in the Islamic World*, 13–20. University Park: Penn State Press, 1988.

Brookes, John. *Gardens of Paradise*. London: Weidenfeld and Nicolson, ca. 1987.

Brown, Percy. *Indian Architecture (Islamic Period)*. Rev ed. 1944; reprint, Bombay: D. B. Taraporevala, 1981.

Bulatov, M. S. "The Tomb of Sultan Sanjar." *Architectural Heritage* 17 (in Russian). Moscow, 1964.

Burkett, Mary. "Tomb Towers and Inscriptions in Iran." *Oriental Art* 11 (1965): 101–6.

Burton, Richard, trans. and ed. *The Book of the Thousand Nights and a Night*. S.l: The Burton Club, 1885.

Butzer, Karl. *Early Hydraulic Civilization in Egypt*. Chicago: University of Chicago Press, 1976.

Cabanelas Rodríguez, Darío. "La Madraza árabe de Granada y su suerte en época cristiana." *Cuadernos de la Alhambra* 24 (1988): 29–54.

Cahen, Claude. "Notes pour une histoire de l'agriculture dans les pays musulmans médiévaux: Coup d'oeil sur la littérature agronomique musulmane hors de l'Espagne." *Journal of the Economic and Social History of the Orient* 14 (1971): 63–68.

Cambazard-Amahan, Catherine. "Dar al-Batha." In Jacques Revault et al., eds., *Palais et Demeures de Fès, III – Époque Alawite (XIXeme-XXeme siècles)*. Paris: CNRS, 1992.

Cantacuzino, Sherban. "Azem Palace." In S. Cantacuzino, ed., *Architecture and Continuity*, 164–69. New York: Aperture, 1985.

Caronia, Giuseppe. *La Ziza di Palermo: Storia e restauro*. Palermo: Editori Laterza, ca. 1982.

Carr, Stephen. *Archaeology and Monumental Remains of Delhi*. Simla, 1876.

Castejón, Rafael. "El pavimento de la Mezquita de Córdoba." *Boletín de la Real Academia de Córdoba, de Ciencias, Bellas Letras y Nobles Artes* 54 (1945): 327–30.

——. "Mas sobre el pavimento de la Mezquita." *Boletín de la Real Academia de Córdoba, de Ciencias, Bellas Letras y Nobles Artes* 55 (1946): 233–34.

Çelebi, Evliya (d. 1679). *Narrative of Travels*, trans. J. von Hammer. London, 1834.

Cerasi, Maurice M. "Open Space, Water and Trees in Ottoman Urban Culture in the XVIIIth-XIXth Centuries." *Environmental Design* 2 (1985): 36–49.

Clavijo, Ruy Gonzalez de. *Embajada a Tamorlán*. Ed. F. López Estrada. Madrid: Consejo Superior de Investigaciones Científicas, Instituto Nicolás Antonio, 1943.

——. *Embassy to Tamerlane, 1403–1406*. Trans. Guy Le Strange. New York: Harper & Brothers, 1928.

Clerget, Marcel. *Le Caire: Étude de géographie urbaine et d'histoire économique*, 2 vols. Cairo: Imprimerie E. & R. Schindler, 1934.

Clifford, Derek. *A History of Garden Design*. Rev. ed. New York: Frederick A. Praeger, 1966.

Colin, G. S. "Filaha: Muslim West." In *Encyclopaedia of Islam*, new ed., 2 (1965): 901–2.

Conan, Michel, ed. *The Middle East Garden Traditions, Unity and Diversity: Questions, Methods, and Resources in a Multicultural Perspective*. Washington, D.C.: Dumbarton Oaks, 2007.

Consejería de obras públicas y transportes de la Junta de Andalucía, Consejería de cultura de la Junta de Andalucía, et al. *Plan especial de proteccion y reforma interior de la Alhambra y Alijares*. Granada: Patronato de la Alhambra, 1986.

Constable, Olivia. *Trade and Traders in Muslim Spain*. Cambridge: Cambridge University Press, 1994.

Coomaraswamy, A. K. *The Treatise of al-Jazari*. Boston: Museum of the Fine Arts, 1924.

Cortés García, Manuela. "Ziryab, la música y la elegancia palatina." In *El Esplendor de los Omeyas cordobeses, Estudios*, 240–43. Granada: Fundación El Legado Andalusí, 2001.

Cousens, Henry. *Bijapur and Its Architectural Remains*. Bombay: Archaeological Survey of India (vol. 37), 1916; reprint, New Delhi, 1976.

Creswell, K. A. C. *Early Muslim Architecture*, 2 vols. Oxford: Clarendon Press, 1932–40.

——. *A Short Account of Early Muslim Architecture*. Rev. ed. James Allan. Aldershot: Scolar, 1989.

Crowe, Sylvia, Sheila Haywood, Susan Jellicoe, and Gordon Patterson. *The Gardens of Mughal India*. New York: Thames and Hudson, 1972.

Cuadernos de la Alhambra 36 (2000).

Cuadernos de Madirat al-Zahra', Various articles.

Damluji, Salma Samar. *The Architecture of Oman*. Reading, UK: Garnet Publishing, 1998.

Daneshvari, Abbas. *Medieval Tomb Towers of Iran: An Iconographical Study*. Lexington, Ky.: Mazda, 1986.

Dar, Saifur Rehman. *Historical Gardens of Lahore.* Lahore: Aziz Publishers, 1982.

Davies, Philip. *Splendours of the Raj: British Architecture in India, 1660–1947.* Harmondsworth: Penguin, 1987.

Demiriz, Yıldız. "Tulips in Ottoman Turkish Culture and Art." In Michiel Roding and Hans Theunissen, eds., *The Tulip: A Symbol of Two Nations*, 57–75. Utrecht: M. Th. Houtsma Stichting, 1993.

Diba, Darab, P. Revault, and S. Santelli, eds. *Maisons d'Ispahan.* Paris: Maisonneuve & Larose, 2001.

Dickie, James. "Garden and Cemetery in Sinan's Istanbul." *Environmental Design: Journal of the Islamic Environmental Design Research Centre* ("Sinan and the Urban Vision"), 1–2 (1987): 70–85.

——. "Granada: A Case Study of Arab Urbanism in Muslim Spain." In Salma K. Jayyusi, ed., *The Legacy of Muslim Spain*, 88–111. Leiden: E. J. Brill, 1992.

——. "The Hispano-Arabic Garden: Its Philosophy and Function." *Bulletin of the School of Oriental and Asian Studies* 31 (1968): 237–48.

——. "The Islamic Garden in Spain." In Elisabeth Macdougall and Richard Ettinghausen, eds., *The Islamic Garden*, 89–105. Washington, D.C.: Dumbarton Oaks, 1976.

——. "Palaces of the Alhambra." In Jerrilynn D. Dodds, ed., *Al-Andalus: The Art of Islamic Spain*, 135–51. New York: Metropolitan Museum of Art, 1992.

Dioscorides. *Pedanii Dioscuridis Anazarbaei de materia medica.* 2 vols. Paris, 1935.

Dodd, Erica C. "On a Bronze Rabbit from Fatimid Egypt." *Kunst des Orients* 8 (1972): 60–76.

Dodds, Jerrilynn D. "Ahmad Ibn Baso." In *Macmillan Encyclopedia of Architects*, 4 vols., 1: 38. New York: Free Press, 1982.

Dodds, Jerrilynn D., ed. *Al-Andalus: The Art of Islamic Spain.* New York: Metropolitan Museum of Art, 1992.

Dozy, Reinhart, ed. *Le Calendrier de Cordoue*, new ed. in Arabic and Latin with additional French trans. by Charles Pellat. Leiden: Brill, 1961.

——. *Scriptorum Arabum Loci de Abbaditis, nunc primum editi.* 3 vols. in 2. 1846; reprint, Hildesheim-New York: George Olms Verlag, 1992.

Dubler, C. E. *La "materia medica" de Dioscórides, transmisión medieval y renacentista.* 6 vols. Barcelona: Tipografía Emporium, 1953.

Écochard, Michel. "Le Palais Azem de Damas." *Gazette des Beaux-Arts*, 6th ser., 13 (1935): 231–41.

El Faïz, Mohammed. *Jardins de Marrakech.* Paris: Actes Sud, 2000.

——. *Les jardins historiques de Marrakech: Mémoire écologique d'une ville impériale.* Florence: EDIFIR, 1996.

El Faïz, Mohammed, Manuel Gómez Anuarbe, and Teresa Portela Marques. *Jardins de Maroc, d'Espagne et du Portugal.* Madrid: Actes Sud and Fondation Telefónica Maroc, 2003.

Eldem, Sedad H. and Feridun Akozan. *Topkapi Sarayı bir Mimari Araştırma.* Istanbul: Millî Eğitim Basımevi, 1982.

Esin, Emil. "An Eighteenth-Century 'Yali' Viewed in the Line of Development of Related Forms in Turkic Architecture." In *Atti del Secondo Congreso Internationale di Arte Turca.* Naples, 1965.

Ettinghausen, Richard. *Arab Painting.* 1962; 2nd ed., New York: Rizzoli, 1977.

——. "Introduction." In Elisabeth MacDougall and Richard Ettinghausen, eds., *The Islamic Garden*, 3–10. Washington, D.C.: Dumbarton Oaks, 1976.

Ettinghausen, Richard, O. Grabar, and M. Jenkins-Madina. *Islamic Art and Architecture, 650–1250.* Pelican History of Art. New Haven: Yale University Press, 2001.

Fahd, Toufic. *L'agriculture nabatéenne, traduction en arabe attribuée à Abu Bakr Ahmad b. Ali al-Kasdani connu sous le nom d'Ibn Wahsiyya (IV/Xe siècle)*, 2 vols. Damascus: Institut Français de Damas, 1993–95.

Fat, Leslie Tjon Sie, and Erik de Jong, eds. *The Authentic Garden: A Symposium on Gardens.* Leiden: Clusius Foundation, 1991.

Fernandez Puertas, Antonio. *The Alhambra I, From the Ninth Century to Yusuf I (1354).* London: Saqi Books, 1997.

Findly, Ellison Banks. "Nur Jahan's Embroidery Trade and Flowers of the Taj Mahal." *Asian Art and Culture* (Spring–Summer 1996): 7–25.

——. *Nur Jahan: Empress of Mughal India.* New York: Oxford University Press, 1993.

Flood, Finbarr. *The Great Mosque of Damascus: Studies in the Making of an Umayyad Visual Culture.* Leiden: Brill, 2001.

Forkel, Hermann, et al., eds. *Die Gärten des Islam.* London: H. Mayer, 1993.

Fowden, Garth. *Qusayr Amra: Art and the Umayyad Elite in Late Antique Syria.* Berkeley: University of California Press, 2004.

Franke-Vogt, Ute, K. Bartle, and Th. Urban. "Bagh-e Babur, Kabul: Excavations in a Mughal Garden." In Ute Franke-Vogt and Hans-Joachim Weisshaar, eds., *South Asian Archaeology* (Proceedings of the Seventeenth International Conference of the European Association of South Asian Archaeologists, 7–11 July 2003, Bonn. 541–57). Aachen: Linden Soft, 2005.

Gabriel, Albert. "Kasr el-Heir." *Syria* 8 (1927): 302–29.

Gallotti, Jean. *Moorish Houses and Gardens of Morocco.* 2 vols. New York: William Helburn, 1926, esp. vol. 2.

García Sánchez, Expiración. "Agriculture in Muslim Spain." In S. K. Jayyusi, ed., *The Legacy of Muslim Spain*, 987–99. Leiden: E. J. Brill, 1992.

Gayangos, Pascual de, ed. and trans. *History of the Mohammedan Dynasties in Spain*, 2 vols. London: Oriental Translation Fund, 1840–43 (a translation of al-Maqqari; *Nafh al-tib*).

Gleason, Kathryn, and Naomi Miller, eds. *The Archaeology of Garden and Field.* Philadelphia: University of Pennsylvania Press, 1994.

Glick, Thomas. *Islamic and Christian Spain in the Early Middle Ages.* Princeton: Princeton University Press, 1979.

Goblot, Henri. *Les Qanats: Une technique d'acquisition de l'eau.* Paris: Mouton, 1979.

Goetz, H. "An Irruption of Gothic Style Forms into Indo-Islamic Architecture." *Artibus Asiae* 22 (1959): 53–58.

——. "The Nagaur School of Rajput Painting." *Artibus Asiae* 12 (1949): 89–98.

Goldschmidt, A. "Die Favarades Königs Roger von Sizilien." *Jahrbuch der Kgl. Preuszischen Kunstsammlungen* 16, no. 3 (1895): 199–215.

Golombek, Lisa. "From Tamerlane to the Taj Mahal." In A. Daneshvari, ed., *Essays in Islamic Art and Architecture in Honor of Katharina Otto-Dorn*, 43–50. Malibu, Calif.: Undena, 1981.

——. "Gardens. ii. Islamic Period." *Encyclopedia Iranica* 10, 3 (2000): 298–305.

——. "The Gardens of Timur: New Perspectives." *Muqarnas* 12 (1995): 137–47.

——. *The Timurid Shrine at Gazur Gah*. Toronto: Royal Ontario Museum, 1969.

Golombek, Lisa, and Renata Holod. "Preliminary Report on the Isfahan City Project." In *Akten VII. Internationalen Kongresses für Iranische Kunst und Archäologie (Munich, 1976)*, 578–90. Berlin: D. Reimer, 1979.

Golvin, Lucien. *Recherches archéologiques à la Qal'a des Banu Hammad*. Paris: Maisonneuve et Larose, 1965.

Goodwin, Godfrey. "Gardens of the Dead in Ottoman Times." *Muqarnas* 5 (1988): 61–69.

——. *A History of Ottoman Architecture*. New York: Thames and Hudson, 1971.

Grabar, Oleg. *The Alhambra*. 1978; reprint, Sebastopol, Calif.: Solipsist Press, 1992.

——. "The Earliest Islamic Commemorative Structures. Notes and Documents." *Ars Orientalis* 6 (1966): 7–46.

——. *The Formation of Islamic Art*. Rev. ed. New Haven: Yale University Press, 1987.

——. *The Illustrations of the Maqamat*. Chicago: University of Chicago Press, 1984.

——. "The Islamic Dome, Some Considerations." *Journal of the Society of Architectural Historians* 22 (1963): 191–98.

——. "Qasr al-Hayr Ash-Sharqi." In *The Oxford Encyclopedia of Archaeology in the Near East*, 5 vols. 4: 379–80. New York: Oxford University Press, 1997.

——. *The Shape of the Holy: Early Islamic Jerusalem*. Princeton: Princeton University Press, 1996.

——. "Symbols and Signs in Islamic Architecture." In Renata Holod and D. Rostorfer, eds., *Architecture and Community*. Millerton, N.Y.: Aperture, 1983.

——. "Umayyad 'Palace' and Abbasid 'Revolution'." *Studia Islamica* 18 (1962): 5–18.

Grabar, Oleg, R. Holod, J. Knustad, and W. Trousdale. *City in the Desert: Qasr al-Hayr East*. Cambridge, Mass.: Harvard University Press, 1978.

Graf von Bothmer, Hans-Caspar. "Archittekturbilder im Koran – eine Prachthandschrift der Umayyadenzeit aus dem Yemen." *Pantheon* 45 (1987): 4–20.

Gray, Basil. "A Fatimid Drawing." *British Museum Quarterly* 12 (1938): 91–96.

Grierson, Philip. "The Tombs and Obits of the Byzantine Emperors (337–1042)." *Dumbarton Oaks Papers* 16 (1962): 3–63.

Grunebaum, Gustave von. "The Response to Nature in Arabic Poetry." *Journal of Near Eastern Studies* 4 (1945): 137–51.

——. *Themes in Medieval Arabic Literature*. London: Variorum, 1981.

Gulbadan Begum. *The History of Humayun*. Trans. Annette Beveridge. 1902; reprint, Delhi: Idarah-i Adabiyat-i Delli, 1972.

Gupta, Sankar Sen, ed., *Tree Symbol Worship in India*. Calcutta: India Publications, 1965.

Hali 5 (1982–83).

Hämeen-Anttila, Jaakko. *The Last Pagans of Iraq: Ibn Wahshiyya and his Nabatean Agriculture*. Leiden: Brill, 2006.

Hamilton, Richard W. *Khirbat al-Mafjar: An Arabian Mansion in the Jordan Valley*. Oxford: Clarendon Press, 1959.

Hammudi, Khalid Khalil. "Qasr al-khalifa al-Mu'tasim fi Samarra." *Sumer* 38 (1982): 168–205.

Hanaway, William, Jr. "Paradise on Earth: The Terrestrial Garden in Persian Literature." In Elisabeth MacDougall and Richard Ettinghausen, eds., *The Islamic Garden*, 43–67. Washington, D.C.: Dumbarton Oaks, 1976.

al-Hassan, Ahmad Y., ed. *Kitab al-Hiyal: The Book of Ingenious Devices*. Aleppo: University of Aleppo, 1981.

al-Hassan, Ahmad, and Donald Hill. *Islamic Technology: An Illustrated History*. Cambridge: Cambridge University Press, 1986.

d'Henry, Gabrielle. "Scafati (Salerno): Monumento funerario." *Bollettino d'Arte* 4th ser. 49 (1964): 368–69.

Hernández-Bermejo, J. Esteban, and E. García Sánchez. "Economic Botany and Ethnobotany in Al-Andalus (Iberian Peninsula: Tenth-Fifteenth Centuries), an Unknown Heritage of Mankind." *Economic Botany* 52 (1998): 15–26.

Hernández Giménez, Félix. *Madinat al-Zahra': Arquitectura y Decoracion*. Granada: Patronato de la Alhambra, 1985.

Hernández Núñez, Juan Carlos, and Alfredo J. Morales. *The Royal Palace of Seville*. London: Scala, 1999.

——. "Mitteilungen über die Arbeiten der zweiten Kampagne von Samarra." *Der Islam* 5 (1914): 196–204.

Herzfeld, Ernst, and F. Sarre, *Erster vorläufiger Bericht über die Ausgrabungen von Samarra*. Berlin, 1912.

Hill, Donald. *Arabic Water-Clocks*. Sources and Studies in the History of Arabic-Islamic Science, History of Technology Series, 4. Aleppo: University of Aleppo, 1981.

——. *On the Construction of Water-Clocks* (*Kitab arshimidas fi 'amal al-binkamat*). Turner and Devereaux Occasional Papers, 4. London, 1976.

Hillenbrand, Robert. "The Arts of the Book in Ilkhanid Iran." In Linda Komaroff and Stefano Carboni, eds., *The Legacy of Genghis Khan: Courtly Art and Culture in Western Asia, 1256–1353*, 135–67. New York: Metropolitan Museum of Art; New Haven: Yale University Press, 2002.

——. *Islamic Architecture: Form, Function and Meaning*. New York: Columbia University Press, 1994.

Hoag, John. *Islamic Architecture*. New York: Rizzoli, 1987.

Hodge, A. T. *Roman Aqueducts and Water Supply*. London: Duckworth, 1992.

Hodgson, Marshall. "The Role of Islam in World History." In Marshall Hodgson and Edmund Burke III, eds., *Rethinking World History*, 97–125. Cambridge: Cambridge University Press, 1993.

Holod, Renata. "Luxury Arts of the Caliphal Period." In Jerrilynn Dodds, ed., *Al-Andalus: The Art of Islamic Spain*, 41–47. New York: Metropolitan Museum of Art, 1992.

Holod, Renata, ed. *Iranian Studies*. Special issue: *Proceedings of The Isfahan Colloquium*. 7 (1974).

Honarfar, L. *Historical Monuments of Isfahan*, 3rd ed. Isfahan: Emami Press, 1964.

Hourani, Albert, and S. M. Stern, eds. *The Islamic City*. Philadelphia: University of Pennsylvania Press, 1970.

Hoyland, Robert. *Seeing Islam as Others Saw It: A Survey and Evaluation of Christian, Jewish and Zoroastrian Writings on Early Islam*. Princeton: Darwin Press, 1997.

Hunt, Eva, and Robert C. Hunt. "Irrigation, Conflict, and Politics: A Mexican Case." In Theodore E. Downing and McGuire Gibson, eds., *Irrigation's Impact on Society*. Anthropological Papers of the University of Arizona, no. 25, 129–57. Tucson: University of Arizona Press, 1974.

Hussain, Mahmood, Abdul Rehman, and James L. Wescoat, Jr., eds. *The Mughal Garden*. Lahore: Ferozsons, 1996.

Ibn 'Abd al-Hakam. *See* Robert Hoyland.

Ibn al-Shihnah. *"Les perles choisies" d'Ibn ach-Chihna*. Ed. Jean Sauvaget. Beirut: Institut français de Damas, mémoires, 1933.

Ibn 'Arabshah. *Tamerlane or Timur the Great Amir*. Trans. J. H. Saunders. London: Luzac, 1936.

Ibn Bassal. *Tratado de agricultura*. Trans. J. M. Millas Vallicrosa and M. Aziman. Tetuan: Instituto Muley el-Hasan, 1955.

Ibn Battuta. *Travels in Asia and Africa, 1325–1354*. Trans. H. A. R. Gibb. Abridged version. New Delhi: Manohar, 2001.

—— . *The Travels of Ibn Battuta, A.D. 1325–1354*. Trans. H. A. R. Gibb, 3 vols. Cambridge: Cambridge University Press for The Halkluyt Society, 1958–71.

Ibn Ghalib. *Kitab farhat al-anfus fi-akhbar al-andalus*. Ed. Lutfi 'Abd al-Badi' in *Majallat Ma'had al-makhtutat al-'arabiya* vol. 1 (Cairo, 1955): 272–310.

—— . "La descripción de Córdoba de Ibn Galib." Trans. Joaquín Vallvé Bermejo. In *Homenaje a Pedro Sainz Rodríguez*, 3 vols., III: 669–79. Madrid: Fundación Universitaria Española, 1986.

Ibn Habib. *Kitab al-Ta'rij (La historia)*. Ed. Jorge Aguadé. Madrid: Consejo Superior de Investigaciones Científicas, 1991.

Ibn 'Idhari. *Histoire de l'Afrique du Nord et de l'Espagne musulmane intitulée kitab al-bayan al-mughrib*. Ed. E. Lévi-Provençal and G. S. Colin, 2 vols. Leiden: E. J. Brill, 1948–51.

—— . *Histoire de l'Afrique et de l'Espagne*. Trans. E. Fagnan. 2 vols. Algiers: P. Fontana, 1901–4.

Ibn Luyun. *Ibn Luyun: Tratado de Agricultura*. Ed. and trans. Joaquina Eguaras Ibáñez. Granada: Patronato de la Alhambra, 1975.

Ibn Qutayba. *Kitab al-Anwa'*. Ed. Hamidullah and Charles Pellat. Hyderabad: Dairatu'l-Ma'arifi'l-Osmania, 1956.

Ibn Shuhayd. *El Diwan de Ibn Shuhayd al-Andalus, 382–426 H = 992–1035 C., Texto y Traducción*. Ed. and trans. James Dickie. Cordoba: Real Academia de Córdoba, 1975.

Ibn Wafid. *See* Millás Vallicrosa.

Ibn Wahsiyya. *See* Toufic Fahd.

Ibn Zaydun et al. *Diwan*. Ed. Kamil Kilani and A.R. Khalifa. Cairo: Mustafa al-Bahi al-Halabi, 1932 (1351 AH).

Imru al-Qays. *See* A. J. Arberry, *The Seven Odes*.

'Inayat Khan. *The Shah Jahan Nama*. Ed. W. E. Begley and Z. A. Desai, based on earlier edition of A. R. Fuller. Delhi: Oxford University Press, 1990.

INTACH. "Lodi Gardens" (map). New Delhi: Indian National Trust for Art and Cultural Heritage (INTACH), Heritage Education and Communication Service, n.d.

Irving, Robert G. *Indian Summer: Lutyens, Baker, and Imperial Delhi*. New Haven: Yale University Press, 1981.

Jacobs, Michael. *The Alhambra*. New York: Rizzoli, 2000.

Jahangir, Nur al-Din. *The Jahangirnama: Memoirs of Jahangir, Emperor of India*. Ed. and trans. Wheeler Thackston. Washington, D.C.: Freer Gallery, 1999.

Jain, Minakshi, and Kulbhushan Jain. *The Fort of Nagaur*. Jodhpur: Mehrangarh Museum Trust; Ahmedabad: CEPT School of Architecture, 1993.

Jakobi, Jürgen. "Agriculture Between Literary Tradition and Firsthand Experience: The *Irshad al-zira'a* of Qasim b. Yusuf Abu Nasri Haravi." In Lisa Golombek and Maria Subtelny, eds., *Timurid Art and Culture*, 201–8. Leiden: E. J. Brill, 1992.

Jashemski, Wilhemina. *The Gardens of Pompeii*, 2 vols. New York: Caratzas Brothers, 1979–93.

—— . "Town and Country Gardens at Pompeii and Other Vesuvian Sites." In William Kelso and Rachel Most, eds., *Earth Patterns*, 213–25. Charlottesville: University of Virginia, 1990.

Jashemski, Wilhemina, and Elisabeth MacDougall, eds. *Ancient Roman Gardens*. Washington, D.C.: Dumbarton Oaks, 1981.

Jashemski, Wilhemina, and Frederick Meyer, eds. *The Natural History of Pompeii*. Cambridge: Cambridge University Press, 2002.

al-Jaziri, Ibn al-Razzaz. *The Book of Ingenious Mechanical Devices*. Ed. and trans. Donald Hill. Dordrecht: D. Reidel, 1974.

—— . *See also* A. K. Coomaraswamy.

Jellicoe, Susan. "The Development of the Mughal Garden." In Elisabeth MacDougall and Richard Ettinghausen, eds., *The Islamic Garden*, 109–29. Washington, D.C.: Dumbarton Oaks, 1976.

Jenkins, Marilyn. "Al-Andalus: Crucible of the Mediterranean." In *The Art of Medieval Spain, A.D. 500–1200*, 73–84. New York: Metropolitan Museum of Art, 1993.

Jiménez Martín, Alfonso. "El Patio de los Naranjos y la Giralda." In *La Catedral de Sevilla*, 83–132. Seville: Ediciones Guadalquivir, 1984.

Joffee, Jennifer. "Art, Architecture, and Politics in Mewar, 1628–1710." Ph.D. diss., University of Minnesota, 2005.

Joffee, Jennifer, and D. Fairchild Ruggles. "Rajput Gardens and Landscapes." In Michel Conan, ed., *The Middle East Garden*

Traditions, Unity and Diversity: Questions, Methods, and Resources in a Multicultural Perspective, 269–285. Washington, D.C.: Dumbarton Oaks, 2007

Johnson, Mark J. "Late Imperial Mausolea." Ph.D. diss., Princeton University, 1986.

Joshi, M. C. *Dig.* 3rd ed. New Delhi: Archaeological Survey of India, 1982.

Kaul, H. K. *Historic Delhi: An Anthology.* New Delhi: Oxford University Press, 1985.

Kausar, Sajjad, M. Brand, and J. L. Wescoat, Jr. *Shalamar Garden Lahore: Landscape, Form and Meaning.* Islamabad: Department of Archaeology and Museums, Ministry of Culture, Pakistan, 1990.

Keenan, Brigid. *Damascus: Hidden Treasures of the Old City.* New York: Thames and Hudson, 2000.

Kernan, Michael. "Turning a New Leaf." *Smithsonian*, August 2000.

Khallaf, M. *Watha'iq fi shu'un al-'umran fi'l-Andalus.* Cairo, 1983.

Khan, Ahmad Nabi. "Conservation of the Hiran Minar and Baradari at Sheikhpura." *Pakistan Archaeology* 6 (1969).

Khangarot, R. S., and P. S. Nathawat. *Jaigarh: The Invincible Fort of Amber.* Jaipur: RBSA Publishers, 1990.

Khansari, Mehdi, M. Reza Moghtader, and Minouch Yavari. *The Persian Garden: Echoes of Paradise.* Washington, D.C.: Mage, 1998.

al-Khatib al-Baghdadi. *Ta'rikh Baghdad*, 14 vols. Cairo: Maktabat al-Khanji, 1931. 1: 100–104.

Khokhar, Masood-ul-Hassan. "Conservation of Lahore Fort Gardens." In Mahmood Hussain, Abdul Rehman, and James L. Wescoat, Jr., eds., *The Mughal Garden*, 129–32. Lahore: Ferozsons, 1996.

Kiby, Ulrika. "Islamische Gartenkunst." *Der Islam* 68 (1991): 329–64.

King, David. Review of Charles Pellat, *Cinq Calendriers Égyptiens* (1986). *Journal of the American Research Center in Egypt* 25 (1988): 252–53.

Koch, Ebba. *The Complete Taj Mahal and the Riverfront Gardens of Agra.* London: Thames and Hudson, 2006.

———. *Mughal Architecture.* 1991; reprint, Oxford: Oxford University Press, 2002.

———. "Mughal Palace Gardens from Babur to Shah Jahan (1526–1648)." *Muqarnas* 14 (1997): 143–65.

———. "The Mughal Waterfront Garden." In Attilio Petruccioli, ed., *Gardens in the Time of the Great Muslim Empires: Theory and Design*, 140–60. Leiden: E.J. Brill, 1997.

———. "Notes on the Painted and Sculptured Decoration of Nur Jahan's Pavilions in the Ram Bagh (Bagh-i Nur Afshan) at Agra." In Robert Skelton et al, eds., *Facets of Indian Art*, 51–65. London: Victoria and Albert Museum, 1986.

———. "Pietre Dure and Other Artistic Contacts Between the Court of the Mughals and that of the Medici." *Marg* 39, no. 1 (s.d.): 30–56.

———. *Shah Jahan and Orpheus.* Graz: Akademie Druck und Verlagsanstalt, 1988.

———. "The Zahara Bagh (Bagh-i Jahanara) at Agra." *Environmental Design* no. 2 (1986): 30–37.

Komaroff, Linda. "The Transmission and Dissemination of a New Visual Language." In Linda Komaroff and Stefano Carboni, eds., *The Legacy of Genghis Khan: Courtly Art and Culture in Western Asia, 1256–1353*, 169–95. New York: Metropolitan Museum of Art; New Haven: Yale University Press, 2002.

Koran. See *al-Qur'an*.

Kritovoulos. *History of Mehmed the Conqueror by Kritovoulos.* Trans. Charles Riggs. Princeton: Princeton University Press, 1954.

Lambin, Denis. "Garden, §VIII, 4(ii): France, c. 1550–c. 1800." In *The Grove Dictionary of Art Online*. Oxford University Press, *www.groveart.com*, accessed 20 April 2004.

Lang, Jon, Madhavi Desai, and Miki Desai. *Architecture and Independence: The Search for Identity – India 1880–1980*. Delhi: Oxford University Press, 1997.

Latif, Syed Muhammad. *Lahore: Its History, Architectural Remains, and Antiquities.* Lahore, 1892.

Lehrman, Jonas. *Earthly Paradise: Garden and Courtyard in Islam.* Berkeley: University of California Press, 1980.

Leisten, Thomas. "Between Orthodoxy and Exegesis: Some Aspects of Attitudes in the Shari'a Toward Funerary Architecture." *Muqarnas* 7 (1990): 12–22.

Lentz, David. "Botanical Symbolism and Function at the Mahtab Bagh." In Elizabeth Moynihan, ed., *The Moonlight Garden: New Discoveries at the Taj Mahal*, 43–57. Washington, D.C.: Arthur M. Sackler Gallery; Seattle: University of Washington Press, 2000.

Lentz, Thomas, and Glenn Lowry. *Timur and the Princely Vision.* Los Angeles: Los Angeles County Museum of Art; Washington, D.C.: Arthur M. Sackler Gallery, 1989.

Lévi-Provençal, E. *Histoire de l'Espagne Musulmane*, 3 vols. Paris: G. P. Maisonneuve, 1950–53.

Littlefield, Sharon, with Introduction by Carol Bier. *Doris Duke's Shangri La.* Honolulu: Honolulu Academy of Arts, 2002.

Littlewood, A. "Gardens of the Palaces." In Henry Maguire, ed., *Byzantine Court Culture from 829 to 1204*, 13–38. Washington, D.C.: Dumbarton Oaks, 1997.

López, Angel C. "Vida y obra del famoso polígrafo cordobés del siglo X, 'Arib Ibn Sa'id." In Expiración García Sánchez, ed., *Ciencias de la naturaleza en al-Andalus: textos y estudios*, 2 vols. 1: 317–47. Granada, 1990.

Lowry, Glenn. "Humayun's Tomb: Form, Function, and Meaning in Early Mughal Architecture." *Muqarnas* 4 (1987): 133–48.

Lowry, Glenn, and Susan Nemazee. *A Jeweler's Eye: Islamic Arts of the Book from the Vever Collection.* Washington, D.C.: Arthur M. Sackler Gallery, 1988.

MacDougall, Elisabeth, and Richard Ettinghausen, eds. *The Islamic Garden.* Washington, D.C.: Dumbarton Oaks, 1976.

Maguire, Henry. "Imperial Gardens and the Rhetoric of Renewal." In Paul Magdaline, ed., *New Constantines: The*

Rhythm of Imperial Renewal in Byzantium, 4th-13th Centuries, 181–98. Aldershot: Variorum, 1994.

Maguire, Henry, ed. *Byzantine Court Culture from 829 to 1204*. Washington, D.C.: Dumbarton Oaks, 1997.

Mango, Cyril, and Stephan Yerasimos, *Melchior Lorichs' Panorama of Istanbul, 1559*. Facsimile edition. Bern: Ertug & Kocabiyik, 1999.

Manucci, N. *Storia do Magor by Niccolao Manucci*. Trans. William Irvine. London: John Murray, 1907.

Manzano Martos, Rafael. "Casas y palacios en la Sevilla Almohade. Sus antecedents hispánicos." In Julio Navarro Palazón, ed. *Casas y Palacios de al-Andalus*, 315–52. Granada: El Legado Andalusí, 1995.

al-Maqqari, Ahmad. *Analectes sur l'histoire et la littérature des arabes d'Espagne*. Ed. R. Dozy et al. 2 vols. in 3. Leiden: E. J. Brill, 1855–61; reprint, London: Oriental Press, 1967.

——. *History of the Mohammedan Dynasties in Spain*. Ed. and trans. Pascual de Gayangos, 2 vols. London: Oriental Translation Fund, 1840–43.

Maqrizi, Ahmad. *Kitab al-khitat*. 5 vols. Ed. Gaston Wiet. Cairo: Imprimerie de l'Institut français d'archéologie orientale, 1911–1924.

Marçais, Georges. *L'Architecture musulmane d'occident*. Paris: Arts et Métiers Graphiques, 1954.

——. "Les jardins de l'Islam." In Marçais, *Mélanges d'histoire et d'archéologie de l'Occident musulman*, 2 vols. 1: 233–44. Algiers: Imprimerie officielle du Gouvernement générale d'Algérie, 1957.

Marg. Special issue on Fatehpur-Sikri 38, no. 2 (1986).

Marg. Special issue, "Landscape Architecture and Gardening of the Mughals." 26, no. 1 (1972).

Marín Fidalgo, Ana. *El Alcázar de Sevilla*. Seville: Ediciones Guadalquivir, 1990.

Marshall, P. J. ed. *The British Discovery of Hinduism in the Eighteenth Century*. Cambridge: Cambridge University Press, 1970.

Martín-Consuegra, E., J. L. Ubera, and E. Hernández-Bermejo. "Palynology of the Historical Period at the Madinat al-Zahra Archaeological Site, Spain." *Journal of Archaeological Science* 23 (1996): 249–61.

Martín-Consuegra, E., E. Hernández-Bermejo, and J. L. Ubera. *Palinología y botánica histórica del complejo arqueológico de Madinat al-Zahra*. Monografías del Jardín Botánico de Córdoba 8. Cordoba: Jardín Botáníco de Córdoba, 2000.

Mashmud, Muhammad Khalid. "The Mausoleum of the Emperor Jahangir." *Arts of Asia* 13 (1983): 57–66.

Masson, Charles. *Narrative of Various Journeys in Balochistan, Afghanistan, and the Panjab*, 3 vols. London, 1842.

Maury, Bernard. "La Maison damascène au XVIIIe siècle et au début du XIXe siècle." In *Habitat traditionnel dans les pays musulmans autour de la Méditerranée (Aix-en-Provence, 6–8 juin 1984)*, 3 vols. 1: 1–42. Cairo: Institut Français d'Archéologie Orientale, ca. 1988–91.

McChesney, Robert D. "Some Observations on 'Garden' and Its Meaning in the Property Transactions of the Juybari Family in Bukhara, 1544–77." In Attilio Petruccioli, ed., *Gardens in the Time of the Great Muslim Empires*, 97–109. Leiden: E. J. Brill, 1997.

McKay, A. G. *Houses, Villas and Palaces in the Roman World*. Ithaca: Cornell University Press, 1975.

Meier, Hans-Rudolf. "... 'das ird'sche Paradies, das sich den Blicken öffnet': Die Gartenpaläste der Normannenkönige in Palermo." *Die Gartenkunst* 5, no. 1 (1994): 1–18.

Meisami, Julie Scott. "Palaces and Paradises: Palace Description in Medieval Persian Poetry." In Oleg Grabar and Cynthia Robinson, eds., *Islamic Art and Literature*, 21–54. Princeton: Markus Wiener, 2001.

Menjili-De Corny, Irène. *Jardins du Maroc*. Paris: Le Temps Apprivoisé, 1991.

Metcalf, Thomas. *An Imperial Vision: Indian Architecture and Britain's Raj*. Berkeley: University of California Press, 1989.

Meunié, Jacques, Henri Terrasse, and Gaston Deverdun. *Recherches archéologiques à Marrakech*. Paris, 1952.

Meunié, Jean. "Le grand Riad et les bâtiments saâdiens du Badi' à Marrakech selon le plan publié par Windus." *Hespéris* 44 (1957): 129–34.

Michell, George, and Antonio Martinelli. *The Royal Palaces of India*. London: Thames and Hudson, 1994.

Millás Vallicrosa, José. "La traducción castellana del 'Tratado de agricultura' de Ibn Wafid." *Al-Andalus* 8 (1943): 281–332. *See also* Ibn Bassal.

Miller, Susan G. "Finding Order in the Moroccan City: The *Hubus* of the Great Mosque of Tangier as an Agent of Urban Change." *Muqarnas* 22 (2005): 265–83.

Mir, Muhammad Naeem, Mahmood Hussain, and James L. Wescoat, Jr. *Mughal Gardens in Lahore: History and Documentation*. Lahore: Department of Architecture, University of Engineering and Technology, 1996.

Moaz, Abd al-Razzaq. "Domestic Architecture, Notables and Power: A Neighborhood in Late Ottoman Damascus: An Introduction." In *Art turc/Turkish Art (Tenth International Congress of Turkish Art, Geneva, 17–23 September 1995)*, 489–95. Geneva: Fondation Max van Berchem, 1999.

Mostyn, Trevor. *Egypt's Belle Epoque: Cairo 1869–1952*. London: Quartet, 1989.

Moynihan, Elizabeth. "The Lotus Garden Palace of Zahir al-Din Muhammad Babur." *Muqarnas* 5 (1988): 135–52.

——. "'But What a Happiness to Have Known Babur!'" In James L. Wescoat, Jr., and Joachim Wolschke-Bulmahn, eds., *Mughal Gardens: Sources, Places, Representations, and Prospects*, 95–126. Washington, D.C.: Dumbarton Oaks, 1996.

——. *Paradise as a Garden in Persia and Mughal India*. New York: George Braziller, 1979.

Moynihan, Elizabeth, ed. *The Moonlight Garden: New Discoveries at the Taj Mahal*. Washington, D.C.: Arthur M. Sackler Gallery; Seattle: University of Washington Press, 2000.

al-Muhassin ibn 'Ali al-Tanukhi. *The Table-talk of a Mesopotamian Judge, being the first part of the Nishwar al-Muahadarah, or Jami' al-Tawarikh of Abu 'Ali al-Muhassin al-Tanukhi*.

Ed. and trans. D. S. Margoliouth. London: Royal Asiatic Society, 1921–22.

Mukerji, Chandra. *Territorial Ambitions and the Gardens of Versailles*. Cambridge: Cambridge University Press, 1997.

Mukherji, Anisha S. *The Red Fort of Shahjahanabad*. Delhi: Oxford University Press, 2003.

Müller, Christian. "Judging with God's Law on Earth: Judicial Powers of the *Qadi al-jama'a* of Cordoba in the Fifth/Eleventh Century." *Islamic Law and Society* 7, no. 2 (2000): 159–86.

Murphy, Veronica. *The Origins of the Mughal Flowering Plant Motif*. London: Indar Pasricha Fine Arts, 1987.

Nanda, Ratish, and Jolyon Leslic. "Rehabilitating the Garden of Babur and Its Surroundings in Kabul." In Aga Khan Historic Cities Programme, *Urban Conservation and Area Development in Afghanistan*, 21–41. Geneva: Aga Khan Trust for Culture, 2007. www.akdn.org/hcsp/afghanistan/Afghanistan%20Brochure.pdf.

Nath, Ram. *The Immortal Taj: The Evolution of the Tomb in Mughal Architecture*. Bombay: D. B. Taraporevala Sons, 1972.

Navagero, Andres. *Viaje por España (1524–1526)*. Spanish trans. Antonio Fabie. Madrid: Turner, 1983.

Navarro Palazón, Julio, ed. *Casas y Palacios de al-Andalus*, Granada: El Legado Andalusí, 1995.

Navarro Palazón, Julio, and P. Jiménez Castillo. "El Castillejo de Monteagudo: Qasr Ibn Sa'd." In Julio Navarro Palazón, ed. *Casas y Palacios de al-Andalus*, 63–103. Granada: El Legado Andalusí, 1995.

Necipoğlu, Gulru. "Anatolia and the Ottoman Legacy." In Martin Frishman and Hasan-Uddin Khan, eds., *The Mosque*, 141–53. London: Thames and Hudson, 1994.

——. *Architecture, Ceremonial, and Power: The Topkapi Palace in the Fifteenth and Sixteenth Centuries*. Cambridge, Mass.: MIT Press, 1991.

——. "The Suburban Landscape of Sixteenth-Century Istanbul as a Mirror of Classical Ottoman Garden Culture." In Attilio Petruccioli, eds., *Gardens in the Time of the Great Muslim Empires*, 32–71. Leiden: E. J. Brill, 1997.

Nieto Cumplido, Manuel, and Carlos Luca de Tena y Alvear. *La Mezquita de Córdoba: planos y dibujos*. Cordoba: Colegio de arquitectas de Andalucia occidental, 1992.

Northedge, Alastair. "Creswell, Herzfeld and Samarra." *Muqarnas* 8 (1991): 74–93.

——. "An Interpretation of the Palace of the Caliph at Samarra." *Ars Orientalis* 23 (1993): 143–70.

——. "The Palaces of the Abbasids at Samarra." In Chase Robinson, ed., *A Medieval Islamic City Reconsidered: An Interdisciplinary Approach to Samarra*, 29–67. Oxford: Oxford University Press, 2001.

Norwich, John Julius. *The Normans in Sicily*, 1970; reprint, London: Penguin, 1992.

al-Nuwayri. *Historia de los musulmanes de España y Africa*. Ed. and trans. M. Gaspar Remiro. Granada, 1917.

——. *Nihayat al-arab*. Cairo, 1943.

Nykl, A. R. *Hispano-Arabic Poetry*. Baltimore: J. H. Furst, 1946.

——. *Historia de los amores de Bayad y Riyad*. New York: Hispanic Society, 1941.

Ocaña Jiménez, Manuel. "La Basílica de San Vicente y la Gran Mezquita de Córdoba: nuevo examen de los textos." *Al-Andalus* 7 (1942): 347–66.

O'Donovan, Edmond. *The Merv Oasis*, 2 vols. London, 1882, 2: 259–61.

Okada, Amina, and Jean-Louis Nou. *Un Joyau de l'Inde Moghole: Le mausolée d'I'timâd ud-Daulah*. Milan: 5 Continents Éditions, 2003.

O'Kane, Bernard. "The Arboreal Aesthetic: Landscape, Painting and Architecture from Mongol Iran to Mamluk Egypt." In Bernard O'Kane, ed., *Iconography of Islamic Art: Studies in Honor of Robert Hillenbrand*, 223–251. Cairo: American University in Cairo Press, 2005.

——. *Early Persian Painting*. London: I. B. Tauris, 2003.

Orihuela Uzal, Antonio. *Casas y palacios nazaríes. Siglos XIII-XV*. Barcelona: El Legado Andalusí and Lunwerg Editores, 1996.

Ostrasz, Antoni A. "The Archaeological Material for the Study of the Domestic Architecture at Fustat." *Africana Bulletin* 26 (1977): 57–87.

Otto-Dorn, Katharina. "Grabung im Ummayadischen Rusafah." *Ars Orientalis* 2 (1957): 119–33.

Pal, Pratapaditya, and Janice Leoshko, eds. *Romance of the Taj Mahal*. Los Angeles: Los Angeles County Museum of Art; London: Thames and Hudson, 1989.

Pant, Chandra. *Nur Jahan and Her Family*. Allahabad: Dan Dewal Publishing, 1978.

Parpagliolo, M. T. S. *Kabul: The Bagh-i Babur*. Rome: Istituto Italiano per il Medio e l'Estremo Oriente, 1972.

Parker, Richard. *A Practical Guide to Islamic Monuments in Morocco*. Charlottesville: Baraka Press, 1981.

Patil, D.R. *Mandu*. New Delhi: Archaeological Survey of India, 1992.

Pavloskis, Zoja. *Man in an Artificial Landscape: The Marvels of Civilization in Imperial Roman Literature*. Leiden: E. J. Brill, 1973.

Pavón Maldonado, Basilio. *Estudios sobre la Alhambra. I: La Alcazaba, El Palacio de los Abencerrajes, Los accesos a la Casa Vieja, El Palacio de Comares, El Partal*. Granada: Patronato de la Alhambra y Generalife, 1975.

——. *Estudios sobre la Alhambra. II* (supplement to *Cuadernos de la Alhambra*). Granada: Patronato de la Alhambra y Generalife, 1977.

——. "Influjos occidentals en el arte del califato de Córdoba." *Al-Andalus* 33 (1968): 205–20.

Pavord, Anna. *The Tulip*. New York: Bloomsbury, 1999.

Pedersen, Johannes. *The Arabic Book*. Trans. Geoffrey French. Princeton: Princeton University Press, 1984.

Pellat, Charles. *Cinq Calendriers Égyptiens* (Textes arabes et études islamiques, XXVI). Cairo: Institut Français d'Archéologie Orientale du Caire, 1986.

Pertusier, C. *Promenades pittoresques dans Constantinople et sur les rives du Bosphore*. Paris, 1815.

Petruccioli, Attilio. *Il giardino islamico: Architettura, natura, paesaggio*. Milan: Electa, 1994.

———. "Gardens and Religious Topography in Kashmir." *Environmental Design*, nos. 1–2 (1991): 64–73.

Petruccioli, Attilio, ed. *Gardens in the Time of the Great Muslim Empires*. Leiden: E. J. Brill, 1997.

Pieper, Jan. "Arboreal Art and Architecture in India." *Art and Archaeology Research Papers* (AARP) 12 (Dec. 1977): 47–54.

Pinder-Wilson, Ralph. "The Persian Garden: *Bagh* and *Chahar Bagh*." In Elisabeth MacDougall and Richard Ettinghausen, eds., *The Islamic Garden*, 71–85. Washington, D.C.: Dumbarton Oaks, 1976.

Pope, Arthur Upham, and Phyllis Ackerman. *A Survey of Persian Art*, 6 vols. 1938–39; reprint, Tokyo: Meiji-Shobo, 1964.

Porter, Yves, and Arthur Thévenart. *Palaces and Gardens of Persia*. Paris: Flammarion, 2003.

Prasad, H. Y. Sharada. *Rashtrapati Bhavan: The Story of the President's House*. New Delhi: Publication Division, Ministry of Information and Broadcasting in association with National Institute of Design for Rashtrapati Bhavan, ca. 1992.

al-Qur'an. Trans. Ahmed Ali. Princeton: Princeton University Press, 1988.

Rabbani, Ahmad. "Hiran Munara at Shekhupura." In S. M. Abdullah, ed., *Armughan-e 'Ilmi, Professor Muhammad Shafi' Presentation Volume*. Lahore, 1955.

Rani, Abha. *Tughluq Architecture of Delhi*. Varanasi: Bharati Prakashan, 1991.

Rapp, George, Jr., and Christopher L. Hill. *Geoarchaeology: The Earth Science Approach to Archaeological Interpretation*. New Haven: Yale University Press, 1998.

Raymond, André. "Les porteurs d'eau du Caire." *Bulletin de l'Institut Français d'Archéologie Orientale* 57 (1958): 183–202.

Redford, Scott. *Landscape and the State in Medieval Anatolia: Seljuk Gardens and Pavilions of Alanya*. Oxford: Archaeopress, 2000.

———. "Seljuk Pavilions and Enclosures in and Around Alanya." *Arastirma Sonuçlari Toplantisi* 14 (Ankara), (1997): 453–67.

Reifenburg, A. *The Struggle Between the Desert and the Sown: The Rise and Fall of Agriculture in the Levant*. Jerusalem: Jewish Agency, 1955.

Reuther, Oskar. *Indische Paläste und Wohnhäuser*. Berlin: L. Preiss, 1925.

Revault, Jacques. *Palais, demeures et maisons de plaisance à Tunis et ses environs: Du XVIe et XIXe siècle*. Aix-en-Provence: Édisud, 1984.

———. *Palais et résidences d'été de la région de Tunis (XVIe-XIXe siècles)*. Paris: Éditions du Centre National de la Recherche Scientifique, 1974.

Rich, Vivien. "Mughal Floral Painting and Its European Sources." *Oriental Art* n. s. 33 (1987): 183–89.

Richards, John. *The Mughal Empire*. New Cambridge History of India, 1.5. Cambridge: Cambridge University Press, 1995.

Riggs, Charles. *See* Kritovoulos

Rizvi, S. A. A. and Vincent Flynn. *Fatehpur-Sikri*. Bombay: D. B. Taraporevala Sons, 1975.

Robinson, Chase, ed. *A Medieval Islamic City Reconsidered: An Interdisciplinary Approach to Samarra*. Oxford: Oxford University Press, 2001.

Robinson, Cynthia. "The Lover, His Lady, Her Lady, and a Thirteenth-Century Celestina." In Oleg Grabar and C. Robinson, eds., *Islamic Art and Literature*, 79–115. Princeton: Markus Wiener, 2001.

Robinson, Frances. *Islam and Muslim History in South Asia*. New Delhi: Oxford University Press, 2000.

Rogers, J. M. "Samarra: A Study in Medieval Town Planning." In Albert Hourani and S. M. Stern, eds., *The Islamic City*, 119–55. Philadelphia: University of Pennsylvania Press, 1970.

Rosen-Ayalon, Myriam. *The Early Islamic Monuments of al-Haram al-Sharif: An Iconographic Study*. Jerusalem: Hebrew University, 1989.

Rubiera Mata, María Jesús. *La arquitectura en la literatura árabe*. Madrid: Editora Nacional, 1981.

Ruggles, D. Fairchild. "The Alcazar of Seville and Mudéjar Architecture." *Gesta* 43 (2005): 87–98.

———. "Arabic Poetry and Architectural Memory in al-Andalus." *Ars Orientalis* 23 (1993): 171–78.

———. "The Eye of Sovereignty: Poetry and Vision in the Alhambra's Lindaraja Mirador." *Gesta*, 36 (1997): 182–91.

———. "The Framed Landscape in Islamic Spain and Mughal India." In Brian Day, ed., *The Garden: Myth, Meaning, and Metaphor*. (Working Papers in the Humanities, 12), 21–50. Windsor, Ont.: University of Windsor, 2003.

———. "Gardens." In Frederick Asher, ed., *Art of India*, 258–70. Chicago: Encyclopaedia Britannica, 2003.

———. *Gardens, Landscape, and Vision in the Palaces of Islamic Spain*. University Park: Pennsylvania State University Press, 2001.

———. "The Gardens of the Alhambra and the Concept of the Garden in Islamic Spain." In Jerrilynn Dodds, ed., *Al-Andalus: The Arts of Islamic Spain*, 162–71. New York: Metropolitan Museum of Art, 1991.

———. "Il giardini con pianta a croce nel Mediterraneo islamico." In Attilio Petruccioli, *Il giardino islamico: Architettura, natura, paesaggio*, 143–54. Milan: Electa, 1993. German edition: *Der Islamische Garten: Architektur. Natur. Landschaft*. Stuttgart: Deutsche Verlags-Anstalt, 1995.

———. "Humayun's Tomb and Garden: Typologies and Visual Order." In Attioli Petruccioli, ed., *Gardens in the Time of the Great Muslim Empires*, 173–86. Leiden: E. J. Brill, 1997.

———. "Making Vision Manifest: Frame, Screen, and View in Islamic Culture." In Dianne Harris and D. Fairchild Ruggles, eds., *Sites Unseen: Landscape and Vision*, 131–56. Pittsburgh: University of Pittsburgh Press, 2007.

———. "Mothers of a Hybrid Dynasty: Race, Genealogy, and Acculturation in al-Andalus." *Journal of Medieval and Early Modern Studies* 34 (2004): 65–94.

———. "Vision and Power at the Qala Bani Hammad in Islamic North Africa." *Journal of Garden History* 14 (1994): 28–41.

———. "What's Religion Got to Do with It? A Skeptical Look at the Symbolism of Islamic and Rajput Gardens." *DAK: The*

Newsletter of the American Institute of Indian Studies no. 4 (Autumn 2000): 1, 5–8.

——. *See also* Jennifer Joffee.

Sack, Dorothée. *Damaskus: Entwicklung und Struktur einer orientalisch-islamischen Stadt*. Mainz: P. von Zabern, 1989.

Safran, Janina. "From Alien Terrain to the Abode of Islam: Landscapes in the Conquest of Al-Andalus." In John Howe and Michael Wolfe, eds., *Inventing Medieval Landscapes*, 136–49. Gainesville: University Press of Florida, 2002.

——. *The Second Umayyad Caliphate*. Cambridge, Mass.: Center for Middle Eastern Studies and Harvard University Press, 2000.

Saladin, Henri. *Tunis et Kairouan*. Paris: H. Laurens, 1908.

Salmon, G. "Marabouts de Tanger." *Archives Marocaines* 2 (1905): 115–26.

al-Samarrai, Qasim. "The Abbasid Gardens in Baghdad and Samarra (7th–12th Centuries)." In Leslie Tjon Sie Fat and Erik de Jong, eds., *The Authentic Garden*. Leiden: Clusius Foundation, 1991.

El-Samarraie, Husam Qawam. *Agriculture in Iraq During the Third Century, A.H.* Beirut: Librairie du Liban, 1972.

Samsó, Julio. "Un calendrier tunisien d'origine andalouse?" *Cahiers de Tunisie* 24 (1978): 65–82.

——. "La tradición clásica en los calendarios agrícolas hispanoárabes y norteafricanos." In *Actas del II Congreso para el Estudio de la Cultura en el Mediterráneo Occidental (1975)*, 177–86. Barcelona, 1978.

Sanders, Paula. *Ritual, Politics, and the City in Fatimid Cairo*. Albany: State University of New York Press, 1994.

Sanderson, Gordon, with Maulvi Shuaib. *A Guide to the Buildings and Gardens: Delhi Fort*. 4th ed., 1936; reprint, Delhi: Asian Educational Services, 2000.

Saqi Must'ad Khan. *Ma'asir-i 'Alamqiri*. Trans. Sir Jadunath Sarkar. Calcutta: Royal Asiatic Society of Bengal, 1947.

Sauvaget, Jean. "Châteaux Omeyyades de Syrie." *Revue des Études Islamiques* 39 (1967): 1–42.

——. *La Mosquée Omeyyade de Médine*. Paris: Vanoest, 1947.

——. "Le plan antique de Damas." *Syria* 26 (1949): 314–58.

——. "Les ruines omeyyades du Djebel Seis." *Syria* 20 (1939): 239–56.

——. *See also* Ibn al-Shihnah

Scanlon, George T. "Housing and Sanitation: Some Aspects of Medieval Egyptian Life." In Albert H. Hourani and S. M. Stern, eds., *The Islamic City*, 185–94. Philadelphia: University of Pennsylvania Press, 1970.

Scheindlin, Raymond. "El poema de Ibn Gabirol y la fuente del Patio de los Leones." *Cuadernos de la Alhambra* 29–30 (1993–94): 185–89.

Schiøler, Thorkild. *Roman and Islamic Water-Lifting Wheels*. Denmark: Odense University Press, 1971.

Schlumberger, Daniel. "Les fouilles de Qasr el-Heir el-Gharbi (1936–1939)." *Syria* 20 (1939): 195–238, 324–73.

——. *Lashkari Bazar: Une residence royale ghaznévide et ghoride. 1a L'architecture*, 2 vols. in 3. Paris: Diffusion de Boccard, 1978.

Serjeant, R. B., and Husayn 'Abdullah al-'Amri, "A Yemeni Agricultural Poem." In *Studia Arabica et Islamica* (festschrift for Ihsan 'Abbas), ed. Wada al-Qadi, 407–27. Beirut: American University of Beirut, 1981.

Seyrig, Henri. "Antiquités Syriennes: Les Jardins de Kasr el-Heir." *Syria* 12 (1931): 316–18.

Shah Jahan. *See* 'Inayat Khan.

Sharma, Y. D. *Delhi and Its Neighbourhood*. New Delhi: Archaeological Survey of India, 1990.

Shaw, B. D. "The Noblest Monuments and the Smallest Things: Wells, Walls and Aqueducts in the Making of Roman Africa." In A. T. Hodge, ed., *Future Currents in Aqueduct Studies*, 63–91. Leeds: F. Cairns, 1991.

Shephard-Parpagliolo, M. T. *Kabul: The Bagh-i Babur*. Rome: Istituto Italiano per il Medio e l'Estremo Oriente, 1972.

Shokoohy, Mehrdad, and Natalie Shokoohy. *Nagaur: Sultanate and Early Mughal History and Architecture of the District of Nagaur, India*. Royal Asiatic Society Monographs, 28. London: Royal Asiatic Society, 1993.

Siddiq, W. H. "The Discovery of Architectural Remains of a Pre-Mughal Garden at New Delhi." In B. M. Pande and B. D. Chattopadhyaya, eds., *Archaeology and History: Essays in Memory of Shri A. Gosh*, 2: 573–77. Delhi: Agam Kala Prakashan, 1987.

Simpson, Marianna Shreve. *Sultan Ibrahim Mirza's "Haft awrang": A Princely Manuscript from Sixteenth-century Iran*. New Haven: Yale University Press, 1997.

Sims, Eleanor. *Peerless Images: Persian Painting and Its Sources*. New Haven: Yale University Press, 2002.

Singh, A. P. and Shiv Pal Singh. *Monuments of Orchha*. Delhi: Agam Kala Prakashan, 1991.

Singh, Patwant. "The Tragedy of the Lodi Tombs." *Design* 15 (April 1971): 15–26.

Sinha, Amita. "The Cosmic Tree in Buddhist Landscapes." *Geographical Review of India* 63, no. 1 (2001): 1–15.

——. "Nature in Hindu Art, Architecture, and Landscape." *Landscape Research* 20 (1995): 3–10.

Sinha, Amita, and D. Fairchild Ruggles. "The Yamuna Riverfront, India: A Comparative Study of Islamic and Hindu Traditions in Cultural Landscapes." *Landscape Journal* 23, no. 2 (2004): 141–52.

Siraju-l-Islam, Muhammad. "The Lodi Phase of Indo-Islamic Architecture." Ph.D. dissertation, Freie Universität, Berlin, 1960.

Skelton, Robert. "A Decorative Motif in Mughal Art." In Pratapaditya Pal, ed., *Aspects of Indian Art*, 147–52. Leiden: E. J. Brill, 1972.

Smart, Ellen. "Graphic Evidence for Mughal Architectural Plans." *Art and Archaeology Research Papers* (AARP) (December 1974): 22–23.

Smith, Edmund W. *Akbar's Tomb, Sikandrah near Agra, Described and Illustrated*. Archaeological Survey of India, New Imperial Series, no. 35. Allahabad: Superintendent Government Press, United Provinces, 1909.

——. *The Moghul Architecture of Fathpur-Sikri*, 4 vols. 1894–98; reprint Delhi: Caxton, 1985.

Smith, Jane I., and Yvonne Y. Haddad. *The Islamic Understanding of Death and Resurrection*. Albany: State University of New York Press, 1981.

Smith, Jonathan Z. *To Take Place: Toward a Theory of Ritual*. Chicago: University of Chicago Press, 1987.

Smith, Vincent A. *A History of Fine Art in India and Ceylon*. 2nd ed. rev. K. de B. Codrington. Oxford: Clarendon Press, 1930.

Solignac, Marcel. "Recherches sur les installations hydrauliques de Kairouan et des steppes tunisiennes du VIIe au XIe siècle (J.-C.)." *Annales de l'Institut d'Études Orientales, Alger* 11 (1953): 60–170.

Spear, T. G. P. *Delhi, Its Monuments and History*, 2nd rev. ed. Updated by Narayani Gupta and Laura Sykes. Delhi: Oxford University Press, 1994.

Staacke, Ursula. *Un palazzo normano a Palermo. La Zisa*. Palermo: Ricerche et documenti, 1991.

Stronach, David. "Parterres and Stone Watercourses at Pasargadae: Notes on the Achaemenid Contribution to Garden Design." *Journal of Garden History* 14 (1994): 3–12.

——. "The Royal Garden at Pasargadae: Evolution and Legacy." In Louis vanden Berghe and L. de Meyer, eds., *Archaeologia Iranica et Orientalis. Miscellanea in Honorem Louis Vanden Berghe*, 475–502. Ghent: Peeters, 1989.

Subtelny, Maria. "Agriculture and the Timurid *Chaharbagh*: The Evidence from a Medieval Persian Agricultural Manual." In Attilio Petruccioli, ed., *Gardens in the Time of the Great Muslim Empires*, 110–28. Leiden: E. J. Brill, 1997.

——. "A Medieval Persian Agricultural Manual in Context: The *Irshad al-Zira'a* in Late Timurid and Early Safavid Khorasan." *Studia Iranica* 22 (1993): 167–217.

——. "Mirak-i Sayyid Ghiyas and the Timurid Tradition of Landscape Architecture." *Studia Iranica* 24 (1995): 19–54.

——. "The Poetic Circle at the Court of the Timurid Sultan Husain Baiqara, and Its Political Significance." Ph.D. diss., Harvard University, 1979.

"Sultan Qaboos University." *Mimar* ("Architecture in Development") 37 (1990): 46–49.

Tabales Rodríguez, Miguel Angel. "El Patio de las Doncellas del Palacio de Pedro I de Castilla: génesis y transformación." *Apuntes del Alcázar de Sevilla* 6 (May 2005): 6–43.

Tabbaa, Yasser. "The Medieval Islamic Garden: Typology and Hydraulics." In John Dixon Hunt, ed., *Garden History: Issues, Approaches, Methods*, 303–30. Washington, D.C.: Dumbarton Oaks, 1989.

——. "The 'Salsabil' and 'Shadirvan' in Medieval Islamic Courtyards." *Environmental Design: Journal of the Islamic Environmental Design Research Centre* 1 (1986): 34–37.

Taeschner, Franz. *Alt-Stambuler Hof- and Volksleben*. Hanover, 1925.

Taft, Francis. "Honor and Alliance: Reconsidering Mughal-Rajput Marriages". In Karine Schumer, Joan Erdman, Deryck Lodnick, and Lloyd Rudolph, eds. *The Idea of Rajasthan: Explorations in Regional Identity*, 2 vols. 2:217–41. New Delhi: Manohar, 1994.

Tagher, Jeanette. "Le jardin de l'Ezbékieh." *Cahiers d'Histoire Égyptienne* 5–6 (1951): 413–21.

Tandon, B. "The Architecture of the Nawabs of Avadh, 1722–1856." In Robert Skelton et al, eds., *Facets of Indian Art*, 66–75. London: Victoria and Albert Museum, 1986.

Tavernier, Jean Baptiste. *Tavernier's Travels in India*. Trans. and ed. V. Ball. London, 1889.

Tchalenko, Georges. *Villages Antiques de la Syrie du Nord: Le Massif du Bélus à l'Époque Romaine*, 2 vols. Paris: Paul Geuthner, 1953.

Tengberg, Margareta. "Research into the Origins of Date Palm Domestication." In *The Date Palm: From Traditional Resource to Green Wealth*, 51–62. Abu Dhabi: Emirates Center for Strategic Studies and Research, 2003.

Thackston, Wheeler. *See* Babur

Thompson, J. P. "The Tomb of Jahangir." *Journal of the Punjab Historical Society* 1 (1911): 12–30.

The Thousand and One Nights. See Richard Burton, trans.

Tillotson, G. H. R. *The Rajput Palaces: The Development of an Architectural Style, 1450–1750*. New Haven: Yale University Press, 1987.

Titley, Norah. *Plants and Gardens in Persian, Mughal and Turkish Art*. London: British Library, 1979.

Titley, Norah, and Frances Wood. *Oriental Gardens*. San Francisco: Chronicle Books, 1991.

Tito Rojo, José. "Permanencia y cambio en los jardines de la Granada morisca (1492–1571). Los jardines de los palacios nazaríes: La Alhambra y el Generalife." In Carmen Añón and José Luis Sancho, eds., *Jardín y Naturaleza en el reinado de Felipe II*, 363–79. Madrid: Sociedad Estatal para la Conmemoración de los Centenarios de Felipe II y Carlos V, 1998.

Topsfield, Andrew. *The City Palace Museum, Udaipur: Paintings of Mewar Court Life*. Ahmedabad: Mapin, 1990.

——. "City Palace and Lake Palaces: Architecture and Court Life in Udaipur Painting." In Giles Tillotson, ed. *Stones in the Sand: The Architecture of Rajasthan*, 54–67. Mumbai: Marg Publications, 2001.

Torres Balbás, L. *Artes almorávide y almohade*. Madrid: Consejo Superior de Investigaciones Científicas, 1955.

——. "Monteagudo y 'El Castillejo', en la Vega de Murcia." *Al-Andalus* 2 (1934): 366–72.

——. "El Oratorio y la casa de Astasio de Bracamonte en el Partal de la Alhambra." *Al-Andalus* 10 (1945): 440–49.

——. "Patios de crucero." *Al-Andalus* 23 (1958): 171–92.

Turner, Howard R. *Science in Medieval Islam*. Austin: University of Texas Press, 1995.

Ulbert, Thilo. "Ein umaiyadischer Pavillon in Resafa-Rusafat Hisam." *Damaszener Mitteilungen*, 7 (1993): 213–31.

Vallejo Triano, Antonio. "Madinat al-Zahra', capital y sede del califato omeya andalusí." In *El Esplendor de los Omeyas cordobeses*, 386–97. Granada: Fundación Andalusí, 2001.

——. "Madinat al-Zahra': The Triumph of the Islamic State." In Jerrilynn D. Dodds, ed., *Al-Andalus: The Art of Islamic Spain*, 27–39. New York: Metropolitian Museum of Art, 1992.

Varisco, Daniel. "Agriculture in Rasulid Zabid." *Journal of Semitic Studies. Supplement 14. Studies on Arabia in Honour of Professor G. Rex Smith*, ed. J. F. Healey and V. Porter, 323–51. Oxford: Oxford University Press, 2002.

——. *Medieval Agriculture and Islamic Science: The Almanac of a Yemeni Sultan.* Seattle: University of Washington Press, 1994.

——. "A Royal Crop Register from Rasulid Yemen." *Journal of the Economic and Social History of the Orient* 34 (1991): 1–22.

Vázquez Ruíz, José. "Un calendario anónimo granadino del siglo XV." *Revista del Instituto de Estudios Islámicos en Madrid* 9–10 (1961–62): 23–64.

Ventura Villanueva, Ángel. *El abastecimiento de agua a la Córdoba romana. I. El Acueducto de Valdepuentes.* Cordoba: Universidad de Córdoba, 1993.

Vesel, Ziva. "Les traits d'agriculture en Iran." *Studia Iranica* 15 (1986): 99–108.

Vigil Escalera, Manuel. *El jardín musulmán de la antigua Casa de Contratación de Sevilla. Intervención arquitectónica,* 2 vols. Seville: Junta de Andalucía, Consejería de obras públicas y transportes, 1992.

Vílchez Vílchez, Carlos. *El Generalife.* Granada: Proyecto Sur de Ediciones, 1991.

Villiers-Stuart, Constance Mary. *Gardens of the Great Mughals.* London: A & C Black, 1913.

Viollet, Henri. "Description du palais de al-Moutasim à Samara" and "Fouilles à Samara." *Memoires de l'Academie des Inscriptions et Belles-Lettres,* ser. I, v. 12, pt. 2 (1909, 1911), 567–94, 685–717.

Volwahsen, Andreas. *Imperial Delhi: The British Capital of the Indian Empire.* Munich: Prestel, 2002.

Von Hantelman, Christa, and Dieter Zoern. *Gardens of Delight: The Great Islamic Gardens.* Cologne: DuMont Buchverlag, 2001.

Wagoner, Phillip. "Sultan Among Hindu Kings: Dress, Titles, and the Islamicization of Hindu Culture at Vijayanagara." *Journal of Asian Studies* 55, no. 4 (1996): 851–80.

Watson, Andrew. *Agricultural Innovation in the Early Islamic World: The Diffusion of Crops and Farming Techniques.* Cambridge: Cambridge University Press, 1983.

——. "The Arab Agricultural Revolution and Its Diffusion, 711–1100." *Journal of Economic History* 34 (1974): 8–35.

Watson, William, ed. *Landscape Style in Asia: A Colloquy held 25–27 June 1979.* London: University of London, School of Oriental and African Studies, 1980.

Watt, W. Montgomery. "Iram." In *Encyclopaedia of Islam,* 2nd ed. III (1975): 1270.

Weber, Edgar. "La ville de cuivre, une ville d'al-Andalus." *Sharq al-Andalus* 6 (1989): 43–81.

Weitzmann, Kurt. "The Greek Sources of Islamic Scientific Illustrations." In G. Miles, ed., *Archaeologica Orientalia in Memoriam Ernst Herzfeld,* 244–66. Locust Valley, N.Y.: J. J. Augustin, 1952.

Welch, Anthony. "Gardens That Babur Did Not Like: Landscape, Water, and Architecture for the Sultans of Delhi." In James L. Wescoat, Jr., and Joachim Wolschke-Bulmahn, eds., *Mughal Gardens: Sources, Places, Representations, and Prospects,* ed. 59–93. Washington, D.C.: Dumbarton Oaks, 1996.

——. "Hydraulic Architecture in Medieval India: The Tughluqs." *Environmental Design* (1985): 74–81.

——. "A Medieval Center of Learning in India: The Hauz Khas Madrasa in Delhi." *Muqarnas* 13 (1996): 165–90.

Welch, Stuart Cary. *Persian Painting: Five Royal Safavid Manuscripts of the Sixteenth Century.* New York: George Braziller, 1976.

Wescoat, James. L., Jr. "Early Water Systems in Mughal India." *Environmental Design* 2 (1985): 50–57.

——. "Lahore." In *The Grove Dictionary of Art Online.* Oxford University Press. *http://www.groveart.com* (accessed 19 April 2004).

——. "Picturing an Early Mughal Garden." *Asian Art* 2 (1989): 59–79.

——. "Waterworks and Landscape Design at the Mahtab Bagh." In Elizabeth Moynihan, ed., *The Moonlight Garden: New Discoveries at the Taj Mahal,* 59–78. Washington, D.C.: Arthur M. Sackler Gallery; Seattle: University of Washington Press, 2000.

——. *See also* Kausar, Brand, and Wescoat.

Wescoat, James L., Jr., Michael Brand, and Naeem Mir. "The Shahdara Gardens of Lahore: Site Documentation and Spatial Analysis." *Pakistan Archaeology* 25 (1993): 333–66.

Wescoat, James L., Jr., and Gilbert White, *Water for Life: Water Management and Environmental Policy.* Cambridge: Cambridge University Press, 2003.

Wescoat, James L., Jr., and Joachim Wolschke-Bulmann, eds. *Mughal Gardens: Sources, Places, Representations, and Prospects.* Washington, D.C.: Dumbarton Oaks, 1996.

White, Lynn, Jr. *Medieval Technology and Social Change.* Oxford: Clarendon Press, 1962.

Wiet, Gaston. *Catalogue général du Musée de l'Art Islamique du Caire: Inscriptions historiques sur Pierre.* Cairo: Imprimerie de l'Institut Français d'Archéologie Orientale, 1971.

——. *See also* al-Ya'qubi.

Wilber, Donald. *Persian Gardens and Garden Pavilions.* 1962; reprint, Washington, D.C.: Dumbarton Oaks, 1979.

Wilson, Andrew. "Water Supply in Ancient Carthage." In J. T. Peña, et al., eds., *Carthage Papers (Journal of Roman Archaeology,* Supplementary series 28), 65–102. Portsmouth, R.I.: 1998.

Wittfogel, Karl. *Oriental Depotism.* New Haven: Yale University Press, 1957.

Woodbridge, Kenneth. *Princely Gardens: The Origins and Development of the French Formal Style.* London: Rizzoli, 1986.

al-Ya'qubi, *Les Pays.* Ed. and trans. Gaston Wiet. Cairo: Imprimerie de l'Institut Français d'Archéologie Orientale, 1937.

Yazdani, Ghulam. *Mandu: The City of Joy.* Oxford: Oxford University Press, 1929.

Yildiz, D. "Tulips in Ottoman Turkish Culture and Art." In Michiel Roding and Hans Theunissen, eds., *The Tulip: A Symbol of Two Nations.* Utrecht: M. Th. Houtsma Stichting, 1993.

Zajadacz-Hastenrath, Salome. "A Note on Babur's Lost Funerary Enclosure at Kabul." *Muqarnas* 14 (1997): 135–42.

Index

Acknowledgments

I AM DEEPLY GRATEFUL to historians, architects, conservators, and administrators who allowed me access to the sites and to their knowledge of them.

Many friends and colleagues lent support to this project. Catherine and Frederick Asher offered support and encouragement for work in India on Rajput palaces, and Cathy gave the book manuscript a thorough reading at draft stage with the result that it is much improved. My colleagues at the University of Illinois have provided congenial enthusiasm for landscape history, and, in particular, James L. Wescoat, Jr., also generously provided plans and photographs of sites. Jerrilynn D. Dodds and David Powers read portions of an early draft of Chapter 8. George Scanlon kindly provided information on the excavations and interpretations of Fustat. Nancy Micklewright gave me a large collection of materials on the Ezbekiyah gardens. Carol Bier read the complete manuscript and gave valuable comments. Shawkat Toorawa gave me a full bibliography for Imru al-Qays.

Norah Titley corresponded with me regarding some Mughal miniatures of mutual interest. Particular thanks to Robert Ousterhout for our many discussions on Byzantine and Islamic architecture, and to Kathryn Gleason for steering me toward recent studies on Roman gardens and for our many discussions on the subject over the years. The incomparable Mercedes Maier took me to the recent excavations at the Seville Alcazar in 2004 and shared her insights on that and other Andalusian garden monuments.

Finally, I owe profound thanks to two graduate assistants: Binaifer Variava, who cheerfully and capably redrew a great many of the plans and drawings for this volume and devoted a great deal of time to the project, and Lobsang Chodon, who picked up where Binaifer left off to work on the final stages.

The writing of the book was initially supported by the Graham Foundation. The volume's completion was achieved through my appointment to the Center for Advanced Study at the University of Illinois, where I was supposed to be working on a different project altogether. I am indebted to series editor John Dixon Hunt and art editor Jo Joslyn at the University of Pennsylvania Press for embracing the book before it was completed. Without the support and faith of such institutions and individuals, the work could not have been written.

This book reflects cumulative experience, thinking, and teaching about gardens and landscape from the mid-1980s to the present. It is both a cultural history as well as a meditation on the act of gardening and its power to transform the designated space of a simple backyard, a palace courtyard, and an entire landscape. Human beings change landscape, but a landscape can profoundly change an individual. It is in this cumulative and metaphoric sense that I profoundly thank my visionary colleague Dianne Harris, my husband and partner, Oscar Vázquez, and my daughter, Isabel Fairchild Vázquez. Scholarship is ultimately a human effort, and its heart and soul depends on such friends and family.

This book is dedicated to my parents who have always encouraged me both to cultivate my own garden and to see the world. They generously supported and sometimes participated in many of my first forays to study Islamic gardens.